The Tree of Liberty

CRITICAL CONDITIONS: FIELD DAY ESSAYS AND MONOGRAPHS

Edited by Seamus Deane

Critical Conditions: Field Day Essays

The Tree of Liberty

Radicalism, Catholicism and the
Construction of Irish Identity
1760–1830

Kevin Whelan

UNIVERSITY OF NOTRE DAME PRESS
in association with
FIELD DAY

for Anne, Bébhinn, Fionn and Ruaidhrí

Published in the United States in 1996 by
UNIVERSITY OF NOTRE DAME PRESS
Notre Dame, Indiana 46556
All Rights Reserved.

and in Ireland by
CORK UNIVERSITY PRESS
University College Cork, Ireland

*The paper used in this publication meets the minimum requirements of the
American National Standard for Information Sciences–Permanence of
paper for Printed Library Materials, ANSI Z39.48–1984*

Library of Congress Cataloging-in-Publication Data

Whelan, Kevin.
  The tree of liberty : radicalism, catholicism, and the construction of Irish identity,
1760–1830 / Kevin Whelan.
      p. cm. — (Critical conditions)
  Includes bibliographical references and index.
  ISBN 0-268-01894-4 (alk. paper)
    1. Ireland—Politics and government—1780–1820.   2. National characteristics,
Irish—History—18 century.   3. Group identity—Ireland—History—18th century.
4. Radicalism—Ireland—History—18th century.   5. Catholics—Ireland—History—18th
century.   6. Ireland—Civilization—18th century.   7. Ireland—Civilization—19th century.
I. Title.   II. Series.
DA948.4.W47 1996   96–11879
941.507—dc20   CIP

CONTENTS

The Rights of Man

It is now towards the middle of February. Were I to take a turn into the country, the trees would present a leafless winterly appearance. As people are apt to pluck twigs as they walk along, I perhaps might do the same, and by chance might observe that a *single bud* on that twig had begun to swell. I should reason very unnaturally, or rather not reason at all, to suppose that *this* was the *only* bud in England which had this appearance. Instead of deciding thus, I should instantly conclude that the same appearance was beginning, or about to begin, everywhere; and though the vegetable sleep will continue longer on some trees and plants than on others, and though some of them may not *blossom* for two or three years, all will be in leaf in the summer, except those which are *rotten*. What pace the political summer may keep with the natural, no human foresight can determine. It is, however, not difficult to perceive that the spring is begun.

THOMAS PAINE (1792)

PREFACE

These four independent but interlocking essays revolve around the 1790s, arguably the pivotal decade in the evolution of modern Ireland. The 1790s witnessed the emergence of separatism, of popular republicanism and loyalism, of the Orange Order and Maynooth College, and culminated in the Act of Union, which defined subsequent relations between Ireland and Britain. The decade also presents an arresting amalgam of internal and external forces, where Irish events were inseparable from a wider international process. From a fulcrum in the 1790s, these essays swivel to explore both the eighteenth-century Ireland of which they were the dramatic and unexpected climax, and the nineteenth-century world which they ushered in in an equally surprising manner. The 1790s cast a long shadow, and the names of Tone, Russell, FitzGerald, McCracken and Emmet were to reverberate down the echo-chambers of Irish history, enjoying a resonant afterlife in the two centuries following their physical defeat.

If the 1790s can be seen as the pivotal decade in the evolution of modern Ireland, then an understanding of it is not just of scholarly interest, but has repercussions for current political and cultural debates. It is precisely because of that enduring relevance that the 1790s have never passed from the heat of politics into the shadier groves of history. These essays look again at the window of opportunity which opened and was forcibly closed in the 1790s, a window which beckoned to the still unattained prospect of a non-sectarian, democratic and inclusive politics adequately representing the Irish people in all their inherited complexities. That project remains uncompleted; understanding the reasons for its momentous defeat in the 1790s can help in ensuring that history does not repeat itself in the 1990s.

In the anxious aftermath of 1798 and the Act of Union, control of the interpretation of the 1790s became a vital component of many political agendas; the resulting miasma of (deliberately) confused meanings has to be dispelled before we can once more see the 1790s in their context. By stripping that decade of its disabling jungle of adventitious growth, these essays aim to reveal it more clearly. Relieved of that oppressive weight, the 1790s cease to be divisive, and become available in a fresh way, opening a generous space which has been artificially constricted. As the bicentenary of 1798 approaches, the creation of that available and permeable space is both desirable and necessary.

Theoretically, this work derives from an array of scholarly influences: from historical geography as practised by Tom Jones Hughes and Donald Meinig; from the radical history of C. L. R. James, E. P. Thompson and Peter Linebaugh;

from post-colonial and subaltern studies, as mediated through Irish filters like Seamus Deane, Terry Eagleton, Luke Gibbons and particularly David Lloyd; from the recent prolific advances made in the field of Irish history, especially as practised by Louis Cullen and Tom Bartlett. In an Irish context, the informing perspective of these essays is post-revisionist, an empathy with oppositional cultural formations, a dialogic understanding of the relationship between past and present, a refusal of stereotyping and essentialism, a non-talmudic irreverence to textual authority, and a self-conscious heave beyond the comforting polarities of 'nationalist' and 'revisionist' history. These essays are also deliberately askance to and freely transgressive of disciplinary boundaries. Ultimately they try to formulate the right questions, rather than rehearse pat answers.

The joy of scholarship is the never-failing generosity of fellow-practitioners, and the 1790s is astonishingly hospitable terrain. I have learned from and been helped by many fine scholars, most heavily felt in the cases of Louis Cullen and Tom Bartlett. My work has benefited from creative exchanges with Richard Aylmer, Kevin Barry, Bernard Browne, Nicholas Canny, Brian Cleary, Billy Colfer, Linda Colley, Peter Collins, Pat Cooke, Bill Crawford, Seamus Deane, David Dickson, Luke Dodd, Terry Eagleton, Marianne Elliott, Hugh Fenning, Nicholas Furlong, Dan Gahan, Luke Gibbons, Tommy Graham, John Gray, Jenny Harrison, Lory Kehoe, Dáire Keogh, Anna Kinsella, Peter Linebaugh, David Lloyd, Rolf Loeber, Gerry Lyne, Peter McDonagh, Brian MacDonald, Perry McIntyre, David Miller, Máirín Ní Dhonnchadha, Breandán Ó Buachalla, Eamonn Ó Ciardha, Michael O'Dea, Ruan O'Donnell, Cormac Ó Gráda, Jane Ohlmeyer, Kevin O'Neill, Peter O'Shaughnessy, Gary Owens, Trevor Parkhill, Bob Scally, Dan Scanlon and Christopher Woods. I have also enjoyed the unfailing civility and congenial atmosphere of the Royal Irish Academy, the National Library and the National Archives. My gratitude also extends to the many libraries which have facilitated my work, notably the Burns Library (Boston College), the Beinicke Library (Yale), Notre Dame University Library, the W.L. Clements Library (Ann Arbor), the Houghton Library (Harvard), the Lewis Walpole Library (Farmingham), the American-Irish Historical Society (New York), the New York Historical Society, the Mitchell Library (Sydney), the Linen Hall Library (Belfast), the Public Record Office of Northern Ireland (Belfast), the National Museum (Dublin) and Kilmainham Jail (Dublin). I am grateful to Brian MacDonald (Taighde), Eamonn Ó Ciardha and Mathew Stout for their patience with a last Luddite, and to my publishers, especially Seamus Deane at Field Day, Jim Langford at Notre Dame Press and all at Cork University Press. As always, my work is facilitated by a supportive matrix of family; my parents, Patricia and Bill; my sisters Esther, Eileen, Kathleen, Frances and Rita, and my brothers Liam, Patrick, Tom, James and Eamonn. My Wexford connections always recharge a nourishing exchange between nature and nurture. The greatest debt is to my partner Anne Kearney and our children, Bébhinn, Fionn and Ruaidhrí, who constantly circumvent the selfish shadow cast by scholarship and who cheerfully accompany unending croppy forays between the Bastille and Boolavogue.

Ireland House
New York, 1995

On Seeing a 'Hunger-Bitten' Girl

. . . and at the sight my friend
In agitation said, ''Tis against that
That we are fighting.' I with him believed
That a benignant spirit was abroad
Which might not be withstood, that poverty
Abject as this would in little time
Be found no more, that we should see the earth
Unthwarted in her wish to recompense
The meek, the lowly, patient child of toil,
All institutes for ever blotted out
That legalised exclusion, empty pomp
Abolished, sensual state and cruel power,
Whether by edict of the one or few;
And finally, as sum and crown of all,
Should see the people having a strong hand
In framing their own laws; whence better days
To all mankind.

WILLIAM WORDSWORTH (1793)

AN UNDERGROUND GENTRY?
Catholic Middlemen in Eighteenth-Century Ireland

Introduction

Was eighteenth-century Ireland a typical colony, or was it simply a representative *ancien régime* society? This question can only be answered by looking carefully at a wide range of relationships affecting the island.[1] While the political and economic history of the period are now reasonably well established, its social and cultural history is still in an embryonic phase. There has been little effort to apply in an Irish context the range of questions and methods used by French scholars of the *Annales* school: with the honourable exception of work by Cullen, Bartlett and Connolly, this is still largely untilled ground.[2] This study reconstructs the *mentalité* of one significant group in eighteenth-century Irish life – the descendants of the old Catholic landowning families, reduced to the level of middlemen and farmers. As the *de facto* leaders of Catholic society, in a situation where vertical attachments persisted after their landed power was broken, such families had a pivotal brokerage role to play in the articulation of political and popular culture. The continuing valency of the question of landownership was of enduring significance in these special conditions, and its implications for the political crisis of the 1790s becomes apparent in this context.

Throughout the eighteenth century, land in Ireland remained stubbornly a political issue, not just an agrarian or economic one. Ultimate control of landownership and therefore of political power had been the subject of two disturbingly recent challenges in the 1640s and 1690s – remembered in exquisite detail by both conquerors and conquered. Landownership functioned as a concrete indicator of the realities of Irish life in the eighteenth century, but it was also a resonant symbol. The visibility of the seventeenth-century upheavals, the enduring elite and popular memory of a previous ownership regime, the existence of an Irish Catholic nation-in-waiting overseas (with its colleges, its army, its wealthy diaspora) created an instability over the issue of landownership. The descendants of the old proprietors mutated into an underground gentry, the shadow lords of eighteenth-century Ireland. Their existence set Irish society on a divergent trajectory from that of Wales, Scotland or England. This anterior landed order and its potent afterlife in the Catholic middleman milieu provided an access to alterity, to a potentially different order, a matrix of memory which encoded an attainable future enabled by the available past.

As that vision refocused from residually Jacobite to incipiently Jacobin forms in the late eighteenth century, it retained its demotic force by remaining obsessively grounded, Antaeus-like, in the land. In England the appeal to the land and its organic continuities had a seductive effect as a soothing sedative to excitable and deracinated radicalism. In Ireland, as Edmund Burke knew only too well, both intellectually and emotionally, the jagged edges of the land question chafed at the superficially smooth patina of eighteenth-century life. At moments of high intensity, as in the 1760s and 1790s, that brilliant but brittle surface cracked and through the interstices poured a scalding surge of angry energy, erupting from a pent-up reservoir of memory and threatening to erode the existing political landscape. Anxious issues hovered around the land question – the illegitimacy of the new gentry, access to political power and its denial, the sectarian state, the Catholic question: these issues provided an eighteenth-century bridge across which Catholic sensibilities made the transition from the seventeenth to the nineteenth century in a unique fashion. In this was to lie the long-term political legacy of the land question.

The origins of the middleman system

The origins of the middleman (or head tenant) system are simple: in the turbulent 1690s and the cash-starved early decades of the eighteenth century, landlords sought to stabilise their rentals by attracting resident, substantial, improving Protestant head tenants, who could guarantee cash rent payments, and were (through lease covenants) responsible for developing their holdings.[3] Looking back in 1773, a Presbyterian tenant in County Derry noted the conditions under which middleman perpetuity leases had originated: 'the country not very long settled, waste farms plenty, Protestant tenants scarce, and the Protestant yeomanry absolutely necessary to secure the persons and properties of the landlords'.[4] As late as 1746, an agent advised his Kilkenny landlord 'whether it be not better to set a farm so that a man can live on it than to set it at a rackrent to one who has little or nothing to lose, for these people will take lands at any rate, not at all considering whether they are able to stock or cultivate it'.[5] In other words, it was more in the landlord's interest to attract reputable solvent tenants than to gamble on unknown ones, even if this meant accepting less than the 'going' or cant rent. This created a favourable environment for tenants who had prospered under 1690s leases: they acquired additional leases in the depressed 1720s and 1730s, not infrequently on multiple estates. These accumulated leases laid the basis for the striking success of middlemen in the more expansionary conditions from the 1740s onwards. In exceptional circumstances, as with the O'Mahonys on the Petty estate in Kerry, the O'Reillys on the Plunkett estate in Cavan, or the Whites on the Wingfield estate in Wexford, an entire estate could be leased to a single individual.[6] The actual work of landscape modification devolved on middlemen: delineation of tenancy boundaries, enclosures, permanent hedges and ditches, clearance of scrubland, liming, draining, construction of stonewalled and slated dwellings, planting of orchards and deciduous trees. As well as performing this exemplary role, head tenants were also responsible for the recruitment and organisation of sub-tenants.

While some middlemen held perpetuity leases (for lives renewable forever) which made them *de facto* owners, most were on leases for three lives. Landlords favoured these rather than fixed terms because the element of uncertainty prevented tenants from deliberately exhausting the land in the last years of the lease, and because leases lapsed individually and episodically, thereby spreading administrative costs and income generation, while preventing combinations against the landlord in the matter of upward adjustment of rent. Leases for lives also conferred voting rights, always an important species of landlord property. The reverse aspect of these advantages was that their irregularity made large-scale landlord interventions difficult or protracted. Overall, however, granted the emphatic political bias towards Protestantism, this policy was weighted in favour of immigrant tenants at the expense of native ones. Josiah Bateman, agent on the Boyle (later Devonshire) estate in the 1730s, describes the result of this policy on the evolution of this estate:

> This is a fine English colony, which the late Richard Boyle took such pains and cost to plant here by bringing with him families out of England and encouraging those of English extraction, whose industry he liked, for their improvements, and would not set a lease to a native, because they are quite the reverse to improvement.[7]

This bias against non-Protestant tenants for perceived laziness was widely shared. A Cork agent in 1710 described an unimproved townland as being 'like a papist's farm without bounds made up or a bush on the same'.[8] 'Improvements', as implemented by these Protestant head tenants, had a symbolic as well as a utilitarian purpose. They would articulate in the landscape the visible signs of a stable and civilising Protestant presence, a self-conscious assertion of superior values to those of the indigenous population. Architecturally, for example, this would be reflected by using slate rather than thatch, brick and stone rather than mud, isolated as opposed to clustered dwellings, and formal rather than vernacular architectural styles. In this case style would be substance, and the medium would be the message.

While landlords tended to have a preference for Protestant head tenants, it was not always possible to obtain them. A Tipperary landlord concluded in 1737: 'I and every other gentleman would have good substantial Protestant tenants if we could get them, but as they are not to be had we must take the best we can get.'[9] The only alternative in many cases was Catholic middlemen recruited from the ranks of the dispossessed landowners. The new landlords opted for them as a stabilising force, guaranteed of local acceptability and able to smooth the transition from the old to the new regime. Catholic middlemen were found where the old landlords survived, where the small size of estates militated against large-scale reorganisation, or where it was impossible to recruit solvent immigrants. The survival of Catholic or crypto-Catholic landlords was especially significant in nurturing Catholic middlemen. It is now increasingly evident that such survival was greater in extent than was previously assumed.[10] The inaccurate and flawed formulation of the Protestant Ascendancy has by linguistic sleight-of-hand caused Catholic landlords to disappear from our conception of eighteenth-century Ireland.

Simms's figure of five per cent Catholic ownership of land in 1776 has been frequently cited to 'prove' that such survival was of minimal importance.[11] Yet, based on claimants under the Articles of Limerick, there were as many as 350 landed Catholic families in Ireland in the early eighteenth century.[12] Additionally, it can no longer be safely assumed that 'converts' were a loss to the Catholic interest. Hemmed in by legal restrictions, Catholics quietly discovered loopholes, and felt very little moral qualms about squeezing through them. Ignatius Gahagan, a 'convert' from Catholicism in 1757, made the point succinctly: 'I would rather at any time entrust God with my soul than the laws of Ireland with my lands.'[13] In these circumstances, the convert laws were soon being expertly manipulated. In 1752 a commentator noted that 'the acts relating to purchases made or leases taken by papists are so eluded by perjuries, trusts in Protestant names and other contrivances, that they are of little significance'.[14]

Collusive discoveries (made with the consent of the owner for merely legal reasons) became the accepted method of evading the penal laws on property. Plotting the relationship between eighteenth-century 'conversions' and 'discoveries' demonstrates a synchronicity of the two curves which is astonishing. Behind the black letter of the law a subversive strategy had been devised and implemented by a group of lawyers specialising in convert business. By the mid-eighteenth century, conversion/discovery proceedings were a routine branch of conveyancing.[15] Thus 'conversions' from Catholic to Protestant cannot be taken as an erosion of the Catholic position; rather, in many cases, they strengthened it. It permitted, for example, a convert interest in parliament which was sympathetic to Catholic claims, including well-known figures like Anthony Malone, Lucius O'Brien and John Hely-Hutchinson, and interests like the Dalys in Galway or the Mathews in Tipperary. Edmund Burke should also be located in this tradition. If one includes 'convert' estates, the figure for 'Catholic' ownership of land reaches about 20 per cent. Almost one-fifth of the island therefore remained in relatively undisturbed ownership; even more importantly, these undisturbed estates were concentrated heavily in certain regions – notably the Pale and the Galway/Clare/Mayo area.

The tantalising theme as to how a non-colonised Ireland may have evolved can be partially studied on these estates. Some conclusions seem clear. These estates nurtured (as in Scotland) proliferating kin-based lineages which controlled the strategic leaseholds. A symptomatic example is the Kavanagh of Borris estate in south Carlow.[16] This estate, because it remained in Catholic hands, attracted no planters (indeed, in the 1660 poll tax, Borris is the only town in south Leinster with no New English presence).[17] Even more strikingly, the head tenants remained totally Catholic, with many being recruited from junior branches of the Kavanaghs. In 1747 there were five principal Kavanagh middlemen who held almost a quarter of the estate at very low rents (Ballybeg, Marlay,

Ballynattin, Ballinacoola, Turra, Drummond, Rocksavage, Ballybur, St Mullins). Other Catholic families – Rossitters, Blackneys, Cloneys, Corcorans – dominated the remaining leases and had in turn an overwhelmingly Catholic sub-tenantry. Just as the MacMurrough Kavanaghs sheltered minor branches of their family, so did the Clanricardes in Galway with junior Burke branches, the Ormondes in Kilkenny and Tipperary with Catholic Butlers under their aegis, and the MacDonnells of Antrim.[18] On the Butler (Cahir) estate for example, in the period 1720–50, 97 of 141 leases were to Catholics, like the Sheehys, Buxtons, Farrells, Keatings, Nagles, Dohertys and Prendergasts, some of whom were old proprietors.[19] Dispossessed Catholics were easily accommodated as middlemen on these Catholic estates, and could also be incorporated on Protestant-owned estates. In County Dublin, for example, over sixty of the old landowning class can be traced in the 1660s hearth-money records still living on their ancestral lands.[20] In south County Wexford, a classic region of small estates inherited directly from the medieval landowning system, one can trace twenty-six former landowning families in the role of middlemen in the eighteenth century. If this transition from landowner to middleman is plotted spatially, a striking degree of continuity is manifested.[21]

The pattern in County Wexford is one of lateral translation, an internal low-key dislocation. In this transition from tower-house to farmhouse, and from small landowner to middleman, social and cultural conservatism was ensured. This is reflected across a series of parameters – the survival of farm villages and of vernacular housing styles, the retention of pre-Reformation traditions in the eighteenth century (Christmas carol singing, carrying wooden crosses in funeral processions, mumming) and the survival of the Yola dialect. At a political level, these gentlemen farmers of County Wexford saw themselves and were seen by their communities as an underground gentry, with more authentic roots than the Protestant mushroom gentry around them. As early as 1658, a frequent grievance was the return of transplanted old proprietors to their native districts, receiving 'contributions from their former followers', reflecting the unquestioned acceptance 'amongst the people of their ancient lordly power, the breaking of which was one great end of the transplantation'.[22] These men imbibed the world-view of their Munster counterparts, described by Robert Southwell in 1682 as those who 'expect to be regarded as unfortunate gentlemen, who yesterday lost an estate and were to be restored tomorrow'.[23]

Dispossession and the Jacobite moment

The willingness of others to acknowledge the self-image of the displaced landowners was crucial, generating a residual respect, which cushioned their decline and allowed these families to replicate their traditional status and leadership role. Archbishop King commented:

> They reckon every estate theirs that either they or their ancestors had anytime in their possession, no matter how many years ago and by their pretended titles and gentility they have such an influence on the poor tenants of their own nation and religion who live on those lands that these tenants look on them still tho' out of possession of their estates as a kind of landlord and maintain them after a fashion in idleness in their coshering manner. These vagabonds reckon themselves great gentlemen and that it would be a great disparagement to themselves to follow any calling or trade or way of industry.[24]

In 1738 Samuel Madden commented specifically on this attitude as an Irish trait, 'our nation, above all others, as being the most addicted to follow their great lords and gentlemen of distinction of any in the Christian world'.[25] Culturally, these middlemen families set the tone, as the apex of the surviving social structure. Especially in remote areas, or on the estates of absentee landlords, these old families retained effective cultural control of their communities. The Kerry/Cork borderland provides a good example. The irate letters of Richard Hedges, a new settler in Macroom in the early eighteenth century, link topography ('all mountains, boggs and rocks') to the population composition ('intirely inhabited by Irish') and the lack of Protestants ('from Dunmanway to Canturk which is 40 miles of a barbarous country there is not an English gentleman of note that lives there, except Wm Brown, minister of Macromp'). The end-product was the uninterrupted sway of the old families:

> I think it is my duty to let ye Govt know in what an ill state ye publick peace in this pt of ye Co. of Kerry and some neighbouring parts of ye Co. of Cork is, by means of some heads of Irish clans who not only carry arms and harbour unregistered non-jurist popish priests in defiance of ye laws of the late proclamacion, but have gained ye ascendant over ye civil power by their insolence and principles, so that the ordinary course of ye law cannot be put in force against them, without hazard to ye lives of such as go about to do it, there being very few Protestants and they overawed by ye multitude of papists.[26]

Aodhagán Ó Rathaille picked out Hedges and his fellow-planter Griffin for particular excoriation:

> Gríofa is Heidges, gan cheilg im scéalaibh,
> I leabaidh an Iarla, is pian 's is céasta!
> An Bhlárna gan áitreabh acht faolchoin!
> Is Rath Luirc scriostaithe nochtaithe i ndaor-bhruid.[27]

> Griffin and Hedges – without deceit is my narrative –
> In the place of the Earl, it is pain and torture,
> Blarney deserted except for wolves
> And Charleville destroyed, stripped bare and in deepest desolation.

Even in their reduced circumstances, the older gentry-derived families had a well-developed distaste for 'new' men, whether Catholic or Protestant. The post-

Cromwellian Book II of *Pairlement Chloinne Tomáis* mocks the vulgarity and social affectations of upwardly mobile labourers and cottiers, exhibiting insufficient deference to the descendants of the old nobility: 'Is eagóir go mbiodh mac bodaigh nó lóiminigh ar aonnós le mac duine uasail nó deaghathar'[28] [It is not right that sons of churls or labourers should behave as the son of the gentleman or well-born]. Nicholas Plunkett of the Fingall family, in his Jacobite tract 'The Improvement of Ireland', makes the same point:

> I could wish that there were established a solid distinction between the gentry and those who really are not so . . . I speake this because of an observation made by certain persons how in these late tymes, insolency has crept into the minds of people very mean in their descent but endowed with wealth; some with more, some with less, acquired by industry, whether just or unjust. 'Tis true all honest industry should be encouraged and may they wear the effects of it since they have won it. Yet, let them not turn the same to the abuse or undervalue of such persons to whom there is a respect due for gentility-sake, tho' they should not prove so wealthy, as these new men. Wealth is no lasting companion to nobility[29]

Irish poets also peddled this line of argument; witness Art Mac Cumhaigh's two satires on the Callaghans of Culloville in Armagh, a typical rising Catholic family, investing in milling and leases, but dismissed by the poet as 'bodaigh na heorna' (churls of the corn). *Saeva indignatio* also marks his poem on Arthur McKeown[30] and Peadar Ó Doirnín's 'Tarlach Cóir Ó hÁmaill'.[31] Eibhlín Dubh Ní Chonaill, in her *caoineadh* for her husband Art Ó Laoghaire, regretted the passing of the traditional humility of the *cos-mhuintir* in the presence of her husband:

> Mar a n'umhlóidh romhat mná is fir
> Má tá a mbéosa féin acu
> 'S is baolach liomsa ná fuil anois.[32]

> [Where men and women would bow before you,
> If they have their proper manners,
> But I'm afraid that they don't now.]

A Limerick poet consoled a member of the Burke family who had been reduced to a mere cattle-farmer and who had been insulted because of it:

> Ní masladh ná tarcaisne dhon Bhúrcach
> Bheith ag casadh ná ag múscail a bhó
> Mar dá athair ba chleachtach d'réir dúthchais
> Fairsinige phunnach 'n-a gcomhair:
> A eachra chapallaibh lúthmhar,
> Ba mhinic é a gcúrsa i dtigh an óil,
> An fhaid bhí an aicme seo a dubhairt é
> Ar fuaid gharraidhthe is dronn ortha ag tóch.[33]

> It is no insult or disrespect to Burke
> To be minding and driving his cows,
> For his father inherited extensive sheaf-covered lands for them.
> His team of powerful horses
> Frequently made their way to the drinking-house,
> While the crowd who uttered the insult
> Were bent-backed, grubbing in the fields.

Catholic middlemen families were obsessed, almost to the point of neurosis, with ancestry, family background and the Cromwellian rupture. Miles Byrne of Monaseed described how his father 'told me of the persecutions and robberies that both his family and my mother's had endured under the invaders; how often had he shown me the lands that belonged to our ancestors now in the hands of the sanguinary followers of Cromwell'.[34] John O'Keeffe, the dramatist, describes a childhood visit to Knockdrim, near Edenderry, 'where my father with pride, not unmixed with dejection, led me over tracts of fine land, once the property of his ancestors. My mother had much the same remark to make of her family losses in the county of Wexford.'[35] Contempt for the *arriviste* Cromwellian landlords – a gentry by conquest not by blood – was embedded in the world-view of the families descended from the old proprietors. These sentiments also percolated into the general consciousness. A Dublin tanner was imprisoned in 1714 for sympathising with Jacobites arrested for recruiting: 'Who would blame them for endeavouring to get estates if they could, for that fellow that came over in leathern breeches and wooden shoes now rides in their coaches?'[36] Denis Taaffe, the fiercely partisan historian, expressed similar opinions about the new gentry a century later: 'Ireland proved to them another India, suddenly enriching men of straw, who came here without a good shirt or a coat to their backs.'[37] The convert George O'Malley of Snugborough was proud to note in 1776 that he was 'the direct lineal descendant of the antient famelye of the O'Malleys of Bellclaire in the said Kingdom who were for many centuries sovereign princes there of a large fertile territory that to the present time carryes their name'. He then contrasts his lineage with that of 'the upstart Cromwellian race that infest the country'.[38] Such sentiments were echoed two years later by Rickard O'Connell (of the normally impeccably circumspect Derrynane family); an officer in the Irish Brigade, he referred to his desire to 'make the rascally spawn of damned Cromwell curse the hour of his birth'.[39]

These attitudes continued through to the late eighteenth century. On the Lansdowne estate in Kerry, the agent Joseph Taylor reported in 1775 that 'there are some whose family in former days governed absolutely and who seem to wish still to govern in opposition to my Lord's rights'.[40] Charles Vallancey in 1778 was struck by the fact that 'the bond of vassalage is not yet dissolved among them'.[41] The social pretensions of the Sullivan middleman families on the Lansdowne estate in the late eighteenth century impressed the French traveller Coquebert de Montbret: 'The Sullivans are full of personal vanity. They have their children taught English, which they speak with great purity and they also speak Latin. They dress well and affect an air of good breeding and affluence that is quite astonishing.'[42] These examples also indicate that the Irish sense of gentility was much wider than that of the English or French and that the spectrum was broadened by the scale of the seventeenth-century upheavals, which created this underground gentry milieu, blurring the social categories so readily apparent in England or France.

This obviously had resonances for the land question as well, with an insistent case being made for the legitimate aspirations of the old landed elite. Such aspirations did not stay fenced within the polite precincts of poetry. A remarkable manuscript volume in the National Library of Ireland contains a carefully bound and meticulous transcript of 1733 of every deed and indenture dealing with the 'ancient inheritance of the Waddings of Ballycogly' in County Wexford. This volume was passed to his son by Thomas Wadding in Tenerife, with a rousing admonition to guard it carefully in anticipation of a Stuart restoration, when the 'Cromelian rebbles' would be displaced and the Waddings restored to their rightful position, 'although we enjoy nothing at present but the bare title, having lost all for our loyalty and Catholic religion (to the glory of our family)'.[43]

It was within this context – the displaced Irish elite nexus of patron, poet and priest, and its political typology of rupture, restoration and renewal – that Irish Jacobitism flourished. Janus-headed, its obsessive backward glance to monarchical rupture was balanced by a forward-looking emphasis on restoration. The power of its voice in Gaelic Ireland, the *aisling* (allegory), lay not in its elegiac cadences and dream-world mistiness, but in its allegorical and prophetic intent, which could easily shade into a radical rhetoric of the reversal of the 'ins' and 'outs' of Irish society – English/Irish, Protestant/Catholic, Hanoverian/Jacobite.[44] Consider the culture of complaint embedded in the litany of questions in the eighteenth-century poem 'A fhir chalma sa teangain sin na nGaedhal':

> An fada bheidh na *fanatics* ag réabadh ceall?
> An fada bheidh ag seasamh cnuic le faobhar leann?
> An fada bheidh ár mainistreacha maol gan ceann?
> An fada bheidh ár n-aifrinn fé ghéagaibh crann?[45]

> How long will the fanatics be tearing down churches?
> How long will they be haunting the hills with sharp swords?
> How long will our monasteries be denuded and roofless?
> How long will our masses be held under the branches of a tree?

The same sentiments appear in Aodhagán Ó Rathaille's 'An milleadh d'imthigh ar mhór-shleactaibh na hÉireann' [The destruction that fell on the celebrated families of Ireland]:

> Tír gan triath de ghrian-fhuil Éibhir!
> Tír fá ansmacht Gall do traochadh!

Tír do doirteadh fá chosaibh na méirleach!
Tír na ngaibhne – is treighid go héag liom![46]

A land without a prince of the bright blood of Éibhir!
A land suffocating under foreign oppression!
A land trampled under the boots of boors!
A land in fetters – it sickens me to death!

In the prophetic vein of Irish Jacobitism, Donnchadh Caoch Ó Mathghamhna wrote:

Tiocafaidh an aicme cé fada dá shíor-mhaidheamh sinn,
Is cuirfidh chun reatha lucht trascartha an fhir-dhlíghe chirt:
Bainfidh 's grafaidh nó seasfaidh i ndíg-draoibe –
Sinne ina mbailtibh 's an ghramaisc fá chríon-daoirse.[47]

They [the Jacobites] will come, although we have been endlessly promising them,
And they will expel those who have trampled on the true just law.
We will be in their homes, and they will be
Mowing and hoeing or down in dirty ditches.

Irish Jacobitism therefore provided indigenous ideological ingredients for the subversion of landed title, well in advance of the imported radical recipe from France.

The middleman lifestyle

Looked at by those internal to the culture, it seemed natural for displaced Catholic gentry to retain their status as 'heads of Irish clans'. As late as 1747 fifteen Cork gentlemen supported the future Catholic bishop of Cloyne's nomination by refuting the charge of obscure origins against his family:

They have never degenerated by following any vile or mechanical profession, but have always lived in a decent and creditable manner, in the farming way, as all other Roman Catholic gentlemen in this kingdom are generally obliged to do, ever since the Cromwellian and Revolution forfeitures of Irish estates.[48]

These families were also the bedrock of the Catholic Church in Ireland.[49] Bishop Francis Moylan, reporting to Rome on the diocese of Ardfert (Kerry) in 1785, was worried by the potentially negative impact on the church of the progressive undermining of these middlemen families: 'In these dioceses up to recently, Catholics held the greater portion of the land on terms that were reasonably fair so that there was available to them the wherewithal to exercise their hospitality for which they were renowned and to generously support their pastors.' Now, when leases expired, they were either ejected or forced to pay increased rents, so that 'there scarcely was left to them the means by which they could provide for their families the most meagre subsistence'.[50]

Early in the eighteenth century, William Molyneux described the lifestyle aspirations of the middlemen: 'They think themselves too much gentlemen to put their sons to trade or breed them up to anything that is laborious . . . but sometimes walk about enquiring for news, heretofore concerning the French king and his successes.'[51] Half a century later, in 1755, in a frequently cited diatribe, the Catholic Lord Kenmare accounted for the unimproved state of his estate by reference to the cultural characteristics of his own middlemen:

> This is in a great measure owing to the pride, drunkenness and sloth of the middling sort among the Irish. Every one of them thinks himself too great for any industry except taking farms. When they happen to get them, they screw enormous rents from some beggarly dairyman and spend their whole time in the alehouses of the next village. If they have sons, they are all to be priests, physicians or French officers; if daughters, they are bred up to no kind of industry but become encumbrances on their parents and the public and this sloth and beggary are transmitted from generation to generation.[52]

Kenmare's views were far from singular. In 1773 Joseph Taylor, the agent on the neighbouring Shelburne estate, reported:

> It is really shocking . . . to see how these poor wretches spend their time – parents sauntering about the roads doing nothing and their sons and daughters going to a dancing school at three shillings a quarter, when they might be spinning or carding, digging or plowing or sowing.[53]

As an almost constant refrain, Taylor isolates 'pride, insolence and idleness' as the distinguishing characteristics of the Kerry middlemen of the old stock. Arthur Young was equally censorious in his celebrated depiction of the lifestyle of the Munster middlemen:

> This is the class of little country gentlemen, tenants who drink their claret by means of profit rents, jobbers in farms, bucks, young fellows with round hats edged with gold, who hunt in the day, get drunk in the evening and fight the next morning. These are the men amongst whom drinking, wrangling, quarrelling, fighting, ravishing etc. are found as in their native soil.[54]

Young's pen-picture is a remarkable echo of the contemporaneous 'Caoineadh Airt Uí Laoghaire', where Art is celebrated as a flamboyant custodian of the old Gaelic tradition, eliciting respect and fear in equal measure; he wears a silver-hilted sword, riding-boots to the knee, a gold-banded Caroline hat edged with lace, gloves, a brooch, a cambric shirt and an immaculate suit.[55] These attitudes could surface in various guises. The English land agent Samuel Nelmes had a tough time on the Lansdowne estate in Kerry and was universally disliked, 'his disposition being rather too hot and overbearing among a people who consider themselves as gentry, tho' indeed they have no right to it'.[56] In a revealing couplet,

Eoghan Rua Ó Súilleabháin observed: 'Ní ins an ainnise is measa linn bheith síos go deo, ach an tarcaisne a leanas sin'[57] [It is not being sunk in misery all the time that is worst, but the scorn that accompanies it]. Nevertheless, abundant accounts demonstrate the continuing valency of the old titles. At Callan, County Kilkenny, in 1748 a visitor was struck

> by the respect paid to a man on a little horse and was told that he was a man of an ancient race and derived his birth from some of the most noted clans in the county. Even when the patrimony of such men was gone, the old Irish gave him the title of his ancestors, make him and his lady (if he has one) little presents, cultivating his spot of ground, not suffering him to do the least work to degrade his airy title.[58]

From the same county, Thomas Russell, the United Irishman, reported on the strong feelings excited by the visit of his grandmother, an O'Clear, to Ballyraggett:

> In my father's time, the recollections of these matters were so fresh that he remembers when riding before his mother through Ballyraggett which had been the estate of her family, all the poor people coming out of their cabins clapping their hands and crying out her name.[59]

Near Ballyshannon in 1752, Bishop Pococke met an O'Donnell, supposedly descended from the Earl of Tyrconnell who, 'although he has only leases, yet he is the head of the Roman Catholics in this county and has a great interest'.[60] Colla Dubh MacMahon, a lineal descendant of the Gaelic ruling dynasty of the area, was regarded as the unofficial lord of Dartry barony in County Monaghan until he died in 1724. At the burial of his grandson many years later in Clones, 'the people struggled to get some of his bones as relics or souvenirs'.[61] This later Colla had distinguished himself in a 1790 dispute over the addition of an aisle to the Catholic chapel at Lisnalee in Currin parish on the Madden estate. John Madden, as landlord, tried to prevent the new aisle being opened and came in person to the consecration. MacMahon, as the recognised leader of the local Catholic community, publicly confronted him, faced him down, and physically ejected him from the chapel.[62] The frequency with which newspaper obituaries refer to the old titles also indicates their continuing valency: 1770: 'Died, Donagh O'Brien of Ballyvaghan in County Tipperary esquire, the last of the antient family of the Mac O'Brien in said county.' 1774: 'At Athy died, James Purcell, commonly called Baron Purcell of Loughmoe.' 1790: 'Died near Blarney, Owen McCarthy Esq., commonly called Master-na-Mora.' 1793: 'At Coolavin, County Sligo, died Miles McDermott Esq., commonly called the Prince of Coolavin.'[63] *Faulkner's Dublin Journal* of 29 February 1752 provided a classic example:

> Lately died in the barony of Iveragh and County of Kerry, Daniel Buee McCarthy esq. of a very ancient family. . . . For these seventy years past, when in company, he drank plentifully of rum and brandy which he called 'naked truth'. His custom was to walk eight or ten miles on a winter's morning over mountains with greyhounds

and finders and seldom failed to bring home a brace of hares. He was an honest gentleman and inherited the social virtues of the ancient Milesians.[64]

Such families enjoyed immense social prestige, especially in areas distant from Dublin, where the tendency persisted to regard personal and territorial claims as more legitimate than impersonal state ones. In 1697 the entire estate of Henry Petty, amounting to 20,000 acres in the baronies of Dunkerron and Iveragh in Kerry, was leased to John O'Mahony. Dying in 1706, he was succeeded by Donal of Dunloe (Domhnaill Dúnlúiche), who amassed further leaseholds on the Evans, Kenmare, Pritty and Stopford estates, involving a sub-tenantry of at least 3,000 people. He held almost 300 ploughlands on lease, paid £1,500 per annum in rent, and was agent of the Kenmare property.[65] In the second decade of the eighteenth century, O'Mahony controlled his vast Kerry fief unchecked:

> The said Daniel Mahony for these seven or eight years past contrived a way to make himself great and dreadful in this county; wheresoever he or those under him had any disgust or animosity, his tenants which are very numerous about 4,000 persons and all papists rises out in great numbers by night smocked and black in their faces and give an onset in the nature of fairesses.[66]

Other Kerry middlemen held sizeable leaseholds at this stage which conferred considerable social prestige when combined with a distinguished ancestry. The Bonane O'Sullivans, for example, held 4,666 acres and had been in possession for fourteen generations; the O'Sullivan Mac Fínín Dubh (a 400-year-old title) held 3,111 acres, and the Lynes of Kilmakilloge held 2,900 acres.[67] If necessary, as in the case of O'Mahony, such families could muster formidable 'clans'. In 1740 a hostile Cork observer noted how this power was used by a middleman of this type: 'He has a popish clan that must swagger and must be protected and whoever does not stick his colours to this clan and its patron, the tyrant prime minister, must sink.'[68] In the 1750s that 'clanning' practice (a precursor of the faction-fight?) was still being deprecated by Lord Kenmare,[69] and in the 1770s the agent of the Shelburne estate, Joseph Taylor, had to run the gauntlet against the O'Sullivan families in Tuosist, Creeveen and Bonane. In 1774 his posse was obliged 'to retire from the superior number of people in arms brought against them by the O'Sullivans of Tuosista, against whom there is no standing without an army of soldiers . . . These Sullivans are a desperate and dangerous gang, so connected and related that there is no breaking them without a military force.'[70] In Taylor's opinion, the Kerry middlemen were 'still as uncivilised as in the days of Oliver [Cromwell] and must be handled in the same way. I don't think there is such another set of ungovernable, clamorous, left-handed people in the universe.'[71]

The moral economy

The middleman influence could be exerted unchecked in regions of absenteeism. In 1811 Anthony O'Flaherty held the whole of the Blake estate at Renvyle in Connemara and was 'the acknowledged chief':

> A middleman, possessing an income of £1,500 per annum and surrounded by a numerous and untutored peasantry, utterly unconscious of any other claims on the land, must have undoubtedly been a person of consequence in this county. . . . His authority had an additional sanction from claiming to be a lineal descendant of the old kings of the west, the O'Flaherty of centuries long since gone by.[72]

From Connemara in 1794 a letter of Richard Mansergh St George describes the O'Malley smuggling enterprise:

> Martin O'Malley a tenant of [Richard] Martins is a notorious smuggler, at one time owner or principally concerned in five vessels. He is in a state of defence on a peninsula in Connemara difficult of access from the land by a morass, Great Mans Bay on one side, Costello on the other. He has, I understand, forty stand of arms in his house and has, it is said, committed many illicit acts besides smuggling. He has great influence in that country and may be considered a chief of outlaws, which he attaches to him by presents of run liquors, distributing on holydays casks of spirits among them and is much esteemed for his hospitality and munificence. He rents about £900 a year under Mr Martin's father. . . . Martin O'Malley is connected with most of the merchants in Galway whose trade is smuggling.[73]

The respect enjoyed by such families conferred power. The Freneys of County Kilkenny, now middlemen at Tullagher, continued to regulate clothing (an external marker of social pretensions) by inspecting mass-goers each Sunday and ripping any items that they found offensive.[74] These shadow gentry were avidly sought as sponsors by local families – supplying prestige and patronage and perhaps facilitating access to jobs, subleases, conacre or cottier holdings. They were also used to settle disputes, to act as lubricants if the local social or economic cogs were clogging up. That informal arbitration could blossom into a professional role as estate agent: a classic example is Peter Walsh on the Bessborough estate in south Kilkenny. The same mentality was present in the evolution of the rí (king) concept in the west of Ireland. The rí regulated internal customary practices and represented the community to the outside world. The rí was frequently the scion of an ancient landed family – as with Edward Joyce at Leenane, Edward O'Malley on Clare Island, or Pádraig Ó Flaitheartha of Cill Mhuirbhigh on Aran in the early nineteenth century.[75]

These families also performed a leading role in the Irish version of moral economy. In the late seventeenth century it was already noted that the old proprietors had a much greater grip on the loyalty of the common people than the new landlord class: 'The prime nobility and best gentry of Munster (of which province I am) have a far more commanding and natural ascent over the inclinations of the mob in the respective counties they live in (even in poverty) than the best lord of English birth in Ireland'.[76] Edward Wakefield noted in 1812 that they

> possess a very peculiar influence over the common people which is not enjoyed by Protestants of the same rank. A Roman Catholic gentleman of fortune has thus a paternal character and is looked up to with affection by the population of a very extensive district. Towards the Protestant landlords, there is no such feeling; their influence is limited to their own immediate tenants.[77]

A century later Violet Martin, discussing the Galway method of social control, observed that 'it was give and take, with the personal element always warm in it; as a system, it was probably quite uneconomic but the hand of affection held it together and the tradition of centuries was at its back'.[78]

These Catholic middleman families were also brokers across a series of parameters – political, cultural, social and economic. They were amphibian, at ease in different cultural streams, facing simultaneously into both local and cosmopolitan life, straddling archaic and modern modes. An example may be taken of the Sweetman family.[79] Displaced from their ancestral estate at Castle Eve in Kilkenny, the family had moved to the Catholic Leigh of Rosegarland estate in County Wexford. The Sweetman house at Newbawn is a visual representation of this polyvalent world expressed in architectural terms. The house which they built there in the 1690s still survives – a fine two- storeyed, five-bayed structure of imposing dimensions. It is an instructive example of the blend of traditional and formal in architectural styles: the traditional elements encompass the thatched roof, the mud and coarse rubble walls, the iron window-bars and the central chimney; the formal elements include the symmetrical façade, the Gibbsian doorcase and the sashed windows. The house embodied exactly the social position of the Sweetman family, partaking of both the gentry and common traditions. Alongside the house is a massive cobbled farmyard or bawn surrounded by an array of diverse farm buildings. The complex is located centrally in the townland approached by curving lanes. The Sweetmans bridged two worlds and were brokers on a number of levels – cultural, social and political. They were the hubs around which Catholic society revolved, the solid backbone of the emerging Catholic nation in the eighteenth and early nineteenth centuries.

An equivalent role was played by them in the Catholic Church. These families supplied the senior clergy, the financial support and the chapel sites, and also underpinned the educational system. A symptomatic example is the way in which Catholic chapels were so frequently located on the edges of their lease-holds.[80] The Sweetmans' prominence in the local community is reflected in the fact that the Catholic chapel of Newbawn was sited on their farm, a nucleus around which the chapel village of Newbawn subsequently developed. In the chapel the Sweetmans had their own reserved gallery and a special tea-room was built by them in the chapel yard where the different branches of the family assembled after Sunday mass to maintain family ties.[81] Thus the families saw themselves as patrons of the church, a role accentuated by the heavily domestic character of the institutional church under the impact of the penal laws. Bishop Sweetman's pronouncement in 1771 throws an oblique shaft of light on the acknowledged social dominance of these families in the local church: 'No pastor or ecclesiastick whatsoever must presume to keep a flock or congregation waiting for any person whatsoever; at least, this compliment must not be paid to any one oftener than three times in one year.'[82]

Almost inevitably, such families assumed political roles; a striking feature is how this inherited leadership role could be maintained across a series of movements. In cases like the Sweetmans, Downeses and Kavanaghs in County Wexford, a political leadership role can be traced from a Jacobite phase, through the Catholic Committee into the United Irishmen, and from there into the O'Connellite, tithe and Young Ireland campaigns. These families lent local pres-tige and social solidity, orchestrated crowds, petitions and voters, interpreted the national political process at a local level, and acted as local tribunes of the people. In many senses, they were the penetration point of Catholic politicisation, from whom a radiating effect emanated, deepening the social profile of the politicised group and thereby facilitating the transition from elite to popular politics.[83]

The respect paid to the old families had as its reciprocal the dispensing of patronage. The bonds of affection were tightened by the intimate immersion of these families in the popular culture of their communities, essentially as patrons. In the early eighteenth century Denis O' Conor, head of the family descended from the last High King of Ireland, maintained an Irish master, fencing master and dancing master, while patronising the harpers, Catholic clergy and 'reduced gentlemen' of his neighbourhood. Turlough O'Carolan, for example, was a fre-quent visitor to the house. On Christmas Eve in 1723, he is described as 'taking his harp in a fit of rapturous affection for the family of Belanagare' and 'singing extempore the fall of the Milesian race, the hospitality of old Denis O'Conor and his grandness of soul'.[84] As late as the 1770s, Arthur Young, commenting on the special place of the O'Conors in local affection, noted that 'the common people pay him the greatest respect and send him presents of cattle etc. upon various occasions. They consider him as the prince of a people involved in one com-mon ruin.'[85] The O'Conors themselves were equally conscious of their role as custodians of the culture. A 1786 newspaper report noted that O'Conor 'always appeared contented with the degree of deference and respect from his neighbours and acquaintances which they voluntarily paid him (as knowing him to be a representative of the Royal Connacian race)'.[86]

A concomitant was immersion in popular culture – an immersion that remained strong until the last quarter of the eighteenth century; witness the patronage of music and poetry, the profuse hospitality and heavy drinking, the enthusiastic espousal of hunting, horse-racing, hurling and cock-fighting. This could give an almost consciously archaic feel to the lifestyle, evoked in this description of an Iar-Chonnacht middleman house in the 1750s:

There were two long cabbins thatch'd opposite to one another. In one was the kitchen and apartments for the family. The other was his entertaining room neatly strew'd according to the Irish fashion with rushes, and at the upper end of the room was a kind of platform rais'd above the ground with boards and two or 3 blankets on each which was the lodging for strangers and visitors. A bottle of brandy was the wet before dinner, and the entertainment was half a sheep boil'd at top, half a sheep roasted at bottom, broil'd fish on one side, a great wooden bowl of potatoes on the other and an heap[ed] plate of salt in the middle. After dinner, [there was] some pretty good claret and an enormous wooden bowl of brandy punch which, according to the old as well as the modern Irish hospitality, the guests were pressed to take their full share of; neither did his hospitality allow him to forget their servants and boatmen, but gave a bottle of brandy between every two of them. Towards evening, when the chief began to grow mellow, he call'd in his favourite girl to sing which she did very well and was a neat handsome jolly girl. Before he call'd her in, he stipulated with his guests that they were welcome to any liberties with her from the girdle upwards but he would not permit any underhand doings. A bagpiper likewise attended and towards evening an old Irish bard came in, who for their entertainment made verses in rhyme on any subject they gave him and sung several songs on the virtue of and great prowess of the ancestors of this chief.

In the morning the exhausted guests finally managed to slip away, but the chief 'happening to be awake and, finding them gone immediately mounted a horse bareback'd and pursued them. But they had just reach'd the boat and put off from the shore as he came up; he pour'd upon them vollies of execrations as uncivil scoundrels and milk sops.'[87]

In 1732 Mary Delany visited a thatched cabin in County Galway belonging to 'a gentleman of fifteen hundred pounds a year'. She was startled by the bareness of the house, but its owner 'keeps a man cook and has given entertainment of twenty dishes of meat! The people of this country don't seem solicitous of having good dwellings or more furniture than is absolutely necessary – hardly so much, but they make it up in eating and drinking.'[88] A similar emphasis is evoked eighty years later in the 1811 account of the O'Flaherty middleman house at Renvyle. Their 'Big House' was a long thatched cabin, sixty by twenty feet, only one storey high to all appearances, containing an eating-parlour, a sitting-room twenty by sixteen feet, two reception rooms with two small bed-chambers off each, and also a loft. There were at least two dozen people present at dinner, including two priests, clansmen and relatives. The 'profusion of hospitable board', 'bright turf fire', 'dulcet tones of the bagpipes', 'wine and spirits' were all described as part of the dinner ceremony.[89]

Laurence Whyte's poem *The Parting Cup or The Humours of Deoghedorus* describes the lifestyle of these types of families in County Westmeath c.1710. His preface describes the poem as 'setting forth the great hospitality and good entertainment formerly met with in Irish families, many of whom did not assume to be above the rank of common farmers, whilst some others who were second brothers or the descendants of the nobility and gentry, being for the most part little acquainted with any other kind of industry, turned farmers also and lived very hospitably: these retained the title of gentlemen and were esteemed as such at least whilst they could maintain it'. The subscribers' list to Whyte's *Original Poems* (1740) is a veritable directory of the Catholic gentry of the Pale area, illustrating the appeal that this type of poetry had in that milieu.[90]

Noticeable in these accounts is how the Gaelic stress on profuse hospitality as a marker of gentility survived into the eighteenth century. A 1788 account of the Kavanagh middlemen lifestyle in south Carlow makes the same point:

> The hospitable tables of the inhabitants are furnished with the utmost plenty and elegance. Their principal joy consists in entertaining those who visit them. As soon as any company comes to their houses, word is sent to most of their relations, who join and make the sweetest concord in the world. After two or three days spent in innocent pleasure, you are all invited to another gentleman's with the same agreeable round of mirth and so on till you have gone through the whole race. The day of parting is the only day of grief or discontent. This is the end and manner of what is called coshering so much mistaken by several authors.[91]

There were also widespread kin obligations. In 1748 Charles Carroll of Carrollton in Maryland replied to a letter from Daniel O'Carroll, a distant kinsman in London, remarking on

> the pleasure I have in hearing the health of a gentleman of my name and so nearly related in famyly tho' by the destiny and revolution of time and states separated from our native soil where our predecessors time immemorial inherited both ample estates and honours. Nothing more contributes (next to Christian patience) to alleviate my concerns for such misfortunes than the consideration that the Macedonian and Roman empires are no more, that the Grecian states with many more within the compass of Europe have been overturned. I therefore comfort myself and endeavour to get a livelyhood in this wild part of the globe. [Family misfortune] leaves me the only son of the family you mention but by this I do not expect to inherit Clonlisk, Ballibrit, Leap, Castletown or any other part or a foot in Ely O'Carroll. Transplantations, sequestrations, acts of settlement, explanations, infamous informations for loyalty and other evils forbid.[92]

At times these kin obligations extended to 'the wide concatenation of a Kerry cousinhood'. In April 1783 Maurice O'Connell, an officer in the Irish Brigade, wrote from France to acknowledge his obligations which, as a bachelor, weighed heavily upon him:

> Let me know of any young relatives of our name between fifteen and twenty years of age, of a good figure, size and behaviour who wish to get into some of the Irish houses of our order abroad [the French army]. I shall endeavour to place them on recommendation from you.

Within two years the Kerry deluge had so inundated him that he had to call a halt: 'It becomes impossible to engross the whole of the vacant employments for County Kerry people only, and indeed there's already no proportion in that line, for there are three Kerry people in the Irish regiments for one of any other county in Ireland.'[93]

The importance of the Jacobite tradition also lay in the close links which it maintained between Catholic Ireland and the continent, not least through military recruiting. The activities of professional genealogists were necessary for those Catholics wishing to pursue a military career at a high level in the continental armies, which required proof of noble descent as an entrance requirement to the highest echelons of their societies.[94] The Stuart papers contain many examples of attestations of nobility. In March 1732, for example, Ambrose O'Callaghan, the Bishop of Ferns, wrote in favour of the daughters of Sir Peter Redmond, who had formerly owned Redmond Hall in Wexford. He described them as being 'of as good, noble and gentle family as are in the Kingdom':

> Not only for their lineal descent, without blot or interruption from ancient and illustrious families, ever since ye first coming of the English into Ireland with Strongbow nearly six hundred years ago, but for their ancestors loyal adherence to their lawful kings and to the holy R.C. religion, without it ever being said or known that any of them ever deviated from either ye principles or policies of men of honour. They never undertook any mechanick or loose calling and yet ever since their being wrongfully divested by the usurper Cromwell of their sumptuous houses, patrimonies and estates, they have lived in decency and respect and in good repute among ye best Catholic gentry of the Kingdom who still claim them for their kin and relations.[95]

This milieu created a market for pedigrees, real or embroidered. The degree to which Irish Catholic families with reduced patrimonies looked to officer service abroad to retain status was one of the principal reasons why genealogy retained such a central role in their lives. The French diplomat Coquebert de Montbret was astonished to find on visiting Ireland that even famous French army families like Dillon and Lally were mere tenant farmers on Richard Kirwan's estate at Cregg in Galway, while the Mullallys were simply 'peasants'.[96]

The social pressures on these old landed families to be hospitable was intense. George Ryan of Inch in County Tipperary, inheriting the encumbered ancestral estate in the 1780s, eventually retreated to Toulouse in France, where he could live quietly and frugally without the ruinous expenses of ostentatious entertaining expected of him in his native County.[97] A sympathetic observer, Rev. James Little, described the trajectory of the old Catholic gentry families of the Mayo region. He considered that short (thirty-one-year) leases cramped their successful accumulation of wealth, but that their 'family pride and affection, as well as a certain sense of honour' meant that they had to be magnificently hospitable, as well as maintaining many relatives at their houses. The result was the eventual mortgage and sale of their leases, the dispatch of their sons into foreign military service and their 'dwindling into declining farmers . . . til their names which formerly denoted a parish or a barony have become eclipsed by men in some instances of no name and no origin'. Little cited the Maguires of Crossmolina as a classic example, 'men who have little left to them except the mortifying recollections of the great names of their ancestors'.[98]

However, until well into the nineteenth century, the old attitudes survived. In 1837, John O'Donovan described his encounter with Edmund O'Flyn near Castlerea in County Roscommon:

> [O'Flyn] walked with me to the source of the Suck from the esker over which he shewed me his ancient principality of which he now holds but a few townlands in fee-tail. He knows the names of every bush in the parish of Kiltullagh, the names of which he pronounced for me sitting on Eiscir Uí Mhaonagáin over Bun-Suicín in the townland of Cul-fearna, the parish of Annagh and County of Mayo, from which we had an extensive view of O'Flyn's country of Loch Uí Fhloinn, Sliabh Uí Fhloinn and of the parish of Kiltullagh. As soon as O'Flyn learned that I was one of the ould stock, he commenced to give me a most curious account of his own family and of himself; the poor fellow is very much embarrassed and when I met him, was hiding from the Sheriff who will arrest him for debt as soon as he can.[99]

His Ordnance Survey colleague, Thomas O'Connor, met Patrick Sarsfield of Newtown-Monasterboice in Louth, then aged over eighty years. He was the grandson of Thomas, brother of Patrick of 1690 fame, who had been killed at the Battle of the Boyne and whose gun, bayonet and sword his grandson still possessed. He prided himself on his descent, on his brother in the Spanish army, on his command of the Irish language, on his part in the Defender movement of the 1790s and his subsequent role in the anti-tithe campaign, and his hospitality.[100] In 1798 Sarsfield had sheltered Charles Teeling, who described him as 'not having lost a particle of the pride of his ancestors'.[101]

Popular culture

In the first half of the eighteenth century, the Catholic middlemen had been centrally involved in popular culture and lost no social caste from it. Jonah Barrington identified them as 'half mounted gentlemen', describing how they 'exercised hereditarily the authority of keeping the ground clear at horse racing, hurling and all public meetings'.[102] Laurence Whyte's poem 'The Parting Cup' emphasises how these families were immersed in local life in the early decades of the eighteenth century.

> They seldom did refuse a summons
> To play at football or at commons,
> To pitch the bar or throw a sledge,
> To vault or take a ditch or hedge,
> At leisure hours to unfold a riddle,
> Or play the bagpipes, harp or fiddle.[103]

In May 1749 John O'Connell wrote to his bookish younger brother Maurice, advising him to involve himself in the quotidian culture of the Derrynane area:

Learn ye methods of ye country with regard to dry and dairy cattle – how got and disposed of; how ye ground is tilled and managed. . . . You can read at night and sometimes by day. Goe visit ye workmen: goe fish of a fair day in ye boat: sometimes ride and see ye herdsman and cattle: see waste grass and corn and sometimes rush, leap, run, play ball. . . . By this you'll inform yourself, you'll do ye ffamily a service, you'll exercise yourself, and wch is more than all you'll please your ffather thoroughly upon whom your future welfare depends, and whom (believe me) you cannot otherwise please.[104]

Looking back nostalgically, Michael Whitty captured the closeness of his father to popular culture in the mid-eighteenth century, at Nicharee in Duncormick parish, County Wexford:

My father was a substantial farmer and lived in the low thatched house which his great grandsire had erected about a century before in a little valley which is at the right hand side of the road that runs from Wexford to Bannow. . . . At chapel, he occupied the most prominent form [wooden seat] at the left hand side of the altar and his name headed the priest's list whenever a charitable collection was made. Such a man was looked up to by his neighbours with somewhat of reverence and he was not a little formal in all his proceedings. But above all, he prided himself in following the hospitable example of his father . . . brewing at home; the black and white puddings which lined the capacious chimney showed that the pig had been for some time in salt, the bullock slaughtered at Christmas, the [brick] oven, the hemlock which polished the pewter dishes, the gritty sand spread over the parlour floor (all were part of the lifestyle). . . . There was midnight mass in the little low thatched chapel at Rathangan, with its humble roof, a wooden cross stuck on the gable end, little painted altar, the crucifix, the holy water pots and the fourteen stations. The old Christmas carols were sung here. . . . After mass, the house was filled with friends, followers and neighbours, who ate brown barley bread, bacon and gritty, roast beef, boiled beef, ducks, chickens, pullets and turkeys. . . . The mummers were the main point of attraction at Christmas, when their first performance always took place in a field adjoining the chapel, composed of twelve decent young men dressed in gay ribbons and silk handkerchiefs in snow white shirts going through their artful evolutions. Their company was an honour which was conferred only on the select few. My father's house was the first they usually visited and on this occasion, the friends and relatives of the family were invited to enjoy the dance and the amusement, and it was then the truly substantial black oak table groaned with the weight of the feast, whiskey punch and rich home-brewed ale thrived in goblets brimming full, sparkling even through the opacity of earthen bowls. The twelve days of Christmas were devoted to mumming, hurling and dancing, every door stood open and every table was covered to abundance.[105]

A 1764 description of a wedding in the barony of Forth in the same county presents a comparable picture:

They first find a large waste cabin, malthouse or barn, where they place tables, benches etc., with wadds of straw in several different parts of it. After the couple are joined by the priest's hand and a ring is exchanged, and every person present has heartily smacked the bride, they make a collection for the priest, and for the piper and last for the itinerant beggars who have all assembled to make merry with the happy pair on the joyful occasion. This ceremony over, they seat themselves to dinner, the bride at the upper end of the table, the priest at the lower, the brides-men, bride's maids etc. all seated in proper order, with the bridegroom as an attendant or butler, who does not presume to sit at table but takes a bit, now and then, behind backs. They all eat and drink very heartily, especially the priest, who does the honours of the table and diligently helps himself to the titbits – the two legs and wings of the goose, the biggest one of the puddings etc. After dinner, the bride is handed from the table by the head bridesman, who has the favour of danc-ing with her; then there is an apple thrown up, and whoever recovers it is favoured with dancing second. When they have danced and drank a great deal, the brides-men form a party to carry off the bride, which they commonly accomplish. There is immediately a hue and cry after them, in which most part of the night is spent. The bridesmen never do her the least injury; it is only a kind of old custom or formality used among them.[106]

By the late eighteenth century, these common ties in the informal intimacy of collective engagement in popular culture had snapped, to be replaced by a more formal, distant relationship. The provision of pews and even private galleries in Catholic chapels for the local elite was a graphic representation of the transition. Already by the 1770s it was considered that those who had not disengaged themselves were losing social caste. By 1786 Roderick O'Connor, at the centre of controversy, could be dismissed peremptorily as a nonentity because he was 'a man rather of a mean disposition and rustic education, frequenting hurling greens and football matches, intermingling with the populace at fairs and patrons, drinking to excess spirituous liquors'.[107] O'Connor belonged to that Connacht class described by W.H. Maxwell as 'proprietors of little properties called fodeeins [Irish: fóidín], who continued the names and barbarisms of their progenitors. Without industry, without education, they arrogated a certain place in society, and idly imitated the wealthier in their vices.' By the early nineteenth century, they had 'fortunately disappeared'.[108] Arthur Young's famous attack on middlemen mingled annoyance at their profit rents with distaste for their lifestyle. His analysis quickly became conventional and newspaper accounts continually harped on it. In 1787 Finn's Leinster Journal reported:

Trade is too vile an employment, too grovelling an item for youth, if raised but one step above the surface of beggary. The exalted pursuits of cock-fighting, horse-racing and debauching female innocence are only worthy of their attention. Upon a farm of £200 or £300 a year, it is not at all uncommon to see six or seven gentlemen reared. At length, the little patrimony is divided among them and just as much falls to the share of each as will enable him to subsist without annual labour, to wear a laced waistcoat, once a year to kill a wretched horse with hard riding, to get intoxicated every night with whiskey punch, to be insolent to his superiors and the scourge of them below him.[109]

In 1788 the newspaper returned to the attack:

> What is called hospitality swallows up everything: eating, drinking and rural sports fills up the whole time of our Irish country gentlemen. The principal point of ambition is to outdo his neighbours in hospitable profusion. He retires to support his pseudo-dignity by cock-fighting, card-playing, scheming and skulking among his circle of acquaintances, bullying and cheating every tradesman, running away with an heiress, falls into the road-eating train of some harum-scarum fox-hunter and dies as he lives, despised by that rank to which he vainly aspired.[110]

The newspaper deplored the 'two legacies bequeathed to us by our Milesian forefathers – pride of ancestry and contempt of commerce. Family pride in this country betrays its shabby and fantastic form here and there in the character of a petty despot surrounded by a wretched peasantry, racked and oppressed for the support of his vanity – a tenantry whom he considers his vassals.' Because of the 'contempt of commerce', 'money is wasted on learning to fence, dance, ride, drink, hunt and wench'.[111]

By 1793, when Samuel Crumpe wrote his prize-winning *An Essay on the Best Means of Providing Employment for the People* for the Royal Dublin Society, the attack on middlemen had become a strictly conventional set-piece:

> The yell of a pack of starving beagles is more pleasing to their ears than the song of the ploughman. The sight of their fellow sportsmen, drenched to insensibility in whiskey, more pleasing to their eyes than luxurious crops and well cultivated fields. They are the class amongst whom what remains of the ferocious spirit of drinking which formerly disgraced this kingdom is still to be found.[112]

The cultural, social and spatial distancing illustrated here may have been heralded too by sharpening economic antagonisms. The accelerating social divide was part of a modernising process, a process which eventually killed the archaic middleman world. As early as 1738, though perhaps with a strong element of wish-fulfilment, Samuel Madden observed that Catholics who made money 'were running fast into the neatness and plenty of the English way of living'.[113] But that transition out of the old, local, domestic world really occurred on a large scale between 1760 and 1840, when a second category of middleman emerged – the large-scale speculator in leases who appeared when economic prospects were buoyant but while rents still lagged behind the market value. In these conditions, cash-strapped landlords welcomed lease speculators who could pay a high entry fine. These mercenary middlemen, once in possession, were anxious to maximise profits from their investments as quickly as possible. In the 1760s, this created three effects: a sharp jump in sub-tenants' rents; the expansion of commercial farming, especially in cattle; and the enclosure (in effect privatisation) of commonages to bring them into commercial production. In these circumstances, the smallholders and cottiers lost out badly. They were forced to pay higher rents to the middlemen, who simultaneously deprived them of their commonage rights, and therefore of their cows, hence stripping milk and milk products out of an already depleted diet. In other words, it was the weakest element in local society which bore the brunt of full-blooded commercialisation. The speculative middlemen fattened at their expense. In the rich grazing grounds of Tipperary and Limerick, huge ranchers emerged, holding up to 8,000 acres and outbidding the small tillage farmers, who often rented on partnership leases which protected commonage rights. A Munster commentator noted the result for these small farmers, who

> have generally for several years past been obliged to betake themselves to the mountains, where they took little farms at exorbitant rates, often at the second or third hand, which they planted chiefly with potatoes, of which they endeavoured to make their rents, and with which and some oats they generally maintained their numerous families.[114]

Some of these new middlemen did exceptionally well. The Scullys of Tipperary, for example, were deriving a profit rent of £6,700 from their leases by 1803; from a single lease of Springhouse, the McCarthys in the same county had a profit rent of £1,000 by 1806.[115] Richard Musgrave, at the end of the century, commented on the 'nabob fortunes' which these Catholic families had acquired in the expansionary conditions after 1760.[116] These disparities also fuelled agrarian secret societies. The great redresser movements, the Whiteboys and Rightboys, sought a return to the days when the moral economy blunted the impact of the real one, and when the yawning chasm between rich and poor Catholics had not been so wide. That chasm opened ever wider in the late eighteenth century.

One can see this in a number of key transitions. It is at this stage that the 'cabin' is relinquished in favour of the two-storyed slated farmhouse, and the new house is carefully distanced from the cottiers' cabins. The house becomes mimetic of more formal fashions, signalled by the presence of an avenue, decorative trees and gardens, a miniature demesne. The newer social pretensions are symbolised by the assigning of a name to the farm, usually that of the townland – like 'Johnstown House' or 'Ballymore House'. The transition is also reflected linguistically (the decisive break to English-speaking accelerates during this period); politically (for the first time, farmers begin to play a major role in national politics); and culturally (diet, leisure patterns, clothes, furniture – all begin to change in response to new expectations). We are heading towards the nineteenth-century defining characteristics of the big farmer: 'a priest in the parish, a pump in the yard, a piano in the parlour, and bulled his own cows'.[117]

Above all, these changes are reflected in shifting social attitudes. Throughout Europe in the late eighteenth century, elite groups began to distance themselves from popular culture. In Ireland the sharpening political divides sundered the links, especially in the late eighteenth and early nineteenth centuries. The old allegiances – to calendar custom, hurling, cock-fighting, horse-racing, hunting, patterns, wakes, traditional music, dancing and poetry, public drinking – faded in the face of this modernising thrust. In a way, once Catholic big-farm families had disengaged themselves from this culture (oral, local, archaic, pre-modern), it inevitably withered, degenerating into disorder, without the social discipline and patronage to regulate and replicate itself. Across the board in the late eighteenth century, the sinking social centre of gravity of participation in popular culture can be traced; hurling and abductions are two well-documented examples.[118] Abductions at the middleman level effectively ceased after 1780, in the wake of the much-publicised exemplary executions of Garret Byrne and James Strange in Kilkenny for their involvement with the Kennedy sisters.[119]

The withdrawal from and subsequent assault on vernacular religion is part of the same process, mainly inspired by the Catholic clergy, themselves recruited from exactly the same class which was then abandoning its older mores.[120] The newly respectable voice of Irish Catholic culture can be heard in Father Mathew Horgan, parish priest of Blarney, whose denunciations of wakes led him to new heights of vituperation:

> Irish wakes, I say, are synonymous with everything profligate, wicked, wasteful and disgraceful to a christian people, and every lover of religion, morality and good order should cooperate to abolish such a foul stain on the Irish character. As I was well aware of the difficulty of rooting out old customs and prejudices, I earnestly proceeded to the task for the good of the people whose governor I am. I cursed in the chapel those who allowed wakes and those who frequented them, knowing their business there was neither sorrow or sympathy, but to have a glorious night's fun in eating, drinking and smoking nasty tobacco, and I found that those who frequented wakes, like executions, become hardened villains who could not be trustworthy. I have so well succeeded that the people are grateful and unanimous in their suppression. For this I had a facility which few others could boast of; in the building of my round tower, I left a vault of ten feet in diameter in the base, to which, as soon as a coffin is procured, the body is conveyed to remain there for a time.[121]

Compare this with the traditional *caoin* uttered by the people of Kilmac-killoge in Kerry on the death of the Mac Fínín Dubh in 1809, as recounted by Lady Louise Lansdowne;

> The moment our boat reached the land, all the inhabitants of the bay, who had assembled themselves on some high ground near the shore, began to howl and lament McFinnin and continued to bewail him the whole time we staid and till our boat was well out of sight. The howl is a most wild and melancholy sound and impresses one with the idea of real sorrow in the people, and as we heard it at Kilmacalogue echoed by the rocks and softened by the distance, nothing could be more striking and affecting.[122]

The rise of the Catholic big farmer

One can contrast the Catholic middleman families derived from the displaced gentry with those who advanced socially from the small-farm ranks in the expansionist economy of the eighteenth century. Both carried their values with them, and the embryonic Irish big-farm class formed an arresting amalgam of downwardly and upwardly mobile groups, each of them taking their old world-view with them into their new situations.[123] William Tighe's *Statistical Observations relative to the County of Kilkenny* (1802) provides a classic description of one such rising family – the Aylwards' dairying empire in the Walsh Mountains in the late eighteenth century:

> This family consist at present of five branches who hold among them over 2,000 acres including Knockmeilin [Knockmoylan], Ballybrishan and other large townlands. Their houses are small and near each other and till lately were little better than those of the poorest farmers but they have now slated them to guard against malicious burnings [by Whiteboys] or robbers. The women of the family constantly marry in it and for this purpose are obliged to buy dispensations at a high price and if a widow marries a stranger, she loses all except what she brought with her. For one farm of 900 acres, they paid a few years ago a heavy fine amounting to more than 2,500 guineas for a new lease of three lives or 31 years, and £600 a year rent. This money was given in hard gold which lay by them and this is the mode in which the profits of such farms are applied. They slaughter their pigs generally at home and eat the offal which is the only animal food they usually make use of, living principally on potatoes and some griddle bread. Their incomes are probably not less than £600 or £700 a year.[124]

In contrast to the ostentatious, flamboyant lifestyle of the displaced gentry, frugality, hard work and reticence were bywords for these families. Even the most successful, like the Aylwards, enjoying a gentry-like income, were slow to engage in conspicuous consumption, and communities dominated by these types of farmers, as in south Kilkenny, remained conservative. In 1815 the tourist Atkinson was surprised to find prosperous Kilkenny farmers speaking only Irish. In particular, he commented on the 'extensive pig breeders and dairymen of the Walsh Mountains who cannot speak a single sentence of plain English'. He also noted how their clothes differed from the more modernised districts to the north and east, with the frieze coat still universally popular.[125] When John O'Donovan of Slieverue visited Thomas Larcom for the first time in 1828, Larcom was struck by O'Donovan's 'peasant garb' – his frieze *cóta mór*.[126] In 1732 John Loveday had observed that in Kilkenny most of the men wore a dark frieze of Irish manufacture and that 'the men affect Spaniard-like to walk ye streets with their great coats thrown over their shoulders, by way of a cloak'.[127] It was only in the 1830s, according to James Graves, that the local people abandoned their blue frieze coats and mantle in favour of factory-produced textiles.[128]

A similar reticence applied to the housing of these big farmers. Until the 1780s, estate maps show a surprisingly high percentage, often above ninety per cent, of farmers living in 'cabins' – in eighteenth-century parlance, small, mud-walled, clay-floored, thatched, single-storeyed houses. That predeliction partially reflected a cultural preference; Amhlaoibh Ó Súilleabháin in 1831 was lyrical in his praise of the vernacular house: 'Snug is a low, sheltered cabin, on which the thatch is laid on thick, and in which are food and fire. No house is so comfortable as a thatched, mud-walled cabin, with a solid door, small windows, a big fire, and plenty of provisions.'[129] The preference may also have reflected a typically cautious, low-profile attitude among Catholics. Bishop Patrick Ryan of Ferns in 1812 contrasted the limited numbers of Protestants as opposed to their highly visible public expression:

> They appear more numerous than they really are, because they have power and can make a show; we are without it and make none. Look to the chapels on Sundays and look to the churches. They have law on their side and can speak out: we have it against us and must be silent.[130]

For these rising families, a coherent family strategy, founded on primogeniture and the successful dispersal of surplus children was crucial. Only a prudent management of family resources and alliances could achieve these twin aims. The family strategy of the traditional farm depended on a dual allegiance – to the ancestors of the past and the inheritors of the future. Family continuity was crucial: the individual farm-holder was merely the baton-carrier in the relay race of family destiny. In order to succeed, the acquisition, retention and transmission of leases was vital. Indeed, the most striking achievement of these big-farm families was precisely their ability to insert primogeniture as a controlling principle of family organisation into the very heart of landlordism – the leasing system. A favourable landlord was essential. In 1729 Robert Keating of Knockagh in Tipperary bequeathed 'to my Lord Cahir's eldest son, a young grey mare, now grazing on the lands of Cnocknefalling, as a token of my love to him and his father'.[131]

The acquisition of leases was helped by a number of eighteenth-century developments: the widening distinction between farmer and labourer; the tendency to bypass middlemen and lease directly to the sitting tenant; and the less privileged position of Protestants, increasingly forced to play on a level tenurial pitch. In the background, help also came from the menacing (landlord) or comforting (farmer) phenomenon of customary law (enforced by intimidatory and exemplary violence), which again reinforced the sitting tenant's position. Above all, the expanding eighteenth-century economy distributed wealth to leaseholders. The long period of price rises between 1740 and 1810 laid the basis of a comfortable farming class. Dispersal of surplus family members ensured that the original leasehold remained intact. The ensuing mobility broadened the kinship network and cultural horizons of the family, frequently distributing surplus sons to the church, trade or the professions. The astonishing dominance of the Cork dairying industry or the Wexford malting trade by Catholic families from this background has to be understood in the context of this kinship process.

The marriage patterns of these families were carefully controlled to nurture family interests. The central feature was its endogamous character – like marrying like – within a narrow social and spatial ambit. In the course of time the group of big-farm families in particular areas tended to become a self-perpetuating caste because of repeated intermarriage. Family discipline was maintained by recourse to wills, dowries and marriage settlements. A typical will clause regulated daughters' marriage behaviour. In 1829 John Browne of Big Barn in County Wexford made his will in which he bequeathed 'to my daughter Ann £250 sterling and to my daughter Margaret £250 sterling. Should any of my daughters aforesaid transgress before marriage or marry contrary to the consultation of the Reverend James Brown[e], my son, she or they shall be cut off to one shilling.'[132]

Given close parental control, the paramount obligations of kin, and the obsession with the maintenance of property interests, the arranged match was a *sine qua non*. Women became the pawns of an elaborate chess game: favoured gambits were cousin marriages, double marriages and marriages across a series of generations. This endogamous, carefully structured marriage network held the constellation of family interests together, creating a web of reciprocities and obligations, evolving out of the soft intimacies of kin, but embedded in a hard legal carapace of wills, marriage settlements, dowries and trusteeships. If disputes arose, the ubiquitous priest in the family tree was called down to act as arbitrator. Caution was the watchword for these acquisitive families. According to his son, the Tipperary farmer James Scully's 'principal object was that of acquiring wealth, his next that of preserving it. His views on public subjects were dependent on these objects.'[133] By 1796, pursuing this strategy, Scully had accumulated a lease-hold interest of 15,000 acres.[134] James Downes, a Wexford strong farmer pressed on all sides regarding the disposal of £3,000 he had on his hands in 1801, stated his own preference: 'If I can, I will lay it out in land for my children.'[135]

The emphasis on tight control of family resources was necessitated by the desire to place other family members off the home farm. This demanded resources, especially for education, the key to a successful career. In the eighteenth century, these families sustained the so-called hedge-school system, usually by a system of patronage-cum-tutelage. That education paved the way for openings in trade, the church or abroad. The Whittys of Nicharee, County Wexford, in the 1790s offer a paradigmatic example: 'My father, like other Catholics of means, determined one of his sons for the Church and, not to say it prophanely, he imported a profound teacher, learned in Greek and Latin, from the then classic region of Ireland, Munster.'[136] In the late eighteenth century, these families sustained the great Catholic teaching orders for boys and girls, which spread rapidly under their patronage in the Catholic big-farm region of east Munster and south Leinster. Reflecting the symbiosis, the Presentation and Mercy nuns, and the Christian Brothers, like the diocesan clergy, were overwhelmingly recruited from these same families.[137]

Given their wealth and increasingly assured position, these families often blended in a surprisingly inconspicuous way into the background. Their typically understated farmhouses could escape an unobservant eye. The hurrying traveller, passing rapidly through the roadside raggle-taggle of miserable cabins, was overwhelmed by images of poverty; he failed to notice the discreet world of the big farmer, embedded in the centre of their farms, and insulated from the perimeter of poverty around them. Viewed from this perspective, Arthur Young's cantankerous grumble appears to be a simple misreading of the Irish social landscape: 'I have in different parts of the kingdom seen farms just fallen in after leases of three lives, of the duration of fifty, sixty, and even seventy years, in which the residence of the principal tenant was not to be distinguished from the cottared fields surrounding it.'[138] John Burrows, an English clergyman touring Ireland in 1773, was equally baffled by the 'unaccountable circumstances that though you see a very large extent of country covered with corn, your eye cannot discover one farmhouse or one rick of last year's produce, either of hay or corn. When you ask where the tenants live of such demesnes, you are shown a hovel or two of a cabin, which seem incapable of containing a thousandth part of the produce!' Equally bewildered was Thomas Creswick, who returned from a visit to Ireland in 1837 puzzled at having seen 'no sturdy yeoman, distinguished from his labourers both by the respectability of his dress and the air of command with which he looks around him'.[139]

Owing to the lack of conspicuous consumption, the social cleavages of Ireland were immersed in a deceptively homogeneous landscape, as Patrick Knight describes from Ballycroy, County Mayo:

> In 1813 I slept in a man's house who had 100 head of black cattle and 200 sheep, and there was not a single chair or stool in his home, but one three legged one, no bed but rushes, no vessel for boiling their meals but one, the madder [mether] which was handed around indiscriminately to all who sat around the potato basket (myself among the rest) placed up on the pot for a table; yet this man was said to be very rich, besides the stock named above.[140]

Caesar Otway, reporting from Joyce's Country in County Galway in 1839, picked up on the same point: 'I was also informed that there was much ignorance and contented destitution of all that a better informed people would call comforts, so that a man when he became wealthy did not by any means exhibit it in his living, his house or his furniture.'[141] An Irish proverb expressed this succinctly: 'Dá mbéadh prataí is móin againn, bhéadh an saol ar a thóin againn' [If we had potatoes and turf, we would have life at our ease]. The seat behind the coachman was therefore a biased one in pre-Famine Ireland. It is in this broad sense, perhaps, that one should interpret the concept of the 'Hidden Ireland'. Corkery's twin insistence of approaching it only from the evidence of Gaelic poetry and of locating it largely in west Munster is misleading. The Hidden Ireland of the eighteenth century was not incarnated in the cos-mhuintir – the proliferating, poverty-stricken base of the social pyramid – nor in the flamboyant but restricted world of the Munster middlemen; the crucial custodians of tradition were the comfortable, Catholic, big-farm class (a Norman-Gaelic hybrid) of south Leinster and east Munster, who provided stability and continuity.[142]

Reactions

These developments created a perplexing paradox in the relationship between landlord and tenant in Ireland. At a superficial level, there was the apparently unrivalled power of the landlord which so startled Arthur Young: 'It must strike the most careless traveller to see whole strings of cars whipt into a ditch by a gentleman's footman to make way for his carriage.'[143] At the same time, gentry coming from England to Ireland were struck by the independence of the tenantry's private lives from landlord scrutiny or control, as was noted, for example, by Elizabeth Smith of Baltiboys in 1840:

> There was nothing struck me so remarkably when I first came here as the tenants marrying their children, setting them up in different trades etc. without ever saying one word about it to their landlord. It went through their whole conduct – we were to them only the receivers of a much grudged rent.[144]

Given the evidence of a dispossession mentality in Ireland and of the continuing competition for hearts and minds by an alternative underground gentry, it is not surprising that the official gentry of the country felt uneasy. Even apparently innocuous wake-games could carry a subversive subtext. The game known as 'Sir Soipín' (the Knight of Straw so called from his diagnostic súgán headdress), as described by J. C. Walker in 1789, contrasted an Irish landlord representing an ancient family in the neighbourhood with an English landlord.[145] Their barbed repartee offered obvious opportunities for satire and for historical and political commentary, in which the 'Irish' landlord always had the upper hand.

Faced with the continuous presence of these barely submerged sentiments, Protestants could only deplore the false premises upon which these pretensions rested. Castigating the impact of the Gaelic poems and genealogies which sustained the claims of the old landed class, one early commentator made use of the memorable image of the 'pucán' to make the point:

> In the north of Ireland, the Irish have a custom in the winter when milk is scarce to kill the calf and preserve the skin, stuffing it with straw and set it upon four wooden feet, which they call a puckaun, and the cow will be as fond of it as she was of the living calf. She will low after it and lick it and give her milk down. . . . These writings will have the operation of this puckaun, for wanting the land to which they relate, they are but stuffed with straw, yet they will low after them and lick them over and over in their thoughts and to teach their children to read by them instead of horn books. And if any venom be there, they will give it down at the sign of these writings.[146]

One remedial response was to try to convert the old landed class. In 1708, for example, Lord Weymouth was keen that the newly established Charter School on his estate at Carrickmacross should target the MacMahons 'the ancient proprietors of the barony of Farney'.[147] In the 1730s Arthur Dobbs observed that the old native proprietors still 'always pretend a claim to their ancient properties'.[148] If these claims were accompanied by a flamboyant lifestyle, they were seen as a political affront and those concerned were warned about their behaviour. Richard Cox's charge to the Cork grand jury in 1740 put the point succinctly to the county's Catholics: 'Patience, resignation and humility become men daily exposed to the legal power of their adversaries. These virtues would better recommend them to pardon and impunity than pride, stubborness and insolence.'[149] Protestant nerves tended to jangle at any suggestion that these pretensions might be encouraged. In 1736, for example, Lord Clancarty, a British naval officer and former governor of Newfoundland, sought to persuade the British cabinet to revoke a bill of attainder against his father, which had involved lands now worth £60,000 per annum. Archbishop Hugh Boulter of the Irish Privy Council immediately warned the English Prime Minister that any acquiescence in Clancarty's suit would 'be a great blow to the Protestant interest here, and will very much shake the security Protestants think they now have of the enjoyment of their estates. . . . I think the affair of the first magnitude to the Protestant interest here'.[150]

The insecurity elicited by living in the penumbra of an alternative gentry can frequently be felt under the superficial calm of landlord life. Even the most obsequious demonstrations of Catholic loyalty were still suspect; their fidelity to a Protestant state was 'only from the teeth outwards':[151] 'Even though they seemingly show a great respect and submission to the English, yet we must remember that all this is but forced . . . a feigned obedience and, therefore, but an unwilling subjection.'[152] After the Jacobite scare of 1745, the Catholics were described as 'an enemy within . . . who lies in wait for our estates'.[153] Anxiety can be seen, for example, in the frequency with which visitors to the country were regaled with stories bearing on the old proprietors. Thus, when Baron Edward Willes visited County Clare in 1761, the local M.P. Francis Burton told him about Charles O'Brien, sixth Viscount Clare (1699–1761), whose family had lost their estate as Jacobites. Burton had met O'Brien in Paris and discovered that he still 'claims a great part of the county of Clare as his patrimony . . . that he knew all the gentlemen and the estates of the county and their private affairs as well as if he had lived among them . . . that he had an exact rent roll of all his own estates, that he kept a register of every part that was sold and to whom and for what'.[154] Travelling in Ireland in the 1770s, Arthur Young picked up similar stories from the dinner tables of the landed gentry:

> The lineal descendants of the old families are now to be found all over the kingdom, working as cottiers on the lands which were once their own. In such great revolutions of property, the ruined proprietors have usually been extirpated or banished. In Ireland the case was otherwise, and it is a fact that in most parts of the kingdom the descendants of the old land-owners regularly transmit by testamentary deed the memorial of their right to those estates which once belonged to their families.[155]

Examples of this scenario can be found. In the late eighteenth century, the Dalton heir to the estate of Kildalton (renamed Bessborough) was living as a cooper in Carrick-on-Suir. The Ponsonbys' agent, Peter Walsh of Belline, visited him in his old age, offering him £400 to relinquish all claims to the estate, but was peremptorily refused.[156] In the Ballina area a common toast in the eighteenth century was 'Súil Uí Dhubhda le Árd na Riach' [O'Dowd's expectation of Ardnaree] – a reference to the O'Dowd family's hopes of resuming their ancestral property in the event of a successful Jacobite coup.[157]

Landlord obsessions with these threats to their legitimacy were stimulated by the protracted debate on the validity of leases for lives renewable forever (perpetuity tenancies), a debate culminating in the 1780 Tenancy Act, which was a major victory for such tenants, confirming their legal status. Under the penal laws, leases of this type, if enacted before 1704, were not subject to discovery proceedings, and many Catholic families retained a sub-gentry status by virtue of such leases.[158] The Hay family of Ballinkeele in Wexford and the MacMahon family of Dartry in Monaghan are good examples.[159] In the 1770s landlords were keen to undermine such leases, which were pegged at artificially low levels and which therefore redistributed income from landlords to leaseholders. Part of the landlord campaign focused on the political threat posed by these families: in Munster in particular, Arthur Young was privy to this type of exaggerated commentary. In Cork he was told that 'all the poor people are Roman Catholic and among them are the descendants of the old families who once possessed the country, of which they still preserve the full memory, in so much that a gentleman's labourer will regularly leave to his son by will his master's estate'.[160]

It is noticeable that it was in Munster that the four great *causes célèbres* of conflict between old and new families erupted: the Cotter execution in 1720, the Sullivan-Puxley conflict in the 1750s, the Nicholas Sheehy judicial murder in 1766, and the Art Ó Laoghaire / Abraham Morris saga in 1773.[161] These episodes generated cycles of related poems in the Gaelic tradition.[162] On the eve of his own execution, on 28 April 1754, for example, Daniel Connell composed a lament for Murty Óg O'Sullivan which conveyed the popular sentiment:

> A Mhurtaighe, a ríogh-mhaistir, is cruadh an cás tú bheith ró-lag
> Do cheann geal ó'd corp aluin, is é in airde mar show 'cu.
> Do chonnac-sa féin lá thú is do chloideamh sáighte chun chomhraic,
> Agus go ndeanfá-sa bearna trí gardaibh Rí Seóirse.[163]

> O Morty, regal master, it is a hard case that you are lifeless,
> Your blond head off your fine body, exposed on high as a show by them.
> I saw you myself one day and your sword drawn for conflict,
> Clearing a swathe through King George's soldiers.

It is also noticeable how wealthy Catholic middleman families ('the bucks') were targeted by the Munster gentry in the Whiteboy pogroms, including the Sheehys, Buxtons and Farrells who had prospered on the benign Butler (Cahir) estate.[164] Cork and Tipperary were two of the leading Irish counties for recruitment into the French army in the eighteenth century; this may in part explain why the *aisling* figured so prominently in the poetic tradition of Munster. It may also help explain why the adoption of the traditional Stuart colour (white) by the agrarian redresser movements of the 1760s instantly conferred a political coloration on Munster Protestants' attempts to understand the phenomenon, and on their hardline political response, in which lurid Jacobite plots and collusive Catholic gentry figured prominently.[165] This was despite the fact that the Whiteboys and Rightboys (whose campaign equally targeted Catholic landlords and middlemen) never overtly included a reversal of the land settlement among their aims.[166] Yet, as late as 1770, Shelburne, seeking the establishment of a garrison at Nedeen (Kenmare), described the inhabitants in conventional Jacobite terms: 'Roman Catholics of fierce and uncultivated manners, accustomed to hate and despise civil government, and from many of them having been in the French and Spanish services and other circumstances, inured to arms'.[167]

This consistent sense of irrelevance, of having their legitimacy only grudgingly conceded, of being an embattled minority rather than the nation of Ireland, haunted the landlord psyche in the post-1798 period when their position seemed ever more precarious in a newly volatile, politicised, sectarianised and strife-torn island. But at times of stress, even in the eighteenth century, the spectre of being merely a colonial elite could also haunt them. John Scott, the future Lord Clonmell, gave a classic exposition of this insecurity in 1774:

> A man in station in Ireland is really like a traveller in Africa, in a forest among Hottentots and wild beasts: but a cautious man may subdue them and defend himself, but he must be eternally on the watch and on his guard against his next neighbours, men and beast, at every step he takes, at every thing he does, at every word he utters. Irish government resembles extremely the state of the Hottentots in Africa. The common Irish, divided, oppressed, pillaged and abused as they are, are the Hottentots: the English administration are the Dutch planters: the followers of Lord Lieutenants are the bushmen or spies and swindlers: and their wild beasts viz. lions, tigers etc. are the Irish satraps.[168]

In political terms, this insecurity expressed itself in a fear that any tampering with the constitution would undermine the landed class; as Fitzgibbon pointed out in 1789, 'The Act by which most of us hold our estates was an act of violence . . . an act subverting the first principles of the common law in England and Ireland . . . the Act of Settlement.'[169] Meddling with the constitutional status quo would, in the words of the Attorney General in 1782, 'loose the bonds of society and leave the whole island to be grappled for by the descendants of the old proprietors'.[170] Sir Edward Newenham observed in the same year that 'they have an old claim on our estates'.[171] In such a climate of opinion, even genealogy was suspect as a pursuit. The Chevalier O'Gorman, for example, was suspected in 1786 of 'collecting accounts of Irish estates of which the Roman Catholics were dispossessed in the time of Cromwell and of the Revolution'.[172] The Irish Lord Lieutenant, Rutland, assured London that O'Gorman's 'conduct has been regularly watched and his correspondence intercepted'.[173] In the same year it became known that a French privateer had captured the ship carrying the Cromwellian Down Survey maps to England. As the administrative basis of forfeitures, there was great official disquiet that 'a work so valuable is in foreign hands'.[174]

In the aftermath of the first Catholic relief acts, in the early 1780s, there was renewed Protestant anxiety at the spate of Catholic families seeking reversal of outlawries or recognition of Jacobite titles – including Fingal, Gormanston, Dunsany and Kenmare – and a panic gripped the House of Commons in 1782 (even at the height of its aspiration towards legislative independence) when a poorly drafted clause in the relief bill gave scope for intimations that it could conceivably undo the seventeenth-century acts upon which landownership depended.[175] These paranoid attitudes were also fed by a much-publicised incident in County Roscommon in January 1786. According to newspaper reports, Roderick O'Connor, claiming to be a descendant of 'Cahal Crubdarg' of the old royal family of Connacht, had peremptorily resumed control of a 20,000 acre estate (formerly in O'Connor hands but now owned by the Burkes) in defiance of legal title, and supported by 2,000 followers. The *Dublin Evening Post* reported that his father had had in his possession the ancient crown of the Irish kings, but had been forced by penury to part with it.[176] The incident caused a sensation, being loudly debated in parliament and even being monitored by the Vatican.[177] The controversy forced a Catholic response. The Catholic gentlemen of Roscommon, headed by his brother, repudiated O'Connor's claims to the estate, dismissing his supporters as 'an ignorant rabble, actuated by intoxication'. This was quickly followed by a general address of the Catholics of Ireland to the Lord Lieutenant, Rutland, disclaiming any hint of a claim to the forfeited estates:

> We also look upon all claims or pretenses of claims to any lands or estates, on account of their having been in former ages in the possession of our ancestors, if unsupported by the laws and statutes now in being of this realm, as unjust, and highly subversive of that good order and government which it is not only our duty but our intent to support.[178]

This address mollified Rutland.[179] O'Connor himself was quietly acquitted at the September assizes in Roscommon, having been guilty only of the common ploy of retaining possession of a leasehold after the expiry date, hoping by so doing to apply pressure on the landlord to renew the lease.[180] The exaggerated response was a revealing insight into the insecurity of the existing landed class.

The most intriguing contribution to the debate on the Catholic question in Ireland in the late eighteenth century came from Edmund Burke; it is intriguing precisely because he presented the Jacobite argument that the authentic Irish gentry were indeed the Catholics. Burke pleaded eloquently for Irish Catholics as a local application of his defence of the integrity of traditional society.[181] Extending his espousal of family and local loyalties against abstract claims, he argued that Irish Catholics represented those rooted communities whose presence alone sustained the *ancien régime*. Catholic traditions, beliefs and habits were so engrained in the fabric of Irish culture that a political system which failed to recognise them would inevitably lack the crucial bonding force that gave political systems their endurance – the affection of the people who lived under them. In the Irish system, these well-founded Catholic claims were reduced or denied by a narrow ruling group whose claims to supremacy were based solely on religious persuasion. That ruling group of Irish Protestants was not a rooted, respected aristocracy, but merely a plebian and parvenu ascendancy, a bogus facsimile whose scornful, narrowly based pursuit of power and privilege achieved only resentment and loathing. Like the French Jacobins, they violated the customary affections and rooted relations which made society adhesive and stable.[182] Only by admitting Catholics fully to the political nation could Ireland be pacified, as their innately deferential and monarchical tendencies would then be expressed in support of the status quo, and they would no longer be a prey to factious Dissenters or Jacobin United Irishmen. Burke's scathing critique of the Irish Protestant gentry stemmed in large part from his bruising involvement in the 1760s with Munster Protestants determined to implicate the Catholic gentry, sub-gentry and leading merchants in the Whiteboys. His efforts on behalf of his kinsmen, especially the Nagles, convinced Burke of the reactionary, vindictive and squalid character of their antagonists – gentry families like the Maudes, Bagwells, Kings, Boyles, Beresfords and Hewetsons. He never lost his scalding sense of partisan indignation derived from this close encounter with 'red-hot' Munster Protestantism.

By an unintended inversion, Burke's arguments, conservative in an English setting, became subversive once transposed to the narrow ground of Ireland. In England the past was a stabilising, even a sedating, political presence. In Ireland an appeal to the past inevitably worried old wounds on which the scar tissue had never fully congealed. In England support for the state church was a unifying gesture; in Ireland it was horribly divisive. In England the gentry were acceptable authority figures, embodying the cultural and political gravitas of their tradition, the conservative force-field of custom and precedent. In Ireland the *arriviste* gentry were a standing rebuke to such considerations. In England the common people could be seen as a bulwark against radicalism, a phalanx of stolid complacency. In Ireland the common people were envisaged as a seething mass of barely suppressed sedition.

Old resentment and the new radicalism

One of the most fascinating aspects of eighteenth-century Ireland was the way in which the new radicalism grafted onto older stocks of resentment, growing out of a heightened sense of identity, consciousness of exclusion, and antipathy to the public political culture. In families like the Byrnes of Ballymanus in Wicklow, or the O'Learys and O'Sullivans in Cork, this fusion produced an attitude of aggressive truculence. A typical example occurred in 1784. Count John O'Rourke, born 'in 1735 in the parish of Oghteragh in Breffny' had gone abroad to serve in the French and Prussian armies. In 1784, in the aftermath of the Catholic relief act which ushered in an 'enlightened age', O'Rourke submitted an extraordinary petition to the king, seeking restitution of 57,200 acres in Leitrim (in fact the total area of the county) taken from his family 'by the usurper Oliver Cromwell'. The family had been forced until now 'to submit in silence', but as the representative of the third generation since the confiscation, he now felt it right to claim assistance 'to support in some degree the honour of his birth and the dignity of his family'. O'Rourke's pamphlet was accompanied by detailed genealogies (supplied by the O'Cornins, 'hereditary antiquarians and genealogists to the family').[183] Such latent sentiments could be easily politicised, as happened in the 1790s. John Keogh summarised Catholic resentments: 'Our grievance is that many men beneath us in birth, education, morals and fortune are allowed to trample upon us.'[184] This had political connotations. Miles Byrne commented on these middleman families in Wexford:

> Among those who took part in the insurrection of 1798, there were a great number of Catholic gentlemen, holding land as farmers, but descended from those who had been deprived of their property in land at the time of the Reformation and under Cromwell and above all under William III, merely because they were Catholics.[185]

In the aftermath of the repeal of the penal laws from 1778 onwards, which restored the full rights of landed property, a dichotomy opened in Catholic circles. Those with prospects of landownership within the new dispensation rapidly jettisoned their earlier Jacobite ambitions in favour of an ostentatiously Hanoverian line. Wolfe Tone attacked those, especially the Catholic gentry, who slavishly welcomed the new accommodation, describing them as willing to sell their less advantaged brethren 'to be called "my Lord" at the Castle or to wear a bigwig and a black gown at the Four Courts'.[186] The Catholic bishops, fearful of their flocks catching the 'French disease' from their promiscuous political contacts, also rushed to the side of the state. The Catholic Committee continuously reiterated its renunciation of 'all interest in and title to all forfeited lands resulting from any rights of our ancestors or any claims, title or interests therein'.[187] One of the consequences of this redefinition was that the Jacobite claim of aboriginal ownership was discarded by the top echelons of the Irish Catholic class structure. However, the discarded ideology was picked up and espoused by the Catholic middle and lower classes, in two different forms. The rising big-farm class donned the middleman mantle and with it acquired an ancestry, an ideological pedigree and a rhetoric. Given their tendency to settle locally and the rapid proliferation of such families in the expansionary conditions of the eighteenth century, the mechanism by which this displacement mentality percolated down the generations in a widening stream can be easily identified, as can its diffusion across a broad stratum of Catholic society.[188] This consciousness, spread by generational and spatial shift, was widely present by the late eighteenth century, potently so in the case of middleman families.

In Ulster a different ideological trajectory developed for Catholics. The aloofness of Ulster from national Catholic politics in the period 1760–1830 can be ascribed to the absence of wealthy Catholic families there. By the mid-eighteenth century, there was no landed Catholic interest to provide a shield and a seedbed for these families, equivalent to the Kavanagh, Ormonde, Clanricarde or Kenmare role in the south, with the partial exception of the MacDonnells in Antrim, who succeeded in keeping the Glens predominantly Catholic. The extent of immigration in seventeenth-century Ulster had been such that there was simply no room for the survival of the old landowners as head tenants. The differential experience is well expressed in the experience of the Dohertys of Kinea in Clonmany parish in Inishowen. In 1765 they ran into trouble on the Chichester estate, falling foul of the agents, the Harveys, just as their leases fell in. George Doherty complained of 'the enmity of those in whose power we are as agents and the leases now out'. His father, John, shared his thoughts with Morgan O'Connell of Derrynane:

> The original Irish are very happy in your part of the country: the wicked brood of black-hearted heretics have got no foothold there as yet. . . . Here are few except hewers of wood and drawers of water. In short, we are in the most abject slavery in this barony of Inishowen and not a foot of land to be renewed to any as prime tenant to our landlord, the Earl of Donegall, that is of the old stamp.

The old man concluded: 'Though people advanced in years are generally fond of making their exit in their native soil, yet I am tired of mine and would rather traverse the globe than live under such tyranny.'[189] The family subsequently sold their leasehold interests and emigrated to America.[190]

Deprived of the profits of a substantial leasehold interest, Ulster Catholics were subsequently unable to finance their penetration of the more lucrative branches of the linen industry. Thus the highest social roles to which Ulster Catholics aspired were those of publican, shopkeeper, cattle-dealer, butcher or schoolteacher. Edward Wakefield in 1812 made the wider observation: 'The Protestant gentry of the north, in estimating the character of Roman Catholics, are frequently disposed to form a general opinion from the habits and manners of the wealthier class in Ulster, whose occupations seldom rise higher than that of a grocer or retailer of spirits.'[191] The inherited leadership cadre of the Catholic community elsewhere did not exist in Ulster, where the Catholic experience was radically different, and where deprivation and degradation were much in evidence. The Catholic *mentalité* in Ulster, therefore, was totally different from its southern and western counterparts. Because of the compressed social range of Ulster Catholicism, it was much easier to maintain solidarity than in the more class-based Catholic communities of the south and east. This solidarity facilitated the emergence of the Defender movement, the south-Ulster-based secret society which evolved in the 1780s and flourished in the 1790s and which reflected grassroots Catholic opinion.

While the United Irishmen rode the cusp of an Enlightenment wave and saw themselves as advancing purposefully and inexorably forward with the momentum of inevitable historical progress, the Defenders wished not to repudiate but to embrace history. They saw Catholics as the authentic, aboriginal inhabitants of the island. Time's arrow was not for them the United Irishmen's untroubled progressive projectile: the Defenders wished to flex time, to bend it back to a pre-plantation idyll, to suture the earlier lesions inflicted on the Irish body politic. Their potent sense of dispossession expressed itself in hopes of avenging their seventeenth-century setbacks: 'They can never forget that they have been the proprietors of this country . . . they look upon or talk of the English settlers as not of their nation.' They wished 'to plant the true religion that was lost since the Reformation'. They were encouraged 'by the hope of being what they called uppermost'.[192] Their solution to Ireland's ills was to reverse their seventeenth-century setbacks by overturning the church establishment, the land settlement and the social hierarchy which rested on their defeats. Thus they were fundamentally historicists, looking to the past for explanations of their traditional grievances – tithes, taxes, rents, labour and living conditions. Their millenarianism could also be interpreted in this way: apocalyptic change would be equally subversive of time, again eliding the present. Their levelling tendencies – 'the cobbler and the Caesar made level' – was derived from a historically based sense of social injustice, applicable to the obvious disparities in eighteenth-century Irish life. 'We have lived long enough upon potatoes and salt; it is our turn now to eat beef and mutton.'[193] In these circumstances, the Defenders saw in the French Revolution a possibility of casting off old oppressions, of reverting to a version of the *status quo ante*. It was easy for them to give a sectarian gloss to their readings of Irish history in the hothouse atmosphere of Ulster. Their sense of ethnic allegiance and identity was sharpened by the abrupt juxtapositions of Catholic, Presbyterian and Anglican (or Irish, Scottish and English) in Ulster and especially in the cockpit of Armagh. Thus the Defenders could also practise the politics of the grudge, develop an adversarial sense of collective awareness, and unify themselves through their hostilities.

Yet one should be wary of an overconfident matching of economic and political alignments. The Defenders can never be explained in simplistic agrarian/sectarian terms.[194] Their roots lie equally in the high politics of south Ulster, linked to volunteering and electioneering disputes and to national politics, especially the resurgence of the Catholic question on the active political agenda. All accounts agree in locating firearms at the centre of the initial disputes. Arms, not the franchise, constituted the fundamental badge of citizenship in a pre-democratic state, and the bearing of firearms was, therefore, a pivotal political issue. If Catholics asserted their right to bear arms publicly, they asserted their right to full participation in the political nation. If such assertions went unchallenged, their claim was implicitly conceded. It was opposition to this stance which motivated the Peep o' Day Boys and subsequently the Orange Order. The Defenders signalled the democratisation of the political culture of Catholics, the transition from Jacobite to Jacobin, and a break with the century-old Catholic strategy of deferential supplication. Defenderism could be simultaneously reactive and proactive, looking to the past and the future and it was this bifocal perspective which gave it its protean and resilient qualities.

In considering the Defenders, however, it is necessary to emphasise that the organisation had developed a two-tier leadership structure by the 1790s. The local leadership came from the top of the restricted Catholic class spectrum – 'alehouse keepers, artisans, low schoolmasters and a few middling farmers'.[195] But above them a further leadership tier operated at a regional level, providing overall political direction. This group was drawn from the close-knit (and often interrelated) handful of really successful Catholic families in the Ulster borderlands – the Teelings of Lisburn, the Quigleys of Loughgall, the Coyles of Lurgan, the O'Callaghans of Cullaville, the Rices of Tyholland, the Carolans and McDonnells of Carrickmacross, the Kearnans of Enniskillen, the Maginnises of Ballymacarbery, the Byrnes of Castletown. Where even a handful of such families survived, as on the Downshire estate, they could play an important role in stiffening the backbone of the local Catholic community. The Downshire agent blamed the 'insolence' of the cottiers on the estate in 1799 and their 'refractory disposition' on 'the contumaceous example of the McArdells, Magenises and Byrnes (the descendants of the old proprietors) instilling into the minds of a numerous banditti of cottiers under them that you are only entitled to a chiefry upon the lands and cannot dispossess them'.[196] Charles Teeling defined the Defender leader John Maginnis principally in terms of his ancestry: 'Maginnis was of an old and respectable Irish family, the lineal descendant of the ancient lords of Iveagh. The blood of his ancestors ran pure in his veins and purer never flowed from a generous heart.'[197] Anxious to stress his respect for such individuals, Teeling added that he had 'always been attached to the ancient names of my country and when associated with national achievement, they are doubly objects of my respect'.[198]

These families had also been active in the Catholic Committee. A striking feature of the Defender movement in the 1790s is the way in which its distribution matched that of two clusters of counties with a pronounced anti-Catholic political profile at parliamentary level – one in south Ulster (Armagh, south Down, Monaghan, Louth, Meath), the other in north Connacht (Roscommon, Leitrim, Sligo).[199] This political dimension to Defenderism helps explain why its activities surged and subsided in rhythm with the national progress of the Catholic question: witness the peaks in 1792–3 and 1795. It also explains the strength of Defenderism in towns with a Catholic middle class, notably Dundalk, Newry and Carrickmacross.

The existence of this top-level leadership group facilitated the ease with which the United Irish/Defender merger was accomplished in the mid-1790s.[200] The leadership group of both organisations had had informal contacts since 1792, had mingled freely at the Catholic Convention, and had shared similar interests in electoral politics, especially in south-east Ulster. Given the obvious coincidence of their interests in the post-Fitzwilliam, post-Orange Order period, the merger made practical sense. It was struck initially at this leadership level and then transferred to the rank-and-file membership. The smooth transition is evident in the leadership role which was quickly exercised within the United Irishmen by Defender recruits like James Quigley and the Teeling brothers. It is also evident in the complete disappearance of the Defenders as an active organisation in 1797 and 1798 (despite conservative propaganda which attempted to highlight alleged splits within the alliance along the old sectarian lines).

One should also note that in Ulster the Catholic big-farm class did not exist to act as an intercepting filter to appropriate the Jacobite claim on aboriginal ownership of Irish land. As a result, the claim descended to the popular level. In Ulster by the late eighteenth century a consciousness of dispossession, latent or overt, was widely diffused at the popular level. Robert Bell described this attitude in the 1780s:

> Ignorant and obscure as they were, many families among them used to trace their pedigrees back to a very remote period; they knew the rank and estates which their ancestors once held in the country and they felt no small degree of pride at the recollection that noble blood still flowed in their veins. These families could ascertain every spot of ground which was said to have belonged to their forefathers and of which they looked on the modern possessors as so many usurpers. Their gross understandings were satisfied with learning by tradition that the lands had once belonged to their ancestors who had been driven out by powerful invaders: and they never lost sight of the prospect of being one day reinstated in them.[201]

Defenderism represented a potent fusion of this demotic Irish tradition with some fashionable French imports to create an arresting if not entirely coherent amalgam of Jacobite and Jacobin sentiment. The impact of the French Revolution made Catholics 'a prey to angry recollections and devouring wishes'.[202] This amalgam also spawned an embryonic cultural nationalism, in an inchoate, dissolute form.

The conservative recoil

Thus one of the ironies of the late eighteenth century was that two classes who had no historic claims to it – the rising big farmers and the Ulster poor – inherited the Jacobite version of Irish landownership from the Catholic gentry and middlemen who had initially elaborated it but who were now discarding it as they eagerly reached towards an accommodation with the Hanoverian state. The bona fides of the rich Catholics were not accepted by the hardline Protestants as being genuine. They continued to deploy the old comforting shibboleths, claiming that the Catholic Committee, the Defenders and United Irishmen all harboured the aim of overturning the Glorious Revolution and building a vindictive Catholic state on the ruins of Protestant Ireland. The concept of an imminent resumption of the ancient estates was put into general circulation by the constant scaremongering of loyalists such as Richard Musgrave, Patrick Duigenan and George Ogle. In the early 1790s, it received additional currency from being also linked to the restoration of 'popery' as signalled by the repeal of the penal laws. In a speech to the House of Commons on 4 February 1793, in the aftermath of the Catholic Convention, Duigenan attacked the radicals as a 'levelling, independent, republican, deistical faction, whose apostles are Paine, Price and Priestley', but he focused especially on the Catholics:

> The Irish Catholics to a man esteem all Protestants as usurpers of their estates: they to this day settle these estates on the marriages of their sons and daughters: they have accurate maps of them. They published in Dublin within these ten years a map of the kingdom cantoned out among the old Irish proprietors. They look for political power only to enable them to assert their claims with effect, which they will do if ever they have power, not by tedious forms of law, but acts of parliament or the sword. They abhor all Protestants and all Englishmen as plunderers and oppressors.[203]

Even so apparently innocuous a map as Charles O'Conor's of the location of the old Irish clans caused a flutter.[204] Originally published in 1770, it was reissued (by Patrick Wogan, also printer to the Catholic Committee) in 1792 at a sensitive time for Irish Protestants. Westmorland, the Lord Lieutenant, was troubled by the map, reporting to Pitt on 18 February 1792 that 'I have sent you a map of Ireland describing the estates of the ancient possessors before the forfeitures. The circulation of this has given fresh alarm to the Protestant possessors of these forfeited lands.'[205] William Todd Jones replied to these charges in *A Letter to the Societies of United Irishmen of the Town of Belfast* (1792):

> 'But there is a map!' whispers some English prelate to some English chaplain, aide de camp, or private secretary . . . 'Oh, Sir, there is a *map* would singe your eyebrows but to smell the fiery fragment . . . you would bless yourself to peruse the hideous barbaric names with which it abounds . . . published, Sir, by that dangerous Catholic O'Connor [sic], for the sole purpose of reminding herdsmen and ditchers what great folks were their grandams: – Yes Sir, a *map*, with the charming popish pedigrees as long as the Birdcage Walk, and at their root, the old sanguinary Irishmen themselves, lying extended each upon his own Milesian seignory.'

Todd Jones then deflates the hysteria surrounding the map by a detailed description of what it *actually* shows, as opposed to what its critics *supposed* it to show:

> It is a fragment of taste – an obscure and imperfect delineation; a map for a poring antiquary, an abstract chronological curiosity, a map without boundaries of barony, townland or parish, composed of names for the greater part unannexed to any description of territory but the naked counties without pedigrees, branches of families, christian names, or any possible clew to direct particular descendants of houses to trace, or bring evidence of their claims, or of their origins.[206]

Charles O'Conor's map is also referred to in an anti-United Irish piece of doggerel published in the spring of 1798, in which the map is used to put words into the mouth of the United Irish organiser as he tries to persuade a generic 'Paddy' to join the organisation:

> 'Tis hard indeed and harder still but our good rulers have their will
> That many families should be reduced to lowest poverty
> Perhaps to beg upon the lands once wrested from their father's hands
> Now held by those who will not know them and hardly charity bestow them
> This is a truth, Paddy you know it, and ——'s map does fully show it
> There you may see tho' we're derided, how Ireland's lands are all divided
> Marked with the names of the old proprietors, which in pretence they were rioters,
> Were forfeited, were seized, were given, to any scoundrel under heaven.[207]

Anti-United Irish and anti-Defender rhetoric was obsessed with this issue of the ancient estates. There is a typical passage in the 1795 *An Irishman's Letter to the People called Defenders*:

> Your seducers tell you that you shall recover the forfeited estates. If you mean to keep possession of them, your object is open war and you must first subdue the armed forces of both countries. If you mean to give them to the persons you call their owners, you must in like manner support their possession; consider also that a great number of these forfeited estates are now in the possession of Catholics who will unite with the civil and military powers against you.[208]

Baron Yelverton's charge to the County Antrim grand jury on 17 June 1797 spelled out clearly the common conservative perception of the aims of the United Irishmen, who have 'marked out properties to be confiscated and the uses to which the produce of these confiscations are to be applied. . . . Your servants and dependants should wade thro' your blood into the possession of your estates.'[209]

Such preoccupations were also fed to visiting English politicians by the conservative Dublin Castle establishment. Westmorland reported back in 1793 to the Home Secretary, Henry Dundas, that 'the lower orders of old Irish consider themselves as plundered and kept out of their property by the English settlers and on every occasion are ready for riot and revenge'.[210] John Fitzgibbon, Earl of Clare, was particularly prone to use these arguments. In 1787, when proposing hardline measures, Fitzgibbon had focused on the pernicious influence of the old families, whom he saw at the centre of the Rightboy disturbances and whom he ironically termed 'the gentry': 'The gentry for whose perusal I particularly intended the clause are that ruinous set of men called middlemen, who stand between the inheritor and occupier of the land, to the injury of both, and who I know, for their own base purposes, abetted outrage.'[211] In a 1795 speech he declared that 'Great Britain can never conciliate the descendants of the old Irish to her interests upon any other terms than by restoring to them the possessions and the religion of their ancestors in full splendour and dominion'.[212] He was able to use his own convert background to dramatise this for Gothic effect, as in this reported conversation with Lawrence Parsons:

> My father was a popish recusant. He became a Protestant and was called to the bar but he continued to live on terms of friendship with his Roman Catholic relations and early friends, and he knew the Catholics well. He has repeatedly told me that if ever they had the opportunity, they would overturn the established government and Church, and resume the Protestant estates.[213]

Accordingly, the political role of the old elite was surveyed continuously and suspiciously. Landlords were wary of the degree of independence exhibited by middlemen who were doing well. Joseph Taylor, the Shelburne agent, considered the local middlemen in the 1770s to be 'the old Milesian breed who are full of laws and wrangles'.[214] Walter Kavanagh of Borris regretted having granted long leases in the last quarter of the eighteenth century on the grounds that it made his tenants 'too independent'.[215] The activities of such families were closely monitored in the 1790s. At the Roscommon assizes in August 1795, Arthur Wolfe was delighted to have secured a 'conviction of consequence' – that of James Sheridan, 'the son of a farmer of some wealth and connection, who has been a great inciter of this sedition [Defenderism] and a great leader of the seditious. . . . He is what is called a buckeen, his sisters appeared in handsome riding dresses with hats and feathers. . . . If examples of this type could reach the rich, this would be a very effectual one.'[216] An incident in County Meath in April 1797 showed the depth of fear produced by these preoccupations. Benjamin Chapman, the local M.P., reported:

> The house of one O'Flynn was searched for arms during the Assizes; he was charged to be a captain of the Defenders, but instead of arms there was found a large parcel of his family's antient title deeds before the rebellion of 1641 to the estates of Killyan, now belonging to Mr Loftus in whose employ O'Flynn was at this time. This matter is much magnified by some zealots.[217]

Denis Browne was perturbed in 1807 at the prospects of one of these middlemen, the United Irishman Edward Garvey, being allowed to return to County Mayo: 'In Connaught, the return of such a man as Mr Garvey is particularly dangerous in its example, when the resident farmers are mostly of the class, description and religion of Mr Garvey, where there are few resident gentry to control or interfere with the influence of the middlemen over the peasantry.'[218]

The radical riposte

The United Irishmen were insistent that any confiscation would not be general but selective, targeted only at church land and at those who actively fought against the revolution. The Donaghadee United Irishmen resolved in 1797 that 'there are a great many inimical and will no doubt prove hostile to the cause of liberty: their estates or property shall be confiscated and converted to the national benefit'.[219] Miles Byrne, the Wexford United Irishman, made essentially the same observations: 'The church property becoming immediately the property of the state and the estates of all those who should emigrate or remain in the English army fighting against their country, being confiscated, the revenue arising from these funds would have been employed to provide for and defray all the expenses necessary for the defence and independence of the country.'[220] Only the most advanced of United Irish thinkers, such as Arthur O'Connor, were prepared to go further. In *The State of Ireland* (1798) O'Connor argued that the whole legal basis of property had become 'a barbarous mass of complexity, chicane and fraud' and that it therefore needed reform. To achieve this, he argued, 'we must look to those laws of primogeniture, entails and settlements which have been set up to secure and perpetuate the despotism of the few, and to ensure and perpetuate the exclusion of the many'.[221]

Such perceptions led to a social radical perspective in which the very idea of a landed gentry itself became problematic. This could easily acquire a quasi-theological exegesis. Earlier in the century, the Catholic priest John Fottrell had preached against riches, using metaphors which in an Irish context carried a subliminal attack on the Protestant gentry. Riches were 'turned into stately palaces, and beautiful gardens, into rich furniture and equipage, into the most exquisite meats and most delicious wines'.[222] By the 1790s *The Press* published elegant epigrams:

> Say you who perch on lofty pedigree,
> What fruit is gathered from the parchment tree?[223]

Arthur O'Connor attacked the gentry for their lack of humanity, induced by excessive wealth, describing them as

> men who have made themselves slaves to the meanest and most contemptible wants, desires and habits – miserable if their bed is too hard or too soft, their pillow too high or too low, their dinner too much done or too little, regardless of how many millions corruption and tyranny have left without beds to lie on, or food to allay the gnawings of ravenous famine.[224]

This Paineite-Jacobin streak could also fuse with millenarian sentiment to produce a levelling challenge to the landowning class. Witness *The Cry of the Poor for Bread*, a handbill circulating in Dublin in 1796:

> Oh lords of manors, and other men of landed property, as you have monopolised to yourselves the land, its vegetation and its game, the fish of the rivers and the fowls of heaven . . . in the present condition of things can the labourer who cultivates your land with the sweat of his brow, the working manufacturer, or the mechanic support himself, a wife and five or six children? How much

comfort do you extort from their misery, by places, offices and pensions, and consume in idleness, dissipation, riot and luxury?[225]

A typical millenarian tract, *Christ in Triumph coming to Judgement*, published in Strabane in 1795, contained similar sentiments:

> Those who on earth have sumptuous palaces and wardrobes full of embroidered garments; who every day are hurried thro' the streets in thundering coaches and chariots glittering with gold, shoals of footmen running by, troops of flattering gallants before them, trains of attendants galloping after them: these shall at these sessions [the last judgement] stand shivering, dejected and naked. These proud titles of high and mighty, right honourable, most heroical, thrice illustrious, most revered, truly noble, worshipful, valourous, renowned etc. will be laid by and disregarded. A cobbler and Caesar shall stand at this bar on equal terms.

It concluded with a levelling message: 'The courts of kings, the seats and palaces of noblemen, the banqueting houses of the luxurious, the full barns of farmers, the cottages of husbandmen and the stalls under which beggars lie, will be as one and come to nothing.'[226]

In the aftermath of the failure of the rebellion, the revamped United Irish organisation in Dublin city, dominated by social radicals, made a very explicit attack on landed property in their *Poor Man's Catechism*:

> Q. How would you alter the property in land: preserving the country from anarchy?
> A. By dividing the ancient estates, among the descendants of those Irish families who were pillaged by English invaders, giving to every person without exception a competent share to enable him or her to get a comfortable livelihood, this provision not to extend to any person who impeded the deliverance of the country by cowardice or treachery; the remainder to be sold by public cant, and the money applied to paying off the debts contracted by the former confederacy, and for rewarding the citizens who fought for their country, and providing for their wives and mothers, and giving education to their children and infant relations.[227]

Wolfe Tone, explaining the situation to the French, emphasised that the properties and titles of the Irish Protestant gentry were 'founded in massacre and plunder and being as it were but a colony of foreign usurpers in the land, they saw no security for their persons and estates but in a close connexion with England, who profited of their fears, and as the price of her protection exacted the implicit surrender of the commerce and liberties of Ireland'.[228] The *Poor Man's Catechism* was even more explicit about the Irish gentry, borrowing heavily from Thomas Paine:

> The whole of them may be said, within the last century to be the descendants of English ruffians, adventurers whose crimes or obscurity denied them a livelihood in their own country, but were the cruel agents of foreign force or foreign seduction. The origin of nobles in every country is the same, but time and revolutions have concealed their hateful origin.[229]

Thus in the charged atmosphere of the 1790s, specifically Irish concerns were linking up with a wider international agenda to produce a threat to the landed gentry. The gentry responded by interpreting the radical challenge as simply a war of 'poverty against property', devoid of serious ideological substance.[230] But they were haunted by the threat of insidious undermining from within by their servants and dependants. In January 1797, in the anxious aftermath of Bantry Bay, the government informer Francis Higgins reported to Dublin Castle: 'It is also well known that numbers of farmers and many of lesser note have been employed in making out titles to estates and grounds as belonging to their ancestors which they conceive the French would reinstate them in.'[231] After the rebellion of 1798, horror stories soon circulated of perfidy of this type. Musgrave dwelt on the case of the Minchin family of Grange in County Dublin: on the night the rebellion started, a party of rebels, headed by their gardener Curran and gatekeeper McDonogh, marched down the avenue, where Curran declared he would 'take possession of the house and demesne as his own'.[232] Musgrave also provided an account of the background and pretensions of Colonel O'Doude, who joined the French at Killala: 'Considering himself the head of a clan or family, he despised taking a christian name and always subscribed himself O'Doude Captain and latterly he had the vanity to assume the title Baron, perhaps from his uncle Baron Wipler in Germany'.[233] John Kelly of Killann was reported by Musgrave as having 'made a will by which he left Captain Blacker's estate to a relation, in case he should be killed in the rebellion'.[234] In the Ballymena area an anecdote about a local mendicant, Jack McDowell, went into circulation after 1798. After the fall of Ballymena to the insurgents, he headed straight for Sir Robert Adair's demesne, observing: '"First come, first served." This place is the Adair's no more, it is the property of Mr Jack McDowell forever.'[235] The fears which lie behind these stories are expertly represented in Maria Edgeworth's *Castle Rackrent*, a parodic masterpiece of the 1790s, in which the landed class is subverted by the aboriginal owners. The central character, Thady Quirke, was based on John Langan, the steward at Edgeworthstown.[236]

The official unease about forfeitures can be seen in the secretive archival practices concerning the records of the forfeiture proceedings of the Cromwellian and Williamite period. In 1802, for example, when the English genealogist George Beltz sought access to the outlawry lists of these periods, he was initially informed that an inspection warrant could only be issued by the Attorney General in consultation with the Lord Chancellor, and was then refused the warrant. The stated cause was 'the errors in the judgements upon outlawries which were the basis of these forfeitures, and the fear of renewing ancient animosities in families and disturbing the grants of the crown'.[237] As late as 1822 the Ulster King of Arms, Sir William Betham, reprobated the indiscretion of the Irish Record Commissioners in publishing seventeenth-century inquisitions 'which would foment discontent among the descendants of the attainted proprietors'.[238]

That same impatient insecurity was still there in 1842 when a disgruntled Munster Protestant chastised the Ordnance Survey because they had 'persons sent from this office engaged in taking down the pedigree of some beggar or tinker and establishing him the lineal descendant of some Irish chief whose ancient estate they most carefully mark out by boundaries, and they have actually in several instances, as I have seen by their letters, nominated some desperate characters as the rightful heirs to these territories'.[239] These complaints were stimulated by the type of comment presented, for example, in the Ordnance Survey Memoir of Enniskillen parish:

> The name of Maguire predominates in the town of Enniskillen. Though most of them move in rather an humble sphere, they take no small share of pride in tracing back their ancient lineage to the early lords of Fermanagh. Mr Thomas Maguire, ironmonger (according to his own reckoning) is the nearest heir to the forfeited title and estates of the last Lord Maguire, who was beheaded in London in the year 1644 and to the present day entertains strong hopes of their inheritance.[240]

The elimination of the middleman system

Because Catholics had generally a more restricted lifesyle then Protestants, they were able to pay higher rents. This Catholic advantage was of pivotal significance when the middleman system was undermined in the late eighteenth and early nineteenth centuries. Inevitably, the assault on the middleman system fell disproportionately on the Protestant sub-gentry, whose favoured status had previously been assured by long leases at low rents. The removal of this middleman layer strengthened the Catholic farming interest, because it was occurring practically simultaneously with the dismantling of the penal laws. Catholic farmers were in general more frugal and therefore more solvent and could now avail of long leases as landlords became more pragmatic in the letting of their estates. Especially in the southern two-thirds of the country, the Protestant middle interest contracted, squeezed in the pre-Famine period between landlords adopting a more mercenary approach, and a rising Catholic farming class with lower outgoings. To this one could also add the anxieties caused by the instability of the 1790s, which had literally unsettled many Protestants. Jane Barber, from outside Enniscorthy, observed the bad effects which a military life had had on her brothers, who were rendered incapable of settling back on their farms:

> And [they] continued the same careless, easy life till they became quite unable to pay their rents. They then emigrated to America and on the very ground which thirty years ago was in the possession of old Protestant families, there now lives the descendants of those rebels who may be said to have been the origin of all this evil.[241]

Andrew Meadows, writing from Wexford town in 1822, concurred, following it with a prophetic warning: 'Since 1798, great numbers [of Protestants] have emigrated, which has thinned the ranks of our once-numerous yeomanry, and I say it with great regret that in a few years hence, a Protestant yeomanry in the county will not be found; the gentry, as a certain consequence, must follow them.'[242] The pressure on Protestants in retaining leases is reflected in the threatening notices against Catholics bidding for leases, posted in the Blackwater and Oulart areas of County Wexford in the aftermath of the rebellion.[243] The altered position of Protestants was a profound shock for them, heightened in the 1820s and 1830s when Catholicism seemed to be increasingly taking on a crudely triumphalist face. As an agonised Protestant observed to the French traveller Alexis de Tocqueville: 'They want to put us in the position of a conquered people, in which we long held them. That is what we are not able to endure.'[244]

The elimination of Protestant middlemen as economic and political anachronisms strengthened the role of Catholic tenant farmers and, in retrospect, can be seen as a major step on the road to 'peasant proprietorship'. It was also part of a process of simplification of the social structure, which was accelerated even more by the post-Famine decline of the cottier class and the legislative euthanasia of the gentry. The consequences of these changes are described in a letter of the second Earl of Rosse, writing from Birr Castle, in 1822:

> The lower orders are much more formidable now than they ever were on this island, from their great increase in numbers, from fewer gentlemen residing, from the extinction of the great farmers who were Protestants and the descendants of the English. . . . Forty years ago the land of Ireland was let in farms of 500 or a 1,000 or 1,500 acres: now, landlords, finding that they can get higher rents and have more voters, let them to Catholics in portions of 20, 30 or 40 acres and these as they multiply fast again, subdivide them among their sons and daughters as they marry. Therefore the old modes of preserving order and enforcing obedience to law will not do now.[245]

The consequence of this was 'the expulsion of the middlemen who were in fact the yeomanry of the country, respectable farmers, Protestants, descendants of Englishmen and attached to the government. Numbers of these have latterly gone to America.'[246] This assessment echoes the sentiments of the Offaly agent James Brownrigg, writing from Edenderry in 1815, concerning the demise of the Protestant head tenant:

> The misfortune is that the landlords in general don't understand this matter, and that their agents think they are bound to let the land to the highest bidder and that in doing so they are doing their landlords the utmost justice, when in fact they are ruining their estates and the country by dispossessing the real yeomanry of the lands and letting them to the mere beggars of the country . . . thereby overspreading the whole country with a miserable, discontented and ungovernable peasantry . . . having few persons of any respectability living amongst them to repress crime and to make the laws to be respected.[247]

William Armstrong, a disgruntled Armagh middleman on the Trinity College estate, made essentially the same points in his letter to the college bursar in 1850, on hearing that he was about to lose his lease:

> The lands have been held by my family since originally granted by the Crown. By my ancestors these lands, then a wilderness, were brought into a state of cultivation. . . . If the resident gentry be banished from your estates who, permit me to ask you, will be left to impart knowledge to your tenantry or provide civilisation amongst them?[248]

In Cavan, in the aftermath of the post-Napoleonic depression, Protestant tenants were squeezed out, being incapable of sustaining the payment of inflated wartime rents:

> The landlords have been so hardhearted that the most of them emigrated and those fertile plains are peopled in their stead by Catholics, who were only 'hewers of wood and drawers of water' to the Protestants before, from their frugality or rather austerity in retaining what they earned hard from the former occupiers; with which they tempted the covetous landlords and promised rackrents, besides which none but those who were in the habit of mortifying their bodies internally and externally could pay. My informant lamented and remonstrated with those landlords for being the cause of forcing their old tenantry out of the country, who replied that from the miserable way the Catholics were contented to live, they could pay ten shillings per acre more than the Protestants, who liked good things as much as themselves, and did not care a fig about the professors of any creed but those who could pay them the most money.[249]

In the pre-Famine period, almost half a million Protestants emigrated from Ireland, especially from the midlands and south Leinster.[250] Canada, and Ontario in particular, was the main destination, and protracted, intense chain migration occurred. The decimation of the southern middle interest was crucially predicated on the dissolution of the middleman system. Their functions had been eroded by the professionalisation of estate administration (through surveyors, agents, engineers, architects, valuers, and not least the police) which usurped their previous functions. They were now seen as economically parasitic in an expanding, rather than a sluggish, economy. Landlords developed a heightened sense of seriousness in the early nineteenth century, partially politically induced ('property has its duties as well as its rights'), and they became less willing to underwrite a Protestant cultural ethos if it hurt them economically. The disappearance of middlemen invariably led to reduced opportunities for servants and labourers, and poor Protestants could no longer rely on an unfailing source of patronage. They too left. Simultaneously the collapse of proto-industrialisation and especially of small town industries exposed many more Protestants who had been involved in these activities. The decimation of Dublin's surviving textile industries in the 1820s when British and Irish tariffs were equalised had a disastrous effect on

Dublin's popular Protestant base. Thus there were economic and social motives to encourage emigration, as well as the erosion of political confidence in the face of resurgent Catholic influence.

All of this could be interpreted as demonstrating the absence of an Irish middle class. As Lord Henry Petty reported from Kenmare in 1805 to the English M.P. Francis Horner: 'The great want of Ireland is not middlemen, but a middling class in society – something to fill up the chasm and soften the asperity that now exists between the nominal gentleman and the dependent drudge who tills the soil for his daily subsistence.'[251] Edward Wakefield commented in 1812 on the missing political link in Ireland – 'a middle class of persons, possessed of wealth, enlightened by education and free from aristocratical pride: these are the most valuable members of society and form the best bulwark of liberty'.[252] This lack of a middle class rapidly became a cliché explaining everything from agrarian disturbance to the failure of the novel in Ireland. In fact it was partially an optical illusion – an inability to recognise the low-key Catholic big-farm group. It also derived from an obsession with an impossibly glamorised English yeoman class, whom all were agreed constituted the enduring glory of England. Nationalists pointed to them (and their Irish absence) as proof of the iniquity of the Anglo-Irish relationship. Unionist and English commentators used them to illustrate the casual Celtic waywardness of Ireland, its wilful wallowing in an archaic, unstratified and slovenly society, which lacked the Protestant and Saxon values of thrift, perseverance and relentless accumulation. In part, it also derived from the elimination of the middleman system, which brought anxious landlords and their proliferating tenantry into a much more intimate and (for landlords) shocking proximity.

Middlemen had previously softened the potentially abrasive interface of landlord and tenant, interposing 'a necessary barrier', or a 'valuable mediation', in their own words, between authority and alienation.[253] While much agrarian agitation in the eighteenth century had an anti-big-farmer/middleman agenda, ignoring the landlords, the nineteenth century saw a sharpening anti-gentry profile, because landlords now dealt directly with the vast bulk of the population and were no longer shielded by an intermediate screen. The elimination of the Protestant middleman interest removed an influential buffer between Catholic tenant and Protestant landlord, strengthened the Catholic interest and homogenised the population in a way which allowed it to be more effectively penetrated by mass mobilisation techniques, such as those perfected in the O'Connellite campaign. It also meant that there were no rivals to the Catholic farmers who were increasingly the political arbiters and organisers at a local level. The removal of middlemen, then, while serving short-term economic interests, had a negative long-term social, cultural and political effect on landlordism.

However, one should not infer from all this that the rise of the Catholic big farmer had occurred without incurring substantial social costs. From the seventeenth century, when social differences among native occupiers were limited, Irish society evolved to a situation where the farmer/labourer split became decisive, especially in the more developed regions. By 1841 in County Cork, for example, there was a 7:3 ratio of labourer to farmer, the product of a more complex farming structure which sharpened the social divide between farmer and labourer.[254] The segregation of farmers and labourers into separate settlements was an eighteenth-century phenomenon. On the mid-seventeenth century Down Survey maps, the cabin cluster around the tower-house was a settlement expression of a society where the classes shared a site. As capitalist penetration prised these elements apart, labourers were dispersed to the edge of the farms, which performed a fly-catcher function. This created a cottier necklace around the perimeter of the tillage farms, the social dichotomy mirrored in the micro-segregation. Robert Bell described the process in 1804:

> The master never fed a labourer of this description [cottier]. It was, on the contrary, a chief object with him to keep such a person as far away from his dwelling as possible. He therefore allowed him to occupy, at some remote corner of his farm, a miserable hut, a mere shell formed of mud or sods, without loft, apartment or partition and sometimes without any other covering than that of straws, without any other chimney than the door.[255]

The transformation of popular culture also stemmed from increasing divisions within the Catholic community. The early penal period had created a strong communal bond. A Cork commentator in 1740 noted of Catholics that 'they are an united band and take care of each other as if one family'.[256] Edward Wakefield in 1812 observed that 'the persecuted and proscribed form a compact body, distinct from their oppressors, and the union which common misery produces is firm and lasting'.[257] From the 1760s that solidarity was fracturing under the insistent pressure of economic change, widening class differentiation and increased hostilities. By mid-century the acquisitive strong farmer was increasingly seen as a mere land-grabber or land-shark by those he displaced, and therefore could become a legitimate target for exemplary violence. In 1778 four hundred inhabitants of Kilcullen, County Kildare, marched in solemn procession to the hanging in effigy of a local land-jobber.[258] No wonder that by 1812 it should be noted that wealthy Catholics were 'afraid of the populace' and that farmers moved to slate their potentially vulnerable thatched roofs.[259] In the early nineteenth century the older middleman system was contrasted with the new type which had emerged during the Napoleonic boom. In Wexford it was claimed that 'the middlemen of the present day are themselves but low farmers, a set of harpies who spread misery and oppression on the unhappy creatures who are compelled to live under them', while a Cork observer stigmatised them in 1816 as 'a multitude of upstart gentry without manners or education, oppressive to the poor'.[260] From Waterford in the 1820s, James Connery described these new middlemen as 'landsharks or pirates' whose emergence had been facilitated by the war boom, an 'upstart gentry' who were undermining the underground gentry:

> In these, Ireland has abounded by the late fatal advance in land which was quite unnatural and which caused the hordes of semi-squires in the country who became a multitude of upstart gentry, without manners or education, oppressive to the poor and frequent instigators to riots and disturbance.[261]

Even tenancies of one hundred acres could sustain a middleman in the crowded pre-Famine decades. A witness to the Devon Commission in 1844 noted: 'When you come to a farm of 100 acres, you get a creature between a hawk and a hound and it is difficult to know how to deal with him. He is not a gentleman and not a farmer.'[262] In one of the most land-hungry regions of Europe, in which the stigma of being landless was fiercely resented, the strengthening big-farm interest had good reason to feel uneasy, as they accumulated grudges and spites along with their leases and acres. The 'midnight legislators' could always call on them, because 'we will know you the darkest nights when you will not know us the brightest day'.[263] In Carlow in 1833, one Whitefoot leader commented:

> The law does nothing for us. We must save ourselves. We are in possession of a little bit of land which is necessary to our and our families survival. They chase us from it. To whom do you wish we should address ourselves? We ask for work at 8d a day; we are refused. To whom do you want us to address ourselves? Emancipation has done nothing for us. Mr O'Connell and the rich Catholics go to parliament. We are starving to death just the same.[264]

Edward Wakefield astutely noted the awkward sensibility of the middle-class Catholics, both urban and rural, especially those who had become wealthy in the Napoleonic boom:

> They are afraid of the populace and being uncertain which may gain the ascendancy, the government or the people, they frequently censure the government in order to ingratiate themselves with the community at large. But if the day of trial should come, self-interest would induce them to cling to the power that was successful. The truth is, these people will unite with those who are best able to secure to them the enjoyment of their property.[265]

Conclusion

However, this new big-farm group had consolidated its interests in Irish economic and political life by the early nineteenth century. In so doing, its members also inherited the Catholic middleman mantle and with it the conviction that their claim to the ownership of the land of Ireland was prior to and superior to that of the *arriviste* gentry around them. The Irish big-farm class, although a new social formation, had acquired an older cultural mantle which they now wove seamlessly into their own self-image. They constructed themselves, not as a peasant class but as proprietors-in-waiting, who would reclaim a patrimony of which their noble ancestors had been unjustly stripped.

This rhetoric gained resonance in the post-Famine period, when it contributed powerfully to the dismantling of the Irish landed gentry and their replacement by peasant proprietors. Colonial chickens had come home to roost, but the perches on which they alighted were new, not old ones. That big-farm class also constituted the backbone of the emergent Catholic nationalist project which was largely constructed and given organised political form by O'Connell. This diverged markedly from the classic Enlightenment project of the United Irishmen, which reached Ireland late and at a period when it was already being redefined by an emergent romantic nationalism. O'Connell's Catholic nationalism appealed to history for authenticity and legitimacy, using an idealised past to destroy the decadent present, thereby liberating the desirable future. In other words, it would utilise (or invent) tradition as the binding force shaping and perpetuating the Irish nation. That paradigm would flourish in the nineteenth century, as the Enlightenment politics of the United Irishmen lost impetus and definition under the challenge of romanticism, nationalism and sectarianism, and as Irish society petrified into sectarian rigidities.

These influences slowly fused into an Irish version of that cultural nationalism which valorised societies with a long past, claiming that they produced citizens who practised traditional, uncorrupted virtue. It queried the universality of law when confronted by cultural heterogeneity, questioned the imperative of a cosmopolitan future when faced with the primacy and potency of a particularist past. Romanticism believed that a renovated society could not be achieved by law alone; instead one needed to re-create the people, by recuperating their cultural identity. In this sense, the nation was to be assembled organically, not artificially by the law or state. A nation was a people bound by blood, cemented by custom and a desire for political autonomy. If a nation is without an enabling set of political institutions, it retains its cohesion and collective order by cultural means. In Ireland cultural nationalism tended to become implicated with Catholicism, an inevitable intersection because Catholicism could represent itself as the traditional, customary and therefore 'national' religion of the Irish, and the principal repository of a distinctive Irish nationhood. By the nineteenth century the big-farm class had become the custodians of Catholic culture, wrapped in the mantle of the underground gentry. O'Connell himself emerged precisely from this milieu, which he intimately understood both instinctively and intellectually. His campaign conferred political power on this reading of Irish history, which built more on Burke and the Defenders than on the United Irishmen. The O'Connellite campaign, for example, inherited from Defenderism the concept that the Catholics were the people of Ireland, and from Burke the idea that Protestant Ascendancy was an incorrigible sham.

In either formulation there was no need for the Protestant gentry, whose subsequent legislative euthanasia merely confirmed the proleptic writing on the demesne walls. Thus, despite the fact that it remained a profoundly agrarian society, Ireland was the first European country to shed its landed gentry.[266] In this sense, the seemingly stable seventeenth-century settlement proved in the long term to be surprisingly brittle. The ultimate winners were the big-farm class; their resilience and stability derived substantially from their self-image as an old landowning class, displaced in the seventeenth-century upheavals. This sense of identity gave them a different character to that of other European societies and complicates any simplistic recourse to the word 'peasant' to describe their society. It also created an ambiguous position for the Irish gentry of that time. As Arthur Browne memorably phrased it in a 1787 debate: 'Elsewhere landed title was purchase, in Ireland it was forfeiture. The old proprietor kept alive the memory of his claim. Property in Ireland resembled the thin soil of volcanic countries spread lightly over subterranean fires.'[267] These seismic ambiguities make it difficult to manipulate Ireland into an *ancien régime* model and restore colonial contexts as a defining feature of eighteenth-century Irish life.

United Irish Catechism

What is that in your hand?   It is a branch.
Of what?   Of the Tree of Liberty.
Where did it first grow?   In America.
Where does it bloom?   In France.
Where did the seeds fall?   In Ireland.

CORK, DECEMBER 1797

THE REPUBLIC IN THE VILLAGE:
The United Irishmen, the Enlightenment and Popular Culture

The United Irishmen and the Enlightenment

The United Irishmen were bearers of the European Enlightenment, freely importing ideas from England, Scotland and France. They believed that they were moving in tandem politically with the inevitable laws of historical evolution, which would sweep away the existing Gothic political situation. Tone observed, in characteristic imagery, that 'a new age had dawned. These were the days of illumination at the close of the eighteenth century.'[1] Samuel Barber, moderator of the Presbyterian General Synod of Ulster, claimed: 'Before science, sooner or later, all tyranny will fall.'[2] Accepting the Enlightenment's claim to eliminate particularism in favour of universalism, the United Irishmen's function would merely be to spread this message from European core to European periphery and from top to bottom of the Irish political spectrum. Once Enlightenment principles had permeated the Irish body politic, they would result in clear, simple, unambiguous law, in line with the modern spirit of the age. These laws would allow cosmopolitan Enlightenment principles to achieve their correct dispositions; benevolence, civic virtue, beauty would come into play, and there would be a harmony between national character (Montesquieu's *l'esprit*) and its laws (*les lois*), between *res* and *publica*.

Very conscious of the French Revolution's claim to have annihilated history, the United Irishmen subscribed to the revolutionary orthodoxy of repudiating the past, and specifically the Irish past: 'We have thought much about our posterity, little about our ancestors. Are we forever to walk like beasts of prey over the fields which these ancestors stained with blood?' 'Mankind have been too retrospective, canonised antiquity and undervalued themselves.' 'It [the society of United Irishmen] will not by views merely retrospective stop the march of mankind or force them back into the lanes and alleys of their ancestors.'[3] They adopted the relentlessly modernising rhetoric of the Enlightenment, suffused with images of light, of rationality, of progress, of Utopia.[4] This repudiation of the divisiveness of the Irish past had also a pragmatic political value: the United Irishmen's collective amnesia stressed the enabling rather than disabling forces in Irish history. Thus they consciously agreed to develop a political programme solely on agreed issues, and to tacitly ignore divisive ones: 'Our principal rule of conduct has been to attend to those things in which we agree, to exclude from our thoughts those on which we differ.'[5] The United Irish repudiation of the past was different from the standard radical reading, which saw the past in Burkean terms as a stabilising, and therefore sedative, political agent. In the Irish context, the United Irishmen wished to repudiate the past for precisely the opposite reason – its potentially destabilising effect.

In Montesquieu's classic Enlightenment statement of the relationship between *l'esprit* and *les lois*, every society had its own innate characteristics (dictated by climate, geography, diet), which determined its *esprit* or national character.[6] Thus the historical evolution of every society is inscribed in its origin and development, and this should be crystallised in its laws. The central problem for the Irish Enlightenment was that this simple equation between *l'esprit* and *les lois* did not exist: the calculus was fundamentally disturbed by the position of Catholic Ireland. This could represent itself (especially from the mid eighteenth-century historiographical innovations initiated by Charles O'Conor) as a legitimate cultural entity, with its own specific *esprit* derived from a lengthy and authentic history, but which was excluded from political power as *incapax libertatis*. Ireland was therefore not a simple *tabula rasa*, on which Enlightenment principles could be unproblematically inscribed. Until Catholics were admitted to the polity, there could be no consonance between *l'esprit* and *les lois*. Two options then presented themselves to Irish politicians: to reform the people (i.e. the Catholics) so that *l'esprit* became congruous with *les lois*, or to change *les lois* to make them reflect the Irish *esprit*. The option of reforming the laws only presented itself as feasible once the French Revolution seemed to demonstrate that Catholics (having shaken off their addiction to despotism and priestcraft) were now *capaces libertatis*. Thus, for the late eighteenth-century bearers of the European Enlightenment in Ireland, reform of the laws and system of government, not reform of the people, became the preferred option, as projected by the United Irishmen. These reforms would create a natural consonance between cultural identity and government practice, generating a harmony which would allow for the unimpeded expression of beauty, benevolence and civic virtue. Without this consonance, only a disjointed, corrupt, unrepresentative politics could operate. William Michael Byrne, in his dying declaration from 'Newgate Bastille' on 24 July 1798, highlighted the centrality of the concept of virtue to the United Irishmen: 'No one political action or sentiment of my life has ever been actuated by any other motive than a wish to promote the cause of virtue.'[7]

In practical political terms, the United Irishmen identified the lack of a natural relationship between *l'esprit* and *les lois* as the principal irritant in Irish life, provoking inevitable and recurrent conflict. In particular, the exclusion of Catholics guaranteed the unrepresentative nature of Irish government. In the United Irish analysis, a small privileged handful could thereby run the country in their own corrupt and self-serving interest, facilitated and copperfastened in so doing by the English connection which propped up this same unnatural handful to ensure that English policies could be smoothly implemented in Ireland. This arrangement created a logjam which stymied reform, denied a representative, reformed parliament, and left the country in the hands of a junta. The United Irishmen identified the junta as straw men, buttressed solely by the English connection; remove that link and they would topple overnight, without bloodshed or anarchy. This is what Tone meant when he referred to 'breaking the connection with England, the never-failing source of all our political evils'.[8]

When this despotic and arbitrary government had been removed, the new representative Irish parliament would enact legislation which would bind the nation together, bringing *l'esprit* and *les lois* into harmony again. In the United Irish view, divisions within Irish society were artificial, deliberately exacerbated by the junta (or faction) to maintain their own corrupt regime. William Drennan, the most self-conscious Enlightenment figure among the United Irishmen, observed: 'The faction traduces one half of the nation to cajole the other and by keeping up distrust and division wishes to continue the proud arbitrators of the fate of Ireland.'[9] Arthur O'Connor asked rhetorically: 'Has it not been by sowing, maintaining and fomenting division that Irish administrations have governed Ireland?'[10] Thus, in classic Hutchesonian terms, the United Irishmen attacked despotism, which destroyed the internal cohesiveness of society, and thereby prevented the exercise of virtue. The United Irishmen believed that the balance could be rectified by simply changing the mode of government, and their programme was anchored insistently on this point: 'With a parliament thus reformed, everything is possible.'[11] There is accordingly only a muted articulation of social, economic or cultural reforms within early United Irish rhetoric. Such issues could safely be left to a reformed, representative parliament, which would, because it represented the national *esprit*, inevitably enact suitable legislation in these arenas.

The United Irishmen felt that there was no need to recast the people, to reform them in advance of the laws; no need therefore to adopt a cultural nationalist position, although by the end of the eighteenth century, Romanticism was already beginning to undermine the Enlightenment's faith in law as the sole vector of historical change. Romanticism, and its political offshoot cultural nationalism, reversed the horse and cart in the motor of historical change. If *l'esprit* of the people was nurtured, fortified and stabilised, *les lois* would inevitably yield to the pressure of its insistent presence. Cultural nationalism therefore celebrated the customary, the regional, the particularist, at the expense of the new, the cosmopolitan, the universal. Despite a few decorative gestures in this direction – such as the Belfast Harp Festival of 1792 and the publication of *Bolg an tSolair* in 1795 – the United Irishmen only tentatively represent this intellectual tradition in Ireland. In 1795 William Drennan sneered at Bishop Thomas Hussey's and General Maurice O'Connell's brogue, which 'kept its native broadness and vulgarity'. He was surprised to find that both men, despite their European experience, should 'smack so strongly of the bogtrotter'.[12] The United Irishmen's necks were set in concrete, staring relentlessly forward. They saw their project in Ireland as simply to accelerate the reception of Enlightenment principles. Their relationship with popular culture therefore was radically different from a cultural nationalist programme: they wished not to valorise but to politicise it.

Text and context

Looking at the United Irishmen in the light of this analysis, one can claim that they were simply not interested in popular culture *per se*, but only in politicising it, in using it as one more weapon in the battle for public opinion and especially in 'the race for the Catholic' that was being run at breakneck speed in the early 1790s. The central (and novel) achievement of the United Irishmen was the creation of public opinion as the pivotal political force. As in revolutionary France, the press would be the seminal architect of the arena of public opinion, a novel public space in which competing claims and discourses could be mediated. In Habermas's terms, the United Irishmen were intent on creating a culturally produced social sphere, in which public opinion acted as the arbiter of political rectitude, and in which the press could plausibly pretend to represent a diversified public. They were equally keen to place their ideological imprint on public opinion. Their literature therefore could not transcend the partisan pressure of politics; art for the United Irishmen was a mould, not a mirror or lamp, hence the overtly didactic tone of all their productions. For the United Irishmen, therefore, the Republic of Letters offered the precondition for a political republic, a moral school where republicans could be shaped internally prior to their political incarnation.

For their literature to fulfil its proleptic role as antenna of the political future, its message needed to be transmitted as widely as possible. Arthur O'Connor made the point forcefully, while invoking a typical litany of Enlightenment figures and placing the Irish experience firmly within the American and French fold:

> *The Press* is the palladium of Liberty. What has heretofore made England celebrated over the nations of Europe? – *The Press*. What overturned the Catholic despotism of France? *The Press*, by the writings of Montesquieu, Voltaire, Rousseau, Diderot, Seyes [sic], Raynal, and Condorcet. What has electrified England, and called down its curses on a Pitt? that Press he in vain attempted to silence. What illumined Belfast, the Athens of Ireland? – *The Press* and the *Northern Star*. Why did America triumph over tyranny? – a journeyman printer fulminated the decree of nature against the giants of England and the pen of a Franklin routed the armies of a King.[13]

In a typical flourish, the *Northern Star*, the United Irishmen's own newspaper, claimed in 1795:

> The present is an age of revolution. Everything is changing, every system is improving and mankind appear to become more wise and virtuous, as they become more informed. This is the consequence of knowledge, the effect of intelligence, the result of truth and reason.[14]

Thus the United Irishmen made impressive efforts to disseminate their ideas at the ground level. O'Connor claimed that 'the increase and improvement of intellect among the poor, not being accompanied by a proportionate amendment of their condition, they became fully sensible of the wretchedness of their state'.[15] Leonard McNally noted in 1795: 'Every man who can read or can hear and understand what is read to him begins in religion as in politics to think for themselves.'[16] In 1796 another commentator noted the politicising effect of a situation 'where the public newspapers are so universally read, and where the events passing on the continent are so generally known'.[17]

To achieve their aim of 'making every man a politician', the United Irishmen relied on the power of print (suitably customised) to shape politics out of doors. Especially successful were populist, scaled-down versions in pamphlet form of classic Enlightenment authors. Two such pamphlets had been 'industriously distributed to the peasantry of the north' between 1795 and 1797 – the first 'compiled chiefly from Godwin, Locke, Paine etc.', the second 'a compilation from Voltaire, Volney and other atheistical writers'.[18] Nor did these activities stop at mere distribution. In 1795 William Putnam McCabe, the charismatic United Irish emissary and organiser, was distributing Paine's *Age of Reason* among mill-workers in Belfast, following that by discussions in which he 'answered their several objections to any part of it'.[19] The United Irishmen drew on an eclectic assemblage of Enlightenment figures for inspiration and authority: Locke, Priestley, Godwin, Holcroft, Paine, Montesquieu, Schiller, Voltaire, Raynal, Condorcet, Rousseau, De Volney, Diderot, Sieyès, Ganganelli. Lockean ideas (especially of the contractual nature of the relationship between the governor and governed, and the revolutionary implications of a breach in that contract) were particularly powerful. Robert Emmet's personal copy of Locke's work still survives; it is copiously annotated having been used by him as a student text in Trinity College. On rereading the book for its political rather than scholarly content, he again annotated it with marginalia from Godwin's *Political Justice*.[20]

Belfast, and more especially Dublin, United Irishmen had access to a well-established printing, publishing, journalistic and distribution network, many of whose practitioners were sympathetic to the United Irish message. In the 1790s there were at least fifty printers in Dublin, thirty-four Irish provincial presses (especially concentrated in north-east Ulster), and at least forty newspapers in print. There were fifteen booksellers and printers in the Dublin Society of United Irishmen (1791–4), including such leading figures as John Chambers, Patrick Byrne, Richard Cross, Randal McAllister, Thomas McDonnell and John Stockdale.[21] At least five Dublin printers surrendered themselves as United Irishmen in 1798 – Patrick Byrne, Timothy Byrne, John Blyth, Robert Connolly and Arthur Loughlin.[22] Publishers had well-defined networks for disseminating their products, and the Dublin Castle executive watched aghast as Dublin and Belfast printed propaganda circulated widely: 'Great pains are taken to disperse their publications and besides the newspapers, there were handbills dispersed to the number of many thousand over the whole kingdom, by every shopkeeper in their society, packed in his bales, by every merchant enveloped in his correspondence.'[23] Pedlars, carmen, country dealers, chapmen and emissaries spread these publications also. A rattled Ulster conservative noted that Paine's publications 'and others equally seditious' were 'showered from the chariots of their emissaries as they passed through the several provinces', and that 'on the common road from fairs and markets in this very province were scattered copies of the modern textbook of infidelity [*The Age of Reason*]'.[24]

As early as 1793 Denis Browne in Westport was already attributing the changed political spirit of the ordinary people to the stream of paper emanating from Dublin, a spirit 'produced by the circulation of Paine's *Rights of Man*, of seditious newspapers, and by shopkeepers who having been in Dublin to buy goods have formed connections with some of the United Irishmen'.[25] In County Kildare, James Alexander considered that, in explaining the changing political atmosphere, 'newspapers went a good way into the business: for I never knew the people in [this] neighbourhood anything like so attached to these vehicles of information and political sentiment'.[26] By September 1795 the spy Leonard McNally observed the effects of this paper deluge:

> So sudden a revolution in the Catholic mind is easily accounted for. I impute it to the press. The publication of political discussions, addresses and resolutions by the Societies of United Irishmen of Belfast and Dublin written to the passions and feelings of the multitude filled them with electrical celerity; these papers prepared the way for Paine's politics and theology.[27]

The chief constable of police in the Athlone district agreed: 'The press is destroying the minds of the people in this country for they wish for nothing else.'[28] A correspondent of Dublin Castle in 1797 was surprised to find that in the remoter parts of County Tipperary 'great numbers of printed papers on half sheets had been dispersed all over the hills'. Closer inquiry showed that 'these papers were mostly distributed by persons appearing as pedlars, whose boxes had underdrawers to them'.[29] An English visitor was struck by the number of political pamphlets on sale in Dublin bookshops.[30]

A bipolar web of communications was spun out of Dublin and Belfast, linking trade, publication and distribution.[31] In 1796 Lord Clonmel defined Dublin as 'the mint for coining treason and circulating it in small parts and making it current', while a year earlier Belfast had been described as 'the centre of motion' to the whole United Irish machine in Ulster.[32] The effectiveness of this propaganda drive depended on a literate populace, and the United Irishmen also encouraged popular education and were instrumental in founding Sunday schools and plebeian book clubs in east Ulster in the 1790s. By 1795 the well-informed Captain Andrew MacNevin reported from Carrickfergus how these bookclubs were being used: 'The United Irishmen, being prevented from meeting publickly, have established clandestine societies who are well supplied with inflammatory publications, some calling themselves Book Clubs, Literary Societies and Reading Societies.'[33] According to Richard Musgrave:

These meetings, formed after the model of the Jacobin clubs in France, were usually held in barns and schoolhouses, and were liberally furnished with inflammatory publications, composed by the literati of the United Irishmen, or extracted from larger treatises of a similar tendency in both kingdoms and published in the form of pamphlets for more general circulation. The pretext of meeting for mutual information and improvement was considered as a plausible motive for the lower class of people to assemble. . . . The rustic orators declaimed, with much vociferation and zeal, to the great edification of admiring audiences. The most fluent speakers went from one society to another, to display their talents and make prosleytes to the new philosophy.[34]

The book clubs ('seminaries of sedition') were viewed with undisguised alarm by conservatives, as mimicked by James Porter in the words of Squire Firebrand:

Oh, how times are changed and all for the worse. Your Catholic College, your Catholic schools, your Catholic emancipation, your Sunday schools, your charter schools, your book societies, your pamphlets, your books and your one hell or another are all turning the people's heads and setting them athinking about this, that and the other.[35]

Indeed, national education was an insistent presence on the United Irish agenda; they constantly encouraged reading as the most salutary weapon against corruption in Irish government. The *Union Doctrine or Poor Man's Catechism* (1798) suggested that the Irish people were deliberately kept poor to restrain them from thought:

By being poor, we must be on the alert to procure the necessaries of life, which makes true the old maxim 'they keep us poor and busy.' Our time will be spent studying to avoid want, instead of enquiring the cause of it, for inquiry is dangerous to tyranny.[36]

Ulster and the *Northern Star*

Conservatives and radicals alike were agreed that the exceptionally high literacy level in east Ulster was conducive to the reception of propaganda: Richard Musgrave associated Presbyterianism, literacy and radicalism, noting that in Counties Antrim and Down 'the mass of the people are Presbyterians, can read and write and are fond of speculating on religion and politics'.[37] The radical Thomas Russell claimed in 1796 that 'there does not exist in Europe a class of people in the same line of life, who possess the same enlarged ideas, or minds as well stored with knowledge, as the farmers and manufacturers in the province of Ulster'.[38] Arthur O'Connor stated that 'the people of Ulster were the best educated peasantry in Europe'.[39] There is some independent evidence to back these large claims. In the summer of 1797 some 6,600 adult males from Belfast and its south Antrim hinterland took the oath of allegiance, initially verbally and then by signature, for those competent to write their names. The proportion able to do so – 76 per cent – would certainly position the Belfast region among the most literate areas of late eighteenth-century Europe.[40]

Right across Ulster, there is good evidence for literacy, the spread of political literature and associated politicisation. In 1793 George Knox reported from Strabane in Tyrone;

> There are little clubs in almost every village in the north which take the *Northern Star* and circulate Payne and such publications of the same tendency as are sent to them gratis from Belfast and Dublin. These clubs form volunteer corps and distribute arms among those who cannot afford to purchase them. Where they get money to do this, I cannot discover. They profess favourable sentiments for the Catholics who however do not join them, being restrained I apprehend by the influence of their priests. Some of them enter into resolutions in favour of reform, others against tythes etc. but whatever their public declarations may be, which are one day constitutional and another republican, being just accommodated to the situation of the public mind and to the strength or weakness of the government, their sentiments and principles are French – lowering rents, and abolishing tythes are the principal objects and those held out most assiduously. The members of the clubs are generally a few tradesmen, the dissenting minister, the attorney and the apothecary of the district.[41]

The most articulate exponent of 'intelligent treason' was the *Northern Star* newspaper. The *Northern Star* reckoned that each of its 4,000 print-run reached at least ten people through collective reading.[42] Its penetration is suggested in a vignette in Thomas Russell's diary: travelling in a remote district in south Down, he 'saw a little girl in quite a wild part near Ballynahinch with a paper in her hand. Ask her what it was. Answered *The Northern Star*.'[43] In June 1796, an English traveller in Ulster noted: 'At every cabin around us, you will see them reading them. I often met Sir John's labourers walking to work and reading their papers as they move along.'[44] Charles Moore of Moira reflected in verse in 1798 on the new phenomenon of the village shopkeeper reading the newspapers to his customers:

> Fearfully wise, he shakes his empty head
> And deals out empires as he deals his thread.
> His useless scales are in the corner flung
> And Europe's balance hangs upon his tongue.[45]

The rise in newpaper reading can be demonstrated statistically. In 1785 the *Belfast Newsletter* sold 2,050 copies per issue; at its peak in the mid-1790s, the *Northern Star* sold 4,200 copies, while the *Newsletter* managed 2,750. Thus the impact of popular politicisation in Ulster in the aftermath of the French Revolution was to more than triple the circulation of newpapers.[46]

In the various legal onslaughts on the *Northern Star*, a substantial segment of the paper's own working archive was seized, and careful analysis of this material allows us to reconstruct in detail its distribution pattern in Ulster in the 1793–4 period.[47] One should initially note the essential modernity of the *Northern Star* as a business enterprise: it was the first Irish newspaper to be run by a board of directors and financed by venture capital. The paper had initially to set up a network of agents. As we might expect, many of these were shopkeepers, inn-keepers and merchants, but there was a surprisingly high number of professional men, especially doctors and clergymen. Once that network was in place, popular and political literature could also travel along it. While pride of place went to the *Northern Star's* own publications (notably its popular ballad collection *Paddy's Resource* and its prose satire *The Lion of Old England*), it also distributed Presby-terian sermons (by the United Irish ministers Thomas Ledlie Birch, William Steel Dickson and William Bryson), and handled orders for the popular periodicals, like *Exshaw's* and the *Masonic* magazines. These were generally ordered in small batches of a dozen or half a dozen copies.

We can also recover information about the number of subscribers in various towns in 1793–4. Two hundred copies were going to Dublin, where they were handled by Oliver Bond, a prominent radical merchant and the son of a Donegal dissenting clergyman. A large town like Lisburn, very close to Belfast, had 107 subscribers; numbers varied in inverse relationship to towns' populations, their distance from Belfast, and the size of their Presbyterian congregations. Thus a large centre like Enniskillen, distant from Belfast and predominantly Anglican in composition, took only twelve copies, while the much smaller but intensely Presbyterian centres of Moneymore and Ahoghill took double that number. A noticeable feature of the subscribers' lists is their trans-sectarian composition. There are, for example, at least a half dozen Catholic priests amongst them. Sales figures from the Belfast office for June 1792 to December 1793 provide a reveal-ing glimpse of the rhythm with which retail sales surged and subsided in synchrony with the political temperature. The peak is in December 1792, when the Back Lane Parliament was in session; there is a minor peak in the spring of 1793, when the Volunteer movement in Ulster was suppressed.

The *Northern Star* notebooks also allow us to reconstruct the sales network and distribution routes for the newspaper in 1793–5. If one compares these patterns with ones showing the hinterlands of the major Ulster ports in the eighteenth century, and the flow of trade into these ports in 1837, one can understand a good deal about these patterns.[48] Firstly, the intense strength of the *Northern Star* in Presbyterian areas is clearly apparent; there is a striking fall off in its penetration once it reaches the (essentially Catholic) hinterland of Newry and the (more heavily Catholic and Anglican) hinterland of Derry. The *Northern Star* was sold in Protestant Rathfriland but not in Catholic Hilltown, in Clough but not Castlewellan, in Coagh but not Coalisland. Its greatest strength lay in south-east Antrim, within easy reach of Belfast, and it was also strong along the busy corridor linking Belfast and Armagh down the Lagan valley, in the Presbyterian crescent stretching behind Lough Neagh from Armagh to Dungannon and Maghera, and in the Presbyterian hearthland of south Antrim and north Down. The *Northern Star* struggled to reach as far west as Bally-shannon, but it had no other foothold in County Donegal. One might conclude that in the Defender territory of south Ulster the *Northern Star* made no headway. It only barely penetrated into County Cavan at Cootehill; there was bitter criticism of Cavan town itself, where no agent or subscribers could be found:

> All we could do had no effect on them for [they are] dead with respect to politics nor they don't care a pin which way the war goes and I verily believe that two-thirds of them does not know that there is a war between England and France.

Its rival, the moderate Whig *Belfast Newsletter* of Henry Joy, had its greatest success in the (Anglican) Lagan valley: one-third of its circulation was in the zone stretching from Lisburn, through Tanderagee, Richhill and Armagh. It was correspondingly weak in the *Northern Star's* Presbyterian heartland (where it lost about half of its subscribers betweeen November 1795 and April 1797, as political divisions deepened and a moderate stance was no longer viable). The *Northern Star* notebooks also offer fascinating glimpses of its cut-throat competition with its competitors. The crucial point was to get the *Northern Star* delivered ahead of the *Belfast Newsletter*, and also ahead of the Dublin papers. The *Northern Star's* agents carefully considered every means of getting the paper more quickly to its subscribers – whether by foot courier, by horse-back, or through the post office. In the immediate vicinity of Belfast, with its dense network of subscribers, delivery took place on foot. Outside of this zone, the papers went by horse. Ulster could be divided into three zones: places which got the paper on the day of publication; those which got it on the second day; and an outer zone where delivery took three days. The people in Omagh, for example, complained that 'the news was stale' by the time it reached them, while in Armagh town 'the people here don't understand the reason they don't get the paper the day they are dated'. From the newspaper's point of view, there were great dangers in irregular deliveries. Subscribers could peremptorily refuse to pay if the paper did not arrive punctually and regularly. A large part of the agent's job was sorting out these muddles and pacifying recalcitrant or disillusioned subscribers. The *Northern Star* tried to systematise its distribution as much as possible. On St Patrick's Day 1794 new regulations were established for distribution in Belfast:

> On Mondays, the boys shall not go out with the paper to town delivery before five striking. No shop sale nor delivery to Belfast subscribers till after the boys are out except in the case of a country subscriber or a carrier of papers to the country.

Reliable couriers were pivotal to successful distribution: if one link in the chain of communication broke, a huge knock-on effect could ensue. Carriers with a drink problem were summarily dismissed, like William Caldwell, on the Armagh to Cootehill route, accused of stopping off at Leslie's of Falkland and getting drunk there among the kitchen servants. The carriers were constantly being supplied with equipment to improve their performance – better horses, new shoes, pumps and greatcoats, leather belts and saddle-bags (ingeniously made from flour-bags, sewn at the mouth and then cut into two pieces 'to make it like two wallets for to lie on the horse's back'). There was also close attention to detail, for example stressing the necessity to seal bags and bundles of papers to prevent them being stolen or sold, or criticising the agency in Hillsborough, a public inn, where 'in the middle of the night they [the newspapers] are thrown into the gateway and servants etc. may take them'.

There are glimpses of the *Northern Star's* other printing commitments in the notebooks. It printed advertising labels for posting in coffee-shops, and it had an active jobbing trade in lottery tickets, militia receipts, hair-powder labels, and notices for fairs. There were also favours to be reciprocated – as when Thomas Russell was requested to return 'Price's book on liberty' to Hamilton in Enniskillen or when 'two cases of long or great primer' were to be sent from Belfast to Mr Hanmer. The subscribers themselves always posed difficulties. There was a surprising number of partnership subscriptions, and there were some members who shirked paying their share. It was difficult to extract money from many ordinary subscribers, who had an inventive list of excuses: some had emigrated to America, others were in jail, or at the spa, at the seaside, or in Dublin, or absent at fairs and markets. Others still refused to deal with the *Northern Star's* agent, Thomas Kean, 'like the half gentlemen in and about Enniskillen, not at home'. Adam Perry of Moira claimed that his father-in-law would not let him read the *Northern Star*, while 'A. Crozier in Enniskillen said point-blank that he won't pay for a seditious paper'. The best excuse came from Thomas Lawrence near Richhill in County Armagh:

> I waited on Thomas Dawson Laurence esq. . . . . I could get no money. I believe he is very poor. He began a blather to me about his qualifications and did I see the resolutions that appeared in Mr Joy's paper from Hallsmill – then he began 'O what eloquent language etc. etc. They were written by me sir!' Next he took me through the house, showing me the pictures of his ancestors, but last of all, he made Mrs Laurence go for a volume of his poems, and desired me to present them to the proprietors in his name, at the same time, granting them liberty to publish any of them – which is most certainly a great honour.

The energising impact of the *Northern Star* is vividly caught in a letter from John Schoales, following a visit to Ulster in the spring of 1797 as a prosecuting counsel:

> The Northern Star [is] the principal and most powerful of all the instruments used for agitating and deluding the minds of the people. Unless you see that infernal paper, you can have no idea of the length to which it goes, of the innumerable falsehoods which it circulates among the credulous populace, of the style of its paragraphs, exquisitely adopted to the taste and understanding of the northerners, of the ability, in short, with which it is conducted, nor of the pernicious effects of its circulation. That circulation too is great beyond example. The lowest of the people get it. It is read to them in clusters. A whole neighbourhood subscribe for it.[49]

William Richardson, an astute observer, noticed the interplay between social class, trade linkages with Belfast, and politicisation. He described the agricultural labourers as

> [The] quietest description of men we have, slowly and gradually mending in their circumstances, and little troubling themselves about politicks or grievances except rarely and under local circumstances, or where they have been lately debauched (particularly in the countys of Derry and Antrim) by the really factious, who are the shopkeepers, petty merchants and innholders in the country towns. A set of men more out of reach of grievance and oppression than any description I know of, yet because parliament does not retain its original purity, seats are bought, places and pensions are lavished on the undeserving and Ireland but an appendage, they are miserable and can submit no longer. By the increased demand for commoditys in an improving country, these shopkeepers have suddenly grown rich, but wealth without power is nothing and this can be obtained only by exterminating those that have it. The nature of their trade connects them with great democrats in Belfast and Newry who furnish them with goods for the country and topics of sedition, and by caresses and flattery excite their zeal and convert them into missionarys of treason and sedition. Of such chiefly are composed at present our Northern United Irishmen, more formidable for their activity, organization and desperate spirit that stops at nothing, than from their numbers.

In a revealing aside he described the impact of the *Northern Star*:

> A set of young merchants in Belfast set up a newspaper called the *Northern Star*, not with a view to gain but almost avowedly for revolutionary purposes. In this point of view, it was ably conducted and its success decisive, the country being compleately corrupted or dangerously infected so far as the delivery of the *Northern Star* extends and no farther.[50]

His Derry namesake, John Richardson, noticed a pronounced difference between the conservative west and the radical east of his county:

> This difference of disposition may be easily traced to the most obvious cause – their distance from and little trade or intercourse with Belfast, for it is apparent that the disposition to rebellion is more or less in proportion to the distance from that seat of mischief.[51]

When the *Northern Star* was finally smashed militarily in 1797, the United Irishmen moved their newspaper operation to Dublin. *The Press*, lent credibility by Arthur O'Connor's name, took over the *Northern Star*'s mantle in September 1797. Hostile commentators noted that it 'had immediately a more extensive circulation than many papers long established'.[52] It soon had an unprecedented print-run of 6,000 copies, and a crowd assembled on the night of publication in Church Lane to read each new issue, amidst 'a revelry of sedition'.[53] The newspaper was aggressively marketed, eventually provoking a clampdown on its vendors, accused of 'bellowing at every corner their treasonable publications'.[54]

Even possession of a copy became a serious misdemeanour: an Offaly priest, Father John Brookes of Shinrone, was court-martialled for having one in his house.[55] One United Irishman in Dublin, Patterson, was confined after the rebellion 'for the *horrid* crime of swearing that there never was a paper printed worth reading but *The Press,* that he had every number of it and by J ... s would have them bound in the most elegant manner possible'.[56] *The Press* was so popular, even after its suppression, that three collected editions were published (under the title *Beauties of The Press)* in London, Dublin and Philadelphia.[57]

Medium and message

The newspaper propagandising was paralleled by specially commissioned political material, generating a paper stream that washed through English-speaking Ireland in the 1790s. As in revolutionary France, this paper flood had three principal effects. The first was to challenge the very style of political discourse. Thomas Paine, in particular, illustrated the possibility of creating a vernacular prose, adequate to political discourse, social responsibility and moral seriousness, in a way which had previously been thought possible only in the classical style.[58] Breaking the inherently elitist link between a classical education and political life made available a fundamental democratisation of style itself. This enhanced the accessibility of the radical message and constituted Paine's greatest achievement. Inspired by this breakthrough, the United Irishmen cultivated a plain, blunt style, whose muscular rhythms approximated the spoken voice, and which was designed to be read by the many rather than admired by the few. Avoiding the conventional Ciceronian flourishes of established political discourse, Paine's *Rights of Man* and Tone's *Argument*, the two most successful pamphlets of the early 1790s in Ireland, were a stylistic as much as a political triumph and set the tone for a flood of populist polemical writing. The *Poor Man's Catechism* mocked the notion of aristocracy in a conceit drawn from Paine, claiming that aristocrats should be immediately recognisable at birth:

> They would come into the world finished statesmen, orators, mathematicians, generals, dancing masters, hairdressers, taylors etc, nay, they would come from the womb covered with embroidery, ribbons, stars and coronets.[59]

The second effect was to diminish the authority of elite culture, by displacing expensive books in favour of cheap pamphlets, newspapers, songbooks, prints and broadsheets, thereby democratising the printed word itself. A favoured ploy was the printing of broadsheets, whose reverse side was left blank; these were pinned in public places (chapel, church and meeting-house doors, trees, pubs) for public perusal. In February 1794 the United Irish plans for parliamentary reform were ordered to be published 'on a single sheet for the purpose of hanging up in cabins'. The *Union Star,* printed on one side only, was ideally suited to public display. One magistrate, having dispersed a seditious meeting under the guise of a boxing match at Sallins in County Kildare, was disappointed that he could not send the Castle a copy of the *Union Star* which had been simultaneously posted upon the canal stores there: 'in taking it down, it has been too much torn to send you'.[60] A report from Baltinglass in County Wicklow in May 1797 shows clearly how the Republic reached the village: 'Our town is overrun with disorder by the means of a republic newspaper now done in Carlow where every Sunday two fellows come after mass is over and read what they please to the ignorant country people.'[61] In the same year a report on the taproom of Lennon's pub in Arran Street in Dublin commented on the avidity with which the clientèle listened to the public reading of the *Union Star* by a United Irish organiser, Joseph Davis.[62]

A third effect was the development of genres which overcame the literacy barrier, which were permeable across the barrier between reading and speech. These included ballads, prophecies, toasts, oaths, catechisms and sermons. Because of the heavy emphasis on orality in Irish popular culture, these United Irish strategies were very successful. Even tunes could be customised to fit a newly politicised context. A military riot was initiated in Belfast in March 1793 by a blind fiddler playing the *Ça Ira*.[63] In the same year Thomas Russell recorded an incident at the Fermanagh grand jury meeting where the M.P. Arthur Cole-Hamilton threw his glass at another blind fiddler's head for inadvertently playing the Jacobite air 'The White Cockade'.[64] 'The Rights of Man' entered the traditional repertoire as a slow air in the 1790s, and the United Irishmen also produced a trenchant parody of 'God Save the King' called 'God Save the Rights of Man'. They often disrupted public performances of the official version – hissing it at the theatre in Wexford in 1792, refusing to take off their hats as a military band performed it in Kells in 1796, and inciting full-scale riots in Astley's Hippodrome and the Fishamble Street theatre in 1797 when the bands there tried to play it.[65] During the short-lived Wexford Republic, the radical version was immediately substituted for the loyal version on public occasions.[66]

The United Irishmen also published a series of songbooks, including at least four separate editions of *Paddy's Resource*.[67] This book was sufficiently popular (so successful in 'galloping about the country' that Squire Firebrand's servant thought its name was 'Paddy's Race-Horse') to provoke the Squire's ire:

> 'Tis songs that is most to be dreaded of all things. Singing, Billy, is a damned bad custom: it infects a whole country and makes them half mad, because they rejoice and forget their cares, and forget their duty, and forget their betters. By heavens, I'll put an end to singing in this part of the country in a short time. And there's whistling is near as bad: do you hear much whistling nowadays?[68]

We need to consider context as well as text in assessing the impact of these performance genres. Above all, these performances signified solidarity, public affirmation, and a means of assessing the political spirit of any gathering. Failure to join in the chorus of a popular radical song was a sure sign of disaffection from the popular cause. Songs had a symbolic as well as ideological freight. Thomas

Handcock, a clerical Wexford magistrate, was conscious of the defiant symbolism of a condemned United Irishman, 'a desperate rebel, and when taken sang a wicked rebel song, which he declared he would sing at the gallows if required and I do not doubt it'.[69] Rebels gathering on the Wicklow/Kildare border on the eve of the insurrection are described as singing 'horrible songs never before heard by any loyalist to excite the rebellion'.[70]

The United Irishmen reached the limits of contemporary literacy by using public readings. From Ross barony in County Galway, Walter Bermingham, a local landowner, voiced his suspicions of William Hamilton, described as 'a great politician' who 'spent his time reading newspapers to the common people'.[71] Viscount Dillon was convinced that the United Irishmen had 'paid interpreters in remote parts to translate for the ignorant'.[72] Lord Chancellor Fitzgibbon expressed the establishment assessment of the United Irish movement as a conspiracy composed of 'a deluded peasantry aided by more intelligent treason'.[73]

The dissenting imagination, nourished on the Book of Revelations, tended to react to extreme pressure by generating images of apocalypse, purgation and the imminent birth of a new order out of the violent destruction of the old.[74] It was easy, and the United Irishmen exploited the ease, to transpose these millenarian tendencies from spiritual to secular circumstances. In Ireland such millenarian perspectives were given added potency by the American and especially French Revolutions.[75] This biblical eschatology formed the substrate for a blending of millenial, Enlightenment and republican ideas about the future, a blend which has been identified as an important ingredient in the development of the American and French Revolutions.

In 1792 the Quaker Abraham Shackleton anxiously sent a 'prophecy said to be found in the vault of a druid' to a colleague in Dublin, soliciting his opinion of what he described as 'an awful alarm'.[76] By the mid-1790s such prophecies were being extensively used by the United Irishmen and Defenders, and were being inserted into the popular consciousness. Rev. James Little described them 'as one of the principal stratagems of the Connaught United Irishmen', who had 'established a mint for coinage of false prophecies, from whence new ones were to issue as fast as old ones should fail'.[77] In 1796 John Beresford complained: 'They have songs and prophecies, just written, stating all late events and what is to happen, as if made several years ago, in order to persuade the people that as a great part of them had already come to pass, so the remainder will certainly happen.'[78] 'Prophecy men' circulated in Ulster and Connacht, carrying with them new radical publications.[79] In 1795 alone, three books of prophecies were published in Belfast, two in Strabane, and one in Monaghan. All used millenarian perspectives to explain the French Revolution and to give ideological impetus to the struggle. The County Down United Irishman and 'New Light' Presbyterian minister, William Staveley, added an introduction to the *Northern Star*'s 1795 reprint of Robert Fleming's *A Discourse on the Rise and Fall of Anti-Christ – wherein the Revolution in France and the Downfall of Monarchy in this Kingdom are distinctly pointed out*. Staveley was keen to make the political message stick: 'That millenium state [is] now fast advancing, when men will cast far off the chains of slavery.'[80] It was relatively easy to transmit levelling principles under this eschatological aegis. In 1795 Andrew Gamble in Strabane produced a small millenarian chapbook for circulation by pedlars at fairs: *Christ in Triumph coming to Judgement*:

> . . . and what happy times will succeed to many people when the poor will be had in equal (or perhaps superior) estimation with the rich. The courts of Kings, the seats and palaces of noblemen, the banqueting halls of the luxurious, the full barns of farmers, the cottages of husbandmen and the stalls under which beggars lie will be as one and come to nothing.

No wonder that the magistrate who arrested the demobbed soldier who was selling the chapbook at Gortin fair near Strabane should comment:

> We think [the work] a very dangerous one at this time, and tho' under a religious idea, yet the ignorant country people will take many meanings out of it that suit their present way of thinking, as there is a levelling principle in it.[81]

These genres were interfaces where authoritative forms of the written word penetrated oral culture and imprinted their shapes on it; assimilated in this public (oral) fashion, rather than in a private (written) way, they created a communal store of knowledge, accessible to all, and hence were inherently democratic modes of communication. Such genres were performance-driven, enacted in contexts of sociability. They were also fluid, portable and malleable, capable of being given a topical or local inflection as occasion demanded, through the alteration of place or personal names, for example. These genres privileged the voice, which in the dissenting and evangelical literary tradition, stood for individual integrity, the primal utterance which as unmediated expression stood close to experience and therefore to truth.

These United Irish strategies were increasingly successful in 'making every man a politician', as Thomas Addis Emmet expressed it.[82] In January 1798, for example, a traveller on the Roscrea to Limerick road noted that there was 'not a village on the road in which the name of William Orr and the cause for which he died is not as well known as in the town of Carrickfergus'.[83] Such awareness was created by popular journalism, by memorial cards, by the dissemination of gold rings with the motto 'Remember Orr', by songs and by William Drennan's poem 'The Wake of William Orr'. In the case of effective politicisation of this type, the medium was also the message. Historians have paid more attention to text than to context in assessing the impact of these performance genres. Finally, the most striking feature of all these genres is their assumption that the culture which they addressed was a shared one. J. R. R. Adams's conclusions from a survey of a wide range of this late eighteenth-century popular literature in Ulster is that 'it is impossible to assign material to a Protestant or a Catholic tradition'.[84]

From edition to sedition

The emphasis on the power of the printed word to alter public perceptions and thereby promote political change was especially pronounced in the early phase of the United Irishmen, in which William Drennan, a quintessential Enlightenment figure, was the dominant ideologue and drafter of documents. However, once the war with France had altered the political climate to a situation where the United Irish organisation was heavily repressed, high-flown rhetoric had an increasingly hollow and bombastic ring. By the mid-1790s, social radicals within the movement, like Samuel Neilson in Belfast and John Burk in Dublin, took the initiative, arguing that the paper war had to be supported by a revolutionary mass movement, capable of seizing the power which, it now seemed obvious, would never be voluntarily relinquished to them through the normal political process.[85] Such a mass movement could only be constructed by politicising poverty, by building bridges into existing organisations such as the Defenders, the artisan combinations, the Freemasons and the popular political clubs, and by accelerating the ideological trajectory of the United Irish-men towards pragmatic and politically subversive issues like taxes, tithes, living conditions and the class structure. This would necessitate addressing, even appealing to, the glaring inequalities in Irish life, and having recourse to the past in order to interpret them. Such a perspective was obviously more closely aligned to the Defender position, and made feasible the merger of the two organisations in 1795–6. This merger was orchestrated and implemented by the social radicals within the United Irish movement and Defenders – Samuel Neilson, Thomas Russell, Henry Joy McCracken, James Hope, James Quigley, William Putnam McCabe, Richard Dry, Alexander Lowry, Charles Teeling and Bernard Coyle. The success of the radicalisation project created the great establishment nightmare of the eighteenth century – the jacobinising of the secret societies, leading to an educated Whiteboyism linked to 'intelligent treason'. For the first time the griev-ances of the secret societies were joined to an effective national programme for sweeping political change.

The radical wing of the United Irishmen thereby anticipated the two-phase model of revolution as theorised by Antonio Gramsci in his *Prison Notebooks*.[86] The first phase would be a war of position – a struggle for dominance within civil society itself, an effort to create an alternative sphere of political discourse, which would highlight the gap between social and economic problems, and the inability of the existing political system to address them. Once this public ground had been prepared, the second phase would be the actual military revolution. The United Irishmen movement can be seen as a classic example, albeit *avant la lettre,* of this phenomenon. The broad front policy of the mid-1790s was the first phase. To implement this new policy, the United Irishmen needed to advance beyond empty rhetoric and beyond the print medium itself. United Irish radical rhetoric skilfully blended international, national and local issues, addressing long-nurtured feelings of exclusion and historical injustice, politicising pre-existing cleavages. As early as 1794 the United Irishmen were generating strikingly radical popular literature:

> You have been told that politics is a subject upon which you should never think: that to the rich and great men of the country you should give up your judgement in the business of government. . . . Who gives this advice? . . . The men who profit by your ignorance and inattention . . . but is there any sensible honest man who will say that the poor man is not as useful to society as the rich? Will he not assent that the poor are the support of the society? Who makes them rich? The answer is obvious – it is the industrious poor. . . . Why not think of politics? Think of [it] seriously; think of your rulers; think of republics; think of kings.[87]

The *Children's Catechism*, published at Belfast, was 'circulated among the common people in 1794 for the purpose of turning legal government into contempt'. It is a neat example of the accessible style, humour and satirical cutting edge of this type of production.

> Q. What is a *parliament*?
> A. A collection of animals – some to play cards, some to loll and sleep, some to roar out sedition and treason in all who do not pray God to send twenty-five millions of people to utter damnation! – whilst others are plotting schemes of taxation to reduce the poor man's daily pay.[88]

That same iconoclastic and strongly oral style permeated all the United Irishmen's prose satires, as for example, Rev. James Porter's *Billy Bluff and Squire Firebrand* with its subversive mimicry of Lord Castlereagh and the Ards magistrate Rev. John Cleland. Here is a passage where Billy reports to the Squire a discussion he had with a United Irishman on the nature of the aristocracy. The United Irishman talks of the advantages of an advancement in the peerage:

> 'What a fine thing', said he, 'to see in one day Mr changed into Lord; Mrs into my Lady; Jack-a-Dandy into my Lord likewise; and all the little Misses turned into my Lady A., my Lady B., my Lady C., my Lady D., my Lady E., my Lady F. Did you ever see mushrooms growing on a dunghill', said he? 'Many a time', said I. 'Then', said he, 'you have seen what our new race of Lords and Earls resembles; they have rotten roots, flimsy stems, spongy heads, and start up when nobody expects it, in 24 hours'. 'Then', said he, 'comes the coronet painted on a coach, on a harness, on the dishes and plates, on the piss-pots; it is stamped on the cow's horns, on the bull's horns, on the spades, on the ploughs, on everything; so that the coach will run without horses, the dishes will always be full of nobility, the piss-pots will never break, the cows and bull will breed a noble two-horned race, the spades will work themselves, the ploughs will go without ploughmen'.[89]

A similar parodic style was used to attack one of the junta, John Beresford who (along with Fitzgibbon and Foster) was a constant United Irish target:

> I believe in John Beresford, the father almighty of the revenue, creator of the North Wall, the Ottiwell Jobb and the coal tax, and in his true son John Claudius, who

was created in the spirit of the Chancellor, born of the virgin Custom-house, suffered under Earl Fitzwilliam, was stigmatized, spurned at and dismissed. The third week he arose again, ascendeth into the cabinet and is sitteth at the right hand of his father, from whence he shall come to judge by Court Martial both the Quick and the Dead, those who are to be hanged and those whose fortunes are to be confiscated. I believe in the Holy Earl of Clare, in the Holy Orange Lodges, in the communion of the commissioners, in the forgiveness of sins by acts of indemnity, in the resurrection of the Protestant Ascendancy and Jobbing everlasting. Amen.[90]

The Dublin political underground

This new abrasive style could obviously generate a far greater plebian appeal among the political underground in Dublin. A host of popular political societies existed in the city in the 1790s, including the Strugglers (so called from the tavern where they met), the Real United Traders, the Union, the States, the Huguenot, Clady, Athenian, Cold Bone, Dexter, Druid, Shamrock, Shoe and Friendly Clubs. In these clubs, ideals of fraternity and sociability were blended with occupational solidarity and territoriality, but they also had a covert, and at times overt, political agenda. No wonder, then, that one judge referred sarcastically to the 'nests of clubs in the city of Dublin', or that Richard Musgrave, surveying the range of societies in Dublin in the mid-1790s, described the city as 'a great shell, fraught with various combustibles and ready to explode on the application of a match'.[91] Others noted the attractiveness of such clubs to young artisans:

> The younger part of the tradesmen, and in general all the apprentices of the city of Dublin (lads from 15 to 25 years of age) by the abominable custom adopted by masters of keeping only outdoor apprentices, in their leisure hours after work, which should be spent in the society of their masters or parents, where they might hope to improve in intellect and morality, have now the mischievous alternative of devoting themselves to youthful intemperance, in assembling in clubs instituted for the specious purpose of improvement under the name of reading clubs, but designed for the corruption of their members. Such clubs the emissaries of sedition have fatally succeeded in establishing.[92]

Judge Robert Day claimed that their 'army of advocates' included 'neglected apprentices, needy journeymen, seditious masters hoping to ride in the whirlwind' who 'familiarly discoursed on rebellion as the sacred birthright of the people'.[93] *Faulkner's Dublin Journal* concurred, designating their leaders as 'profligate, unprincipled men who hang loose on society, keeping up the fainting hopes of their members by Paine and the *Evening Post*'.[94] In these clubs moved men like John Burk (expelled from Trinity for his atheism); Watty Cox, son of a Westmeath blacksmith, a gunsmith, and later progenitor of the *Union Star*; the brothers Thomas and Richard Dry, clothers and radicals; Le Blanc, the Frenchman; Denis Taaffe, Catholic priest, historian and pamphleteer, and a host of other colourful individuals. These men would have fitted easily into any of the radical underworlds of the late eighteenth-century Enlightenment, whether in Paris, Philadelphia or London.[95]

Nor were these men content simply to receive advanced political literature; they also generated and distributed it themselves. Active in the Huguenot Society, for example, were John Burk, Watty Cox, the Dry brothers, William Lawlor and Le Blanc.[96] The rank-and-file membership included brogue-makers, hucksters, tailors, servants, militia men and soldiers. At the meetings on the Exchange steps or in Plunkett Street, the Society heard Lawlor read extracts from de Volney's *Vision of the French Republic*, while 'a motion was made to get more books and papers to enlighten the boys and everyone was asked what they would like to learn'. John Burk wrote, and the Society printed, 2,000 copies of the radical broadsheet *The Cry of the Poor for Bread*. They were pasted up on street corners and 'given away to the people on the street on purpose to enrage them against the government'. In *The Cry*, scriptural references are striking: in content, style and rhythmic cadence, it was closely modelled on the King James Bible. The scriptures were chosen as an available register that could transcend a variety of social classes and linguistic competences, appealing to a widely diffused set of precedents, rather than inherently elitist classical references. *The Cry* was written as much to be read aloud as silently – and consequently was a powerful piece of effective propaganda. The copy preserved in the Rebellion Papers had been exacted by Francis Higgins from a farmer named Russell, who 'had taken it from a large tree near the Naul where it had been posted up'. Russell had produced this during a dinner party in August 1796 at the Naul where Higgins, three priests and several 'opulent' Catholic farmers had been discussing the likely response to a French invasion.[97] The distribution network of these clubs was impressive; one piece from the Philanthropic Society was picked up in Sligo and sent to Dublin Castle.[98]

A broadsheet similar to *The Cry of the Poor for Bread* is *The New Age, addressed to the people of Great Britain and Ireland*, which bears the characteristic Burk style, in a reworking of de Volney's *Ruins of Empire*. This was a favourite Jacobin piece of the 1790s, frequently published in chapbook form, especially its fifteenth chapter, the vision of a 'New Age', with its polemical dialogue between the 'useful' and the 'parasitic' sections of society.[99] In this millenarian piece, the people of Britain and Ireland are envisaged as being divided into

> two groups of unequal magnitude, and dissimilar appearance. The one, innumerable and nearly integral, exhibited in the general poverty of their dress, and in their meagre and sun-burnt faces, the masks of toil and wretchedness; the other, a petty group, a valueless faction, presented in their rich attire, embroidered in gold and silver, and in their sleek and ruddy complexions, the symptoms of leisure and abundance. . . . The large body was constituted of labourers and artisans, tradesmen and every profession useful to society, and in the lesser group there were none but priests, courtiers, public accountants, commanders of troops, in short, the civil, military or religious agents of government.

There ensues a long dialogue between 'the people' and the 'privileged class' about labour, government, religion, monarchy, the army etc. in which the people consistently win the argument. The privileged class eventually concede the case: 'It is all over for us: the swinish multitude are enlightened.'[100]

The relatively sophisticated radicalism of the clubs' rhetoric can be seen in Denis Taaffe's 1796 polemic *Ireland's Mirror*. Consider this passage where he attacks Dublin city as being 'this gorgeous mask of Ireland's distress' because of the oppression of the poor by the rich – an especially effective example of the politicisation of poverty in the 1790s:

> The east part of the capital indeed displays some grandeur in palaces, public buildings and works which instead of disguising rather makes more glaring the huge poverty, the gigantic misery that fills this great city, in every garb, in every shape of human woe, and gradation of wretchedness. Every street, every lane, every place of public resort is crowded with the squalid victims of oppression . . . pomp and property alongside abject poverty, such magnificence in buildings and equipages, coupled with the filth of mud cabins and the rags that disfigure our poor. . . . It is an insult to us in our poverty to withdraw so large a portion of our scanty circulation from the more useful channels in order to rival in the pomp of buildings the opulence of London or Amsterdam. . . . Your colossal edifices are propped on our mud cabins.[101]

A hostile witness claimed that 'at these clubs not only the well-known books of Paine were read but original lectures on the same subjects were delivered and with great industry transcribed and disseminated through the lower order of the people'.[102] Another commentator noted:

> The mode of assembling in clubs or small societies, in which politics were discussed and debated, became general and every porter house could boast a set of statesmen who, without the aid of education or experience, considered themselves competent to every branch of legislative occupation.[103]

The clubs were accused of raising and directing city mobs for political purposes – as in the great riot which marked Camden's arrival as Lord Lieutenant in 1795. No wonder, then, that conservatives should see the reading clubs as 'preparatory schools for the Defenders'.[104] And this was not just establishment paranoia. The United Irishmen in the mid-1790s colonised these clubs, using them as forcing-houses for the revolutionary movement. In 1794, immediately after the 'open' United Irish movement had been suppressed, John Burk set to work to build a network of clubs: 'I formed the Athenian, Telegraph and Philanthropic societies as nurseries from which to procure men of full intellectual growth and patriotism, and in addition to these, I set on foot an armed secret organisation divided into tens.'[105]

The informer Francis Higgins, who kept a sharp eye on these clubs, described them in January 1797 as being composed of 'King killers, Paineites, democrats, levellers and United Irishmen'. He described the States Club, which met at the

Anchor in Poolbeg Street, as 'an association of eating and drinking democratic citizens' who convened in July 1796 to celebrate 'with great festivity' the fall of the Bastille. Higgins also reported in August 1796 that another club, meeting at Ross Lane, under cover of being a Freemasons' lodge, had 'a private printing-press from whence issue various treasonable productions on half and quarter sheets which are distributed among the abettors of sedition'. He identified [Watty] Cox as 'a principal leader' in this enterprise, claiming that 'the conduct of this fellow and his associates deserve or call for close investigation'. By May 1797, when the United Irishmen had incorporated these clubs, Higgins noted the role of printers in producing seditious literature:

> With regards to keeping up the minds of the people and preparing them for their traitorous views, they cause to be distributed various publications and handbills etc. (two of which is enclosed). The poem from the type etc. I am told was worked off at Chambers (a United Irishman), and one of the Common Council. The address signed 'An Irishman' is done by one Fitzpatrick (another of the firebrand crew and the established printer of the R.C. Committee). Byrne of Grafton Street and Moore of College Green are all of the brotherhood and send out a distributive share of this kind of libel.[106]

The conservative response

By contrast with the radicals' easy embrace of literacy and all that accompanied it, conservatives clung to the age-old wisdom that, as in Bernard Mandeville's formulation, reading, writing and arithmetic are 'very pernicious to the poor'. In his *Fable of the Bees*, Mandeville had noted:

> To make the society happy and people easy under the meanest circumstances, it is requisite that great numbers of them should be ignorant as well as poor. Knowledge both enlarges and multiplies our desires. . . . The welfare and felicity therefore of every state and Kingdom require that the knowledge of the working poor should be confined within the verge of their occupations and never extend (as to things visible) beyond what relates to their calling. The more a shepherd, a plowman or any other peasant knows of the world and the things that are foreign to his labour or employment, the less fit he'll be to go through the fatigues and hardships of it with chearfulness and content.[107]

Richard Musgrave, writing in the aftermath of the rebellion, concurred:

> If good wine be infused in a sour cask, it will of course partake of its impurity. Would it improve the morals of the lower class of people to enable them to read the works of Paine, Volney, Godwin and Thelwal, and the Jacobin prints, which give wings to treason, and convey it to the garret and cellar? By far the greatest part of the English militia who came to Ireland during or subsequent to the Rebellion were illiterate, and yet they were religious, sober and industrious. Learning in the abstract will produce no good effect on the mass of the people.[108]

There were pressing difficulties for the conservatives in combating the United Irishmen's successful recourse to popular political literature. Consider the stylistic impediment. Conservatives by definition had to assume that the ordinary populace were utterly incapable of absorbing political arguments, and therefore they could not be addressed in any fashion which conceded this point. The only conservative style available for discourse with the masses, then, was *de haut en bas*, typically in the form of the dialogue, sermon, moral tract, or vituperative attacks on the radicals. Despite the fact that these were produced and distributed in very large numbers, they compared unfavourably with the intelligence, intimacy and immediacy of the radical message. Faced with this dilemma, conservatives could only respond by denigrating the accessible style of radical discourse: Judge Day described it as 'composed in all the jargon, phraseology and pompous vulgar slang of the Jacobin school, made up of the stolen shreds and scraps of their vile vocabulary'.[109] They were equally quick to denounce its cheapness: 'The United Irishmen, by publishing at a penny-a-piece and sending through the country in thousands and ten thousands Paine's detestable book, have cut asunder in many instances those bonds of amity which united persons of every rank.'[110] They attacked the United Irishmen for advancing 'with the Bible in one hand and the *Rights of Man* in the other'.[111] They also attempted to block the spread of this new literature. *Faulkner's Dublin Journal* warned householders against the danger of letting such material into their houses, even for the sake of curiosity, as it 'made favoured servants open to the seduction of sedition':

> The man who contributes to a seditious newspaper by the purchase of its treasonable trash does more mischief than by the mere pecuniary contribution. He circulates among his servants an active and mischievous poison, which dissolves all the ties of domestic gratitude and affection.[112]

The Catholic episcopacy similarly cautioned against the 'French disease' carried by the United Irishmen, who were described by Bishop James Caulfield of Ferns as

> a miserable and desperate crew of uncivilised mountaineers or village politicians, tutored by seditious agents to lessons of democracy, profligacy and insubordination, maddened by ill-digested doses of French principles, injected into their ignorant minds through the dangerous medium of inflammatory newspapers.[113]

Some conservatives accused church and state of not doing sufficient to provide an antidote to the radical poison. James Arbuckle complained to Lord Downshire in 1796:

> Is it not a shame to government, to their Graces and my Lords, the Archbishops and Bishops of this land, that it was left to the munificence, public spirit and religious principle of a private citizen of Belfast to print and publish at his own expense 1,500 copies of Bishop Watson's *Apology for the Bible* in order to contend with the cheap editions of Payne's *Age of Reason* that are industriously circulated throughout the country?[114]

The government's response to the flood of print was initially surveillance, and finally repression. Fitzgibbon noted the effect:

> The press has been used with signal success as the engine of rebellion. Sedition and treason have been circulated with unceasing industry in newspapers and pamphlets, in handbills and speeches, and republican songs and political manifestoes.[115]

The radical newspapers, the *Northern Star*, the *Cork Gazette*, the *Union Star* and the *Roscrea Southern Star*, were all suppressed legally or militarily. Other newspapers – *Finn's Leinster Journal* in Kilkenny, the *Belfast Newsletter*, the *Waterford Herald*, the *Cork Herald* – were given financial inducements to support the government.[116] There was even a plan to stymie Arthur O' Connor's *The Press* by printing a loyalist surrogate of it. By the spring of 1798, there was no radical or opposition paper in print. Castlereagh wrote to Cornwallis: 'The principal provincial papers have been secured and every attention will be paid to the press generally.'[117]

'Ministers of treason': the hedge-schoolmasters

Post-rebellion analyses, however, agreed that while the United Irishmen lost on the battlefields, they had easily won the propaganda war:

> It is certain that you were unable to cope with such adversaries and the cause is obvious – you were not, you could not imitate their base and secret art; these were equally unbecoming and impracticable to you: how were you then to undeceive the people? Was it by publishing the facts, in this way inculcating truth and loyalty? It could not reach them for they could not read. Did you even wish to convince and conciliate them in conversation, they might often as well be deaf, for they did not know your language. Thus was every avenue to their hearts and understandings closed against you.

This pamphleteer drew the obvious conservative conclusion:

> From all this it follows then, that education is your only resource; 'tis this alone can open to you the channels of instruction, and this will enable you to meet the enemy, who has secretly got possession, not only on equal terms, but with superior advantage.[118]

As a result, the informal school system and popular literature became persistent foci of attention. Many commented, for example, on the high proportion of schoolmasters active in the United Irishmen. Whitley Stokes drew attention to the subversive subtext of the chapbook literature, a matter which was to remain constantly at the forefront of conservative concerns in the first two decades of the nineteenth century:

> The lower classes these last few years confined their purchase of books to a particular kind called Burtons, which they got for sixpence halfpenny a piece,

but for which they now pay eight pence. . . . The mischief done by histories of robbers, books of superstition, and by indecent books, will be acknowledged; some will think romances innocent; but these works contribute greatly to keep alive a false admiration of courage, a spirit of war and revenge, and a love of adventure so incompatible with the happiness of mankind.[119]

Others noted the pernicious influence of schoolmasters in spreading the United Irish system:

We find that rebellion was planted and cherished by means of active, artful emissaries dispersed throughout the land, who worked in disguise and spread their doctines in darkness and secrecy. As their assistant in every village, some petty demagogue, whose pride in his superior literature was the cause of his disaffection which must sink as letters grow more common, became the officious minister of treason, and vented his lies and calumnies where he might do it without danger of contradiction, to an illiterate circle who looked up with wonder and implicit belief to the man who could read, and through this polluted channel received all their information and principles.[120]

Judge Day provided an example in the role of John Hurley, a schoolmaster involved in the anti-tithe agitation in Cork in 1794:

He had with several of the country people subscribed for a newspaper. He used to read the French debates and other seditious publications to the multitude at the chapel of Toobane in Drinagh parish and at Ballygurteen village in Kilmeen parish next to Drinagh. This had been his practice for three months before the disturbances. Hence the parishioners became politicians, talked of liberty and equality and appointed a day to plant the Tree of Liberty.[121]

Thus one of the principal impacts of the politicisation of the 1790s was to move education and the state's control (or lack of it) close to the top of the political agenda. But conservative hostility to the informal education sector (the so-called hedge-schools) has led historians of education too easily to endorse these partisan attacks, which came from both the state and the churches, especially the Catholic Church, eager to gain control over it, and therefore keen to demonise it in its existing form. The result has been to underestimate the achievement of this non-state education system. The high rates of literacy and the consequent penetration of popular politicisation in the 1790s are a direct tribute to this achievement. In a more oblique way, so are the strength of the Dublin publishing industry and the surge of Catholic devotional literature in the late eighteenth century.[122]

Examining the popular literature of the 1790s, then, allows us to contextualise its creation, dissemination and reception from both – equally necessary – sides of the equation, from the perspective of the reader as well as the publisher/printer/bookseller. Irish work in this field has been heavily orientated towards the production side, on the book as artefact. We need to move beyond this into the challenging world of ideas, and the role of the book as their vector. The history of the book, after all, must equally be a history of the reader.

The politicisation of popular culture

By the spring of 1798, the architects of the United Irish organisational structure sought to build the advantages of localism into revamped, more streamlined cells: 'No society should consist of more than twelve members and these as nearly as possible of the same street or neighbourhood, whereby they may be all thoroughly well known to each other and their conduct be subject to the censorial check of all.'[123] The new structures worked well in practice. For example, the 'Macamore Boys', from the coastlands east of Gorey in County Wexford, maintained a strong fighting corps right through the rebellion. In Wexford town the rebel corps were derived from the age-old sectors of the town – the artisan John Street corps, the mercantile Selskar corps, and the fisherman Faythe corps.[124] Feeding on the pervasive and intimate localism of Irish life, this territoriality principle stiffened morale and allowed ersatz soldiers to perform competently in an arduous and protracted campaign. In such settings the inherited leadership role of locally potent families came into play, and these families disproportionately supplied the officer corps of the United Irish army; the kinship ties which bound together these endogamous families provided a powerful cementing force in the leadership of the United Irishmen.[125]

The United Irishmen attempted to politicise popular culture, whether this be sport, calendar custom or communal festivities. The fusion of high politics and quotidian life was exemplified by Lord Edward Fitzgerald. An account from 1793 noted that 'he is turned a complete Frenchman, crops his hair, despises his title, walks the streets instead of riding and thence says he feels more pride in being on a level with his fellow citizens'.[126] Such activities brought instant recognition of his role as a tribune of the people. Anne, Countess of Roden, described a Dublin theatrical scene in 1793:

> One of the actors brought in of himself, 'Damn the French!', upon which there was a moderate clap and Lord Edward Fitzgerald stood up in his box and hissed singly; upon which you would have thought they would have tore the house down with clapping, men, women and every creature. He looked bursting with rage and venom. I never saw anything so delighted as they were with it.[127]

In Kildare, Fitzgerald participated enthusiastically in local life and was described there in 1796 as 'dancing among the rustics at bonfires and in short conducting himself among them with such uncommon condescension, freedom and affability that, like Absalom of old, he stole away the hearts of the people'.[128] With Michael Reynolds, Fitzgerald used handball matches to spread the United Irish organisation in County Kildare, and he made a vigorous effort to interact with the ordinary people. *Faulkner's Dublin Journal* describes how 'he used to mix with and participate in the breakfasts and dinners of the meanest peasantry in the county . . . that he used to hold the plough in order to obtain the confidence (i.e. for the purpose of abusing it) of the unsuspecting and ignorant tillers of the land'.[129]

The most striking example of United Irish success in the field of popular culture is the use of the Tree of Liberty. This could easily be grafted onto the indigenous 'May bush' tradition, the festive, decorative bush which welcomed the summer. The transnational and demotic symbols of optimistic regeneration were fused in a potent cumulative symbol, in which the colour green also had a powerful resonance. In August 1795, soldiers had to be called out from Cork to Blarney 'to prevent the planting of a tree of liberty, adorned with ribbons and mounted with the red cap by Irish carmagnoles'. The tree was 'a finely grown birch tree, the most stately found in the wood', and its planting was accompanied by 'the playing of the Marseillaise, Reveil le Peuple, Ça Ira etc' by a specially requisitioned group of blind pipers.[130]

The United Irishmen sought to channel pre-existing factions into their organisation. Collections of young adult males (already group-bonded) would form tight and cohesive United Irish cells. In Carlow town, William Farrell described how the five Mayboy 'factions' (the Quarry Boys, the Clash Boys, the Burren Boys, the Castle Hill Boys and the Potato Market Boys) each rooted in a particular area of the town, were recruited into the United Irish organisation in 1797.[131] In Dublin similar faction groups (the Cross-Lane Boys, the Newmarket Boys, the Marybone Lane Boys, the Light Horse) were similarly absorbed.[132] In the rebellion of 1798 such groups formed the backbone of whole United Irish units. In Wexford, for example, the Duffry, Mulrankin and Kilmallock (Bogtown) units were based around pre-existing hurling teams, and in Dublin the Donnybrook hurlers were a revolutionary front.[133] Given the predominant role of young, unmarried adult males in the rebel ranks, this is understandable and gave cohesion and *esprit de corps* to non-professional fighting men. Miles Byrne described with feeling how localism acted as a bonding agent in the United Irish camps: 'The sweet cry of the name of their native barony or village roused them at once.'[134] At Gorey Hill the 300-strong Ballymanus corps, led by Billy Byrne, marched into the camp chanting 'Ballymanus, Ballymanus'.[135]

Radical Freemasonry and popular mobilisation

The United Irishmen also utilised pre-existing groupings as a necessary cover for political mobilisation, given the restrictions imposed by the Insurrection and Convention Acts which prohibited political meetings. Freemasonry provided the substrate for much of this organised activity – with its secretive character, its codes, symbols, passwords and elaborate catechisms, its mixture of the practical and the arcane, and its strong emphasis on collegiality. Behind its esoteric allegorical veils, Freemasonry has been exposed as a seminal laboratory of revolutionary thought in eighteenth-century France. The Masonic member, stripped of his religious and class identity, was predisposed towards unity and social harmony across class divides; Masonry accordingly acted as a vector of *fraternité* – of social equality. Officially apolitical, Freemasonry almost unconsciously through its organisation and discipline became a precursor of the concept of citizenship, while also indicating proleptically the possibilities of constructing a new social order. In Ireland, after two short pulses of energetic growth in the late 1740s and late 1750s, Masonry grew steadily in the 1780s before entering an explosive growth phase in the 1790s. This involved large-scale creation of new lodges and the revival of moribund ones. Outside of Dublin and the army, this growth was especially apparent in Ulster, and particularly in the Presbyterian belts. By 1798 there were 94 Masonic lodges in County Antrim and 46 in County Down, with a strong concentration along the Lagan and Bann valleys, and in the Lough Neagh basin.[136]

There is little reason to doubt that Freemasonry was used by the United Irishmen as an organisational tool when the 'cell' structure was being actively promoted in 1795 and 1796. In 1796 alone, thirty-three new lodges were created and twelve old ones revived; Lodge No. 845 in Belfast was titled the 'lodge of love and liberty', and activity was concentrated in Antrim, Fermanagh, Tyrone, Derry and Down. United Irish influence in these lodges was soon attracting hostile attention: lodges at Coleraine, Garvagh, Dungiven, Newry, Duleek, Clonfeacle, Coagh and Moy were reported as examples of 'that most dangerous system grafted onto freemasonry'.[137] As a result, government pressure was exerted on the Grand Lodge to curtail its activities, and in 1797 and 1798 there was a massive downturn in the spread of Masonry. Thus one of the most ideologically and organisationally congenial vectors of revolutionary thought was neutralised; in addition, as Orange lodges spread (themselves clearly modelled on a Masonic prototype), Freemasonry could no longer transcend sectarian divides, and a fissile tendency developed. In the 1780s Defenders and Peep o' Day Boys occupied a space only a sectarian fission away from Masonry. In the late 1790s, that split occurred, and faction disturbances between Orange lodges and Masonic (United Irish) lodges begin to be reported. None the less, the conjunction of Presbyterianism, Masonry and radicalism created a distinctive ethos, well represented in the works of the 'rhyming weavers'.[138]

As well as Masonic lodges, confraternities, burial societies and lottery clubs could all be pressed into United Irish service. The United Irishmen even organised their own extensive lottery, running parallel to and subversive of the state lottery. Whole organs of the state were systematically undermined. By 1796 the United Irishmen had infiltrated the watch, described in the *Freeman's Journal* as 'a democratical army in the metropolis under near 200 republican directors'.[139] Clandestine United Irish meetings were held under the aegis of sporting meetings and communal festivities – cock-fights, wrestling matches, horse-races, patterns, dinner parties, pilgrimages, bonfires, wakes, turf-cuttings, dances, balls, spinning bees, confraternities. The informer Thomas Boyle described a typical example – a cock-fight in a barn at Clonard on the Meath/Kildare border, attended by one hundred men, ninety of whom took the United Irish oath, under the tutelage of

Flynn and Tuite, the chairman and secretary of the local corps.[140] From the Kildare/Wicklow border in June 1797, a spy reported that United Irish organisation was proceeding under the cloak of cock-fighting in the Ballymore Eustace, Dunlavin, Donard and Hollywood areas. The fights attracted a crowd which was then proselytised by Dublin and northern emissaries.[141] Confraternities were also considered suspicious: Caesar Colclough wrote to Dublin Castle in January 1799 deprecating their episcopal encouragement, on the basis that 'prior to the rebellion in the county of Wexford, the effects of such societies were very destructive'.[142] Rev. James Little in County Mayo was especially critical of the Carmelite confraternity and its promotion of the scapular: 'I have no doubt this institution was resorted to as a political engine . . . designed for the mere purpose of organising the people, now rendered difficult by the laws prohibiting all popular assemblies.'[143]

In circumstances in which their activities were closely monitored, United Irish emissaries became adept at disguise: the Presbyterian clergyman James Porter posed as an itinerant astronomer, while James Hope organised a fictive linen market to gather a crowd in the Creggan area of south Armagh. The Antrim man James Cochran, while on United Irish business in Tyrone, carried three forged Freemasons' seals and medals and a stolen linen seal, to facilitate his ease of movement. William Putnam McCabe, their most effective, ubiquitous, protean and resourceful emissary, used his acting and mimic powers to pose as a preacher, a recruiting sergeant, a yeoman, a travelling hedge-schoolmaster or a pedlar, as occasion demanded.[144] In June 1797 'a man named O'Kelly, who styled himself a travelling poet' was arrested at Termonfeckin on suspicion of being a United Irishman.[145]

The United Irishmen also understood how to organise politics as theatre. This theatrical sense of political expression could draw on an established repertoire. Elaborate mock funerals bearing a fleece had long been organised by unemployed weavers to dramatise their distress. In August 1782, for example, 'a number of broad loom weavers have, for these days past, perambulated the streets of this city, preceded by the effigy of a golden fleece, borne on a pole covered with crepe, symbolical of the distress they suffer from the stagnation of their business'.[146] Examples of United Irish use of this tactic can be illustrated. In the eighteenth century, the price of a loaf remained fixed, but its size fluctuated in response to market conditions. In May 1795 a procession from the Liberties paraded to the Parliament House, Dublin Castle and the Lord Mayor's mansion,

> preceded by a loaf hung with crepe and sable to signify the distress of the time. This procession was followed by a lean, wretched horse, on which was mounted a chief mourner, who ever and anon looked at the loaf, and then, with no ill-acted shew of horror, applied his handkerchief to his face in token of grief for its diminutive appearance.[147]

In 1795 the Dublin United Irishmen were planning to decapitate the three royal statues in the city, which were throughout the eighteenth century a target for popular opprobrium in politically tense situations.[148] In 1796 a gallows was erected outside the house of the rector of Ardboe in County Derry, who had been active against the United Irishmen.[149] In 1797, when specie (coinage) was in short supply in Dublin,

> One of these ambulatory wags with which this city abounds exhibited as a practical and profitable *jeu d'esprit* a show box with glasses, etc., etc. on Essex Bridge to which all persons were loudly invited at the moderate premium of one penny to behold one of the greatest curiosities that could be exhibited. The opening box displayed on inspection a solitary guinea suspended by a black ribbon under the scroll of – a real, original, golden guinea.[150]

This subversive sense of humour was also demonstrated at the funeral of John Fitzgibbon, when a dead cat was hurled at the coffin – an ironic reminder of his boast that he would 'make the seditious as tame as domestic cats'.[151] A similar cast of mind can be seen in the use of 'Sir John Doe' as a pseudonym on threatening letters – a parody of the conventional name for the typical citizen used in legal textbooks.

The numbers game

Public displays were also used by the United Irishmen to make explicit the power of numbers: political funerals, potato-diggings, harvestings and turf-cuttings were not simply solidarity demonstrations, but a celebration of the local strength of adherence to the cause and a calculated, intimidatory gesture of defiance. Henry Echlin, returning from Balbriggan to Dublin in the spring of 1798, was 'much surprised at seeing at least 200 men on horseback, almost all cropped, pass by me. I found they were going to Lusk to the funeral of a man called Wade, a tanner from Dublin. I have seldom seen such an assemblage.'[152] All gatherings became suspect in this 1790s numbers game. They were seen by conservatives as provocations, a public display of insolent democracy requiring to be kept down. Any public display of Catholic religious observance (patterns, pilgrimages, funerals) fell under similar suspicion. The advent of popular politics added an even greater distrust. As the English Whig George Moore expressed it:

> For a century past, the great body of the nation has been an object of jealousy, suspicion, hatred mixed with contempt to its rulers; on one side are numbers, on the other are property and dominion. Property and dominion must necessarily regard numbers with a jealous eye.[153]

To help undermine the law and order strategy of the government, and to make visible the support for their cause, the United Irishmen made constant appeals to the strength of numbers. The Chief Secretary, Robert Hobart, complained in 1793:

> The pains which have, for these last eighteen months, been taken to persuade
> the people of the irresistible force of numbers, has given them such an idea of
> strength, that until they are actually beaten into another opinion, they will never
> be quiet.[154]

A proclamation by the Lord Lieutenant on 6 November 1796 observed the
dangers of

> The disaffected having adapted a practice of marching in military array, and assem-
> bling in large bodies, in some instances to the number of several thousands, under
> pretence of saving corn, and digging potatoes; but in fact to terrify the peaceable
> and well-disposed, and to compel them to enter into treasonable associations. The
> same system has since frequently been had recourse to by the United Irishmen in
> other parts of the Kingdom under various pretences, such as funerals, football
> meetings, etc with a view of displaying their strength, giving the people the habit of
> assembling from great distances upon an order being issued, and making them
> more accustomed to show themselves openly in support of the cause.[155]

A United Irish ballad succinctly expressed the point: 'We have numbers
and numbers do constitute power.'[156] Such concerns frequently led to an
interest in sectarian calculus. Dublin Castle was intensely alarmed by Edward
Hay's census project in 1795, which aimed to establish the true numbers of
Catholics and Protestants in Ireland on a parochial basis. This, in the Castle's
perception, was simply an exercise in intimidation 'to enforce the power of
numbers' by 'representing the Catholics as the *people* of Ireland and their present political inferiority as tyranny'.[157] Writing to another United Irish activist,
Luke Teeling, Hay himself claimed that his census would show a seven to one
ratio of Catholics to Protestant (demonstrating its essentially political motivation by adding the half-million Presbyterians to the Catholic balance).[158] The
significance of the exercise was also immediately grasped by Edmund Burke:
Hay's census would prove that 'the depression of the Catholics is not the
persecution of a sect, but tyranny over a people'.[159]

Earlier in the decade, in 1792, Edward Sweetman, one of the forward
group in the United Irishmen, was scathing about conservative efforts to damp
down these speculations about Catholic numbers:

> You are angry with these miserable people for stating their numbers at three
> millions: You are then angry that they were born! You are angry that they tread
> the earth, breathe the air or survey the heavens.[160]

Consciousness of the increased political weight of numbers in the aftermath of the French Revolution also lay behind the renewed interest in
petitioning in the 1790s, and especially petitioning at the popular level. Such
exercises mobilised public opinion, while increasing the sense of the political
power of the individual in this public gesture of affirmation. In County
Wexford alone, Hay organised the signatures of over 20,000 individuals in

both 1792 (Catholic relief) and 1795 (the Fitzwilliam recall).[161] These exercises were deeply distrusted by the conservatives. Archbishop Troy noted how Hay's parochial censuses 'excited uneasiness in the minds of the ascendancy and Orange partisans who presented them as records of Catholic numbers to threaten the smaller numbers of Protestants'.[162] One final aspect of the numbers game must be noted: the destabilising impact of demographic growth in itself. The doubling of population between 1700 and 1800 had the effect of making their tenantry more opaque to landowners, especially as the bulk of the new population were sub-tenants, cottiers, agricultural labourers and western rundale farmers, outside the daily surveillance of the landlord class and at one remove from any direct contacts with it.

Public houses and faction-fighting

United Irish meetings were frequently pub-based – because the crowded tenements of the Liberties of Dublin, for example, allowed no scope for domestic socialising. In the 1790s there were at least fifty pubs in Thomas Street, the spine of the Liberties.[163] The city as a whole had 1,300 public houses (one for every eight houses paying the hearth tax) in 1791.[164] In 1789 a newspaper claimed that one in four houses in the Liberties was a dram-shop, and a visitor to the 'St Giles of Dublin, in Meath Street and Thomas Street' in 1804 noted 'the drunkeness, noise, beatings of drums and fifes at the door of alehouses'.[165] As in late eighteenth-century Paris (with its 3,000 bars in 1789), the poorer areas of the city bristled with pubs, where journeymen and immigrants escaped their crowded, cramped rooms.[166] The pub then became a key arena of masculine sociability. Not just the clientèle, but even the names and signboards of public houses could carry the revolutionary message. In Belfast in 1793 drunken soldiers of the 17th Light Dragoons pulled down the signs of Dr Franklin, Mirabeau and General Dumouriez (commander of the French northern army) at the public house owned by the father of the celebrated William Putnam McCabe; he retaliated by putting his own portrait on the sign-board under the title 'McCabe – an Irish slave'.[167]

Public houses loomed large in loyalist perceptions of sedition. At the Kilmainham quarter-sessions in January 1796, Judge Robert Day conjured up a horrifying vision of public houses seething with sedition:

> It is in the dead of night, when all nature seeks repose, all but creatures of prey, that conspirators assemble and hatch dark and bloody treasons and other atrocious crimes. And it is in these hotbeds of corruption and debauchery that the first seeds of vice and criminality are sown, which afterwards ripen into full-blown guilt.[168]

Yet by the spring of 1798, the tightened United Irish organisation was eschewing the use of public houses as meeting-places: 'Avoid as much as possible meetings in public houses, either of societies or committees, because they might be attended with much danger and the occasions of meetings induce no such necessity: a few minutes in any convenient place will be sufficient for a small number of men to confer on the objects of their deliberation.'[169] Two reasons were advanced for avoiding public houses: as well as increasing discipline, it would simultaneously depress government excise revenue. The movement therefore laid great stress on avoiding excessive drinking (a potential source of indiscipline). 'In the pursuit of these great and valuable objects, let not drink and idleness dishonour United Irishmen.' 'Be discreet and avoid drunkeness. Be firm but be patient, and avoid riots.'[170] So successful were the United Irishmen in disciplining their followers that the absence of heavy drinking and faction-fighting was taken as a sign that an area was very well organised. Richard Musgrave considered 'the abstinence of the lower class of people from spirituous liquors to a degree of sobriety too unusual and general not to be systematic' as a symptom of the approaching insurrection, while Judge Day noted that in both 1798 and 1803 'it was observed that the people were never more peaceable, orderly or sober than while the preparations were going forward for the rising'.[171]

While the United Irishmen accentuated some elements in the repertoire of popular culture, they sought to discard others, in particular sectarianism, faction-fighting and excessive alcohol consumption. They invested a considerable degree of organisational energy in attempting to stem the spread of sectarianism in mid-Ulster in the mid-1790s, in line with their own often stated aim of concentrating attention on issues which could be supported by all the Irish people. Thus United Irish rhetoric, as in this example from a 1796 ballad about the Armagh expulsions, stressed the necessity of repudiating sterile, historically based sectarianism: 'We'll throw by all distinctions, what's past never mention, / Join hands with our neighbours, and let all agree.'[172] Accordingly, loyalist observers could be equally shaken by 'infernal calm' as by outright lawlessness; both betokened a dangerous level of organisation.[173] Only a customary level of violence was reassuring. In 1804 a conservative commentator noted with satisfaction that in Wexford and Kilkenny

> Never was there a greater number of broken heads known at any former period, as all the barony bullies headed their respective factions and every evening closed with drunken quarrels. For some time before 1798, a quarrel was not known at any fair or patron and my barometer for the political state of the country is the parish and barony factions fighting with each other. Every fair in the country ends at present with a general engagement between rival factions.[174]

The successful penetration of popular culture by the United Irishmen was possible because Irish elite groups, in common with their European counterparts, had begun to disengage from it in the second half of the eighteenth century. Common ties, which had united the classes vertically in the informal intimacy of collective engagement in popular culture, had snapped. A more formal, distant relationship replaced them. As the gentry adopted metropolitan standards of taste, propriety and refinement, their patronage of hurling, of traditional music, of mumming groups, and their involvement in sociable (dancing, drinking) activities with their tenants withered.[175] In the late eighteenth century this withdrawal from popular culture was accelerated by assaults on its degenerate and lawless character. In such conditions, there was no competitor to the United Irishmen in their quest to colonise popular culture, with the notable exception of the gentry-led effort to support popular loyalism in mid-Ulster in the mid-1790s.[176]

Law and disorder

The disengagement of the gentry from popular culture also completely transformed the administration of law and order, which had been indulgent and personalised, operating within the softening ambit of the moral economy. Given the sectarian nature of the eighteenth-century Irish state, there was always a brittle relationship between authority and alienation. There was also a communal ambivalence towards the law, and considerable hostility to its local agents – the tithe-proctor, the gauger, the crimping sergeant, the police, the press-gang, the soldier. Ability to deflect, bypass or resist the letter of the law could be linked to an alternative, customary or moral code of law. Right across the board, one could trace manifestations of this attitude in the eighteenth century – forcible possessions, smuggling, treatment of wrecks, tithe affrays, abductions, illegal distillation, food riots, resistance to distraint, faction-fighting. There were at least thirty food riots in eighteen different Irish towns in the period 1772–94; there were fifty combinations in twenty-seven different trades in Dublin in the period 1775–95. Great sympathy could be manifested to victims of the official law – convicts, deserters, etc. Robert Bell described the general attitude to the law in the 1780s: 'Their independence consisted neither in tranquillity nor competence, but generally displayed itself in a sort of hostile resistance to superiors, attempting acts of injustice, or endeavouring to enforce the executions of the laws.'[177]

This personalised, localised and demotic sense of the law frequently exercised legal and administrative commentators: Chief Baron Willes in 1760 considered it

> to be the greatest evil of this kingdom – a disobedience and resistance to the law. I don't mean breaches of particular laws as theft etc., but a resistance with armed force to the civil process and magistrates, and the taking or keeping of possession by armed force. There is scarce a day but I have complaints of this kind in my court.[178]

That ability to deflect or bypass the letter of the law also transferred itself down the social spectrum: it linked with an alternative code of law, customary or moral in character, but none the less legitimised or implementable. In Tipperary in 1780 a single incident demonstrates that these old allegiances of family and locality died hard. At Killaneve, near the Silvermines, a family of MacNamaras retained possession of their holding by force, with the strong support of local people, long after their lease had expired: 'The MacNamaras are young men, who have been looked upon among the mountaineers as a kind of half-gentry [buckeens] and brought up in idleness, have followed dissolute courses.'[179] Two decades later George O'Malley, of the Connemara smuggling family, discussed his attitude to law and order in the early nineteenth century:

> I grant that society requires law and order to hold its bonds firmly together and I also hold that this law and order should be respected, but I don't believe that there should be one law for the rich and another for the poor man. When a man is robbed of his properties and title held by his ancestors for no other reason than worshipping the Maker under a certain form of religion, there's nothing Christian in that. . . . They rob the poor first and make them fight after.[180]

This alternative law frequently stood antecedent and antagonistic to the king's writ *per se*.[181] As a statement from Donegal in 1831 expressed it:

> We are bound to obey the law of the land; but we find that in practice, especially among unlettered people, there is a law which is paramount to it; it is the law of nature, which the very worm when trodden upon acknowledges and which disposes men to resent suffering when it exceeds the power of endurance.[182]

Here too was a potent reservoir from which the streams of popular protest could flow. Redresser movements could don the mantle of community with a certain legitimacy given the prevailing attitude to the law, especially if they espoused a communal language and motivation, symbolised by the mask. In all pre-modern cultures the mask signifies the dissolution of the individual identity and the assumption of the communal, the timeless, the impersonal, in an autonomous expression of communal will. Inherited directly from the folk tradition of strawboys, wrenboys, Mayboys and mummers, the mask also conferred the power of judgement, and of exemplary intimidation. That communality and legitimacy could also be asserted by symbolism. By adopting the lexicon of folk dress and idiom, the Whiteboys and Rightboys appropriated a potent non-verbal language, rich in symbolic resonance, and transcending their individual lives under the impersonal aegis of ancestral forces. That impersonal legitimacy also nurtured the *omerta,* the code of silence, essential for success and again inhabiting the space between official law and its local reception.[183] Successful law evasion on a routine level brought entire communities in contact with the powerlessness of the law. This corroded its legitimacy and strengthened the antiauthoritarian tendency at a local level. The United Irishmen were able to politicise these feelings in their propoganda: tithes, for example, a longstanding rural grievance, could be explained as the iniquitous fruits of an oppressive church–state alliance. A republican government would eliminate the linkage, thereby abolishing this parasitic burden.

Prior to the 1790s the gap between perception and practice created a neutral space around the letter of the law which gave room to manoeuvre and allowed for personal intervention by local magnates. Implementation of the fearsome legislative panoply, with its wide range of capital crimes, was subject to considerable discretion. With the withdrawal of the gentry from popular culture in the last quarter of the eighteenth century, concomitant with the advent of a harsher political climate, this personalised, latitudinarian and consensual administration of the law declined rapidly. The Irish gentry turned instead to a more heavy-handed interpretation, requiring a firm display of legal force, often backed by the military, which invaded the neutral gound between the law and its reception, and thereby made the law at once more visible, partisan and abrasive. This was a crucial element in creating the widespread alienation from government in the 1790s. The United Irishmen worked hard to widen this breach between governors and governed, exploiting it for tactical advantage. From the mid-1790s, once Orange attitudes had begun to spread, the United Irishmen were even more successful in this propoganda war, undermining the legitimacy of the state in the crucial law-and-order arena. In efforts to claw back this ground, the government resorted to tougher, increasingly draconian measures, which served as ideal propaganda points for the United Irishmen. Their rhetoric, skilled in humour, invective and vituperation, dislodged Catholics in particular from their deferential frame of mind. Gentry reports in the 1790s poured into Dublin Castle, alarmed at the erosion of paternalistic influence: the people were 'impudent', 'insolent', 'insubordinate', 'sullen', 'surly', 'saucy', 'audacious'. In early 1797 Richard Musgrave reported that in County Carlow

> The insolent looks and haughty demeanour of the peasants, who would not formerly approach a gentleman but with the greatest deference, challenged his attention with a broad stare, often followed by a sardonic grin.[184]

Another commentator noted:

> Ireland is the only country in the world where such a complete separation subsists between the governors and the governed. In England, the public opinion is the law and acts of authority are little more than enunciations of what the most sober and respectable part of the community have already approved in their thoughts. In Ireland, there is no public opinion, or if there is a faint resemblance of one, it is the opinion of those who are most eager to push violent measures against the bulk of the nation.[185]

Given this broader cultural change, government distrust of popular culture was strong. It is remarkable how many flashpoints arose in connection with communal festivities, as, for example, the John Foster-inspired military assaults on patterns in County Louth. As early as 1788, in an effort to prevent the spread of the Defender movement into his county, Foster, heading a troop of soldiers, attacked a pattern at Oldbridge on the Boyne, 'cut up the tents, charged the mob and totally dispersed them', and announced his intention of doing the same at every other pattern and fair.[186] In 1792, in a controversial reprise of this policy, soldiers under Foster's control first fired into, and then charged with drawn swords, a pattern at Tallanstown rumoured to be a Defender display of strength.[187] This disengagement of the gentry was echoed by the institutional

Catholic Church, with episcopal condemnations mirroring government ones: Bishop Caulfield of Ferns wished 'to most earnestly recommend and conjure you to avoid all unnecessary meetings, associations, places of pilgrimage, or patrons, of diversions and dissipation which can tend to no good'. He itemised these as 'dancing, ball-playing, hurling, and assembling in alehouses'.[188]

Conclusion

However, there were failures in the United Irish colonisation of popular culture. Firstly, systematic recourse to the printed word as its political cutting edge had the effect of concentrating its most effective penetration in anglophone and literate areas, which had close links to the main publishing centres of the period, Dublin and Belfast. United Irish strength was greatest in the anglicised east coast area stretching from Antrim to Wexford. This obvious correlation is a warning against the facile splitting of the east Ulster/south Leinster rebellion in 1798. The weakness of the United Irishmen was their inability to penetrate significantly Irish-speaking areas. In counties with an internal linguistic frontier, such as Donegal and Wexford, the United Irishmen's limits of organisation fell neatly astride the linguistic boundaries. Predominantly Irish-speaking counties, even those with a major city such as Kilkenny, Waterford, Limerick and Galway, remained largely impervious to the new radicalism. This correlation between literacy and politicisation also created a relationship between the richer parts of the country and the success of the United Irish organisation. This was recognised by Rev. James Little, an Anglican minister in County Mayo:

> It is not in the poorest but in the richest parts of this kingdom that sedition and a revolutionary spirit prevail and first raised their heads: an extreme degree of poverty and distress will sink the mind of man, divest him of the courage even to complain and bury in silence himself and his sufferings.[189]

Secondly, the United Irishmen did not see popular culture as the basis for a political project – one in which, for example, an abiding sense of a communal Irish identity might be created by recourse to a shared culture. Universally grounded cosmopolitan appeals to benevolence, virtue and other displays of moral fortitude rang increasingly hollow as the local situation deteriorated in the mid-1790s. Rooting these in the narrow ground of Ulster, for example, required a carefully thought-out politics of culture. The United Irishmen's instrumental view of popular culture did not encourage such an approach.

Finally, the United Irishmen overestimated their ability to transcend the inherited politics of religion in Ireland. The United Irishmen's elaborate efforts to elide the divisiveness of the Irish past and religious differences concealed their popular potency and conceded them to conservatives as a political weapon that could be used against them. Once government explicitly endorsed the sectarian card in the post-Fitzwilliam period, popular Protestantism, notably through the Orange Order, was wrapped within a tough ideological carapace. This appeal to disunited rather than united Irishmen had an atavistic, visceral appeal; it was to prove all too potent a counter-revolutionary weapon.

The Tree of Liberty

Upo' this tree there grows sic fruit
Its virtues a' can tell, man:
It raises man aboon the brute,
It mak's him ken himsel', man . . .

Fair Virtue water'd it wi' care,
And now she sees wi' pride, man,
How well it buds and blossoms there,
Its branches spreading wide, man.

Wi' plenty o' sic trees, I trow,
The warld would live in peace, man.
The sword would help to mak' a plough,
The din o' war wad cease, man.

Like brethren in a common cause,
We'd on each other smile, man;
And equal rights and equal laws
Wad gladden every isle, man.

ROBERT BURNS (*circa* 1790)

UNITED AND DISUNITED IRISHMEN:
The State and Sectarianism in the 1790s

The roots of the 1798 rebellion lay in the tangled web of late eighteenth-century politics and the ambivalent position of Ireland within the British state. Too far away to be easily assimilated, like Scotland or Wales, too near to be let float free like America, Ireland's anomalous constitutional settlement gave it its own parliament, but with strings attached which suggested that ultimate political power continued to reside in London. The 1782 settlement, which cut some of these strings, gave the Irish parliament freer control over its legislative processes. However, nagging doubts soon reasserted themselves that English control was just as entrenched as ever, because the Lord Lieutenant could manipulate a parliamentary majority by judicious management of patronage and places. Many therefore claimed that the much-vaunted independence conferred by the 1782 settlement was a hollow shell if it was not accompanied by parliamentary reform to eliminate these manipulative manoeuvres.[1]

However, parliamentary reform inevitably raised the vexed question of the admission of Catholics to the franchise and, therefore, to the political nation. The reform movement of the 1780s, as represented especially by the Volunteers, split on this Catholic issue.[2] Even advanced reformers like Charlemont believed that Catholics were inherently debarred from political participation because they were incapable of exercising independent judgement, being under the thumb of their priests. Other reformers such as Henry Grattan argued that Irish Protestants would be irrevocably locked into an artificially restrictive political system if they did not accept Irish Catholics on an equal footing as part of the political nation:

> The question is now, whether we shall be a Protestant settlement or an Irish nation. So long as the penal code remains, we can never be a great nation; the penal code is the shell in which Protestant power has been hatched, and now it is become a bird, it must burst the shell asunder or perish in it. . . . The question is not whether we shall show mercy to the Roman Catholics but whether we shall mould the inhabitants of Ireland into a people.[3]

The problems entailed in this solution were bluntly outlined by Sir Hercules Langrishe:

> Personal equality of representation, the only equality that I can conceive, would be a pure democracy and in a country like ours, where the democracy does not profess the religion of the state, a democracy subversive of the laws and constitution.[4]

In the Irish context, where Catholics predominated, a freely elected Irish parliament would return a Catholic majority; because Catholicism was inherently and historically a persecuting religion, that majority spelled tyranny and, ultimately, persecution for Irish Protestants. Therefore any tampering with the franchise and parliamentary reform which included Catholics was a dangerous experiment. The second half of the 1780s witnessed a sharpening awareness that the vaunted '1782 revolution' had produced merely the illusion of independence while effectively copperfastening the corrupt English connection. The stumbling-block remained the admission of Catholics to the political nation: the reform movement increasingly diverged around this contentious issue. The heady tide of early enthusiasm receded, exposing a barren political landscape as the decade subsided into a sullen sectarian stalemate.

The United Irish moment

It was within this gloomy context that Wolfe Tone welcomed the French Revolution as 'the morning star of liberty' in Ireland.[5] It released this sectarian gridlock on Irish politics, hitherto immobilised by the intransigent Protestant conviction that Catholics were inherently *incapaces libertatis*. The revolution provided the thrilling spectacle to reform-minded Protestants of French Catholics systematically dismantling the *ancien régime* equation between popery, despotism and political slavery. The Irish implication was obvious: if French Catholics could display such political maturity, so too could Irish Catholics. Almost overnight the political moulds of a century shattered; amidst the debris of discarded certainties, the French Revolution cleared a space which could be occupied by a non-sectarian political movement. The impasse of the reform movement was breached. Once the dust had settled on the 1790 election campaign, the stage was set for a new departure in Irish politics – a non-sectarian organisation which would invigorate and unify the reform campaign by explicitly adopting Catholic Emancipation as an essential part of that programme. The United Irishmen were established precisely for this reason. Its ideological architects drew on American and French precedents to claim that it was possible to dismantle the existing Protestant state and replace it with a secular equivalent which was both inclusive of Catholics and thoroughly reformed.

The seeds of the new organisation were sown at the great Bastille Day celebrations in Belfast on 14 July 1791. While the fall of the Bastille was a potent international symbol of the collapse of the *ancien régime*, the 14 July date was auspicious, allowing the reformers to downgrade the divisive celebrations of 12 July. The well-organised, flamboyant celebrations involved the major Belfast reformers and some from further afield. These included Theobald Wolfe Tone, already close to the Catholic Committee and an essential bridge to their political world. The animated discussions during the celebrations led to general agreement to form a political alliance seeking a representative, reformed parliament. The more cautious senior Presbyterian figures still entertained doubts about the Catholic question and it was to ease their fears that Tone published, in the following month, his *Argument on behalf of the Catholics of Ireland*. This persuasive polemic was written explicitly to convince moderate Presbyterian opinion that the popish leopard could indeed shed its spots: 'Look at France; where is the intolerance of Popish bigotry now? Has not the Pope been burned in effigy in France? Who will now attend to the rusty and extinguished thunderbolts of the Vatican?' Tone argued 'that no reform can ever by obtained which shall not comprehensively embrace Irishmen of all denominations'. He appealed for Protestants to cast aside their inherited perceptions of papists as so much anti-quated lumber:

> Let us for God's sake shake off the old woman, the tales of our nurses, the terrors of our granddams, from our heart. Let us speak to this ghastly spectre of our distempered imagination, the genius of Irish Catholicity. We shall find it vanish among the other phantoms of the brain distempered by fear.[6]

Tone's brisk broadside had an immediate effect in Presbyterian east Ulster, convincing the cautious that Irish Catholics had now attained political maturity and could be safely gathered to the reform fold. In this transformed intellectual climate, a window of opportunity opened for a new political movement.

Belfast intellectuals, especially William Drennan, designed the blueprint for the new political society – for which Tone coined the name 'United Irish-men'. In October and November 1791 societies of United Irishmen were inaugurated almost simultaneously in Belfast and Dublin, an essential step in creating a fully national organisation. Drennan, Tone, Thomas Russell, Samuel Neilson, all those closely involved, were driven by a desire to act as midwives to the impending arrival in Ireland of the new political order. In the aftermath of the American and French Revolutions, it appeared only a matter of time before the enlightened political ideals they had unleashed would be equally influential in Ireland.[7] The United Irishmen's aims were simple; to create a political system that would obliterate the old religious-based antagonisms, guaranteeing the equality of all Irishmen's political rights, regardless of reli-gious affiliation.[8]

Accommodating Catholicism

This rapidly shifting attitude to Irish Catholicism had a destabilising impact on the ideological infrastructure of the existing Irish state. Radical Presby-terians were now making common ground with Catholics, linking the hitherto separate agendas of parliamentary reform and Catholic relief. It is no accident that this development emerged precisely at the period when institutional Catholicism ('popery' in eighteenth-century parlance) seemed to be waning irreversibly and when a millenarian mood swept through radical dissent throughout the anglophone world.[9] In the early 1790s it became received wisdom that popery was visibly wilting: the suppression of the Jesuits in 1773, the difficulties of the papacy, the secularising impact of the European Enlightenment in general and the French *philosophes* in particular all demonstrated this thoroughly.[10] The United Irishmen, then, seemed on firm ground in claiming that popery had shot its bolt on the international political scene, thereby undermining the enduring eighteenth-century argument that Irish Catholics formed an insidious fifth column for their continental brethern and consequently must be kept militarily and politically impotent.[11]

This perceived decline of popery and its protective *ancien régime* shell was a necessary precursor to liberal Protestants, and especially the Presbyterians, making common cause with Catholics. The Whig Henry Grattan could argue that 'the Irish Catholics of 1792 did not bear the smallest resemblance to the Irish Catholics of 1692' and that 'the influence of the Pope, the priest and the Pretender were at an end'.[12] The United Irish 'Declaration to the Irish Nation' in September 1792 confidently asserted that 'popery is no longer to be met with but in the statute book'.[13] Three years later Arthur O'Connor laconically claimed that the 'superstitious power of the Catholic clergy is at an end'.[14] A flavour of this contemporary feeling can be savoured in the advertisement by the Dublin radical and United Irishman John Burk, who had himself been expelled from Trinity College, Dublin, for atheism:

> For Sale. Two red slippers of His Holiness the Pope; a bit of the toe nail of St Januaries; a scrap of the garment of Ignatius Loyola; inquisition racks, just from the Inquisition; crowns, sceptres and crosses of St Louis; cardinals' hats, ducal coronets etc., together with all the wardrobe of royalty. Theatrical gentlemen would do well to attend this auction, for the purpose of increasing their wardrobes, which are useless to their present owners, who are becoming plain citizens. Also, a few Pope's bulls with gilt horns.[15]

The novelty of this redefinition of the position of popery can only be understood with reference to prevalent Protestant stereotypes. William Cobbett, for example, recalled this image of the pope from a dissenting childhood: 'I most firmly believed when I was a boy that the Pope was a prodigious woman, dressed in a dreadful robe, which had been made red by being dipped in the blood of Protestants.'[16] It was, therefore, profoundly unsettling for conservative Protestants when Presbyterian radicals began to make common cause with Catholics in the United Irishmen. These anxieties were exacerbated by the shocking realisation that the British state was increasingly drifting to a position of neutrality between Irish Protestants and Catholics in the aftermath of the French Revolution.

At elite levels in English politics, anti-Catholicism had weakened considerably in the last quarter of the century. The then Irish Catholic priest, Walter Blake Kirwan, summarised the new orthodoxy in a London sermon of 1786:

> There never perhaps was an age so liberal and tolerant as the present. Thanks to the influence of a mild and unprejudiced government, we enjoy the exercise of

our religion in a peaceful security. The brand of fanatical sedition is extinct and philanthropy, the first in the heavenly train of virtues, scatters with a full hand the blessings of universal amity and concord.[17]

The older generation of Irish Protestants (especially those steeped in the Munster 'red-hot' tradition) lamented these innovations. As Lord Longfield rue-fully commented to Shannon in 1778: 'We want an efficient Pretender to recall this King back to those principles which placed his family on our throne.'[18] The new relaxed attitudes also percolated through to the younger, more sophisticated generation. Henry Quin, the son of a wealthy Dublin doctor, on his grand tour in 1785, attended mass at St Peter's on Christmas Day, to see both Pope Pius VI ('an extremely well-looking man of his age') and more particularly the Pretender:

> The Pretender was in a kind of loge next the singing men. After the mass was over, I went to the door of the loge to see him come out; he was so infirm as to be carried into his chair by his footmen. He is now old and pale; the contour of his face is somewhat like Lord Carhampton's. He had the garter but the blue was not sufficiently dark. I could not help feeling for him as he passed by.[19]

By the 1780s it was obvious that, among the fashionable young, the two great bugbears of eighteenth-century Ireland, the pope and the Pretender, were objects of idle curiosity, mere tourist attractions.

The new British attitude to Catholics was also facilitated by the French Revolution's attack on the papacy (which created a flood of goodwill towards the pope), by the subsequent emigration of 1,500 refugee priests to England, and by the enormous prestige of Burke's treatment of the Catholic Church as a stabilising counter-revolutionary force at the very heart of *ancien régime* society. Britain and the papacy shared a common enemy in atheistical France, and Irish Catholics benefited from the novel realignment. Not all were convinced of the honesty of these new sentiments. William MacNeven considered that they represented 'crocodile tears, that fall from the Ascendancy, lay and Churchmen, for the Pope, whom they have ever reviled'.[20] The radical Catholic priest Denis Taaffe sardon-ically noted the *volte-face* that the new stance represented for the British state:

> What sympathy, what sorrow, for the losses of a Church usually stigmatised as popish, idolatrous, anti-Christian, the very scarlet harlot, whore of Babylon, riding on the beast with seven heads and ten horns, quaffing the gold cup of abomination and committing fornication with the kings of earth. Now it is 'alas! alas! Babylon the great is fallen'.[21]

There was also one other effect of the relaxation of anti-popery within British society: it loosened the ties which had bound Protestant opinion of all shades together. Anti-popery had cemented the Protestant consensus in British and Irish life. Presbyterians, for example, hated popery more than they hated the Erastianism and episcopacy of the Anglican Church. With the popish threat in seemingly irreversible retreat in the 1790s, Presbyterians, especially in Ireland, felt freer to refocus on their ancient quarrel with the Anglicans. They were also greatly heartened by the separation of church and state in the American constitution, a victory achieved through the efforts of American dissent, in which the Ulster Presbyterian element loomed large. The result was an accelerating antagonism towards Anglicanism, deepened by Belfast-Dublin tensions, which quickly acquired political overtones. This antagonism greatly benefited Irish Catholicism in the early 1790s and made the Anglican position deeply uncomfortable. It was no longer just the Catholics who regarded conservative Anglicans as *bêtes noires*. William Campbell, unofficial leader of the Presbyterian Synod of Ulster in the 1780s, considered that the 1774 Vestry Act (which had undermined Presbyterian influence) had originated in 'the motherland of superstition and bigotry, the county of Armagh'.[22] Epithets normally used by Presbyterians to describe the Catholics were now transferred to the Anglicans, and the issues of tithes, state establishment and political reform widened the breach in Protestant unity.

The military imperative

The more relaxed imperial attitude to Catholics facilitated a growing realisation of their strategic importance as the long-term consequence of the French Revolution on the nature of war itself began to be slowly absorbed. While Britain in the initial stages of the French war relied on its long-established strategy of co-opting its continental allies to do the fighting, its governing class became ever more aware that the revolution would eventually redefine the terms of warfare. By the mid 1790s it was apparent that war would now be ideological in origin, 'a war of principles' (Burke) rather than dynastic or strategic. Secondly, it would involve mass mobilisation, vastly in advance of the meagre standing armies of the *ancien régime*. Thirdly, the actual war would not be a restrained series of tactical manoeuvres with low casualties, but bloody encounters with massive casualties. As one commentator noted:

> This is not a common war. This is not one of those contests which formerly engaged the attention of Europe, in which the restless, unquiet passions of the human breast were let loose in struggling for some trifling, often imaginary point of interest, often some punctilio of chimerical honour.[23]

The French Revolution, therefore, was not just an internal affair but 'a revolution of doctrine and theoretic dogma' (Burke).[24] It was also eminently exportable, once the French determined (in the Edict of Fraternity, 19 November 1792) that the Rights of Man applied equally to nations as to individuals. That altered the *ancien régime* French attitude to Ireland, which had hitherto interpreted Ireland as lying within the legitimate sphere of British influence, and therefore not an object of French strategy. The sophisticated French diplomat Marc de Bombelles, visiting Ireland in 1784, fully accepted that the penal laws were justified and that Irish Catholics should acquiesce in accepting them:

Il seroit imprudent d'admettre dans telle sorte de magistrature ou d'emploi public d'autre individus que ceux qui professent la religion dominante du pays. L'Irlande est gouvernée par les memes loix que l'Angleterre, et a adopté la meme lithurgie; elle ne pourroit sans s'exposer à de nouveaux troubles, étendre aux Catholiques plus numbreux des deux tiers que les Protestants des prérogatives dont seuls les Protestants doivent jouir.[25]

After the revolution Ireland was reinterpreted as an oppressed small nation struggling to free itself from arbitrary and despotic British rule, and which therefore deserved French sympathy and if possible support.[26] For the British state, these no longer seemed mere paper promises after the Battle of Valmy of 20 September 1792, when the French novices forced an ignominious retreat of the Duke of Brunswick's seasoned troops. The *levée en masse*, the volunteer army, the fight for *La Patrie*, the exportability of the revolution – these were frightening developments for conservatives, creating (in Burkean terms) the absolute necessity of civilising (i.e. subjugating) France, before France barbarised (i.e. spread its revolutionary system throughout) the rest of Europe.[27] These new realities initiated a reassessment of British military strategy.

Before the revolution the British state had already begun to cast avaricious eyes on the Catholic masses in Ireland as a rich reservoir for military recruitment. French events gave an added impetus to plans for tapping this potential. Obviously the principal impediment was the existence of the penal laws; removing this blockage caused the rapid passage, at English behest, of the relief acts of 1792 and 1793 and the linked Militia Act of 1793, which allowed regular soldiers to be withdrawn from Ireland to bolster the British army, and be replaced by a locally recruited militia. In 1793 and 1794, the first two years of the war, sixty-four new regiments were created; of these, no less than thirty (twenty-six infantry, four cavalry) were raised in Ireland, comprising about 25,000 men, half the total force raised in that period. In the longer term, a minimum of 150,000 Irish recruits (overwhelmingly Catholic in composition) joined the British army: the bulk of these were used to staunch the 'Spanish ulcer' which was threatening to bleed the British Napoleonic force dry.[28] Coupling Catholic relief and recruitment therefore had the multiple benefits for the British of a rapid accession of Catholic manpower, a potential neutralising of disaffection among the grateful Catholics (otherwise a permanent invitation to French invasion projects), the splitting of the emerging Presbyterian–Catholic alliance, and the wooing of an incipiently imperial Catholic leadership cadre. The cabinet was keen to outflank the radical Protestant (especially Presbyterian) appeal to the Catholics: by attaching the Catholics to the side of government through a policy of conciliation, the cabinet could trump the radical card.[29] The Catholic relief acts were accordingly pushed through at a speed which alarmed the conservative wing of the Irish Protestant elite, who passed them only grudgingly and in an atmosphere soured by surly sectarianism. The British cabinet, however, had no qualms in sacrificing local sentiments on the altar of imperial expediency, or of advancing ahead of popular Anglican opinion in Ireland, which still clung forlornly to the old familiar political landmarks.

The state's realignment on religious issues can also be gauged from its weakening commitment to the great commemorative occasions of Irish Protestant memory. By the 1780s there was a marked disengagement from formal state celebrations of 4 November (King William's birthday) and 23 October (the outbreak of the 1641 rebellion). In their stead the state began to promote St Patrick's Day as a less divisive and non-sectarian occasion.[30] The disengagement was even quicker among the Whigs and radicals. In espousing Bastille Day (14 July), they signalled their relinquishment of the Williamite tradition and the Glorious Revolution to the ultras, who then redefined them as conservative (not liberal) moments. Thus by the 1790s these state occasions were no longer an uncontested celebration of Protestant political unity and monolithic identity. Thomas Russell, himself a devout Anglican, attacked the whole project of Protestant commemoration: 'The anniversary of those events which led to the degradation of the country were celebrated, strange as it may appear, with martial pomp and festivity, differing in this from all nations, ancient or modern.'[31]

One unpredictable result of the French Revolution, then, was to increase the receptivity of the British state to the claims of Irish Catholics, whom they wished to cultivate as a counter-revolutionary force. This was symbolised most profoundly by the founding of Maynooth College in 1795 under the auspices of the government. The sheer novelty of the rapprochement is captured in the letter of Patrick Plunkett, Bishop of Meath, which describes the laying of the foundation stone at the college by the Lord Lieutenant, Camden, on 20 April 1796:

> The Viceroy was received at the approach of the college by the trustees, a number of the nobility and the fifty students in their gowns. Three of the students pronounced in the presence of Earl Camden the Lord Lieutenant three odes, one in Greek, one in Latin and one in English. His Excellency and suite sat down to a plentiful collation of which we the ecclesiastical trustees had the honour to partake. We received at Maynooth cards of invitation to dine that day with the Lord Lieutenant at the Castle of Dublin, and his Excellency had the goodness to order his carriage to convey the ecclesiastical trustees from Maynooth to Dublin, a distance of eleven miles. Doctors O'Reilly, Troy, Abbé Hussey and I came to the capital in the Viceroy's splendid coach-and-six attended by his servants. We had the honour of dining that day along with the other trustees at the Castle with the Lord Lieutenant. The dinner, you may be sure, was suitable to the place and the occasion: the politeness, attention and affability of the Lord Lieutenant was such as to leave us nothing to wish for.[32]

Plunkett's Roman agent, John Connolly, replied to this glowing account: 'Who could imagine when I left Ireland nearly thirty years ago that some of our Catholic prelates were to go in 1796 in state through Dublin and to dine at the Castle'?[33] Bishop Thomas Hussey aphoristically contrasted the new sentiments with the old: 'An impolitic wall of separation had been raised for some centuries past between the King and the Pope.'[34] As that wall now crumbled with astonishing speed, conservative Protestants could see themselves being buried under its rubble.

Protestant ascendancy

The early 1790s thus saw a stiffening of Protestant self-image. That image, inextricably bound up with their sense of hereditary superiority over Catholics, had been fractured by the failure of the much-vaunted (and still Protestant) constitution of 1782 to safeguard them from unwelcome British initiatives, by the legislative concessions to Catholics, by the United Irish challenge to sectarian politics, and by the seeming detachment of Presbyterians from the Protestant consensus. One conclusion only could be reached by conservative Protestants: the state itself – their state – was disengaging from its Protestantism. This conclusion fundamentally affected the national consciousness of Irish conservative Protestants. Their nationalism could only exist in a climate of self-confidence, predicated on keeping the majority Catholic population in permanent disarray, their political teeth drawn by their 1690s defeat, and the subsequent enactment of the penal laws against them. In those circumstances, and those alone, the Irish Protestants of Swift's generation could see themselves as 'the people of Ireland', an independent sister kingdom of England, with a shared crown, not a mere colonial appendage.

Protestant nationalism peaked in the settlement of 1782, at a period when England was weakest internationally. But this Protestant assertiveness could only flourish in an atmosphere free from fear – especially fear of the Catholics, their superior numbers and their continental allies. All these fears resurfaced in the turbulent 1790s. Protestant nationalism receded almost in tandem with the re-emergence of the Catholic question. The English courted the Catholics for imperial reasons, trading relief for recruitment, while using the Catholic threat to bring over-assertive Irish Protestants to heel. This policy laid bare an anxiety in Protestant nationalism, revealing that it had always been conditional and ambivalent. As the old fissures of Irish society reopened in the 1790s under the destabilising impact of the French Revolution, Protestant Ireland ceased to think of itself as the Irish nation. John Fitzgibbon, the most anglophile of the senior conservative politicians, had pointed out the reason (with his customary brutal clarity) during the regency crisis in 1789: 'When we speak of the people of Ireland, it is a melancholy truth that we do not speak of the great body of the people.'[35] He warned Irish Protestants of the danger of straying too far from the shelter of the British constitution, in a situation where they were in a minority in Ireland at a time of accelerating and unpredictable political upheaval.

Yet all the signals after 1791 were that Britain increasingly regarded Protestants and Catholics as equals in Ireland. One commentator noted the result: 'Among the Protestant party, the cant now is "England has given us up. We must take care of ourselves." '[36] Such a rapid shift forced a commensurate change in the articulation of Protestant identity: Protestants now had to develop a common identity as Protestants, not Irish, once the state seemed to be transforming itself from being solely sectarian. There had been no need to formulate explicitly such a position prior to these developments: British concessions and the radical challenge forced Protestant conservatives to stiffen their ideological stance, which they did in the rapid formalisation and dissemination of the concept of 'Protestant Ascendancy'. While this term had an immediate popularity in Irish domestic politics, it also had a currency in British circles, crystallising as it apparently did what was at stake in the war with France, while drawing emotionally on the memory of the Glorious Revolution, of anti-popery and of francophobia. The term 'Protestant Ascendancy' emerged out of these contexts, defined by Charles Sheridan in 1792 as:

> A Protestant King, to whom only being Protestant we owed allegiance; a Protestant house of peers composed of Protestant Lords Spiritual, in Protestant succession, of Protestant Lords Temporal, with Protestant inheritance, and a Protestant House of Commons elected and deputed by Protestant constituents; in short, a Protestant legislature, a Protestant judicial [sic] and a Protestant executive in all and each of their varieties, degrees and gradations.[37]

In a speech the same year, responding to the proposed Catholic Convention, John Giffard explained the historical context to a meeting of Dublin freemen:

> The question came to this point, whether the assembly were willing now to surrender to the Roman Catholics those birthrights won by their ancestors who bled on the banks of the Boyne, or to alienate the government and legislature of the country to popish hands. By conceding to the Catholics what they now demanded would be to change places with them and place the Protestants exactly in the situation where the Catholics then stood.

He drew the obvious conservative conclusion that 'the Catholics cannot be allowed the smallest influence in the state'.[38]

This anxious articulation was also designed to meet the *conjuncture* of the early 1790s – the changing imperial view of the Catholics and the seeming dismantling of the Glorious Revolution in Ireland. The non-sectarian and, hence, radical message of the United Irishmen would now be countered by an explicitly sectarian conservative message, emphasising that the security of Irish Protestants ultimately rested on their sole proprietorship of a Protestant state. To conservatives, the category of religion took precedence over that of nation, and this was starkly contrasted to the United Irishmen's strenuous efforts to neutralise, or even elide, the religious category. Therefore the rights and privileges of the Established Church in Ireland became one of the principal theatres of political warfare between radicals and conservatives in the 1790s. This resulted in deepening the virulent paper war sparked by the Rightboy attack on tithes in Munster, by the associated effort of Whigs like Grattan to reform the church and especially to remodel tithes, and by the subsequent trenchant defence of church privileges by Bishop Richard Woodward. This debate intensified under the impact of the French Revolution, with its aggressive severing of church and state.[39]

In these debates over sectarianism, the Catholic Church enjoyed one massive advantage. Unique in eighteenth-century Europe, it was completely untainted by any connection with political patronage since severing its linkages with the Stuarts in 1766. Therefore the Catholic Church in Ireland was insulated from radical attack in the 1790s. Catholics and Dissenters could concentrate their polemical fire on newly vulnerable Erastian Anglicanism, with its enormous state endowment for what was obviously a minority church (or 'insignificant sect', as Bishop Hussey famously described it in 1797).[40] That attack came consistently from Belfast where the dissenting interest was dominant, Anglicans weak, and Catholicism only minimally visible and politically impotent.

The United Irishmen wished to follow American and French precedents in separating church and state. Their political creed stated that religion was 'an affair between the conscience of man and his creator' and that 'it ought to be as free as the air in which we breathe'. Accordingly, 'all national churches are national defects'. One of their favourite toasts was 'a speedy divorce to church and state'.[41] Before the French Revolution it had been a cliché that the two main barriers to political freedom were an arbitrary monarchy and priestcraft, which had to be kept in check by a powerful parliament and an Erastian religious settlement, in which the church was firmly subordinated to the state. At a stroke, the French Revolution cut through these Gordian knots and created a new freedom in discussing them.

The United Irishmen concentrated their fire on the Established Church. William James MacNeven, one of their principal leaders, considered that 'all church establishments are injurious to liberty and religion'. Asked by Lord Kilwarden if Anglicanism would not simply be replaced by Catholicism as the established religion in the event of a successful Irish revolution, MacNeven replied vehemently: 'I would no more consent to that than I would to the establishment of Mohometanism.'[42] The United Irish attack was joined by Whig reformers like Henry Grattan. In his address to the citizens of Dublin in 1797, Grattan refuted Fitzgibbon and others who insisted that

> The Irish Catholic was still the bigot of the last century, that with respect to him, the age had stood still, that he was not impressed with the new spirit of liberty but still moped under the old spirit of bigotry and ruminated on the triumph of the cross, the power of the Catholic hierarchy, the riches of the Catholic clergy and the splendour of the Catholic Church.

He then pressed home his conclusion: the reason why 'those ministers alleged that the Catholic mind had stood still was that their own mind had stood still: the state was the bigot, and the people the philosopher'.[43] Burke was equally aphoristic: 'New Ascendancy is the old mastership.'[44]

The appeal to the past

Faced with this potentially debilitating challenge, one conservative response had been the appeal to Protestant Ascendancy. A second conservative response was the almost instinctive appeal to the past, in an effort to stabilise shifting Protestant opinion by reminding it of the inherent duplicity of Catholics, as demonstrated classically in the 1641 rebellion and in the Jacobite period. To assume that Catholicism had changed was grossly naïve, and Presbyterians in particular were culpable in dismantling the century-old Protestant consensus on the exclusion of Catholics from political power in Ireland. For conservatives, Catholics were *semper eadem*, and reformers were self-deluding in concluding otherwise. Amputating the past from the present, as the United Irishmen wished to do, was for the conservatives dangerous, as it would dispense with the ties, loyalties, and shared historical memories which bound together the Protestants, the Irish parliament and the connection with England. The Protestant position in Ireland depended on the English connection and on upholding the Glorious Revolution. Patrick Duigenan put the point succinctly in 1792: 'The Protestants of Ireland are but the English garrison in an enemy's country and, if deserted by the parent state, must surrender at discretion.'[45] The conservative response to the United Irish appeal to the future was therefore an appeal to the past, a backwards glance which emphasised the ethnic and religious fissures in Irish society, the old reliable hatreds which had facilitated stable government in the century following the Boyne. The lesson from history in the Irish context was that a Catholic majority meant persecution for Irish Protestants because Catholicism was inherently a persecuting religion. Edward Newenham, a conservative M.P., claimed in 1795: 'As little could the Ethiopian be washed white as the Church of Rome be taught to endure an equal in power.'[46]

This conservative position hardened throughout the turbulent 1790s. Fitzgibbon, for example, argued in 1795 that the tranquillity of eighteenth-century Ireland had fundamentally rested on these sectarian foundations: 'The penal laws enacted in this country were a code forced on the parliament by hard necessity and to these old popery laws, I do not scruple to say, Ireland stands indebted for her internal tranquillity during the last century.'[47] Therefore it was dangerous in the extreme 'to make experiments upon this giddy country'.[48] And he warned about the danger of a split within Irish Protestant opinion: 'Till the modern Irish patriots had divided the Protestants of Ireland into opposite factions, we never heard of claims to political power advanced by Papists'.[49] In these circumstances, Presbyterians and Anglicans should stick together politically; Protestant disunion had opened the space into which the United Irishmen had adroitly inserted themselves, working hard to hammer in the wedge and to split the consensus of a century. Particularly dangerous was the developing relationship between the issues of parliamentary reform and Catholic Emancipation. Euseby Cleaver, Bishop of Ferns, pointed out in June 1797 how 'our dangerous demagogues in parliament' would proceed:

They doubtless will seize the first opportunity to excite ferment by agitating the question of Catholic Emancipation and Reform of Parliament. They are questions intimately connected, and if the English cabinet shall at any time think it expedient to concede one, the other in a short time will necessarily follow. This connexion between the questions will unite the Papists and the Presbyterians who together I believe comprehend near 7/8 of the Kingdom. If the English government therefore do not support the other eighth, it of course must fall.[50]

Burke and the Catholics

A diametrically opposed analysis was presented by Edmund Burke. He believed that only by admitting Catholics fully into the political nation could Ireland be tranquillised, as their innately deferential and monarchical tendencies would then be expressed in support of the status quo, and they would no longer be a prey to factious Dissenters or Jacobin United Irishmen:

> Suppose the people of Ireland divided into three parts. Of these (I speak within compass), two are Catholic; of the remaining third, one half is composed of Dissenters. There is no natural union between those descriptions. It may be produced. If the two parts Catholic are driven into a close confederacy with half the third part of Protestants, with a view to a change in the constitution in church or state or both, and you rest the whole of their security on a handful of gentlemen, clergy and their dependents – compute the strength you have in Ireland, to oppose to grounded discontent, to capricious innovation, to blind popular fury and to ambitious, turbulent intrigue.[51]

Burke believed that his analysis picked out 'the great danger of our time, that of setting up number against property'.[52] This blunt diagnosis left only three options open. Firstly, if Protestants wished to avoid repeating the bloody excesses of the French Revolution, they would have to relinquish sole proprietorship of the state. Alternatively, if they wished to face down Catholics, they could scurry into the hollow husk of Protestant Ascendancy and seek either a union or a bloody civil war in which they could only hold the country by force with English support. Then 'you may call your constitution what you will, in effect it will consist of three parts (orders if you please) cavalry, infantry and artillery and of nothing else or better'.[53] The three options – Catholic Emancipation, union, civil war – were here starkly delineated. Burke ridiculed Irish Protestant perceptions of popery:

> the fear, or pretence of fear, that, in spite of your own power, and the trifling power of Great Britain, you may be conquered by the pope; or that this commodious bugbear (who is of infinitely more use to those who pretend to fear, than those who love him) will absolve His Majesty's subjects from their allegiance, and send over the Cardinal of York [the Young Pretender's surviving brother] to rule you as his viceroy; or that by the plenitude of his power, he will take that fierce tyrant, the King of the French, out of his jail, and arm that nation

(which on all occasions treats his holiness so politely) with his bulls and pardons, to invade poor old Ireland, to reduce you to popery and slavery, and to force the free-born, naked feet of your people into the wooden shoes of that arbitrary monarch. I do not believe that discourses of this kind are held, or that any thing like them will be held, by any who walk about without a keeper.[54]

He was not optimistic about the ability of Protestant Ascendancy figures in Ireland to make the right decisions. 'These miserable creatures, the zealots of the Ascendancy, have been fed with this stuff as their nurse's pap and it is never to be got out of their habit. Their low and senseless malice makes them utterly incapable of forming a right judgement on anything.'[55] In a despairing trope, he likened these Ascendancy politicians to rats and Ireland to a ship – 'but the ship is kept up for the benefit of the rats'.[56]

The conservative backlash

It was Burkean principles which Fitzwilliam tried to implement during his short viceroyalty in 1795. Full Catholic relief would be accompanied by a yeomanry act, permitting grateful Catholics to express their loyalty to what would now be 'their' state. The ultras would be faced down, signalled in the dismissal of John Beresford, Arthur Wolfe and Edward Cooke. The backlash against these measures led to the collapse of the viceroyalty, the reinstatement of the 'junta' and the espousal of hardline measures. Camden replaced Fitzwilliam as viceroy, with explicit cabinet instructions 'to rally the Protestants' and to resist any further Catholic demands for incorporation into the state.[57] Faced with the French threat, the Catholic account was now closed by the imperial parliament, as military priorities took precedence over political susceptibilities. As long as he could be assured of Protestant loyalty, Camden was quite happy to alienate the Catholics:

> If the great body of Protestants will exert themselves in the contest, I am authorised to give them the most decided and unreserved support and that in conjunction with them, I am ready to make every exertion they can desire to prevent the admission of Catholics to the legislature.[58]

This explicitly sectarian stance was backed by a tougher military policy. The anticipation and advent of the Fitzwilliam viceroyalty had essentially tied the state's hands in dealing with the internal threat represented by the Defenders and the United Irishmen.[59] Once the 'junta' took over policy again in the spring of 1795, they quickly set about re-exerting the authority of the state, if necessary by terror. Among their weapons were litigation, the construction of an intelligence network, and a confrontational security policy. Faced with a mounting Defender threat and evidence of its spread into north Connacht and the midlands, the paralysis of the jury system, the failure of nerve of many country gentlemen, and the possibility of the French using

Ireland as a launching-pad for an invasion of Britain, the administration moved towards purely military solutions. The Carhampton campaign of the summer of 1795 in north Leinster and Connacht marked the first systematic deviation from a legal response to disaffection. Camden excused it as 'a salutary system of severity' which was founded 'upon obvious principles of political necessity'.[60] It emerged out of a growing establishment sense that the situation had spiralled out of their control. Writing in August 1796, John Beresford wailed:

> We are in a most desperate situation: the whole north, Louth, Meath, Westmeath, Longford, Roscommon, Galway, the county and city of Dublin ready to rise in rebellion; an invasion invited by ambassadors; our militia corrupted; the dragoons of Ireland suspected; the United Irishmen organised; the people armed; while we are without military stores, magazines etc. And where things will end, God only knows but our heads are in no small danger, I promise you.[61]

The new legislative programme involved the principle of suspending the constitution to save the constitution, as reflected especially in the Insurrection Act (March 1796) and the Suspension of Habeus Corpus Act (October 1796). This latter act had to be introduced to combat the freedom of movement of the United Irish leadership and the dismal failure of the embryonic spy system to discover high-grade information useable in court. The Insurrection Act gave unprecedented powers to magistrates, and the bench itself was widened to include many new men from the middle interest. These men, now vested with draconian powers, were often inexperienced, with narrow horizons and a poorly developed sense of how local and national political levels interacted. Such men were to be a propaganda godsend to the United Irishmen in succeeding years.

Maria Edgeworth, the novelist, noted in the mid-1790s that 'the magistracy and the yeomanry were peopled by men without education, experience or hereditary respectability', so that 'in their new characters, they bustled and bravadoed, and sometimes in certainty of party support and in public indemnity, they overleaped the bounds of the law'.[62] As tensions heightened, United Irish propaganda focused insistently on men like Thomas Judkin Fitzgerald in Tipperary, Thomas Hugo in Wicklow, Robert Cornwall in Carlow, Hunter Gowan, Archibald Hamilton Jacob, Hawtrey White and Standish Lowcay in Wexford, Thomas Rawson in Kildare, and John Greer and James Verner in Armagh. Verner was acidly described by James Quigley as 'a man who has done everything but what is right and just' and who 'had metamorphosed into a legislator for his country from being a common feeder and handler of gamecocks'.[63] These men were particularly resented in those counties which were riven between 'Whig' and government interests, and where accordingly no consensus existed on law-and-order policy. In the Whig aureoles around Belfast (Antrim, Down, Armagh) and Dublin (Kildare, Wicklow, Wexford, Carlow) there was consequently a highly visible split around law-and-order issues, which ensured that magistrates' actions were closely scrutinised for political bias. This in turn created an intimate link between local and national policy and between high and popular politics, with national debates being refought at local level and political and propaganda advantage being sought out of every local incident. By contrast, in counties where there was no significant split and where control rested with one dominant interest, the same divides on law-and-order issues did not surface (as, for example, in Foster-controlled Louth, Hill-controlled Derry, and Ormonde-controlled Kilkenny). As with the law-and-order debate, so too with sectarianism. Judge Robert Day commented explicitly on the link between high politics and the emergence of sectarianism as an issue on the ground:

> It is only in the counties where political adventurers place themselves at the head of these sects respectively and make religion a stalking horse for elec-tioneering purposes that these sanguinary and atrocious crimes have been committed for the love of God![64]

Arming the Protestants

Given these anxious circumstances, it is not surprising that the Protestant military tradition was reactivated, in a decade which witnessed the classic scenario of threat for them – an external (French) and internal (Catholic) challenge to their state. As Bartlett has pointed out, Irish Protestants had a long memory of 'providing their own military protection, both in the case of invasion from abroad but also, more especially, lest their enemies the Irish Catholics should rise up in rebellion'.[65] The militia of 1793 had ultimately proved disquieting to Protestant opinion, as outside east Ulster, the corps were overwhelmingly (75 per cent) Catholic below the rank of officer, drawn from the poorest layer of Irish society and therefore increasingly suspect as the political temperature shot up in the mid-1790s. That suspicion was exacerbated by the policy of rotating the units away from their home counties, which led to Catholic units being billeted in Pro-testant areas. Far more comforting was the property-based and locally stationed yeomanry created in 1796, who took their religious character from the areas in which they were recruited. They were extremely important in giving public expression to Protestant self-perception. As with the Orange Order, the yeomanry concept originated in the troubled Lough Neagh crescent, with William Richard-son of Armagh and Thomas Knox, the Dungannon M.P. By mid-1796 they had decided that the contest between loyalists and republicans was fast approaching and that 'the question must be decided by the sword'. In such a situation, Knox believed that 'the first up will carry the day' and that it was accordingly essential to arm all loyalists. From Knox and Richardson the idea was transmitted to Dublin Castle by Arthur Wolfe. The Dungannon Association, founded on 12 July 1796, was the first step in testing the concept on the ground.[66]

The new aim, in Beresford's words, was 'arming the Protestants that can be depended on'.[67] The yeomanry provided a rallying-point, allowing conservative Protestants to define and consolidate their common interests. The Irish yeomanry were based on the English yeoman force established in 1794, with great care being taken to prevent the revival of volunteering. They would remain firmly under central control, equipped and commissioned from Dublin Castle, with ruthless screening of their officer class.[68] Their incorporation would release the regular army from routine policing duties to deal instead with the invasion scenario. This necessitated their concentration in large, strategically located camps, rather than being dispatched piecemeal and randomly to succour every neurotic country squire. These isolated detachments on garrison duties had proved ruinous to discipline, easy to infiltrate, impotent in case of an invasion, and impossible to systematise, as their dispositions were made in response to local and political, rather than strategic and military considerations. By mid-1796, of 40,000 regular troops in Ireland, a mere 7,000 were in camps.

Alongside the broad strategic aim of releasing the regulars, it was also hoped that the yeomanry would stiffen the loyalist backbone. Beresford noted the enthusiastic Protestant response to the announcement of the yeomanry: 'The wisdom of the measure appears from the confidence which it raises in loyal subjects.' He also noted:

> If the loyal Protestants are armed, they will keep the people in alarm; they fear them already beyond idea or measure and I have no doubt if the measure be speedily carried into execution, that it will have the best effects.[69]

The yeomanry would provide a rallying-force, defining and consolidating their common interests by defending the stability of the social and political order on which they rested. The rights of property would now be pitted against the rights of man. Within three months of the yeomanry act receiving royal assent on 7 October 1796, there were 18,000 recruits. The numbers soared again in the aftermath of Bantry Bay; by the end of 1797 they stood at 36,854; by 1798 at 43,221, and a post-rebellion surge peaked at 66,082 by 1799.[70]

The origins of the Orange Order

An ancillary effect of all these developments was a marked sectarianising of the political atmosphere from the mid-1790s onwards, a sectarianism deliberately injected by the government as a counter-revolutionary strategy of tension. By the mid-1790s, and faced with a mounting crisis, a further conservative response developed, utilising informal impediments (notably the Orange Order) as a surrogate for crumbling formal impediments (the penal laws) to the Catholics. This strategy of countering the non-sectarian message of the United Irishmen with an avowedly sectarian one was especially important in the aftermath of the Catholic relief acts and of the Fitzwilliam episode. In 1795 Edward Newenham described how the 12 July celebrations of the Williamite victory provided a rallying-point for anxious loyalists in the village of Rathdrum in the great Whig county of Wicklow:

Last Sunday the 12th July was celebrated in this village. Early in the morning, every loyal Protestant house and even many cabins were decorated with Orange lilies: the very roofs were stuck with them: at church, men, women and children, except three democrats, had those loyal emblems affixed to their persons. . . . In the evening, thirty-two Protestants paraded in the market place, opposite the tavern where eighteen of us loyalists dined. They marched around the town, firing twelve vollies and dressed with orange ribbands. Barrels of ale were supplied from the tavern to drink 'The Glorious Memory', 'The Prince of Hanover', 'The King and Queen' and 'Confusion to the French'. At each toast a volley was fired amidst applause. The loyalists then made a bonfire at which a great number of remarkable well-dressed girls appeared, and there was dancing till daylight.[71]

These instincts were soon to be given political codification in the formation of the Orange Order later that year. The Order's initial impetus came from beleaguered Protestants in mid-Ulster, and responded to a profound demotic need. Faced with a mounting United Irish challenge in this very region, gentry and military leaders jettisoned their qualms about its democratic tinge and its predilection for ugly sectarian violence. The elite Anglican layer in mid-Ulster, socially vulnerable and politically isolated, quickly grafted themselves on as the leadership of the organisation. In 1796, when thirty Orange lodges paraded through north Armagh, Lord Gosford turned it into a political display, organising the march to pass through his demesne, reviewing it as it passed, and sending a glowing report to Edward Cooke in Dublin Castle, of the lodges

marching in regular files by two and two, with Orange cockades, unarmed and by companies which were distinguished by numbers upon their flags. The party had one drum and each company had a fife and two or three men in front with painted wands in their hands who acted as commanders. They posted two men at each side of my gate with drawn swords to prevent any persons coming in but their own body. The devices on the flags were chiefly portraits of King William with mottos alluding to his establishment of the Protestant religion and on the reverse side of some of them I perceived a portrait of his present majesty with the crown placed before him, motto God save the King. They were perfectly quiet and sober. After parading through part of my demesne, they took their leave. I was at my gate: each company as they passed me by saluted me by lowering their flags.[72]

The Order especially appealed to Anglicans squeezed between the United Irish (Presbyterian) and Defender (Catholic) challenge, and without any political grouping of their own. It acted as a stabilising force for Anglicans at local level, visibly demonstrating their political loyalties. Parades and marches were rites of both inclusion and exclusion, territorial markers, which wrapped a tough carapace around a suddenly vulnerable group. Its leaders also wished to use the Order to pull Protestant opinion (in Armagh particularly) to the right, and thereby claw back the ground they had been losing to the radicals in mid-decade.

In the early 1790s there had been a three-way split in Armagh politics, with the radicals on one extreme matched by a loyalist party on the other, but with a large moderate middle ground, occupied by the interests of Charlemont and Brownlow. But that middle ground was rapidly eroded in the mid-1790s, exemplified by Brownlow's move from independence to a pro-government and anti-reform stance. The Armagh by-election of 1795 was a close-fought one between the newly conservative Brownlow and the radicals Cope and Stewart, who stood on an overtly Fitzwilliamite (parliamentary reform and Catholic Emancipation) and covertly United Irish platform. Brownlow's narrow victory by a mere handful of votes in a large electorate caused concern in Ulster conservative circles. With another election looming in 1797, it was essential to stop Armagh following Antrim and Down into the Whig camp, because of the boost that this would give to the United Irishmen. The crucial group was the Presbyterians. With Catholics mobilised in the Defenders and Anglicans in the Orange Order, would the Armagh Presbyterians side with their fellow-Protestants, or would they, as their Belfast brethren urged, join the United Irishmen, creating a powerful alliance of rural and urban Ulster? In 1795 and 1796 the stakes were high in terms of recruiting Presbyterians, as the political fate of mid-Ulster rested on it. The United Irishmen (appealing to their radicalism) and the Orange Order (appealing to their inherited anti-popery phobia) competed vigorously for their political and organisational allegiance. The intense propaganda battle waged around the Armagh Troubles also revolved around this issue. Loyalists (both in Armagh and Dublin) tried to pin the blame for the anti-Catholic pogroms on the Presbyterians in an effort to drive a wedge between the two; radicals argued that the disturbances were orchestrated deliberately by the government and conservatives, and that Catholic and Dissenters were actually drawing constantly closer in 'the brotherhood of affection'.

The rapid espousal and spread of the Orange Order must be contextualised within this high political framework; it was as much a 'top-down' as a 'bottom-up' development and emerged out of the peculiar circumstances of 1795 – the strong and vocal Fitzwilliamite rump in parliament, the failure of the Carhampton campaign to subdue Defenderism, the Camden riot, the evidence of United Irish overtures to the Defenders and the French, the rapidly approaching election of 1797, the possibility of Catholics and Presbyterians developing a closer anti-government alliance. It is against this explicitly political background that the emergence of the Orange Order should be set, not exclusively against socio-economic and sectarian backdrops.[73] The suggestive role of John Giffard, the Dublin ultra, in the origins of the Order make sense in this context, as does the early and prominent role of conservative gentry in Armagh. From the start these conservatives were careful to avoid any repetition of the mistakes of the Volunteer period. John Ogle reported to Cooke that as he considered the Order

> to bear a strong affinity to embodying of the old Volunteers I conceive it might
> be much better manag'd by the same means and to keep them in bounds, To

say, the interference of the landlords & gentlemen of popularity & discretion, who would mix with them & point out what was reasonable or otherwise.[74]

The families who quickly put themselves at its head included the Verners of Church Hill, Blackers of Castle Blacker, Atkinsons of Crowhill, Maunsells of Drumcree, Clarkes of Summer Island, Warings of Waringstown, and Brownlows of Lurgan.[75] Anglican clergymen also gravitated towards it, with Philip Johnson of Derriaghy and Thomas Higginson in Lisburn being especially active. Johnson claimed that his parish lay astride the Antrim/Armagh border and therefore directly in the path westwards of the United Irishmen from 'the grand focus of sedition' in Belfast.[76] In consultation with Downshire and Castlereagh, he 'formed five or six parishes, being a principal part of my Lord Hertford's estate, into small armed bodies, including every loyal Protestant, who were in some degree organised and prepared to check the progress of sedition'.[77] These parishes included Derriaghy, Lambeg, Lisburn, Ballinderry and Glenavy. When the yeomanry corps were formed, the Hertford estate was able to supply 1,500 rank and file.[78] Johnson subsequently became Grand Master of the Order in County Antrim, describing it as 'highly useful if properly directed'.[79]

The Orange Order stiffened the will to resist of minor country gentlemen, especially the magistrates and clergymen who had hitherto given the United Irishmen a free rein. Many had fled from the countryside to the safety of towns; others were quiescent and passive in the face of the radical challenge. The spread of the Order allowed pressure to be brought to bear on these waverers. A meeting of the lodge masters at Armagh on 21 May 1797 requested 'the gentlemen to stay in the country and we will form ourselves into district corps under their paternal care'.[80] The Order was therefore crucial in areas of lax political management, where the United Irishmen had hitherto met little opposition. Such areas included large swathes of south Armagh, south Down, and the Charlemont estate west of Armagh city. These areas contrasted with the vigorous political and security policy on east Armagh estates, like the Hertford property, or the Downshire lands in north Down. In these lax areas the Order provided the nucleus of a law-and-order offensive. John Beresford commented on the good effect of this liaison between the Order, the yeomanry and the local gentry: 'Loyal people, who were before afraid to appear, show themselves active and I trust we shall soon have this country quiet.'[81] In a retrospective assessment, William Richardson picked out the crucial role of the Order in 1795 in giving public expression and coherence to loyalism, in opposition to the well-organised Defenders and United Irishmen: 'All parties were now ready to rise but the loyalists, who having no system or point of union or method of showing themselves were supposed by many and asserted by the United Irishmen not to exist.'[82]

The public wearing of Orange insignia provided an important counter to the United Irish wearing of the green. The United Irishmen's brotherhood of affection was now being met by the Orange Order's brotherhood of disaffection – for Catholics, for radicals, for United Irishmen. Their non-sectarian message was challenged by an explicitly sectarian one; their radical appeal to the future was matched by a conservative appeal to the past; their effort to create united Irishmen was rebuffed by a deliberate effort to create disunited Irishmen. But popular loyalism was not just a reflex of conservative politicians; it also had complex roots within Irish Protestant culture. The Orange Order represented a refurbishment of the faded repertoire of commemoration, from which the state had retreated as politically obsolete in the 1780s.[83] The Williamite focus, the emphasis on the Glorious Revolution, anti-popery, the military volunteering – all these aspects of Orangeism lay solidly within the Protestant tradition and touched a responsive chord. In Armagh itself a further ethnic dimension was noted:

> It is to be remarked and very particularly attended to that the O[range] Men are almost entirely composed of members of the Established Church, attached to the established government of this kingdom and its connection with England, by birth, education, habit and prejudices: they are the descendants of English men and the sole cause of all they have of late done has originated from those attachments.[84]

The state and the Orange Order

The astute military commander in mid-Ulster, General John Knox, and his brother, Thomas Knox, M.P., realised that the Order could also be used to solve a major strategic problem – how to prevent the United Irish tide from flooding down the Lagan valley into Armagh, and thence inundating west and south Ulster. The Knoxes, and other conservative Ulster gentry, were able to convince an initially sceptical Dublin Castle (notably Pelham and Cooke) of the political and military utility of the Order. Thomas Knox had, indeed, suggested that in the Orangemen 'we have a rather difficult card to play'. Yet the bottom line was that 'on them we must rely for the preservation of our lives and properties should critical times occur'.[85] His brother, the general, warned that the Orange Order was crucial to his strategy of containing the United Irishmen within their east Ulster heartland. While recognising that their licentiousness constituted a major problem, Knox claimed that 'they are the only barrier we have against the United Irishmen'.[86] Pelham replied:

> You say at the end of your letter that if you are permitted, as you are inclined, to encourage the Orangemen, you think that you will be able to put down the United Irishmen in Armagh, Monaghan, Cavan and part of Tyrone. I do not exactly understand the degree of authority or the sort of encouragement you wish for. Your object is so desirable that we can hardly object to any means for gaining it. At the same time, party and religious distinctions have produced such consequences in the county of Armagh that it will require infinite prudence and dexterity in the management of such an undertaking: but as I am aware that anything I suggest and more will occur to you upon the subject, I believe that the best line of conduct I

can follow is to leave the matter to your discretion, requesting only to be informed of any particular plan you might think proper to adopt.[87]

Knox's policy was to allow Orangemen to enlist *en masse* as yeomanry corps: 'I do not wish the government should give them an avowed protection . . . but that protection may be given silently by permission to enroll themselves in the district corps and by having it generally understood that their meetings (a sort of freemasonry) shall not be disturbed.'[88] Knox subsequently revealed to Dublin Castle how he intended to use them: 'I have approved a plan to scour a district full of unregistered arms: this I do, not so much with a hope to succeed to any extent as to increase the animosity between the Orangemen and the United Irishmen. Upon that animosity depends the safety of the centre counties of the North.'[89] He informed the influential Abercorn that, as the Orangemen were the only pro-government party in Tyrone, 'I have found it necessary to encourage that party'.[90]

Knox subsequently assured Dublin Castle that 'the institution of Orange lodges was of infinite use' and that he 'would rest the security of the north on the fidelity of the Orangemen who were enrolled in the yeomanry'.[91] Further, he claimed that 'were the Orangemen disarmed or put down, or were they coalesced with the other party [the United Irishmen], the whole of Ulster would be as bad as Down and Antrim'.[92] Camden, the ever-anxious Lord Lieutenant, eventually acquiesced in the policy of supporting the Orangemen, but only once it was clearly understood that such measures should be discreetly distanced from Dublin Castle; in this connection, he noted with dismay that 'some of the magistrates have been incautious enough not to carry on this measure so secretly as to have escaped the notice of the public'.[93] By January 1797 Pelham could happily observe: 'In the north, things are growing better. About Dungannon, Knox's activity and knowledge of the country have given courage to the loyalty that was kept down by terror.'[94] Musgrave claimed that in Monaghan, Fermanagh, Donegal, Tyrone, Derry and Armagh 'the Orange Order had a peculiar good effect in detaching Presbyterians from the union'.[95]

A second 'good effect' was to split the Masonic movement along sectarian lines, thereby halting one of the United Irishmen's most effective recruiting, organisational and ideological vectors. By 1797 pressure was being exerted on the Grand Lodge to excise 'that most dangerous system grafted onto Freemasonry', and there was a marked hiatus in the spread of Masonry subsequently.[96] The Orange Order was pivotal to the policy of deradicalising Freemasonry. As Orange Lodges (themselves clearly modelled on a Masonic prototype) spread, Freemasonry could no longer transcend sectarian divides, and a fissile tendency developed. In the late 1790s that split occurred, neutralising an ideologically congenial vector of revolutionary thought. Radical Freemasonry shuddered to a sectarian-induced halt.

By 1797 even liberal Whigs, faced with the polarisation of political opinion in Ulster, swung reluctantly into line behind Knox's argument from necessity in favour of Orangeism. The Whig clergyman Charles Warburton, overwhelmed by the gravity of the Armagh situation, concluded: 'Upon principle, I am an enemy to all kinds of religious party, but the enemies of our establishment have reduced us to make "divide" a justifiable measure.'[97] Ultimately, from Dublin Castle's point of view, the Orange Order's ability to stem the spread of the United Irish system from east into mid-Ulster was a significant counter-revolutionary success. William Richardson drew attention to its strategic significance:

> The Orange country extending from near Dungannon eastward through the county of Armagh [and] a considerable way into the county of Down has served with Lough Neagh as a barrier to stop the progress of the Un[ited] Irish to the west and south-west; while to the north-west, meeting no obstacle in their course from Belfast, they have inundated everything.[98]

He later explained in detail:

> Every mischief diverged from Belfast. Lough Neagh, with the Orange country to the south and south-west, stopped its progress in that direction. It then, like a flood, doubled round the obstacle, passing on one side by Coleraine, Newtown Limavady, Derry, Strabane, Omagh, Aughnacloy, round to the southern parts of Armagh where it was met by the other branch that had taken its course by the county of Down to Newry and thence backwards to Armagh.[99]

Writing from Lisburn at a critical point on the Orange crescent below Lough Neagh, the Anglican clergyman Thomas Higginson noted of the United Irishmen:

> Immediately in this parish, and I suppose thro' Armagh they are outnumbered by the Orangemen and I must evince that I think this distinction of parties under God saves the country; but lower down, towards and below Antrim, they are almost without exception of a contrary sentiment; they openly express themselves, sing the most rebellious songs, drink the most rebellious toasts and swear to plant the Tree of Liberty all Ireland over.[100]

The Orange Order was therefore vitally important in inserting a conservative wedge between two radical regions – the United Irish heartland in Antrim and Down, and the Defender stronghold of south Ulster.

These analyses eventually persuaded the initially sceptical Abercorn of the utility of the Orange disturbances. He wrote to Richardson:

> Instead of thinking, as I used, the part of Ireland you have treated upon, the most turbulent and ticklish part, I now think it rather a bulwark of the North and heartily wish Tyrone and Donegal in a similar situation for when there is energy in the well-affected part of the community, that part will in the worst of times be a rallying point and will be sure to preponderate and prevail at last.[101]

Fear of being abandoned to the aftermath of a successful revolution concentrated the conservatives' minds, haunted by nightmarish images of the French disease inflicting its dreadful ravages on the Irish body politic, sweeping away themselves, their families and their properties. Richardson noted how the diverse spectrum of political opinion in the early 1790s had clarified into a stark polarisation by 1797:

> Revolution becoming the point at issue, no parties were known but Loyalists and United Irish, each branding the other with what names they thought fit, Orange or Papist, as might best serve to inflame. This has reduced our northern differences to a nut shell.[102]

The theatre of terror: the Armagh expulsions

In these circumstances, taking their cue from Knox and from Dublin Castle's tacit approval, local magistrates extended the Orange policy into the administration of law and order. Richard Jephson wrote from Loughgall: 'It is impossible for the Protestant gentry to keep up the farce of impartiality between the parties or to disavow the absolute necessity of giving a considerable degree of support to the Protestant party.'[103] The outcome included the Armagh expulsions of 1795 and 1796, when hundreds of Catholic families were banished 'to hell or to Connacht' by a rampant Orange faction, while the ultras among the gentry offered covert support and Dublin Castle declined to intervene. Sectarianism must be supported, at least covertly, if that was the necessary price to be paid to undermine the radical challenge. Writing from Tynan in County Armagh, John Short described the situation there in January 1796, as the Orange attacks on Catholics reached their height:

> Any of us that are Catholics here are not sure going to bed that we shall get up with our lives, either by day or night. It is not safe to go outside the doors here. The Orangemen go out uninterrupted and the gentlemen of the county do not interfere with them but I have reason to think encourage them in their wickedness. There is a Mr [James] Verner, a gentleman of great fortune who lives near Armagh has so far proved his encouragement as that he has turned off his estate his poor Catholic families who were plundered of every earthly thing they had, even to their wearing apparel. The Orangemen go out in large bodies by day and night and plunder the poor Catholics of everything they have, even the webs of linen out of their looms . . .
>
> Any of the Catholics they do not wish to destroy, they give them two or three days notice to clear out of the place by pasting papers on their doors, on which is written 'Go to Hell or to Connaught. If you do not, we are all haters of the papists, and we will destroy you.' The Orangemen come and after they have taken away everything worth carrying out of the cabins, they then dig round the bottom of them, as the cabins are mostly mud walls and easily dug around, and so let them tumble onto the unfortunate creatures. The houses that are not built with mud walls, these savages go up to the top of them with saws, and saw the beams on which the roof is supported and let the entire roof fall down on top of the poor creatures, by which they are bruised to pieces. I think that you will hardly credit this account, nor would I myself were I not on the spot.[104]

Later in the same year Bridget Brannon of Strabane commented on the great fear which had descended on Ulster Catholics:

> Our Catholic brethren are all either murdered or banished in the county of Armagh and many more on the borders of that county, so that our prospect is very indifferent. If a papist will endeavour to save or defend himself, he is either transported or hanged. God be our guardian for we need not depend on men. The great men of the nation that ought on their own account to put a stop to this in all quarters seem to be in a profound sleep and will not hear of these troubles.[105]

Another victim, John Lennon, forced to flee to Drogheda, later recalled the devastation:

> I cannot forget when six hundred families were banished from their homes, in the county of Armagh, in one year; every Catholic house in Ulster was closed at night, and all their windows built up with stone and mortar, unless weavers' windows, which were filled up at night with bog oak blocks, lest the inmates be shot at their work, as many were. Every magistrate in Ulster, but one or two, was an Orangeman, and no justice could be obtained either in courts of law, or elsewhere.[106]

This Armagh theatre of terror was sponsored by the state. Despite these widely publicised reports, there was no hesitation in Dublin Castle in endorsing the policy, in the aftermath of the near miss at Bantry Bay and the potentially devastating (and supremely embarrassing) Spithead mutiny, when Britain's floating 'wooden walls' were immobilised by United Irish intrigue. Once the 1797 election season was over (and with it the necessity to avoid handing propaganda gifts to the Whigs and United Irishmen), senior figures in the Dublin establishment, notably Edward Cooke and John Beresford, began systematically to implant the order into the suspect crescent of Whig counties south of Dublin – Kildare, Wicklow, Carlow and Wexford. The aim was to strengthen the conservative and pro-government factions in these counties, which would then be sufficiently energised to implement the tough law-and-order policy now being pursued by Dublin Castle.[107] *The Press* described the founding of Orange lodges in County Wicklow in the winter of 1797 as 'intended as a counteraction to United Irish societies' and as being 'countenanced by men high in rank and office'.[108]

The Dublin Grand Lodge was founded on 4 June 1797, and it was especially popular among the Munster gentry (King, Maude, Longfield, Musgrave, Beresford), who had formed the strongest anti-popery, anti-Jacobite, francophobic grouping in Irish society, and especially in parliament, throughout the eighteenth century.[109] Coming from within the Munster tradition and heavily involved in elite Orangeism, Richard Musgrave commented on the gentry role: 'Many gentlemen of considerable talent placed themselves at its head to give the institution a proper direction.'[110] The well-informed pamphlet *Orange Vindicated* offered this justification for the espousal of the Order at the highest levels of Irish decision-making:

In the year 1797, when the system of the United Irishmen had attained a great degree of maturity, and was every day threatening open rebellion, and when Catholics, little grateful for past favours, demanded new concessions, amounting to the surrender of the constitution, under the fantastical name of Catholic emancipation, which stood foremost among the postulata of the rebels, then I say, at that dangerous crisis, a plan was formed, and executed, of transplanting the Orange association from the North to the metropolis, and by regulating and improving the system, and placing at its head men of higher rank and talent, to convert to the support of the Throne and the Constitution, an institution, which from the nature of its origin and formation, might have degenerated into a ferocious spirit of persecution. This plan was the more beneficial and laudable, as any attempt to crush the association, in the place of its origin, would have been highly dangerous and impolitic, and therefore it was wise and expedient to direct the motions and progress of a machine which could not, with safety, be stopped. The detaching of the Presbyterians from the Union, as it was then called, was also a strong motive.[111]

The Orange Order had another valuable use as a military weapon. It popularised oaths of allegiance, which were particularly useful in targeting suspected United Irishmen who had infiltrated militia and yeomanry units, especially those under the control of liberals. General Knox was quick to spot the potential of the Order in disinfecting units of United Irishmen. As tension soared in 1797, he argued for the wholesale incorporation of Orange lodges as supplementary yeomen:

I proposed some time ago that the Orangemen might be armed and added to some of the loyal corps as supplementary yeomen. . . . They are bigots and will resist Catholic emancipation. A W. Atkinson has spoken to me on the subject of arming a body of these men (a hundred) of the Church of England. He is a very loyal man and stout magistrate, but I understand illiterate and of rude manner. A corps might be entrusted to him with good effect. Mr Verner's corps might also be increased.[112]

In summary, then, one can note how effective the Orange Order was as a counter-revolutionary device. It inserted an implacable barrier to the linking of the United Irishmen and Defender territories; it stopped the spread of radical Freemasonry; it pulled Protestants in general firmly to a conservative pro-government stance; it split the nascent Presbyterian–Catholic alliance in mid-Ulster; it checked United Irish infiltration of the yeomanry and militia. Given these advantages, which were soon apparent to strategic thinkers like Knox and Richardson, the government quickly abandoned its earlier wariness and espoused the Order covertly; remaining inhibitions (primarily about the propaganda value of the Order to the Whigs) vanished in the backlash after Bantry Bay and Spithead. As it moved south the Orange Order rapidly ascended the social ladder, gaining in prestige until it reached the very pinnacle of Irish society. From early on, then, initially in mid-Ulster and later nationally, the Orange Order was a gentry-backed organisation, operating within a specifically political context. An Armagh magistrate summarised this explicitly:

I have asserted that religion has nothing to do directly with the tumults and animosities in the county of Armagh and consequently that Orange Men are unjustly branded and for inflammatory purposes with the appellation of bigot and persecutor. Religion and its attachments are not warmer now in the breasts of Protestants than they were forty years ago: yet however severe the laws then were, the people were not persecutors. To what other cause then are we to attribute the present hostility of Protestant against the R. Catholic? 40 years ago there were no Defenders – no R.C. committees – no conventions – no insulting and dangerous demands of Protestant property and political power, and yet the present times have been much more indulgent to the R. Caths. But I firmly believe there has not existed a single religious party in this country for above twenty years. Our partys [sic] are all purely political so that when the terms Protestant, Dissenting, or Roman Catholic interest are used, the meaning is that the person using it wishes to have, or to be supposed to have, that interest to support the point he is pressing, whatever it may be.[113]

In this sense, the Dublin Whig lawyer Peter Burrowes was accurate in his assessment: 'I am well satisfied that the orange boys have been excited and encouraged by the Protestant Ascendancy men.' He claimed that it was the policy of government 'to disunite the people' in order to weaken the United Irishmen, accusing the senior conservative politicians of supporting Orange institutions from 'an union of hereditary and political prejudices'.[114]

Espousal of the Order ran in tandem with a much tougher security policy. Dublin Castle was quite willing to abandon the constitution if, in its judgement, extra-legal measures were required to contain by intimidation and state terror the spread of disaffection. Fitzgibbon, at the heart of hardline strategy formation, believed that 'it would be dangerous in the extreme to damp the ardour of those who may be depended on, under an apprehension that their zeal may become the subject of misrepresentation'.[115] By February 1796, the government's law officer, Sergeant Stanley, claimed that 'a too scrupulous adherence to the tedious terms of law was not commendable policy when the constitution itself was in danger'.[116] A year later Pelham requested General Lake, about to embark on the dragooning of Ulster, 'not to suffer the course of justice to be frustrated by the delicacy which might possibly have actuated the magistracy'.[117] Camden ordered him to take action 'if necessary beyond that which can be sanctioned by law'.[118] General Knox warned Pelham:

This country can never be settled until it is disarmed and that is only to be done by terror – by putting certain districts under martial law until all arms and ammunition are delivered up and by authorising the general officers to declare war upon property.[119]

Pelham himself, briefing Portland on the Insurrection Act, concluded equally bluntly that if it failed, there was no further option but to 'have recourse to the sword'.[120] By early 1798 Fitzgibbon considered that the state of the country required these extra-legal activities, beyond 'the slow and technical forms of a regular government',[121] while Judge Robert Day simultaneously told his juries that 'lenity (were it in your discretion) would be unreasonable, perhaps fatal. Lenity would be cruelty.'[122] In these circumstances, Henry Grattan could plausibly argue that there were 'now two constitutions for Ireland, one for the rich and another for the poor':

> The war is begun in Ireland between property and poverty: it is commenced by the former on the privileges of the latter. . . . The majorities of our House have gotten the spirit of planters, not of country gentlemen. They hate the papist and they hate the people.[123]

By the end of the year Grattan was describing the yeomanry as 'an ascendancy army':[124] 'The idea seems to be blood, the gentry against the common people, the noise and the spirit of hunters in the shape of members of parliament, and their game was the people.'[125] In 1797 he claimed that Dublin Castle employed 'the rich like a pack of government bloodhounds to hunt down the poor'.[126] By early 1798 all pretence had been shrugged off. A shocked Leonard McNally reported from the spring assizes at Maryborough:

> The defences set up by the prisoners were treated too often with inattention, laughter and contempt, everything against them received as truth. In some cases, the judge's authority could scarcely preserve the decorum necessary to a court of justice. Some gentlemen of fortune wore Orange ribbands and some barristers sported Orange rings with emblems.[127]

The United Irish response

The government's reversion to sectarian moulds confirmed every suspicion of the United Irishmen about them. It also seemed to be a perfect demonstration of how baneful English influence actually was in practice. From 1793 the cabinet was on a war footing and left the management of Ireland very much in the hands of the Lord Lieutenant. Like Westmorland before him, Camden was weak and ineffectual, and therefore inordinately dependent on his close advisers – Fitzgibbon, Foster, Beresford and Cooke. These men were essential to the management of parliament, in strategy formulation and in the day-to-day routine of business. The price paid by Camden (and ultimately the British government) for this closeness was that these men were virtually untouchable, and dictated policy and its implementation. Consider, for example, the absolute contempt with which Fitzgibbon viewed Camden:

> What can be said for that chuckle-pated coward, Lord Camden? His head would long since have adorned a lamp post and probably your head and mine might have accompanied it, if it had not been for the exertion of the Protestant loyalists of Ireland. The beast has been in his bed almost from the day of his resignation. It will not very much signify should he remain there.[128]

This 'junta', in the United Irish view, had deliberately conjured up popular loyalism to maintain their grip on corrupt power. That loyalism had no genuine or independent existence beyond these Machiavellian manipulations. The United Irishmen did not understand how these atavistic feelings could have any genuine popular constituency; in their reading, these developments were artificially induced by conservative ascendancy figures (the 'junta') to prolong their divide-and-rule strategy. James Quigley, for example, described how he attempted 'to reconcile the parties' in Armagh 'but was discoursed by several leading gentlemen of that county who have often told me at their tables that it was of great utility to the Irish government that such religious disputes should exist between the Dissenters and Catholics'. Quigley described the Orange Order as simply a 'church and king' mob and claimed that it was deliberately created 'to break the Catholic/Presbyterian alliance which it was much feared might end up in a union of all parties against the said Beresford and co'.[129]

Thomas Russell described the Orange Order as arising from 'the instigation of artful and wicked men', designedly raised to oppose 'the system of brotherly love and union, and a revival of national spirit' which the United Irishmen had created. He saw this as simply one more example of the fomenting of 'religious animosities' as 'the engine by which this country was kept in subjection: this [the Orange Order] may be considered as the last effort of the enemies of Ireland to prevent that union which when once effected will terminate their power'.[130] Attacking the role of the Order in fomenting discord, a 'Presbyterian' from Castlereagh wrote to *The Press* in November 1797, describing its attitude to Catholics:

> If you Catholics will endeavour all that is in your power to rivet your own chains, and the chains of your posterity; if you be sensible of the great grace and favour of us your Orange lords and masters, in allowing you, as you and your forefathers have always done, to creep among our feet, and live upon the dust of our soles, why then we will graciously permit you to live; but if you presume to think of Liberty, of political consequence, of Irish independence, or of being friends with the Presbyterians, consider your awful doom, we have the means in our hands, and we will execute summary vengeance.[131]

In similar vein, *The Press* fulminated in its 'Letter to the Orangemen of Ireland':

> In order to keep themselves in the possession of the whole political power of the country which they have usurped, they will by every infernal means which the Prince of Hell can invent, endeavour to promote that disunion which has long enslaved our country and divided the children of our land into parties. Captain G[iffard] first organised the Break-O-Day boys in Armagh and gave them the name Orangemen. Mr Secretary Cooke and the Dog [John Giffard] are planners of the Orange system.[132]

The United Irishmen invested considerable energy in trying to soothe sectarian tensions in Armagh. Special missions were dispatched there in 1792 and again in 1795, and senior figures like Neilson, Teeling, McCracken, Quigley and Lowry worked the area ceaselessly in the anxious period from 1795 to 1797, when the Armagh Troubles threatened to undermine the whole United Irish project in Ulster. Tone considered that 'that county has always been a plague to us', while Teeling referred to 'the perpetual blister' in Armagh. Teeling was keen that the United Irishmen's 'absorbing' influence would operate successfully on the Defenders, who otherwise were only 'a mere isolated system of self-defence' for Catholics, whom he described as 'the segregated sons of Ulster' and 'the children of the wild'.[133]

The United Irishmen continued to believe passionately in the power of the national concept to harmonise the internal discordances of Ireland. Their mistake was not, as is frequently alleged, a narrowness of sympathy, but an over-optimistic, and therefore false, inclusiveness – a problem which was subsequently to persist stubbornly at the core of the Irish nationalist project. The divisiveness of the failed revolution of 1798 exposed the limits of the United Irishmen's optimistic understanding of the cleavages within Irish society, and the extent to which the 1790s had polarised Irish politics. Simply to state the sectarian problem was not a solution in itself. The United Irishmen consistently underestimated the powerful groundswell of support for conservatism; the popular appeal of the Orange Order and the yeomanry indicated that this was not just a chimera engineered by establishment politicians. Like the French Jacobins confronted with the (to them) incomprehensible opposition of the Vendée's conservative peasantry to the French Revolution, the United Irishmen could not comprehend how there could be a genuine counter-revolutionary impetus of this type; in their reading, it could only be artificially induced by government and Ascendancy connivance. With an analysis based on this reading, which fundamentally misjudged the depth of popular counter-revolutionary sentiment, the United Irishmen unrealistically expected massive defections from the militia and yeomanry once the rebellion actually started. It was to be a fatal mistake; underestimating popular support for the regime, the United Irish revolution turned out not to be a painless coup, but a rancorous struggle, in which the lines of demarcation all too easily split along confessional cleavages.

Detaching the state

Once the United Irish challenge had been seen off in 1798, the state retracted its endorsement of the Orange Order. Judge Day observed: 'In the commencement of the late troubles, the institution was productive of much good, for it served as a rallying point for the well-affected and enlisted all-powerful fashion in the service and cause of loyalty.' But it had outlived its usefulness: 'The Orange institution, like the old Irish Volunteers, was of infinite use for a season; like them, it has degenerated into an invidious faction and ought to be discontinued.'[134] Dean

Warburton considered the suppression of the Order to be one of the greatest problems facing the new Lord Lieutenant, Cornwallis: 'Indeed, his Excellency's chief difficulty seems to be putting down that sad and ruinous system, so unwisely established by his predecessor, and he has greatly succeeded, tho' opposed and abused by those in office who ought to have seconded his honest and honourable endeavours.'[135] George Knox, whose family had been so influential in attaching the Order to the government, argued in 1803 for its detachment, describing it as

> a party which I am convinced by opposing the United Irishmen in the north saved us at one time from a general overthrow but which excited the religious feud which broke out in so sanguinary a manner in the south.

He then assessed them as being 'like all political parties which gain an ascendancy, tyrannical, proud, illiberal and irritating – therefore, God forbid we should be encouraging them, though their zeal at critical moments is very serviceable'.[136]

Conclusion

In defence of the United Irishmen, it should be stressed that blame for the introduction of sectarianism into the political life of the 1790s should not be laid at their door, but at that of the sectarian state itself. It has become fashionable to blame the United Irishmen for entering into an alliance with the Defenders on the grounds that this sectarianised the movement, compromising its earlier secular cosmopolitanism and replacing it with Catholic nationalism; by espousing the Defenders, it has been argued, the United Irishmen's original ideals were betrayed, and the seeds of a bitter sectarian rebellion were sown.[137] That line of argument ignores the deliberate injection of sectarianism by conservatives, and ultimately by the government, as a counter-revolutionary weapon. That omission can be traced to the overwhelming emphasis in work on the 1790s on popular radicalism, and the neglect of popular loyalism, in an obsession with revolutionaries, but not with counter-revolutionaries. We as yet do not possess an analytic narrative of 1790s conservatism, despite the copious sources. Such a narrative would have to confront the endorsement of sectarianism by the state itself. One should not underestimate the success of this strategy: the Irish elite was one of the few within *ancien régime* Europe to withstand the destabilising impact of the French Revolution. They were able to baulk the United Irish project of creating a reformed parliament which would oversee a supra-factional state which could adequately represent the Irish nation in all its inherited complexity.

If this United Irish objective failed, the movement did succeed in bringing down the unreformed Irish parliament. Acquiescing in the Act of Union marked the end of Protestant Ireland's representation of itself as 'the Irish nation': the Union was a devastating defeat for Irish Protestants, as they relinquished their precious Protestant parliament back into the hands of those from whom they had spent a century defending it. In another sense, the United Irishmen's project was displaced in the post-Union period by one based on an embryonic cultural nationalism which validated confessional allegiance as an essential ingredient in national identity. Its secular and republican impulses were negatived and its universalist and international strains were domesticated. The symbiosis of 'nationalism' and 'Catholicism' in Ireland was strengthened by the slow withdrawal of Presbyterians from the equation. The generous current of Irish nationhood, fed by many tributaries, as envisaged by the United Irishmen, was canalised into a narrower Catholic channel by the ruthlessly efficient engineer of the new Irish politics – Daniel O'Connell.[138] There was no site here for the United Irish project; their Enlightenment concept of the neutral state had to yield to the imperious presence of the nation-state. In that sense, the United Irishmen marked the death, not the birth, of a political tradition in Ireland, and O'Connell was their principal gravedigger.

Trees of Liberty

Before 'dying' for your country, think, my friends, in how many quiet strenuous ways you might beneficially live for it.

Every patriotic Irishman (that is, by hypothesis, almost every Irishman now alive), who would so fain make the dear old country a present of his whole life and self, why does he not, for example – directly after reading this, and choosing a feasible spot – at least, plant one tree? . . .

'Trees of Liberty', though an Abbé wrote a book on them, and incalculable trouble otherwise was taken, have not succeeded well in these ages. Plant you your eight million trees of shade, ornament, fruit: that is a symbol much more likely to be prophetic. Each man's tree of industry will be, of a surety, *his* tree of liberty.

THOMAS CARLYLE (1850)

'98 AFTER '98:
The Politics of Memory

The 1798 rebellion was fought twice: once on the battlefields and then in the war of words which followed in those bloody footprints. The struggle for control of the meaning of the 1790s was also a struggle for political legitimacy, and the high drama of the Union debate was dominated by discussion of 1798. The interpretation of 1798 was designed to mould public opinion and influence policy formation: the rebellion never passed into history, because it never passed out of politics. The debate aligned on divisions which predated and postdated 1798 and which the rebellion bisected. The historiography was deeply implicated in the existing political divisions; the war of words was an amplification and extension of the divisive 1790s debate and of the actual war which was precipitated by that politicisation. In his recent book *The Past in French History*, Robert Gildea has probed the uses of the past in French politics and culture. He concludes: 'What matters is myth, not in the sense of fiction, but in the sense of a construction of the past elaborated by a political community for its own ends.'[1] This construction of collective memory is one of the primary tasks of the historian, and the nature of the project can be clearly seen in the shifting and contested meaning of 1798 after 1798.

Sectarian, not secular

For conservatives, the immediate task in the aftermath of the rebellion was to create an exclusively sectarian narrative of the origin and progress of radicalism in the 1790s. By so doing, the revolutionary movement could be stripped of its ostensibly secular mask, revealing instead its real (and ghastly) popish face. As the outbreak of rebellion loomed, an insistent emphasis in conservative rhetoric popularised this interpretation.

By March 1798 John Beresford complacently noted that 'as the United Irishmen style all Protestants Orangemen, by and by we shall come to a war of religion'.[2] Edward Cooke argued that 'the popish spirit has been set up against the Protestant by representing every Protestant to be an Orangeman and by inculcating that every Orangeman has sworn to exterminate the papists'. He argued that 'nothing but real vigour can save us. . . . I fear relaxation and too much clemency, but the snake must be killed, not scotched.'[3] When the rebellion finally broke out at the end of May, loyalist commentators immediately stressed the 'popish plot' interpretation, using alleged southern barbarities to frighten Ulster radicals: 'It is now evident to every man that it is exclusively a popish plot to extirpate all Protestants, which has so terrified most of the Presbyterian republicans that they seem desirous to join with the Protestants of the Established Church in defence of the present state.'[4] Two days later, on 31 May, Fitzgibbon reported favourably to Auckland on the news from the north: 'The republicans there seem at length to have discovered that it is a popish game in the rest of the kingdom, to which they never meant seriously to lend their assistance.'[5] And, as Beresford reported to Auckland on the same day, the 'dreadful accounts from Wexford' in the loyalist press were immensely useful: 'Bad and shocking as the war is, it has its horrid use; for now there is a flying off of many Presbyterians who were united and the north considers it a religious war.'[6]

Lurid massacre stories were deliberately planted in the newspapers to blacken the southern rebels – stories which were circulated antecedent to the major atrocities of Scullabogue and Wexford Bridge, and which were especially aimed at the north. A typical example from *Faulkner's Dublin Journal* of 5 June claimed that the Wexford liberal Protestant Cornelius Grogan (who in reality joined the United Irishmen) had been murdered: 'The first eruption in that county was manifested in the most promiscuous massacres of all the Protestant families whom vigilance or precaution had not withdrawn into Enniscorthy or Wexford. . . . In their fury, no Protestant was spared and accounts even state that Mr Cornelius Grogan was one of their victims.'[7] Two days later the *Freeman's Journal* printed a fabricated rebel oath which had been given a bloodthirsty sectarian tinge: 'I, A.B.. do solemnly swear by our Lord Jesus Christ, who suffered on the cross, and by the Blessed Virgin Mary, that I will burn, destroy and murder all heretics, up to my knees in blood. So help me God.'[8]

In the disturbed context of the 1790s, with its arms raids, arrests, assassinations and obsessive militarism, these reports were successful in alarming Protestants. On the same day that the rebel oath was published, the Methodist preacher Adam Averell wrote to a friend claiming that 'about nine-tenths of the Protestants of County Wexford have been massacred'.[9] Fitzgibbon pointed out why such black propaganda was needed: 'In the north, nothing will keep the rebels quiet but a conviction that where treason had broken out, the rebellion is merely popish.'[10] The alarmist bishop of Ferns, Euseby Cleaver, concluded similarly that the prominent involvement of Catholic clergy had 'kept the Presbyterians quiet', as well as that 'the conduct of the French towards their friends the Americans has somewhat sickened them of that connexion and made them despair of the utopian government which was to have risen under the shade of the Tree of Liberty'.[11] Beresford admitted stoking the sectarian fire on 8 June, but was aware of its limits: 'The northern Protestants now are alarmed but we cannot make them more so lest we disgust the militia and papists of the army.'[12] Next day he noted: 'The only comfort we have is that the northern Protestants begin to see their danger and are arming in our favour, but the truth is that the government, I see, are afraid to trust them [the Orangemen] and particularly lest the papists of the militia and army take affront.'[13] It is at this same stage, and for the same reason, that accounts were spread of dissensions between the Defenders and the United Irishmen in Ulster, allegedly rooted in sectarian squabbles.

While the propaganda campaign was successful in the short term, its long-term consequences were bitterly divisive. In July 1798 Edward Hudson, his local agent, wrote from Armagh to Lord Charlemont: 'The brotherhood of affection is over; rancour and animosity to an increasing degree have succeeded.'[14] A year later he commented on the massive spread of the Orange Order among the Presbyterians who had hitherto held aloof from it: 'The word Protestant which was becoming obsolete in the North has regained its influence and all of that description seem to be drawing closer together. . . . The Orange system has principally contributed to this.'[15]

The matrix of memory: Musgrave's *Memoirs of the Various Rebellions*

Responses to the rebellion in print developed with remarkable rapidity. The first of these portrayed 1798 as the result of a deep-seated popish plot with tentacles stretching all the way to Rome and embedded in Irish history. It sought to establish parallels between 1641 and 1798, to depoliticise the 1790s, and to establish disreputable sectarian motives as the sole grounds of action. In a wider sense, the aim was to reverse, or at least stop, the process of incorporation of Catholics into the state, and especially to argue the case against Catholic Emancipation being part of the Union settlement. The classic formulation of this viewpoint was Sir Richard Musgrave's *Memoirs of the Various Rebellions in Ireland*, a huge compendium of material which quickly became notorious. The first edition, published simultaneously in London and Dublin in March 1801, sold out its 1,250 print-run in two months, despite its high price; a second edition, published later in the same year, sold another 1,250; and a third, Dublin-only edition in two volumes sold a further 1,350 copies.[16] The book's enormous vogue among ultra-loyalists produced an equal and opposite vilification from radicals.

Richard Musgrave came from a family of minor gentry in the lower Blackwater valley in west Waterford and shared to an exaggerated extent the francophobia and partisan popish paranoia which disfigured the Protestant gentry world of Munster. This had ruffled the surface calm of eighteenth-century life in four *causes célèbres* – the Cotter episode in the 1720s, the Morty Óg O'Sullivan case in the 1740s, the judicial murder of Father Nicholas Sheehy in the 1760s, and the Art Ó Laoghaire affair in the 1770s.[17] Thus, although Musgrave did not come from one of the storm-centres of the rebellion itself, his mindset was deeply influenced by these earlier episodes. Sheehy, for example, haunts his narrative, reappearing like Banquo's ghost at regular intervals. Musgrave was also involved in the sharp 1780s debate over the status of the Church of Ireland, crystallised in Bishop Richard Woodward's defence of its prerogatives against attacks on it by the Rightboys and by reformers like Grattan. Woodward's polemic unleashed a paper war and was the inaugurating moment in the debate over Protestant Ascendancy.[18] Woodward consciously refurbished the older protective polemics of John Temple and William King, the master narratives of Protestant Ireland which were regularly resorted to at times of stress, redefinition or Catholic resurgence. Temple's book, for example, was issued seven times in the period 1646–1812, and latterly with King in a cheap single-volume edition.[19]

Musgrave self-consciously worked to provide Protestant Ireland with an interpretation of the 1790s which could be welded seamlessly into the tradition of Temple, King and Woodward. The 1640s, the 1690s and the 1790s were interpreted as the three great traumas of Protestant Ireland. In all three decades Musgrave identified the same recurrent problem – the rooted and inveterate hostility of the Roman Catholic Church to the English Protestant interest in Ireland. Therefore the same style, the same tropes, the same polemics, the same warnings developed by Temple and King were equally appropriate and necessary for the 1790s. In words that could have been lifted directly from his predecessors, Musgrave argued that 'It is not what is erroneously and ridiculously called emancipation that the mass of the Irish Roman Catholics want: it is the extirpation or expulsion of the Protestants, the exclusive occupation of the island for themselves and its separation from England.'[20]

As early as July 1798 he began collecting materials which he modelled on the revered Temple precedent of authenticated affidavits by Protestant sufferers – the celebrated depositions of 1641, the interpretation of which remained at the heart of the historiographical divides of the late eighteenth century. As well as personally paying for the transport and accommodation costs of those (especially from Wexford and Wicklow) who came to Dublin to swear them (allegedly from fears of doing so in their own counties), Musgrave was also supplied with specimens damaging to Catholics by ultra-loyalists in sympathy with his project: from Wexford, Hunter Gowan, Archibald Hamilton Jacob, James Boyd, John Lyster, Richard Newton King, Stephen and Abel Ram and Standish Lowcay; from Carlow, Robert Cornwall and Samuel Carpenter; from Wicklow, Rev. Edward Bayley; and from Dublin, John Beresford. Close examination of the affidavits reveals that they were written down from oral examination of the deponents and that the line of questioning was designed to elicit testimony as damning as possible to the United Irishmen, and even more so to the Catholics.[21]

A second conduit of information for Musgrave was a questionnaire distributed with the co-operation of certain Church of Ireland bishops and their clergy. Musgrave was friendly with William Newcome, Archbishop of Armagh, and with Thomas Percy, Bishop of Dromore, and he also received strong support from the conservative wing of ecclesiastical opinion in the 1790s, especially Euseby Cleaver, Bishop of Ferns, and William Bennet, Bishop of Cloyne. Musgrave's queries fell on stony ground in areas with less doctrinaire bishops – notably with the Whig bishops, William Dickson in Down and Connor, Joseph Stock in Killala, and Thomas Lewis O'Beirne in Ossory. Some of Musgrave's bitterest invective was reserved precisely for these enemies within and for their political fellow-travellers like Grattan and Moira. Grattan acquired the nickname of 'the up-and-down doctor' in Dublin because Trinity College, having commissioned his portrait when his popularity was at its height, refused to hang it when he opposed the Established Church over tithes; it was hung during the Fitzwilliam viceroyalty, when Grattan enjoyed a brief moment of power, but was then removed again and hidden behind the Provost's chair, before being finally banished when Grattan was vilified after the rebellion broke out.[22]

The questionnaire submitted by Musgrave in Ulster shows clearly that he was seeking information to buttress an argument already formed, not to elicit the materials for an interpretation. This is apparent, for example, in a letter written to George Lenox-Conyngham on 27 April 1799:

> I have undertaken to write a history of the rebellion, and I have got very copious information of what passed in Leinster and Munster, but I have little or no knowledge of what occurred in Ulster. May I request then the favour of your assistance as to what happened in the county of Derry? For the sake of per-spicuity, I submit the following queries to you:
>
> 1st   When did the Defenders first appear there?
> 2nd Were they not exclusively of the popish religion?
> 3rd   What seemed to have been their design?
> 4th   When did they join with, and become subservient to, the United Irishmen?
> 5th   Did the papists and Presbyterians ever cordially unite, and at what time, in the rebellion?
>
> From the great antipathy which ever existed between these sects, I am much at a loss to know how they could ever be made to unite. I have been assured that the Presbyterians quitted the papists as soon as they discovered that they were impelled by that sanguinary spirit which was ever peculiar to their religion. Any anecdotes of atrocities committed by the United Irishmen and Defenders will be very acceptable. I don't mention the names of any gentlemen who are so good as to favour me with their assistance.[23]

Musgrave's particular concerns were to depoliticise the northern rebellion, to eliminate any linkage between it and the Leinster one, to erase any signs of a political rapprochement between Presbyterians and Catholics, to stress the overwhelmingly sectarian nature of the United Irishmen, and to demonstrate that the Presbyterians quickly quitted the movement once the errors of their ways became apparent. Musgrave's aim here was to reattach Presbyterians to the fraying Protestant consensus which had unravelled in the 1790s. Musgrave exaggerated or invented stories of Presbyterian–Catholic tension in 1798, repeating with relish a rumour relayed to him by Bishop Percy:

> The rebel army at Ballynahinch consisted of Presbyterians and other denomina-tions of Protestant dissenters, with few, if any, Roman Catholics, as 2,000 of them deserted the night before the battle which inflamed the Presbyterians very much against them. [*Footnote*: They remained about two miles off, on the

> Seaford road, and could not refrain from expressing their satisfaction that the
> Protestants were mutually destroying each other.][24]

James Hope and Charles Teeling were later to refute this *canard*.[25] Musgrave
also emphasised, with dogged determination, the idea that Protestant United
Irishmen at the last moment invariably repented their involvement in the
rebellion – that as the scales fell from their infatuated eyes, they realised they were
being duped by the Catholics. This motif can be seen in his account of Thomas
Bacon, the Presbyterian minister James Porter and Bagenal Harvey, among
others.[26] An extension of this argument lays great stress on the numbers of
erstwhile United Irish Presbyterians who flocked into the yeomanry and Orange
Order once they recognised the true nature of the Catholics: 'General Knox
assured me that numbers of Presbyterians who were united became yeomen and
offered their services and received arms from him in the district he commanded
last summer, about the end of June when the Wexford atrocities were known.'[27]

Musgrave's intentions become transparent once one looks at the allocation of
space within his massive tome of approximately 1,000 pages. A mere 2 per cent
is assigned to Antrim and Down, compared with 62 per cent to Wexford, and
four-fifths of the book is devoted to Leinster. Musgrave's inclusion of Ulster
material came late in the day and was not part of his original conception of the
book. Even within his narrow Ulster focus, Musgrave's theme is that Anglicans
were the sole loyal sect in the 1790s, squeezed between inveterate papists and
foolishly radical Presbyterians. Against the historical record and in favour of this
theme, he depicts the Armagh disturbances of the 1780s and 1790s as being
between Presbyterians and Catholics, not Anglicans and Catholics.

Musgrave's aim was also to paint the rebels in the most unflattering light
possible. Terms like 'rabble', 'barbarous', 'ignorant', 'savage', 'fanatic', 'horrid',
'cruel' and 'vulgar' pepper his descriptions of the United Irishmen and especially their Catholic manifestations. Musgrave explicitly repeats key phrases
out of Temple, while at the lurid high points of Scullabogue and Wexford
Bridge he reaches back into an even older set of tropes derived from Foxe's
Book of Martyrs. The cumulative effect is to represent Irish Catholics as barbarians frozen in the formaldehyde of seventeenth-century antagonisms, steeped
in their superstitious stupor. The ultimate result is to present them as depoliticised, even dehumanised. In describing the rural poor of the 'remote and
barbarous parts' of County Cork, Musgrave claims that they 'were but one
step above animal instinct'.[28] Thus, for Musgrave, the Catholic poor represented the real heart of Irish darkness.

The Union: from Protestant state to Protestant empire

Musgrave was a devout Anglican, and a central theme of his analysis is the
absolute necessity of maintaining the privileges of the Church of Ireland. The
term 'Protestant state' is repeated to mantra-like effect at recurrent intervals in

the text. Musgrave was obsessed by Presbyterian and Catholic attacks on the Established Church and by the possible collusion of a backsliding British government in these attacks. This fear also informs Musgrave's anxieties about the possibilities of betrayal in the Union settlement – Emancipation being dangled as a *douceur* to curry Catholic support for the Union. He was equally afraid that arguments about the nature of Catholicism internationally – in Canada, for example, whose francophone Catholics had been incorporated painlessly into the empire, or in Switzerland and Germany, where Catholics shared a state with seeming benignity – might be imported into the domestic debate with ruinous consequences. He is therefore at pains to depict Irish Catholicism as *sui generis*: 'No parallel can be drawn between the popery of Ireland and that of any other country in Europe.'[29] Refuting the suggestion that Irish Catholics could be incorporated into the British state just as easily as Scotch Presbyterians had been, he argued that

> The lower class of the Irish are traitorous towards the state, and fraudful, ferocious and sanguinary towards such of their fellow subjects as differ from them in religion; and for this reason the Scotch peasant, or mechanic, differs as much from the Irish, as a house dog does from a wolf or a fox.[30]

While Musgrave contemptuously rejected the Union-with-Emancipation scenario, the idea of a Protestant Union had a visceral attraction for him as a necessary corrective in the zero-sum game of sectarian Irish arithmetic, where the oppressive weight of Catholic numbers threatened to obliterate the political control of the frail Anglican minority. It was this distrust of Catholic numbers which allowed the Act of Union to pass. Given Catholic dominance, it was wise for Protestants to negative it by joining the British state. John Wilson Croker put the point bluntly: 'Of Great Britain and Ireland, [Catholics] were an inconsiderable sect; of solitary Ireland, an important majority.'[31] At a stroke, the Union converted Catholics from an 80 per cent majority in Ireland to being at best a 20 per cent minority in the United Kingdom. These revised sectarian sums appealed to Musgrave himself. In July 1799 he noted approvingly: 'In a menacing tone, the papists have told us for some years "we are 3 to 1". With the Union, we may retort "we are 11 to 3".'[32] It was also from this motive that Musgrave could claim that 'my fears for the Protestant religion and the Protestant state have made me a warm advocate of the Union'.[33]

The loss of an independent legislature did not weigh heavily on him; indeed, he was inclined to trace disturbances out-of-doors to incitement from within the portals of the House of Commons, attributing the ignition of smouldering discontent to the parliament, 'a great volcano which sets the country alight'. This was due to 'our political prize-fighters and venal orators', and it was only they who opposed the Union: 'I compare the House of Commons to a ladder which leads to a rich larder and them to be so many monkeys who are afraid of being deprived of the means of ascending to it.'[34]

The Union offered Musgrave another balancing strategy: the word 'empire' was consciously used by him to replicate his earlier insistence on 'state', and both terms were pitted by him against the radical appeal to the 'nation'. The imperial paradigm was welcomed by conservative Protestants as a suitable surrogate for their lost state and as a solution to the identity problem posed by their precipitate abandonment of a national legislature. Musgrave goes so far as to call it the 'Protestant empire', deliberately invoking and reformatting his earlier use of 'Protestant state'.[35] This sense of attachment to a wider imperial elite culture quickly eclipsed the older insistence on national rights. As another Protestant commentator acerbically agreed, 'it was surely safer to assume an imperial identity, rather than reverting to the crude formula of colony and metropolis', especially given the painful lessons of 1798:

> The colony has learned in a bloody school the vanity of her ambitions: she feels that she is not and cannot be independent of this sustaining hand which succours and upholds her. Three millions of natives and Catholics forbid it.[36]

In choosing the empire and copperfastening the position of Irish Protestants within it as a privileged minority, Musgrave (and with him conservative Protestantism in general) effectively ceded the concept of the nation to Irish Catholics. This explains the curious trajectory of Irish political nationalism in the 1790s, which entered the decade as a Protestant phenomenon but exited it as a Catholic one.

In a different context, Linda Colley has stressed that the self-definition of Great Britain emerged essentially from heightened awareness of the intractable other: British identity was invented after 1700, consolidating around what Britons had in common, rather than what divided them. At the heart of this self-definition was Protestantism, envisioning Britain as insular bastion, circled by a seething Catholic sea and constantly besieged by continental, and especially French, Catholicism. War and the threat of war with France unified Britons in an intensely shared hostility. In the nineteenth century the aggressive British imperial mission played the same role, bringing prolonged and pervasive awareness of an alien and recalcitrant empire. From this often anxious contact, self-definition clarified.[37] Extending Colley's argument into an Irish context, one can see how Catholicism became that highly insistent other, even more visible because it was internalised in the state itself, against which British Protestant identity was defined. In this sense, Musgrave's arguments were tailored to suit not just Irish but also British Protestant prejudices about Ireland and, more especially, about Irish Catholics who joined the French as the alien *doppelganger* of British identity. Irish Catholics could then be allocated the role of the enemy within, the brutish barbarians against whom British civility was measured.

Bibles, not beads: the evangelical context

The rebellion stimulated the evangelical wing of Irish and more broadly British Protestantism which argued that the correct response to 1798 was a revamped proselytising mission to Irish papists. This endeavour appealed to English dissent, increasingly aligned to conservative politics and determined to breach the hitherto impervious superstitious shield of Irish Catholicism.[38] The evangelical upsurge met a receptive response, not among Catholics, but among anxious, vulnerable Protestant communities, in south Ulster in particular. Here the triple appeals of providentialism (the 'miraculous' escape of Irish Protestants in 1798), eschatology (a conservative reading of millenarianism) and emotionalism (a personal, born-again Christian faith) led to a doubling of Methodist numbers between 1798 and 1802. Itinerant Irish-speaking field-preachers like Gideon Ouseley, Charles Graham and James McQuigg were joined from Kentucky by the flamboyant frontier preacher, Lorenzo Dow, and by the returned South Sea missionary, William Gregory. And this urgency was not confined solely to Methodism; the Presbyterians founded the Evangelical Society of Ulster in October 1798, also in response to the rebellion and inspired by the American 'Second Awakening'. In their assessment, the 1790s had witnessed a dangerous dilution of religious fervour:

> Formality, lukewarmness, the distemper of the Laodiceans, appears to encase many. Professors are not so cold as to lay aside the profession and form of religion altogether, nor so hot as to have any lively practice of it.[39]

As well as being aggressively anti-Catholic, the revamped evangelical mission linked Protestant morality, social stability and political loyalty. The London Hibernian Society observed in 1806: 'The hope therefore that the Irish will ever be a tranquil and a loyal people, and still more that piety and virtue will flourish among them, must be built on the anticipated reduction of popery.' It was strongly supported from Britain, finding a mission on its doorstep 'in a land of beads not bibles'.[40] The fund-raising propaganda emanating from these Irish missionaries, especially the Methodists, was lurid in the extreme, because bloodthirsty Irish papists had to compete as objects of missionary attention – and funding – with the lascivious South Sea islanders, cannibal Africans and scalping Indians.

It is within this evangelical effervescence that Musgrave's religious arguments must be contextualised. His endorsement of a renewed onslaught on Irish Catholicism, a revamped Reformation, is directed at his perceived British audience. He advocates a panoply of long-discredited instruments to achieve this aim – Charter Schools, the foundling hospital, the creation of strictly Protestant new towns on the model of Bandon, trebling the number of Protestant clergymen, and the reimposition of the penal laws.[41] There is no essential difference in outlook here from that of Temple a century and a half earlier. These political and religious arguments slotted neatly into a pre-existing ideological template – a text-based matrix of memory, ranging from Foxe through Temple and King to Woodward. Fundamental lessons could be learned from all of them, and Musgrave's arguments here re-echoed those of wider Protestant opinion.

One lesson was the unvarying and unrelenting nature of Irish history: 'We find in the atrocities of 1798 a revival of 1641.'[42] Popery was 'the motive of all these wars, the spring of all the massacres which have stained this country from the bridge of Portadown to the strand of Wexford'.[43] A second was the necessity for Protestant unity, especially between Anglican and Dissenter, 'for there is nothing more certain than that they are bound in one sheaf and, should the bond once be loosened, all will be scattered'.[44] At Mullingar on 1 July 1798 the local clergyman preached 'a sermon on Ireland's deliverance from popish slavery' in which he yoked together the 1640s, 1690s and 1790s; dealing with providential precedents, he noted that 'we must not pass by those of the present time; when a cloud hung over the kingdom a few days back, how wonderfully has the tempest been scattered'. The Protestant wind of the Armada period still haunted Irish shores: 'God breathed and they were scattered'. Judge Robert Day praised the 'God of mercy, whose breath had heretofore miraculously dispersed the infidel fleet'.[45]

But providence and prudence were closely linked; the narrow escapes in 1796 and 1798 indicated the necessity both for renewed moral fervour and for Protestant unity to counteract the debilitating lassitude, at once religious and political, which had infected Irish Protestantism in the 1790s, when 'more dangerous than all, many among ourselves began to be infected by a strange apathy and lukewarmness towards things formerly considered as claiming our warmest interest and attachment'. These sentiments strengthened the case for the Orange Order, which 'has given to us an animating and seasonable impulse and has tended to rouse us to a sense of our danger and our duties'.[46] Faced with the reality of what had happened in Leinster, Ulster Presbyterians

> became affrighted at their own misconduct; they awoke from their dreams of reform and separation and each man, shocked at the atrocities of his allies, or fearing for himself, the insurgents of Ulster listened to the voice of truth and reason, and quietly returned to their looms and their senses.[47]

Retribution or appeasement? the post-rebellion debate

Looked at more narrowly, Musgrave's aims were all directed at the opinion-forming and decision-making levels of British high politics – to establish a solely sectarian reading of the rebellion, to prevent any attack on the position of the Church of Ireland, to decouple the questions of Catholic Emancipation and the Union settlement, and to sabotage Cornwallis's lenient line towards the defeated rebels. Musgrave was under no illusions as to the extent of British knowledge about Ireland: 'The mass of the people of England are as ignorant of the real state of Ireland as they are of the most remote regions in the torrid or frigid zones.' Therefore 'I considered it as an important, nay, a sacred duty, to lay before them the real state of Ireland.'[48] His subsequent defence of his book was that 'it was written for the purpose of giving the British cabinet and parliament at present, and posterity hereafter, an accurate narrative of the late rebellion and a fair representation of the state of Ireland for many years previous to that dreadful event'.[49] The book may have successfully influenced British opinion. William Bennet, the Bishop of Cloyne, an experienced political analyst, argued that the book's influence had been felt most effectually outside Ireland: 'In England, certainly, the work was of the utmost service in making the people acquainted with the state of Ireland which opposition speeches, pamphlets and party histories . . . had completely concealed from them.'[50] The historian Edward Gibbon encapsulated perfectly the supercilious metropolitan attitude which Musgrave was trying to educate: 'Of Ireland, I know nothing, and while I am writing the decline of a great empire, I have not leisure to attend to the affairs of a remote and petty province.'[51]

Musgrave's volume was also a very specific intervention in an Irish debate – opposing the Cornwallis line of leniency towards the defeated rebels in the hope of building a consensus on the Union question. To achieve this, Cornwallis had sidelined the old 'kitchen cabinet' of Foster, Fitzgibbon, Beresford and Cooke which had dictated policy to his two weak and easily influenced predecessors, Camden and Westmorland. Cornwallis relied instead on his own judgement, rather than become a prisoner of these wily old hands who had retained a decisive grip on the reins of power since 1795. The British cabinet, preoccupied by war, had left Ireland to its own devices, thereby copperfastening the role of the 'cabinet' around the Lord Lieutenant, who imposed policy on the ineffectual viceroys as recompense for their role in managing both parliament and the daily administrative routine. If the price of British negligence, viceregal incompetence and an over-powerful 'cabinet' was Protestant Ascendancy and junta power, Pitt was willing to pay it – as long as Ireland did not obstruct imperial intentions at a fraught period.

The 1798 rebellion exposed the bankruptcy of the Dublin Castle administration, the arrogance of senior Irish politicians, and the futility of the Irish parliament itself. The decks would now be ruthlessly cleared on the ship of state, and among those swept overboard by Cornwallis's new broom were the old cabinet crew. A Whig commentator remarked on the change of management practice by the Lord Lieutenant: 'He is open to information from every man, but consults no man. He sees the ruinous effect of the late administration and does not favour the opinion of the old cabinet.'[52] His amnesty bill, his deal with the United Irishmen, his abolition of further show-trials, his close scrutiny of courts martial, his overtures to the Catholics and, above all, his independence caused intense flutterings among the conservative dovecotes, distressing even the resolutely anglophile Fitzgibbon. Fears of a sell-out surfaced: Cornwallis – or 'Cropwallis' – was wooing the United Irishmen and the Catholics to a pro-Union stance by his deferential treatment of croppies; even worse, the Emancipation carrot was openly dangled in front of papist noses as a Union incentive. An English militia officer caught the adverse reaction in Dublin loyalist circles to Cornwallis's policy of giving the rebels amnesty: 'The Orangemen, Protestants etc. of whom the yeomanry is principally composed are raving mad at Lord Cornwallis's conciliatory measures.'[53]

Political arguments in the immediate aftermath of the rebellion centred on the treatment of the defeated rebels. A split quickly opened in Protestant opinion between ultra-conservative and more liberal approaches. The loyalists wanted measures 'taken to eradicate if possible the whole deluded race – a horrid necessity but everyone here seems convinced of it and that humanity must be out of the question'.[54] Another commentator described the ultras as follows: 'Gibbets and executions seem to haunt their imaginations: they looked forward with a savage joy to the sufferings which they would inflict on the rebels when they were taken: their whole legislative wisdom was punishment and every punishment was death.'[55] The Marquis of Buckingham reported the tone among this group in July 1798 as being

> a project of extirpation of which all good Protestants talk with great composure as the only cure for the present and the only preventive for the future, nor do I find one who does not believe that it is in the interest and intention of Great Britain to fight that battle *usque ad internecionem*.[56]

By contrast, liberals lauded Cornwallis's policy of appeasement: 'God knows blood enough has been unfeelingly shed already.'[57] The split is neatly summarised in a letter from the Irish M.P. Benjamin Chapman to Shelburne in England on 13 October 1798:

> Even loyalty is divided here into two violent parties. The first may be determined the old, or high Court party; the latter, the new or low Court party. The first breathes nothing but extermination. Mr Pitt is the idol of their worship; with them, he possesses infallibility and omnipotence and all who do not implicitly submit to every operation of his or see or speak in defence of the late Irish administration and do not consider this a war of religion are branded with the appellation of traytors and republicans. Even our present viceroy who seems more inclined to the Catholic party is not spared. The very best virtues of the human heart are traduced as your Lordship remembers in the time of Dion; those virtues are nicknamed and melted down into the contiguous vices. Thus patience becomes stolidity, mercy – pusillanimity, and no man who wishes to be considered well affected dares to compassionate the afflicted or succour the distressed. Popery is worse than witchcraft, and intolerance is the pledge of constitutional attachment. The design of an incorporating union of both kingdoms is at the same time trumpeted by the zealots of the first party in order to explain every concession and to account for every forbearance of the utmost extremity.[58]

Musgrave clearly positioned himself in the hardline camp, claiming that

> Cornwallis has offended the leading members of the Irish Privy Council by the bluntness of his manners and by never consulting them, and all the loyal subjects by his indiscriminate and ill-judged lenity to notorious traitors, which I am convinced he adapted to conciliate the papists. I know that monstrous favours have been promised them to gain their support and that government relies much on it.[59]

In an attempt to apply pressure, Musgrave sought – and received – permission to dedicate his book to Cornwallis. When it appeared in March 1801, Cornwallis was outraged by the transparent effort to derail his conciliation project and immediately rescinded the permission to use his name:

> Had his Excellency been apprised of the contents and nature of the work, he never would have lent the sanction of his name to a book which tends so strongly to revive the dreadful animosities which have so long distracted this country, and which it is the duty of every good subject to endeavour to compose.[60]

Musgrave was philosophical about this rebuke and its subsequent publication: 'I am convinced the Protestants of the north, who are numerous and opulent, will purchase the whole of the second edition in a short time from its publication.'[61] In a wider perspective, Musgrave's efforts were designed to further the invention of a tradition for Irish Protestants, to encode the matrix of memory in distinctly political ways. Text and tradition would be mutually reinforcing; ultimately the Protestant memory of '98 would be filtered and then focused through this partisan prism.

Closing the chasm: the liberal line

While Musgrave, Duigenan and other conservative commentators concentrated on creating this charged reading of the rebellion, their voice was not that of a monolithic Protestant community, but of a faction within it.[62] An opposed reading was articulated by the liberal wing, creating a counterpoise to the damaging weight of Musgrave's text, most notably in the works by James Gordon, Joseph Stock and Francis Plowden.[63] All three addressed the issue of what style of government made sense in a polarised society. If over half a million people had been sworn into the United Irishmen, as the government's own reports claimed, then hardline advocacy of retribution would deluge the country in rivers of blood. Following the Cornwallis line of conciliation rather than coercion, these Whig texts downplayed the rebels' responsibility for the rising, were sympathetic to Catholic rights, and were pro-Union. They belonged to that school of thought epitomised by Lord Altamont: 'It appears to me advisable that the rebellion and all connected with it should be let sink into oblivion to avoid continuous quarrels, animosities and bloodshedding.'[64]

Thus Joseph Stock, an Anglican bishop, and James Gordon, an Anglican clergyman, wrote notably understated accounts of the rebellion which were remarkably vague on the origins and progress of the United Irishmen, but stressed instead the essential loyalty of Catholics, assigning the outbreak of the rebellion to the refusal of parliamentary reform and Catholic Emancipation, consequent military provocations, law-and-order excesses, and the rise of the sectarian Orange Order. These books were explicitly designed to undermine the authority and credibility of Musgrave's account. The Whig view of Musgrave survives in Barrington's much quoted pen-picture, where he is ridiculed as 'generally in his senses, except on the abstract topics of politics, religion, martial law, his wife, the Pope, the Pretender, the Jesuits, Napper Tandy and the whipping-post'. Barrington also related with gusto the tale of Sir Richard's attempt to throttle his sleeping wife, under the apprehension that he was struggling with a popish rebel.[65]

This Whig voice is a valuable reminder that there was no monolithic Protestant identity in eighteenth-century Ireland; not all Anglicans were pro-government, either before or after 1798, and these political splits, which both predated and postdated 1798, were carried over intact into the historiographical debate. Indeed, it was precisely the existence of these damaging splits which heightened tensions within and between the ruling elites in Ireland and Britain. Writing from within this liberal Protestant stance, Stock, Gordon and Plowden all gave enormous offence to more conservative loyalists.[66] Stock's relatively sympathetic account of the rebel occupation of Killala during the French invasion may have led to the blocking of the episcopal advancement of this talented man, leaving him stranded in his poor west-coast diocese until 1810. These Whig historians were seen as apologists for the United Irishmen, overtly pro-Cornwallis and covertly pro-Catholic, and as hired propagandists for the Union. The Union was supported most strenuously by anti-establishment and liberal Protestants and was bitterly opposed by conservatives (like John Foster) who saw in an Irish parliament the only long-term assurance of protection for Protestant privileges and who favoured a tough law-and-order stance. The Union could be carried precisely because of this lack of a monolithic Protestant response, allied to Catholic acquiescence (which derived from Catholics' interpretation of the Union as a necessary precursor to Emancipation).[67]

The Whig historians wrote also to rebuke the rabid Musgrave account. They stressed the rebellion's local and occasional, rather than its political origins, emphasised the loyalty of the Catholics, and argued against further exacerbating the existing divisions within the country. The liberals constantly addressed the issue of governing a country traumatised by political conflict, so deeply riven that the possibility of consensus had disappeared from the political agenda. They tried to disperse the occult and divisive power of the past by projecting the Union as a new beginning, presenting the future, not the past, as the pivotal temporal parameter, and appealing to the electorate of optimism, not of fear. These arguments were reiterated in choric fashion as the Union debate intensified. Fitzwilliam articulated the classic Whig argument in favour of the Cornwallis line: 'The whole system of the country, the principle of conqueror and conquered, of negroes and planters, must be done away.'[68] In that spirit, the Union was initially welcomed by English Whigs as a liberating measure: 'Union will really emancipate the Irish people; it will emancipate them from party government; it will emancipate them from the tyranny of passion, from the despotism of prejudice.' The English Whig George Moore posed the question whether the 'virtual representation' of the English parliament existed in its Irish equivalent: 'Does this kind of representation exist in Ireland? Do our representatives, as they are called, sympathise with the feelings and opinions of the great body of the nation? Can the national pulse be felt through its acts?'[69] The English and Irish Whig judgement was that the unreformed Irish parliament did not represent Irish opinion, but only that small segment of it epitomised by the Orangemen:

> A set of men, whose opinion is the only thing that can be called a public opinion in Ireland, have arrayed themselves in clubs and lodges to maintain this prejudice, to preserve all religious and civil animosities, pure and unmitigated, in the country, and the name of the tolerant and heroic William is made the rallying point of fanaticism and persecution.[70]

In these circumstances, a breach opened between ruler and ruled, between the legislature and the people, between rich and poor, between Protestant and Catholic. It was the task of post-Union Irish political management to close that breach, so spectacularly manifested in the rebellion itself. Even though change might be slow – 'generations must pass over before this chasm, which has swallowed the happiness of so many, can be closed'[71] – public opinion must be coaxed in this direction if Ireland was to enjoy a stable political system:

> It is not from the Castle, or the Viceroy, that amnesty and oblivion must be proclaimed; it must be a mutual compact between the upper and lower orders in Ireland. Let resentment and rebellion sleep in one tomb, and no Gallic incantation shall ever be equal to awake either.[72]

And here the task of the liberal historian was clear with respect to the 1798 rebellion:

> It is the duty of every man, not to widen, but to help to fill up the moral breach, and it must be the aim of every good man, as it lately has been that of the Bishop of Killala [Stock] to counteract a spirit of animosity, bigotry, revenge and distrust, which would most effectually mar every endeavour at improvement.[73]

The English Whig George Cooper, visiting Ireland in 1799, attacked the basis of the Musgrave project:

> I hope that the design which was advertised in Dublin while I was there, of blazoning out the details of that unhappy event, the rebellion, will be given up. When the interests of both parties are on the eve of adjustment, and I trust of reconciliation, past differences should receive a general amnesty.[74]

In this mood, Francis Plowden, an English Catholic lawyer, was hired by the Addington administration to woo Catholic acceptance of the Union, even in the aftermath of the failure to accompany it with Catholic Emancipation. Plowden's reading of the rebellion followed the liberal line of Gordon and Stock, treating their accounts as neutral texts by disinterested Anglican divines. They could then be used to undermine Musgrave. But Plowden also places great polemical stress on Catholic and even United Irish passivity, interpreting the rebellion's origins as a defensive response to mistaken government policy, military excesses and Orange provocations. Active agency is downplayed; instead the Burkean line is reiterated – that Catholics *en masse* had a natural tendency towards loyalty and obedience. Catholics are represented as reluctant participants in the politicisation of the 1790s.

Plowden's analysis was well received among Irish Whigs. Henry Grattan praised this 'manly and able production', written 'against the tide of power and prejudice', endorsing the conclusion that 'the Castle system had caused the rebellion to break out' just as it had 'before created the disaffection'. He also agreed that new government policies allowed Catholics to assert their traditional loyalty: 'Allegiance advances as the system retires.'[75] Similarly, Fitzwilliam believed that 'every man who feels an interest in the unity of the British and Irish people will feel more obligation to him whose literary labours produce principles of harmony, conciliation and goodfellowship, than from all the most skilful artists in coercive retribution'. He endorsed Plowden's conclusion that the real problem in Ireland was 'the divide between conqueror and conquered, a distinction systematically and industriously kept up, not by the animosity of the conquered, but by the policy of the conquerors'.[76]

Walking the tightrope: the Catholic Church's response

A recurrent theme in this liberal approach is to minimise the 'war of religion' argument put forward by Musgrave. This buttressed the Cornwallis policy; soon after his arrival in June 1798, he noted 'the folly which has been too prevalent in this quarter of substituting the word Catholicism, instead of Jacobinism, as the foundation of the present rebellion'.[77] This interpretation played into the hands of the Catholics, who were determined to avoid the odium being cast on them. At this time the papal legate in London could report that 'everybody is fully convinced that the word religion has only been an instrument to seduce the ignorant multitude during the rebellion'.[78] A further possibility existed in this approach: it encouraged a rapprochement between liberal Protestants and Catholics in terms of the legacy of '98 and facilitated the construction of a pro-Union alliance against the anti-Union conservative and Orange faction. In this sense, the Union was, accordingly, a humiliating defeat for Protestant Ireland, which lost its parliament, the most precious emblem of a separate identity, and with it its century-old project of representing itself alone as the Irish nation. The flawed flowering of Protestant nationalism did not survive the boundaries of the eighteenth century, and the rebellion effectively undid the Williamite settlement.[79]

In another sense, the Act of Union could be passed because of Catholic acquiescence, an acquiescence derived from fear of being abandoned to the aftermath of a rebellion for which they were blamed. A vindictive witch-hunt against politically active Catholics, the wave of chapel-burnings in Wexford and elsewhere and the rancorous invective of Musgrave all heightened Catholic fears of a protracted Protestant backlash, connived at by parliament. For Catholics, the Act of Union was initially welcomed as removing what Burke had called that 'crazy and infected structure' which crushed them in the eighteenth century.[80] As Bishop Hussey expressed it, Irish Catholics 'would prefer a union with the Beys and Mamelukes of Egypt to that of being under the iron rod of the Mamelukes of Ireland'.[81] The Union also wiped out the rotten boroughs which had underpinned Protestant control of the Irish legislature. The astute John Foster realised immediately that 'the union has accomplished for [Irish Catholics] the reform without which they could never hope to be of consequence in parliament'.[82]

It was, therefore, essential for conservative Catholics to distance themselves utterly from the rebellion and, in particular, to convince English public opinion of their basic loyalty. Catholic apologists claimed that the geography of the rebellion unequivocally demonstrated that it could not be laid at their door as a religious war. If it were, surely the most Catholic areas would have been the most involved in sedition, whereas they were the least. This was the argument fed to the English Whig visitor George Cooper in 1798: 'It was no war of religion, because none of the Catholics of Cork, Waterford, Limerick, Clare, Galway, or any part of the Kingdom, except those few counties in which the rebellion broke out, were at all implicated in it.'[83] A pamphleteer observed: 'The counties of Wexford and Wicklow, the seat of rebellion, may be considered as Protestant; the provinces of Munster and Connaught, where the Roman Catholics prevail, were never engaged in rebellion.'[84]

But this still left the embarrassing problem of explaining away the well-publicised leadership role of Catholic clergy in Wexford.[85] This issue had, indeed, sparked the initial paper war after the rebellion, when a series of pamphlets (inevitably initiated by Musgrave) had argued the 'popish plot' interpretation in terms of these highly visible priest leaders.[86] Clerical complicity, in this view, reached even as far as James Caulfield, the Bishop of Ferns, who had been resident in Wexford town throughout the short-lived Wexford Republic. Caulfield had therefore publicly to defend both himself and his clergy: in this he allowed himself to be utterly guided by John Thomas Troy, the formidable Archbishop of Dublin, who had developed good contacts with Dublin Castle since the establishment of Maynooth.[87]

Troy encouraged Caulfield to recruit two skilled Catholic pamphleteers, Matthew D'Arcy and James Clinch; they would 'ghost-write' Caulfield's defence with information supplied by the bishop. Their argument presented the rebel priests as unrepresentative, a hot-headed handful who, in Caulfield's own stinging words, were 'excommunicated priests, drunken and profligate couple-beggars, the very faeces of the Church'.[88] These pamphlets also accused loyalists like Musgrave of deliberately keeping the embers of rebellion hot. He was 'still employed in sowing the provocations of warfare, in exciting fear and pretending fearfulness, in dividing the people, in assaulting life and in slandering to death those whom it is not permitted to slaughter'.[89] Caulfield also harped on the idea that the local oppression of Catholics was the sole cause of the rebellion:

> I am persuaded in my own mind we shall be better off than ever if the ruling powers are convinced that the late unfortunate and wicked rising was not on the part of the Catholics a rebellion against the King but against the Protestant Ascendancy and Orangemen.[90]

In this vein, a Castle informer reported Catholic reaction to the first wave of executions of leading Protestant United Irishmen: 'The Catholics exult at the present executions – it takes the odium off them – [and they] say the idea can remain no longer of it being a popish plot or massacre.'[91]

Troy himself was well aware of the torturous path that Catholics had to negotiate in the difficult post-rebellion period, balancing the need to placate English politicians against Roman imperatives. This involved the dreaded issue of the limited crown veto on Catholic episcopal appointments which Troy had reluctantly accepted in principle as a necessary evil in the Union settlement:

> We all wish to remain as we are, and we would so, were it not that too many of the clergy were active in the wicked rebellion or did not oppose it. . . . If we had rejected the proposal in toto, we would be considered here as rebels. . . . If we agreed to it without reference to Rome, we would be branded schismatics. We were between Scylla and Charybdis.[92]

Caulfield was grateful for Troy's masterly public relations campaign against the 'monster' Musgrave; he was even moved to declare that 'St Peter's chair would not be an extravagant reward for . . . [Troy's] great, judicious and zealous efforts'.[93]

Convenient amnesia: O'Connell and '98

Troy's campaign had successfully presented the Catholics as docile and deferential and as the innocent victims of Protestant Ascendancy malevolence in the 1790s. This argument acquired an additional curious twist as the Catholic Emancipation campaign hotted up – that it was the turbulent and disorderly Presbyterians who seduced the law-abiding Catholics into radicalism and then rebellion, before treacherously abandoning them. This convenient amnesia was promoted by Daniel O'Connell, erasing his own past as a sworn United Irish member in the 1790s. The spymaster Francis Higgins described him to Dublin Castle on 7 March 1798:

He waits to be called to the bar here, merely to please a very rich old uncle, but he is one of the most abominable and blood thirsty republicans I ever heard. He is open and avowed in the most daring language. His place of rendevouz is at the Public Library, Eustace Street, where a private room is devoted to the association of the leaders of the United Society. [94]

Faced with imminent arrest, O'Connell had to flee the city, escaping in a potato boat to Clonakilty. He subsequently carefully distanced himself and the Catholics from involvement in a revolutionary movement. Asked in 1825 if there were any Catholics among the United Irishmen, he replied:

There were scarcely any among the leading United Irishmen who were almost all Dissenters. In the North, the lower classes of United Irishmen were at first almost exclusively Dissenters: it spread then among the Roman Catholics and as it spread into the southern counties, and took in the population, it increased its number of Catholics. In the county of Wexford, where the greatest part of the rebellion raged, there were no United Irishmen previous to the rebellion and there would have been no rebellion there if they had not been forced forwards by the establishment of Orange lodges and the whippings and torturings and things of that kind.[95]

In this way political leaders like O'Connell expertly distanced Catholics from the implication of the rebellion's failure. Loyal, monarchical Catholics had been manipulated by wily self-serving Presbyterians who wished to use them only as a cat's-paw to extract parliamentary reform from the blazing inferno of the 1790s. Catholic involvement in 1798 was, therefore, only an example of second-hand sedition, and the rebellion itself had solely defensive and protective aims, into which Catholics had been unwillingly driven by brutal repression. The 1803 insurrection, once more led by Protestants – Robert Emmet and Thomas Russell – demonstrated exactly the same point. By the 1820s this convenient consensus, with its repudiation of the United Irishmen, had become axiomatic among Catholic leaders. By May 1841 O'Connell's line had hardened even further:

As to 1798, we leave the weak and wicked men who considered sanguinary violence as part of their resources for ameliorating our institutions, and the equally wicked and villianously designing wretches who fomented the rebellion, and made it explode in order that in the defeat of the rebellious attempt, they might be able to extinguish the liberties of Ireland. We leave both these classes of miscreants to the contempt and indignation of mankind.[96]

Nor was O'Connell averse to gratuitous attacks on Ulster Presbyterians: 'The Presbyterians fought badly at Ballynahinch – they were commanded there by one Dickie, an attorney, and as soon as these fellows were checked, they became furious Orangemen and have continued so ever since.'[97]

O'Connell was representative of many Catholics whose initial relief at being freed of their local taskmasters by the Act of Union soon frosted over when it became apparent that the expected final removal of their disabilities was not contemplated and that Catholics would not be admitted to the imperial parliament. Catholic frost turned to ice when it gradually became apparent that in order to placate Protestants the Irish administration would be run on strictly Protestant, and essentially Orange, lines. The Emmet insurrection rocked administrative confidence in the placidity of post-rebellion Ireland. The Cornwallis project of appeasing the Catholics was now absolutely dead. Writing in October 1802, Lord Redesdale explained why, using a Caribbean analogy:

> The argument from the numbers professing the R.C. religion in Ireland is weak in the extreme, considering England and Ireland as parts of one kingdom, so far as it extends towards making the Roman Catholic religion the established religion in Ireland, and putting that religion on an equality with the Protestant Church must have that effect. Look to St Domingo. The philanthropists (and you will observe that the philanthropists are the great advocates for the R. Catholics as Mr Plowden observes) determined that the people of colour and the negroes had by nature equal rights with the whites. This once gained, the physical force of the blacks was felt by them, and they have turned the tables and driven the whites out of the island. So will it be with Ireland, unless the English, giving assistance to their Protestant brethren, shall be more fortunate than the French have been in the assistance they have given to the whites of St Domingo.[98]

In choosing this Protestant strategy, the British government ensured that Catholics would be turned from neutrality to hostility towards the Union, that local rancour would be institutionalised, and that the Catholic question would quickly become the Irish question. Once Catholic political activism revived, it would inevitably be pitted against the sectarian administration at home and a hostile, or indifferent, imperial parliament in London. In such circumstances, Catholic Emancipation could only be taken, not granted, and the adversarial stance between Catholic and Protestant and between Catholics and the British state would be hardened and perpetuated. The self-image of the emergent Catholic nation would be formed, or deformed, as much by its enemies as by its internal character.

It was this scenario that Catholic leaders, and especially O'Connell, exploited in various novel ways: in actualising the latent potential of superior Catholic numbers, in building a strategic alliance with the clergy and the institutional church, and in nurturing a powerful Catholic nationalist sensibility.[99] But they did so at the cost of superseding the Enlightenment United Irish project with a Catholic version which stressed confessional allegiance as the prime ingredient in national identity. The United Irishmen's sense of the imperative of a cosmopolitan future was now confronted by a project stressing the primacy and potency of a particularist past, which valorised history, the regional and the customary, at the expense of the new, the cosmopolitan, the universal. In Ireland cultural national-ism became bound up with Catholicism, which could represent itself as the 'national' religion and the principal repository of a distinctive Irish nationhood. Whereas the United Irishmen had challenged Irish Catholics to remodel themselves as embodiments of republican virtue, O'Connell merely flattered them in their inherited identities. O'Connell's pre-eminent role was possible only because of the destruction in the 1790s (by execution, death on the battlefield, transportation and exile) of an entire generation of gifted political activists who would otherwise have contested O'Connell's leadership of the political campaigns of the post-Union period. O'Connell oversaw the obliteration of the United Irish project, an obliteration on which his personal success depended.

By the 1840s the Achilles heel of O'Connell's political strategy was revealed; he consciously avoided campaigning in the northern third of the island during the Repeal movement, repeating a pattern established in the Catholic Emancipation programme. In so doing, O'Connell subliminally proclaimed that his Irish nationalism was a Catholic nationalism and that he was unable, or disinclined, to create a nationalist movement that could transcend his Catholic support base. Reports of the Repeal monster meetings stressed how they 'joined rich and poor, men and women, clergy and laity, town and country' in a powerful display of unity.[100] But what they did not join in any meaningful way was Catholic and Protestant. O'Connell's experiment in participatory democracy failed signally to include Irish Protestants and was an embarrassing failure in Ulster. Viewed from this perspective, the United Irishmen's ability to construct a mass-based, non-sectarian movement was an enormous achievement, elevating Irish politics out of the time-worn sectarian grooves on which it had evolved, and self-consciously brushing Irish history against the grain. O'Connell's success depended on returning Irish politics to those familiar sectarian ruts and then developing a highly effective form of trench warfare from within them.

Retreat from revolution: the Presbyterian aftermath

The post-Union decades saw the dismemberment of the United Irish alliance of Presbyterian and Catholic radicalism. This was hastened by the rancid polemics which peddled sectarian glosses aimed precisely at opening Presbyterian–Catholic divisions. But there were other reasons. Irish Presbyterians were far from being a homogeneous category. There was only thirty miles, but a world of difference, between the cosmopolitan radical chic of Belfast and the drumlin insularity of small-farm mid-Armagh. Radicalism had never been the politics of all Ulster Presbyterians.[101] A strong, if less visible, loyalist tradition existed, both among older, wealthier Belfast Presbyterians and in the small rural congregations of south Ulster – frontiersmen not so heavily influenced by the Scottish Enlightenment, and much more surrounded by Catholics than their east Ulster brethren. Even in Belfast, divergent responses within Presbyterianism became apparent in the 1790s, as the wealthier moved stealthily to side with the forces of reaction, eliciting Henry Joy McCracken's caustic comment: 'The rich always betray the poor.'[102]

In the aftermath of the rebellion, the Burgher Presbytery of Down assigned the defeat of the rebellion to the irreligion of its participants:

> The prediction of God by the prophet Zephaniah appears to meet with its accomplishment in our day – 1/17 – 'and I will bring distress upon men that they shall walk as blind men because they have sinned against the Lord, and their blood shall be poured out as the dust, and their flesh as the dung'.

And it issued a resoundingly conservative conclusion:

> Let us then thank the Lord for all these mercies and pray for their continuance, as also that God would more and more extend the gospel, promote reformation abroad and at home, restore peace, bless our King, establish his throne in right-eousness, counteract his and our foreign and domestic foes, purge away corruption in Church and state, and long preserve our civil and religious liberties. Amen.[103]

A year later Robert Day noted the changed atmosphere in Belfast:

> Treason which not long since paraded your most public streets and braved in public meetings and in open day the laws of the land, has lost the powerful allure of fashion and now skulks and hides its diminished head, stript of its leaders by the gibbet and the sword.[104]

The Act of Union itself could be interpreted as a very advanced act of parliamentary reform. It eliminated the rotten boroughs, increased the weight of the county boroughs, elevated the power of the (mainly Catholic) forty-shilling freeholder, and reduced at a stroke the power of the borough-mongers – and all this a generation ahead of the similarly sweeping reform measure enacted in England in 1832. There was also no serious political divide in Antrim and Down, the United Irish heartland, and therefore no politically motivated historiography emerged after the rebellion – unlike the situation in Wexford, for example, where the polemics emanated out of rival electioneering interests. The absence of an antagonistic historiography allowed the embers of the rebellion to cool quickly. Most importantly of all, anti-popery, which was essential to cementing Protestant unity, revived; once Napoleon made his concordat with the papacy in 1801, popery seemed to be on the march again. This closed the window of opportunity opened by the French Revolution, and the United Irish moment passed.

Despite its initial optimistic auspices, the French Revolution ultimately ushered in a phase of closure, not of opening, in Irish political life. In these cir-cumstances, Presbyterians and Anglicans could gingerly come closer together again in a shared evangelicalism, with its stress on personal religious experience, fashioned to suit a more urbanised, industrialised and individualised society.[105] The failure of Thomas Russell to arouse more than a faint flicker of support in Presbyterian east Ulster in 1803 also helped to narrow the political breach between Anglicans and Presbyterians. Thus religious and political conflicts underwrote rather than undermined Protestant religious allegiance in Ulster. A popular Protestant identity transcending its confessional variety could then emerge, consolidating around shared opposition to Catholic claims and to nationalist ones, once Catholicism usurped that name. However, we should not exaggerate the speed or ease with which the Anglican–Presbyterian divide closed. In some respects, it survived throughout much of the nineteenth century, and the two groups finally came together as a coherent political force only in the 1880s with the advent of popular unionism. A strong liberal element remained active within Ulster Presbyterianism – evident, for example, in the sizeable support that Henry Montgomery enjoyed in his tussle with Henry Cooke for control of the synod in the 1820s.[106]

The enemy within: the United Irishmen's two strands

A further historiographical response to the rebellion came from the United Irishmen themselves. It was not a unified response, and it existed in a number of guises. The United Irishmen were never an entirely homogeneous grouping. The principal division did not break along religious but rather along class lines, and on the desired political trajectory of achieving United Irish goals.[107] One wing of the movement, led by Dublin-based aspiring politicians like William Drennan, Simon Butler and Archibald Hamilton Rowan, envisaged the United Irishmen as high-profile power-brokers, whose rhetorical and publication skills would act as the crucial lever to prise reform from the government. The second wing, led by Samuel Neilson, McCracken, Tone and Russell, believed that this 'talking-shop' principle would achieve nothing and that serious change could only be generated by building a broad-based radical organisation on mass democratic principles. This core group, influential in the Belfast area, had already, as early as 1792, developed links with the Catholic Committee and the Defenders, especially in the south Ulster region.[108] By 1795 the new revolutionary underground was tightened by Neilson into a disciplined, cellular and hierarchical movement. Until then its basic strength was confined to within a twenty-mile radius of Belfast. A new strategy was devised to broaden its social, religious and geographical appeal; this was also necessary to give the United Irishmen a military organisation sufficiently credible to entice the French into partnership. Essentially this involved melting down the Defenders into United Irish cells.[109]

To do this successfully, the United Irishmen had to redefine and broaden their programme, involving a widening range of grievances and a concomitant sharp drop in the social centre of gravity of their membership. The success of the merger was predicated on the ability of the United Irishmen to politicise poverty, which was the essential Defender grievance. The merger achieved at a stroke a number of key United Irish objectives. It immediately boosted the numbers in the United Irish organisation, no longer leaving it a lightweight paper army, utterly dependent on French help. It spread the movement out beyond the Armagh frontier of the Belfast hinterland. By lowering the sectarian temperature, it eased Catholic–Presbyterian tensions in mid-Ulster and made possible renewed United Irish recruiting there. The Defender merger was one component in building a mass-based revolutionary organisation. Other strategies included the infiltration of the militia and army, the forging of links with the Dublin political underground, the adoption of Freemasonry as an ideological and organisational vector, and the diffusion of the United Irish system into the diaspora in London, Lancashire and Lowland Scotland.

However, even within the reorganised United Irish movement, there was still a divide in the leadership about the type of revolution they wished to promote. A conservative wing, represented by Thomas Addis Emmet and William James MacNeven, was adamant that an internal insurrection would only be desirable or feasible alongside a substantial French invasion, because French discipline would keep the ragged hordes of the Irish poor in check. They argued, therefore, for a lightly armed, essentially paper 'army' whose principal function would be to assist the French. By contrast, the radical wing in the movement sought to build a broad-based revolutionary movement, capable of achieving a successful revolution using solely indigenous resources.[110]

These internal divisions simmered right up to, and including, the rebellion itself. Until recently, historians have too readily accepted the Drennan/Emmet/ MacNeven analysis of the 1790s situation. The marvellous run of 1,400 Drennan letters (he was an obsessive paper-keeper, always concerned to put himself in the best light, and with one eye firmly on posterity) and his superb command of rhetoric endears him to historians with their insatiable lust for serial sources and the well-turned phrase. In this sense, Drennan is the Irish equivalent of Francis Place in England, and a similar distortion to that introduced by over-reliance on Place in accounts of English radicalism may similarly have infected Irish scholarship on the 1790s. The question now being posed is whether Drennan's revolutionary model would ever have been more than a Masonic talking-shop, a secretive club of oyster-eaters, if muscle and organisational sinews had not been added by the Belfast 'secret committee' who orchestrated the early society. By contrast with Drennan, figures like Samuel Neilson were strategically cautious to the extent of avoiding paper communication. A deeper silence may have existed beyond the voluble Drennan in which the real power-players of the United Irishmen operated – Neilson, MacCabe, MacCracken and Russell. When the going got tough in 1794, Drennan, Butler and Rowan quickly withdrew from the radical scene; these others stood their chosen ground impressively.

Reluctant revolutionaries: the conservative interpretation

The post-rebellion writing by United Irishmen continued these existing divisions, and the early response was dominated by the conservative MacNeven/Emmet wing, notably in the detailed *Memoir* which they presented to the government in August 1798 as the price of escaping hanging (or, as MacNeven delicately phrased it, 'effecting a retreat from an unsuccessful insurrection').[111] The same argument is presented at more expansive length in the MacNeven-edited *Pieces of Irish History*, which appeared in New York in 1807.[112] This conservative wing was keen to distance itself from culpability for organising a bloody armed insurrection; they presented their role as that of reasonable men caught in the crossfire between an intransigent government and an infuriated peasantry. England, and more especially the corrupt Dublin Castle establishment, are blamed for goading the peasantry into revolt, and the evidence for United Irish conspiracy is toned down in favour of a perspective which presents the leaders as desperately trying to restrain a furious peasantry, driven to distraction by military and Orange excesses. This protective polemic stresses the passivity of the United Irish leadership. Similarly evasive exegetics exaggerate the split between the United Irish movement and the Defenders, deftly using Defender – Orange rivalry to explain the force of the rebellion itself. In these and other ways, their own complicity in organising the rebellion is skilfully masked, and the origins of the rebellion are sought not in the active agency of the United Irishmen but in government cruelty. The rebels appear as reluctant revolutionaries, and the United Irish leadership as reactive, constantly restraining popular fury. The rebellion itself is presented as spontaneous, spasmodic and localised, with no clear central direction or focus, breaking out indiscriminately in response to local oppression.

All this fitted Cornwallis's conciliatory policy and was, indeed, carefully tailored to suit it. In the post-Union period, it acquired another gloss – accusing Pitt of deliberately goading the country into rebellion, using his tools, Fitzgibbon, Cooke and Castlereagh, in order to achieve the Union by Machiavellian means. MacNeven bluntly states that the rebellion was 'intentionally produced by the chief agents of the British ministry'.[113] By the time this perspective developed, the United Irish organisation and revolutionary conspiracy had been allowed to fade well into the background, with an emphasis instead on the early, or constitutional, phase of the movement and the leadership's efforts to ensure a bloodless revolution, even in the face of relentless provocation in the aftermath of the Fitzwilliam episode. This, in turn, leads to an emphasis on the decisive differences between the first and second organisation, presenting the society as a solely constitutional movement which had been driven underground by the abject failure of reform in 1795 and by subsequent unrelenting government oppression. It also ignores north – south links, social radicalism, United Irish intrigues in Great Britain and France, and the effort to construct a merger with the Defenders. This line of reasoning was helped by the arrests of 12 March 1798, which, it was claimed, decapitated the movement, depriving it of responsible leadership; this lack of leadership is then used to 'explain' the bloodiness of the actual insurrection, which is interpreted as 'the convulsive effort of despair' driven solely by 'popular fury'.[114] None of this analysis, as developed by MacNeven, Emmet, Drennan, and later by William Sampson, should be accepted at face value as a representative account of the evolution of the United Irish movement. Instead it is simply the judgement of one faction within the movement on their internal opponents.[115]

This 'reluctant revolutionary' stance was also adopted by some of those centrally involved in the military phase of the insurrection, notably Edward Hay and Thomas Cloney.[116] In both cases their works are a continuation of courtroom forensics, as both had suffered long and malignant prosecutions. Hay prefaces his book with a lengthy account of his imprisonment and trial, while Cloney prints a verbatim transcript of his court martial.[117] Both lay great stress on their veracity as eyewitnesses, while denying involvement in the United Irishmen. Both emphasise their respectable political and family connections, and Hay, especially, is an inveterate name-dropper.[118] These linkages are used to explain their high profile in the rebellion, with their influence deriving from their popularity, an influence exercised solely for moderating purposes. An extension of this argument is used to suggest that the preponderance of high-ranking United Irishmen were press-ganged into leadership roles by insistent gangs of rebels.[119] A real legal point lay behind this claim. While rank-and-file United Irishmen could take advantage of the amnesty, officers remained liable to the death penalty. Proof of officer status was, therefore, literally of life-or-death importance, as a sequence of well-publicised trials and executions showed. The constant emphasis in Hay, Gordon and Cloney on the lack of a United Irish organisation in County Wexford makes sense in this hothouse legal climate. There is a marked lack of specific detail in all three books – a protective device, designed to minimise any legal repercussions. There is absolutely no mention of United Irish military titles in these texts, lest they be used as evidence.

Set in their immediate post-rebellion context, the silences, evasions, even falsehoods, in the Hay and Cloney accounts become more understandable. Writing after the Wexford assizes of 1800, the judge Robert Day, himself a noted conservative, described the prevalent atmosphere in Wexford:

> The magistrates and peace officers are every day employed in dragging offenders to prison in utter contempt of the provisions and policy of the Amnesty Act. If a dispassionate and dignified sense of justice has ceased to operate in that county, a very active spirit of retaliation and revenge supplies its place, and furnishes ample occupation for tribunals and juries, a spirit, however lamentable in its consequences, too grateful it must be owned and too natural, too much influenced by the most unparalleled and barbarous injuries. Hence, religious rancour flourishes in full vigour in that disturbed county and there appears no prospect of returning harmony among its gents and classes. Such in truth was the prejudice which we have had to control in the counties of Wexford and Wicklow that the juries seemed much more disposed to repeal than to give full effect to the Amnesty Act, that most gracious effusion of H.M.'s benevolence and royal favour to his deluded subjects of Ireland.

Day noted that while the favoured loyalist aim of 'an utter and entire extirpation of the rebels' would doubtless, as they argued, restore tranquillity, it would be 'the tranquillity of the tomb'. But this malignant atmosphere was polluting the justice system itself: 'A thirsty spirit of retaliation is now busy.

This vengeance is blind and, if in the pursuit, trifles are magnified to proof, appearances mistaken for guilt, innocence will often be the victim.'[120]

Faced with this onslaught, the Wexford United Irishmen had one stroke of incredible good fortune. Their representative, Robert Graham, carrying with him the details of the county's United Irish organisation, dallied with a barmaid in the White Horse Inn in Camden Street, Dublin, and arrived late for the fateful meeting at Oliver Bond's house on the evening of 12 March 1798, thereby evading the mass arrest of the Leinster directory.[121] When the report of the House of Commons' committee of secrecy was rushed out in August, Fitzgibbon published all the documents seized in the raid, which itemised United Irish membership by county.[122] But Graham's dalliance ensured that there were no figures for Wexford. Hay, Gordon, Cloney and others could then argue, on the basis of the government's own meticulously detailed account, that there was no United Irish organisation at all in the county. Hay wrote that 'it was an incontrovertible fact that before this period, there were fewer United Irishmen in the county of Wexford than in any other part of Ireland'.[123]

One could then argue, as Hay does, that the Wexford rising had nothing to do with the overall United Irish movement and that it was 'a general misrepresentation that the insurrection in the county of Wexford was connected with the disturbances in other parts of the nation'.[124] Blame for the Wexford insurrection could then be neatly laid at the door of Ascendancy bigots in collusion with sectarian Orangemen. Hay argued that 'the Wexford people's first inducement to combine was to render their party strong enough to resist the Orangemen, whom they actually believed to be associated and sworn for the extermination of the Catholics and "to wade deep in their blood" '.[125] The rebellion's leadership only came into the equation then, as they were cajoled or coerced by supplicant or menacing rebel bands after the rebellion had burst out: 'Most of the leaders, throughout the disturbances in Wexford, acted in their several stations, from the irresistible force of compulsion and constraint after it had actually existed.'[126]

A further argument now became available to the secular United Irish leadership: the leaders of the Wexford rising were the Catholic priests (conveniently dead), and this had been amply demonstrated by Musgrave, the loyalist champion. Thus Hay and Cloney are happy to endorse Musgrave's sectarian reading where it suits their case; while reversing the relative culpability of the sects, they are as vindictive about the clerical leaders (notably Father John Murphy and Father Philip Roche) as Musgrave was. The dead priests became, in effect, scapegoats for the secular leadership.[127] But Hay, having established these parameters, is keen to lay the blame at the conservative gentry's door: 'I am still persuaded that the insurrection in the county of Wexford was in a great degree occasioned by the conduct of the magistrates, yeomen and military.'[128] He also vigorously attacks Musgrave and his 'past prejudice entertained against the people of the County Wexford', ascribing it to Musgrave's failed suit at the 1792 assizes in Wexford town against a local gentleman for criminal conversation with his wife.[129]

Hay actively pitched his history at an English audience, giving a free copy to every M.P. and seeking the advice of his patron, Fitzwilliam, as to what other influential people (from the king and Prince of Wales down) should be sent it.[130] Hay tried to influence English opinion and decision-makers into having a more positive view of Catholics under the Union, and he presents himself and his work as purely conciliatory: 'With a view, therefore, of establishing concord, by showing from what has happened that it will be of universal advantage to forget the past, and to cultivate general amity in future, I have undertaken the arduous task of endeavouring to reconcile.'[131] Hostile commentators were not convinced. His work was dismissed by Bishop Bennet of Cloyne as 'a history in which he palliates all the crimes of the rebels and abuses the Protestants and loyalists without mercy. . . . In short, he is to the full as partial as Musgrave, with much less regard for the truth'.[132]

Dublin Castle watched Hay's publication anxiously. Under-Secretary Alexander Marsden wrote to Chief Secretary William Wickham while the book was in the press:

> It abounds with matter which it were best was not published. I got the sheets as they are struck off, and I am just now considering what steps it will be best to take, which shall of course be well weighed by others also. I had rather have the printer to prosecute me for a trespass, than that we should only have the satisfaction of placing him in the pillory after he had distributed some hundred or thousand copies.[133]

Richard Musgrave himself described Hay's volume as 'the grossest libel that ever appeared in a civilised country', lamented the fact that its author had escaped hanging in 1798, and suggested that he was a mere catspaw for more astute agitators: 'From the illiterateness of the author and the great variety of styles which appear in it, there cannot be a doubt that it was composed by different persons and that he had little or no concern in it.' He also noted two sinister circumstances: Hay had boarded with his publisher, the well-known radical John Stockdale, and the book appeared three months before the Emmet rising: 'It is universally believed that it was intended as an incitement to the conspirators and actors concerned in this dreadful event.'[134]

A similar 'reluctant rebel' syndrome dominates another of the key texts of 1798. Joseph Holt, the Wicklow Protestant United Irish leader, dictated his memoirs in 1818;[135] they were subsequently published in 1838 under the supposedly 'impartial' editing of Thomas Crofton Croker, an Irish antiquarian steadily climbing up the literary and administrative ladder to the eventual post of chief admiralty clerk.[136] Croker was personally keen to undermine Holt's account, which he does by 'correcting' him in copious lengthy footnotes which frequently overwhelm the text itself. His stated aim was 'to demolish Holt's history, or at least render it as veritable as that of Robinson Crusoe'.[137] A more serious, because covert, editorial intervention is the addition of interpolated passages of Croker's own invention, designed to depoliticise the text, to fumigate it of any odour of blame attaching to the British connection or the Irish government for the insurrection. In completely fictitious passages Croker carefully covers his own political back and puts an impeccable piece of politically correct 1830s rhetoric into Holt's mouth:

> Self preservation was the motive which drove me into rebellion – respect for the oath of the United Irishmen, which I had taken, kept me faithful to my engagements as one, but as to effecting a change in the government, it gave me little trouble or thought. Reform was much more necessary among the people of all ranks than the government, which was good enough for me. If the laws were fairly and honestly administered, the people would have little reason to complain. It was private wrongs and individual oppression, quite unconnected with the government, which gave a bloody and inveterate character to the rebellion in the county of Wicklow. The ambitions of a few interested individuals to be at the head of affairs first lighted up the flame everywhere.[138]

Such a passage fits neatly with Croker's thesis on the positive impact of the Union in Ireland, and is designed to accelerate the process he identifies:

> England looks towards her with a more gracious aspect; many abuses also in the mode of legislation have been removed and the measure having taken place, it must be the wish of every honest mind that it will be made as beneficial to both as possible, and that the bonds of mutual interest and reciprocal justice will cement the two countries.[139]

Croker also works assiduously to metamorphose Holt into a reluctant rebel through a whole series of fictitious passages:

> I should never have been otherwise than loyal had I been left any alternative than of dying like a dog, a victim to the private malice of those armed with the power of destroying anyone they wished to get rid of, or to make them fly like myself for protection to the rebels in the mountains.[140]

His involvement was, therefore, 'accidental', and 'contrary to my inclination'. He was 'driven from my house and my children, forced into an association I detested', with 'no choice left but continuance'. Croker's interpolation has Holt including himself in the general statement that

> The poor people engaged in the Irish rebellion of 1798 had very little idea of political government. Their minds were more occupied with their own sufferings or enjoyments and many, I say most, were compelled to join in the rebellion on pain of death! They had no choice, therefore, and great allowances should be made for such miserable creatures when they fall into the hands of government. Those who instigate rebellions are the great criminals, not the poor wretches who are driven by circumstances they cannot control into acts of violence.[141]

In total, Croker made 160 substantive changes and added 80 of his own interventions to Holt's text. The cumulative effect is to vitiate it as a source of information about either Holt or the 1798 rebellion. To rescue Holt from Croker, we must revert instead to the original manuscript in the Mitchell Library in Sydney.[142]

Problems of a different kind infect another text by an ex-United Irishman – William Farrell's account of his involvement in the 1790s in Carlow town, which is unrelenting in its attacks on the United Irish system.[143] There are circumstantial and evidential grounds to believe that Farrell may have become an informer (albeit reluctantly to save his own life) in 1798.[144] With unseemly haste, his death sentence was commuted to transportation and then quashed altogether, allegedly to his 'great mortification'. Suspicions about his bona fides are intensified by his later appointment as gatekeeper of Carlow jail, a job in the gift of the local grand jury. The text was written in his old age, in the 1830s, and self-exculpations and special pleadings are so prolific in the text that it can hardly be taken seriously as an accurate account of the United Irish movement.

Revolutionary muscle: the radical response

While this conservative wing of the United Irishmen rehabilitated its politics by pursuing this evasive line, the radical wing remained secretive and unapologetic. Approached to give evidence to the secret committee of the House of Commons, Samuel Neilson stretched out his arm, with his hand clenched, saying: 'I hold in my hand every muscle, sinew, nay, fibre of the internal organisation – nay, every ramification of the United Irishmen', and gradually opening his hand, he added: 'I will make it as plain as the palm of my hand if our terms are complied with.'[145] He subsequently produced a tough-minded defence of his radical career, directly opposed to the apologists of the conservative wing:

> With respect to the progress of truth by discussion and not by arms, I agree with Godwin; but when discussion is utterly at an end, I know no means of resisting tyranny but by arms. While it was possible to persuade the people from this last appeal, I advised every man I know to exert himself to keep the country quiet. But when the horrid cruelties committed by the army – when robbery, rape and butchery and rapine of every kind become a custom, and when I found the country thus maddened into resistance, I did conceive neutrality a crime, and had I been at large, I would have lent my feeble aid to the common cause of my much injured and bleeding country. Death to me has no terrors – slavery accompanied with barbarous cruelty I cannot endure .
>
> As to liberty for Ireland, I die for her. And so far from regretting any political act of my life, I look back upon the whole with infinite pleasure. I die in confidence that truth must triumph and that Ireland must be free. As to my religion, that is a matter between my maker and myself, with which the community has nothing to do. As to my morals, they have ever been – to do to others as I should they should do to me and in this faith I shall depart without a groan.[146]

In the year of his death, 1801, Neilson repeated these sentiments in a letter from America to A. H. Rowan:

> Neither the eight years' hardship I have endured, the total destruction of my property, the forlorn state of my wife and children, the momentary failure of our national exertion, nor the still more distressing usurpation in France, has abated my ardour in the cause of my country and of general liberty. You and I, my dear friend, will pass away, but truth remains. Christ was executed upon a cross, but his morality has been gaining ground these eighteen hundred years, in spite of superstition and priestcraft.[147]

Others from within the radical wing had an equally sharp grasp of the wisdom of the proverb: 'Victory has a thousand fathers, defeat is an orphan.' James Hope, looking back over the histories of the rebellion in his 1843 memoir, was scathing in his judgement:

> It is hard for a man who did not live at the time to believe or comprehend the extent to which misrepresentations were carried at the close of our struggle. . . . The men who flinched and fell away from our cause grasped at any apology for their own delinquency.[148]

This revolutionary disenchantment was also part of a wider international pattern of intellectual withdrawal from the French Revolution, notably among the English romantic poets like Coleridge, Wordsworth and Southey.[149] As the heat of history cooled, *ennui* followed. Coleridge wrote to Wordsworth in 1799:

> I wish you would write a poem in blank verse, addressed to those who, in consequence of the complete failure of the French Revolution, have thrown up all hopes for the amelioration of mankind and are sinking into an almost Epicurean selfishness, disguising the same under the soft titles of domestic attachment and contempt for visionary *philosophes*.[150]

Coleridge, Southey and later Shelley were all drawn in guilty fascination to the figure of Robert Emmet, an accusing surrogate of their abandoned radicalism. Coleridge described him as 'a mad Raphael, painting ideals of beauty on the walls of a cell with human excrement'; Southey wrote a fine poem on him, while Shelley came to Dublin in 1812 in a quixotic attempt to reignite his insurrection.[151]

That great disenchantment did not reach to the popular constituency which had supported the radical element within the United Irishmen. The most socially aware (and radical) document produced by the United Irishmen came after the rebellion had been militarily crushed – *The Union Doctrine* or *Poor Man's Catechism*.[152] In February 1799 John Beresford complained that even Dublin theatre audiences were 'now so insolent as constantly in both playhouses and elsewhere, to clap for the memory of Lord Edward Fitzgerald, the Sheares, Oliver Bond etc.'.[153] Similarly, a crowd of several thousand attended the funeral of Peter Tone, Theobald's father, in August 1805.[154] It was out of this popular radicalism that the two most acerbic commentators on the radical side emerged – Denis Taaffe and Watty Cox.[155] Their abrasive rhetoric is a world away from the polite, almost patrician historians. Writing in 1805, Taaffe complained in characteristically cutting prose that Catholics were forced to 'bow obeisance to every Protestant cobbler who slants about with his leather apron swelling in all the pride of Protestant Ascendancy and exclaiming after washing down the fumes of his anti-popish zeal with a hearty smack of his morning, "The papists are good soles but very bad uppers" '.[156]

Watty Cox's *Irish Magazine* (1807–15) specialised in raking over the embers of '98 in abusive and often scurrilous detail, aggressively and humorously attacking Protestant Ascendancy and Orange figures. Written with great vigour, enlivened by satire and containing a series of daring cartoons by Brocas, the *Irish Magazine* was enormously popular and was continued even from jail by its ebullient editor. He pursued certain characters from 1798 with unrelenting zeal, notably Major Sirr and John Beresford. Cox strengthened the popular image of 1798 as a vicious pogrom against Catholics. A typical entry is an obituary for Sir Thomas Judkin Fitzgerald, notorious for his tough measures as high sheriff in County Tipperary in 1798, including personal flogging of suspects: 'The history of his life and his loyalty is written in legible characters on the backs of his countrymen.'[157] Brocas's cartoons were simplistic, but visually striking, forcefully reversing the prevailing representation of the Gothic horror of 1798. His focus is on the Ascendancy and its cruelties – like the 'walking gallows' (a grotesque visual of Lieutenant Hempenstall, so tall that he could half-hang suspected rebels over his back). Brocas also attacked the pretentiousness of Irish conservative politicians – as in 'The Louth Mower', a pointed allusion to the allegation that John Foster's grandfather had been merely a farmer, and also a bitter pun on his repressive law-and-order stance in 1798.[158]

The *Irish Magazine's* adversarial style, colloquialism, robust sense of humour and demotic style are close to the tone of the contemporary ballads of 1798 and also share their register, vocabulary and political outlook.[159] These ballads are written almost invariably in English: the 1790s politicisation targeted anglicised, not gaelicised, Ireland. Remarkably few poems in Irish survive about 1798, notably the compositions of Micheál Óg Ó Longáin in Cork. He wrote in a self-consciously closet style, recognising that he had no national audience for his political poems. The rebellion of 1798 was an episode in English-speaking, not Irish-speaking Ireland, and the politicisation of the 1790s only lightly touched Irish-speaking areas.[160]

Both Taaffe and Cox had a sharply defined sense of class as a fault-line in Irish society, and 1798 is therefore also construed by them as an attack by the rich on the poor. Taaffe claimed that in Ireland 'the poor were created for the use of the rich as much as the beasts of the field'.[161] He pointed to the obvious disparities in Irish social life, interpreting them politically, assuring the landed gentry, for example, that 'your colossal edifices are propped on our mud cabins'. He interpreted the disparities in Irish cultural life in the same politicised way: 'We are stript bare and then reproached with our poverty.'[162] And, inevitably, he attacked Musgrave:

> Who could expect in the beginning of the nineteenth century, in the midday blaze of toleration and philosophy, to hear or read such impolitic invectives against the whole Catholic Church. . . . Pikes, rebels, traitors and massacres, Scullabogue and Wexford glitter in gloomy array in this dark and daring libel.

Taaffe concluded that the aim of such work was to make Protestants and Catholics in Ireland 'like two cats tied together by the tail across a pole, to bite and scratch each other to death'.[163]

The United Irishmen in America

This aggressive line was also pursued by those émigrés who were writing about Ireland from America, notably John Burk, Thomas Ledlie Birch and Edward Byrne (under the pseudonym Hibernicus).[164] Burk's hurried and confused book is a standard radical reading of the 1790s, but is garbled through reliance on newspaper reports after he left the country in 1795. By contrast, Birch's account is one of the very few written from a Presbyterian perspective, and was based on his personal experience. He was especially keen to refute the sectarian interpretation of the rebellion, as in this long meditation on what the word 'Protestant' meant in the Ireland of the 1790s:

> From the butcheries reported to be committed in Ireland by the Roman Catholics upon the Protestants, you have concluded that the Presbyterians and Catholics are not an united body, as represented, and your honest soul and indignation are roused against the unworthy, persecuting Roman Catholics of Ireland. Alas! how soon does Pharo's chief butler, now at the prison, forget Joseph! It might have been supposed that you Americans, not one hundred years out of the same predicament with Ireland, would have known those whom (using the term once made use of to you) the wise, omnipotent parliaments of Great Britain and Ireland, mean by Protestants. However, for the information of the ignorant and the refreshing of the memories of the forgetful, we must observe that it is much easier to answer in the negative, as to religious professions, and religions they exclude and the religion designed to be pointed out, if there is any religion in the matter, which is disputed. By the name of Protestant is not meant the people of the Presbyterian Christian profession, nor even the descendants of the old Puritans settled in your New England provinces, whose fathers were persecuted out of Great Britain under the 'De Heretice Comburendo' or burning of heretics, in the reigns of Mary and Charles, and whose churches in Boston etc. were (not fifty years ago, as unhallowed cages, because not consecrated) turned (by certain generals) into play houses, barracks and riding houses – neither does the term Protestant intend seceders, called here Scotch Reformed Presbyterians, Baptists, Methodists, Universalists, etc., or even the meek, mild brotherhood called Quakers, who are enemies to all wars, slavery of men, and who permit the loss of

property, or even life, without resistance, when in conscience they cannot comply. No, no, my dear friend, none of these sects are allowed the dignified title of Protestants by the wise masters, unless 'Rule Britannia' or 'Hearts of Oak' have a powerful Roman Catholic rival to combat, some party business in Church or state is to be served, then the shibboleth, the rallying term, the hue and cry, is Protestants! At other times they are ignorant, wild, blind enthusiasts, void of all religion: in a word, those designated by the name of Protestants are members of the Episcopal Church, the legal establishment of Ireland.[165]

These American-published books also consistently claimed that censorship would prevent their publication in England. William Sampson, for example, appealed to American susceptibilities by noting the similarity between British propaganda against both countries:

The printing presses of Ireland have been lawlessly demolished and all who dare write or speak the truth have been hunted to extinction, whilst scouts and hirelings, paid from the Irish treasury, have been maintained in the remotest regions of the Earth to slander Ireland. . . . Let it be kept in mind that the same writers and runners hired to traduce Irishmen in America are those who traduce America in Europe, with this only difference, that in all their clumsy sarcasms, the spirit of the jest is to call the American 'Yankee' and the Irishman 'Paddy'.[166]

These authors were keenly aware of history-writing as an intervention in contemporary politics. William James MacNeven believed that 'history or the present recollection of past events, if properly applied, would emancipate the Catholics or, better still, the Irish'.[167] And these writers could claim the freedom of the American presses as essential to this project. Edward Byrne's *Hibernicus, or Memoirs of an Irishman*, published at Pittsburgh in 1829, contains a vivid account of 1798 in County Carlow – more vivid, he claimed, than anything produced in Ireland: 'I durst not write, nor dare any printer publish these things in Europe, at least in the British dominions: they are not, however, the less true.'[168] Here, for example, is his description of the execution of Father John Murphy:

Murphy was after this executed, or rather butchered, at Tullow, opposite the door of a Catholic merchant; his head cut off, his bowels torn out and burned while an officer, taking the gory head by the hair, placed it on the merchant's counter, saying 'there is some fresh meat for you'.[169]

For the exiled United Irishmen, America was a favoured place. At least 2,000 made their homes there after the rebellion's failure, many of whom became passionately involved in American politics on the Republican side. The events of 1798 remained a constant theme – seen, for example, in the virulence of the campaign waged against Rufus King, who had been hostile to the idea of allowing United Irishmen into the United States.[170] Thomas O'Conor, a United Irishman and a member of the well-known Roscommon family, continued the United Irish line into American politics in his newspaper

The Shamrock or Hibernian Chronicle. Its masthead featured the American eagle, sheltering the United Irish shield of the uncrowned harp, under the motto 'Fostered under thy wing, we die in thy defence'.[171] This Americophilia was a deeply held sentiment, often imbued with Hibernophobia. Thomas Addis Emmet replied in 1807 to a friend's request that he come home by contrasting his American and his Irish life, concluding:

> I am too proud when vanquished to assist by my presence in gracing the triumph
> · of the victor. And with what feelings should I tread on Irish ground . . . as if I were
> walking over graves and these the graves of my closest relatives and dearest
> friends. . . . There is not now in Ireland an individual that bears the name of
> Emmet. I do not wish there ever should while it is connected with England and, yet
> it will perhaps, be remembered in its history.[172]

Reclaiming the rebellion: R. R. Madden and Miles Byrne

During the two decades preceding the granting of Catholic Emancipation, there was a deliberate effort on the part of those managing the campaign to avoid the difficult topic of the rebellion. Thomas Cloney, for example, had been intent on publishing his account in the early 1800s, but had been dissuaded by the politically astute Peter Burrowes.[173] Once Emancipation became a *fait accompli*, there was a renewed burst of writing on the 1790s, but this time with a less apologetic air. The publication of Tone's autobiography in Washington in 1826 inaugurated the new phase, followed by the accounts published by Charles Teeling in 1828, Thomas Cloney in 1832, Joseph Holt in 1838, Archibald Hamilton Rowan in 1840, Lord Cloncurry in 1849, John Binns in 1854, and culminating in Miles Byrne's *Memoirs* of 1863, the last to be written by a direct participant in the events of the 1790s. This new phase in the historiography of the United Irishmen was sealed in 1842 with the publication of the first volumes of R. R. Madden's monumental seven-volume *The United Irishmen: Their Lives and Times* (1842–6).[174] Madden had assiduously corresponded with and interviewed the surviving United Irish leaders, and his books are biographical in focus and hagiographical in tone. A few months after publication of his initial volume, the first issue of *The Nation* appeared on 15 October 1842. Madden's books were a profound influence on Thomas Davis and the Young Irelanders, who celebrated the United Irishmen not as passive victims or reluctant rebels, but as ideologically committed revolutionaries with a coherent political strategy. The United Irish leaders (approximating the Young Irelanders' own self-image) were a vanguard, republicans in the French style, whose brilliantly articulated ideas and committed leadership were then enthusiastically endorsed by a mass populace. For these reasons, Davis tried to infuse the spirit of the 1790s into the 1840s, explicitly hailing Wolfe Tone as 'one of the greatest men that Ireland ever produced'.[175] Madden's volumes were a major intellectual resource, which could be filleted for appropriate themes. Madden, for example, expended considerable effort in demolishing the sectarian interpretation of the rebellion, carefully matching the number of Anglican, Presbyterian and Catholic leaders and balancing the role of the Catholic clergy in the south with that of the Presbyterian clergy in the north (he lists exactly twelve in each group).[176] Davis could then use the inspiration of the United Irishmen to refashion a similarly pluralist conception of identity for the 1840s, seeking an Irish nationality 'which may embrace Protestant, Catholic and Dissenter, Milesian and Cromwellian, the Irishman of a hundred generations and the stranger who is within our gates'.[177]

Inspired by Madden's precise pinpointing in 1842 of Tone's burial place at Bodenstown, Davis visited the site in 1843 and published his poem 'Tone's Grave' in *The Nation* of 25 November 1843 and subsequently in the compilation *The Spirit of the Nation*, which established it firmly in the popular repertoire. Independently, Tone's widow Matilda sought to mark his grave in 1843, and the leading Young Irelanders undertook the task, choosing a plain black marble slab with a simple epitaph by Davis. This was privately erected in 1844 to prevent any embarrassment to O'Connell – indicating that in the 1840s it was still politically sensitive to engage in any open commemoration of the men of '98. The Davis legacy was inherited directly by the Fenians, who equally venerated the memory of '98 and of Tone. It was presumably Fenian sympathisers who chipped away both the older family and later Young Ireland slabs at Bodenstown in quest of souvenirs, thereby necessitating the erection of a locked railing in the 1870s to protect the site.[178]

This positive image of 1798 was strengthened by the publication of Miles Byrne's *Memoirs* in 1863, the same year in which the Fenians launched their newspaper, the *Irish People*.[179] Miles Byrne as a young man had been active in both 1798 and 1803, before embracing a distinguished professional career in the French army. He had been the Parisian correspondent of *The Nation* and, in detached old age, had dictated his memoirs to his very capable wife Fanny, who published them posthumously. Byrne's work was written directly against the grain of the evasive exegetics of the well-known works of Hay, Cloney, Teeling, Gordon *et al.* and often deliberately undermined them. While ostensibly praising Thomas Cloney, for example, he presents him as a sworn and fully committed United Irishman, and gives an eyewitness account of Cloney's involvement with Robert Emmet (an involvement which Cloney had categorically denied).[180] He dismissed Hay as a professional Castle Catholic, and Gordon as a self-serving sycophant, and is at pains to refute their collective authority. Byrne attacks the representation of the rising as sectarian, ascribing it to 'the great pains taken by the enemies of the independence of Ireland to make it appear that the Catholic United Irishmen had no other object in view than retaliation and revenge on their Protestant fellow countrymen during the war'.[181] In Byrne's judgement, 'nothing could be further from their view than a religious war', and the Wexford insurgents showed 'perfect toleration for every creed and religious persuasion – that is to say, civil and religious liberty for all to the greatest extent possible'.[182] He further argued against the tendency to highlight the role of the Catholic clergy in 1798, noting, for example, that the bulk of the Wexford clergy had been bitterly opposed to the United Irishmen and that Father John Murphy himself was a marginal figure in the crucial early stages of the rising: 'Yet, because three or four priests were driven from their neutral position by the blood-thirsty Orangemen to join the people's camp, the English government wished to stamp the war in Ireland of 1798 as merely a religious war carried on by priests.'[183] Byrne also witheringly attacked those who reduced the rebellion to 'a mere revolt of ignorant wretched peasants'.[184]

Moving beyond the protective polemics and evasive exegetics of earlier generations of United Irishmen, and writing from the neutral ground of Paris, Byrne's viewpoint is clear: the rebellion was not a disjointed response to unbearable provocation, but one coherently organised by a secret society with mass popular support, carefully planned under responsible leadership and deriving its mandate from an overwhelming popular will. It is immediately obvious how appealing this view would be to the Fenians, who reprinted the work in parts in the *Irish People*. Young Fenian activists could now adduce compelling evidence of the historically rooted claims of militant Irish republicanism.

Faith, fatherland and Fenians: Kavanagh's *Popular History*

Inevitably, the Fenian challenge caused intense heart-searching among the Catholic clergy, because it contained an arresting mixture of 1798 and 1848 – at once national and international, populist and anticlerical, emotional and intellectual. The Fenians pointedly focused on the advanced role of the priests, especially Father John Murphy, at the centre of an armed republican conspiracy in 1798, and contrasted this with the supine role of the current generation of cringing Catholic clergy. The accusations hurt, precisely because 1798 was so well known. Cardinal Cullen dismissed the Fenians as 'Godless nobodies', worthless Irish representatives of the degenerate anticlerical Mazzini and Cavour faction in Italy.[185] He was equally dismissive of the United Irishmen on the same grounds: 'All our patriots were tinged with infidelity, the two Sheares, Emmet, etc.'[186] The church's ambivalence concerning 1798 can best be seen in the contemptuous refusal by the parish priest of Boolavogue to allow a monument to Father Murphy, planned by Dublin Fenians in 1877, to be erected anywhere near church property. He also banned his parishioners from attending the unveiling – the first public sculpture commemorating 1798 – and forced publicans for miles around to close on that day.[187] One can also sense the uneasiness over the legacy of '98 in W. J. Fitzpatrick, the popular historian of the 1790s in the 1860s, who refused to use material collected by Luke Cullen from surviving participants: 'Owing to the revival of Fenianism in Ireland, we have deemed it more prudent not to use, in the present volume, the exciting details collected by Mr Cullen.'[188] Cullen's meticulous research – the first oral history project in Ireland – was to remain unpublished until the 1950s.[189] The number, volubility and openness of his informants in Wicklow, Wexford and Dublin in the 1840s and 1850s indicates the enduring significance of 1798 at the popular level.[190]

In these circumstances, the institutional church needed to develop its own history of 1798, which would sanitise the clerical role while providing historical sanction for their own unbending opposition to the Fenians in particular and secret societies in general. That challenge was taken up by a Wexford Franciscan friar, Patrick Kavanagh, in his book *A Popular History of the Insurrection of 1798*, published in 1870.[191] This volume is an attempted reconciliation of the conflicting imperatives of Catholicism and nationalism, an effort to rejoin seamlessly what the Fenian wedge had begun to split apart. The United Irishmen in this book figure as a retrospective surrogate of the Fenians. Published in the year of the outbreak of the Franco-Prussian War, and of consequent high Fenian excitement, the book enjoyed an enormous vogue, rapidly going through nine further editions – in 1874, 1884, 1898, 1913, 1916, 1918, 1920, 1923 and 1928. Kavanagh silenced the competing voices: his perspective dominated the interpretation of 1798 both in the lead-up to the centenary and in the creation of the new state itself.[192] His message was simple, even simplistic: Father John Murphy, and he alone, was at the real and metaphysical heart of 1798 in Wexford, the heroic leader of a defenceless, passive people, under attack solely because of their religious persuasion. The United Irishmen, and by extension secret societies in general, are demonised: Kavanagh presents them as riddled by spies and informers, ruined by drink, with self-important leaders who brought the people to the precipice of perdition, pushed them over it, and then callously stood back to watch them fall.

The United Irish obsession with oaths left them wide open to infiltration by spies and to subsequent legal proceedings. The emphasis on the destructive impact of spies on secret societies like the United Irishmen was designed to minimise the attractiveness of the oath-bound Fenians. William John Fitzpatrick, like Kavanagh an ardent Catholic, publicised the spies of the 1790s in his sensation-seeking books, most especially in the hugely popular *The Sham Squire and the Informers of 1798*, which went through at least six editions at the height of the Fenian period. Fitzpatrick was explicit in his preface to the second edition (1865): 'Owing to the recently discovered Fenian conspiracy and the attention which it has excited, this work possesses perhaps more than ordinary interest.' In the preface to the third edition (1866), he cites its 'true moral' as being that 'secret confederacies can do no good, that informers will always be found to betray them, and that no plot which deals in signs and signals can enlist the sympathy of those whose co-operation would be really valuable'. A side-effect of this obsession with spies was to minimise the successful way in which the United Irishmen often dealt with them, notably in the 'turning' of both Edward Newell and John Smith in the winter of 1797, or in the remarkable fact that St John, the person employed in the Dublin post office 'to have the care of searching letters', was actually an United Irish officer.[193] But to suit contemporary agendas, both Fitzpatrick and Kavanagh presented the United Irish movement as riddled with spies from top to bottom and thereby inevitably doomed to failure.

Kavanagh asserts that when the rising erupted, the United Irishmen were nowhere to be seen and left Wexford to suffer its affliction alone: 'When Wexford stood at bay, the United Irishmen were not to be found.'[194] It was then that the Catholic priests stepped self-sacrificingly forward, leading their defenceless people in a crusade for faith and fatherland. Remarkably, Kavanagh reverts almost totally to the old Musgrave interpretation, except with his value-system inverted. To achieve this heroic interpretation, Kavanagh had to ignore or dismiss commentators like Madden, Luke Cullen and Miles Byrne (whose damaging account is rejected on the grounds that he was a callow youth in 1798). In their place, Kavanagh reverts to oral tradition, and in particular the version passed on in his own Wexford family. Once more he isolates the Wexford rebellion from any national context, downplays politicisation and presents the rebel army as simple country people whose courage and determination came from their confidence in their pastors.

That single recurring image – of heroic priest leaders and of a goaded but morally pure peasantry – was literally set in stone and bronze during the 1798 centenary, when Kavanagh was the preferred interpreter. This can be strikingly seen in Oliver Sheppard's magnificent statues at Enniscorthy and Wexford. At Enniscorthy, a flag-furled Father Murphy paternally lays his hands on an insurgent's shoulder, while at Wexford a pikeman strides confidently forward, alone, pure, morally dignified, dressed not in a United Irish uniform but in his workaday rags. These images were created after long, often acrimonious discussions with the local committee, headed by Father Byrne (the founder of the Uí Chinnsealaigh Historical Society, with a 'faith-and-fatherland' emphasis).[195] One revealing instance is recorded of Kavanagh's diplomatic laundering of the Catholic Church's role. A Maynooth College student wrote to him querying his omission of Bishop Caulfield's stinging condemnation of the role of the Wexford priests in the rebellion. Kavanagh replied: 'I thought it better to omit it in the new centenary edition. It is not creditable to that prelate and our people would be no better for reading it. The bishops were then in a critical position and thought prudence the best part of valour.'[196] A similar customising occurred in 1898 when the portrait of Father John Murphy preserved at Boolavogue was sent to Dublin for restoration: a Roman collar was painted over his cravat to give the iconic priest a more recognisable clerical identity.

This view of 1798 was transferred virtually intact into the popular novels, plays and ballads which enjoyed a massive efflorescence in the 1890s. A *locus classicus* is P. J. McCall's stirring anthem, 'Boolavogue', which highlights Father Murphy's role. This, and the earnest simplistics of Robert Dwyer Joyce's 'The Boys of Wexford', completely obliterated the actual songs of the 1790s and immediate 1798 period, driving them from the popular repertoire and usurping the popular imagination of what 1798 meant. That change also impacted in a fascinating way on the mumming tradition of County Wexford. A Bree schoolmaster, Sinnott, rewrote the traditional verses in the 1860s to incorporate a Catholic-nationalist pantheon, in which '98, Lord Edward Fitzgerald and especially Father Murphy figure prominently. These rhymes, printed and put into circulation by Evoy, the Adamstown blacksmith and possessor of a small manual printing-press, quickly gained in popularity and are now the standard version used by Wexford mummers.[197] A similar invention of tradition can be seen in P. J. Bourke's melodrama of 1910, *When Wexford Rose*. It is still there in modern versions like Thomas Flanagan's *The Year of the French*, Seamus Heaney's 'Requiem for the Croppies' or in Brian Friel's *Translations*.[198] One should not underestimate the power of these texts: Heaney's poem was inspirational in radicalising northern Catholics in the Civil Rights period.[199]

Kavanagh's book salvaged 1798 for the Catholic Church, allowing the institution to relinquish its reticence over the rising. By the time the 1938 and 1948 celebrations came round, they were exclusively organised by Father Patrick Murphy, a Wexford parish priest, who became so identified with the period that he was known universally under the soubriquet 'Ninety-Eight'.[200] The contretemps of half a century earlier, when the Wexford priests wanted nothing to do with '98, was now conveniently forgotten. In other ways besides its Catholic-nationalist reading, the centenary was pivotal in knitting together the strands of nationalist opinion which had unravelled in the acrimonious aftermath of the Parnell split.[201] Indeed, it could be interpreted as a necessary precursor to the nationalist resurgence and the cultural revival of the early 1900s. Yeats collaborated with Maud Gonne on commemorative committees and became fired by her enthusiasms.

The Irish Revolutionary Brotherhood, the Fenian inheritor, was the principal organiser of the centenary celebrations, under the co-ordination of Frederick Allan, a Dublin Methodist and I.R.B. activist. As disenchantment with the contemporary political paralysis of the 1890s peaked, there was a rebuking return to the past in the quest for exemplary political heroes. The centenary of 1798 was brilliantly orchestrated as a separatist riposte to the 1897 Diamond Jubilee of Queen Victoria, celebrated in Dublin especially as a copperfastening of constructive unionism and a consolidation of Ireland's place in the Empire. The proposed statue of Wolfe Tone, for example, was to be located at the top of Grafton Street, deliberately planted in the heart of unionist Dublin. On 15 August 1898 the dedication of its first stone by the veteran Fenian John O'Leary was attended by 100,000 people after a massive procession rich in resonance and ritual. The centenary became easily the most spectacular commemorative event of the nineteenth century: in terms of mass participation in a political project, it was matched only by O'Connell's monster meetings and the high point of the Land League campaign.[202]

It was also the I.R.B. who organised the first structured Bodenstown commemoration in 1891, and by the middle of the decade crowds of up to 5,000 gathered there each June, on the Sunday closest to Tone's birthdate. In 1898 a bust of Tone was placed on the grave by John O'Leary, already an iconic figure.[203] By then one thing was certain – no one feared to speak of '98. Even John Redmond, at first reluctant, had gradually been sucked in, until eventually he also felt it necessary to claim the mantle of '98, stressing his maternal ancestor, William Kearney, a committed Wexford United Irishman (and conveniently ignoring his paternal ancestor, Walter Redmond, a Catholic yeoman and loyalist). Redmond's proposed '98 monument – a round tower on Vinegar Hill – had been unceremoniously rejected in his Wexford heartland as a flagrant effort to usurp 1798 for constitutional nationalism, through deliberately replicating O'Connell's monument at Glasnevin.[204] In the aftermath of the centenary, Bodenstown became an ever more important place of political pilgrimage. In 1913 the I.R.B. organised a massive commemoration, at which Patrick Pearse delivered his famous oration, describing Tone as 'the greatest of Irish nationalists'.[205] The wheel had indeed turned full circle from the lonely grave of the O'Connellite era.

Froude and Lecky

Because 1798 ushered in the Act of Union, and because the Union remained at the centre of the Anglo-Irish debate in the nineteenth century, the rebellion remained a high-profile subject in British as well as Irish political circles. This explains the generous allocation of space to the 1790s in the many published collections of correspondence which punctuate the nineteenth century, its second half in particular. This is true of the Castlereagh series (1850), Beresford (1854), Cornwallis (1859), Abbot (1861), Auckland (1861–2), Pitt (1890), Charlemont (1891–2) and Moore (1904), as well as in the H.M.C. Fortescue series (1892–1927).[206]

The high profile of 1798 also figures in the great historiographical battle of late nineteenth-century Ireland, between James Anthony Froude and W. E. H. Lecky.[207] Froude's *The English in Ireland in the Eighteenth Century* (1872–4) devotes all of its third volume to the rebellion, where it repeats the Musgrave line. Lecky's response came initially as part of his *History of Eighteenth-Century England*; reissued as an Irish series in 1892, it ran to five volumes, no less than three of which were concerned with the 1790s. In these, Lecky undermines Froude's account by following the liberal Protestant line of post-'98 historiography. His interpretation was to remain magisterial. Both Froude and Lecky wrote primarily for an English audience, as is shown by the *exordia* to both series, which draw out the contemporary lessons for politicians and administrators from their studies of Irish history. Ironically, given Lecky's own unionist stance, his account of '98 was to be (with Kavanagh's) the major source of the nationalist reading of '98 and especially of the Act of Union. As the Union settlement itself came under increasing pressure, these books were all the more eagerly ransacked for evidence that the whole Union business was flawed, immoral and unworkable from its inception. Its relevance to the contemporary political agenda therefore kept 1798 at the forefront of historiographical debate in the nineteenth century, replacing 1641, which had performed a similar role in the eighteenth century.

Conclusion: post-revisionist perspectives

There are obviously wider implications in this discussion for the constantly shifting narrative of '98 after '98. A simple conclusion is that, whatever this writing was about, it was not directly about 1798 at all. Therefore the standard narrative accounts of 1798 (Musgrave, Gordon, Cloney, Hay, etc.) have to be seen as post-rebellion polemics, not as neutral or objective sources. Accordingly, historians like Thomas Pakenham and R. B. McDowell whose interpretations rest primarily on these accounts present a misleading analysis.[208] Pakenham's *Year of Liberty* is fundamentally wrong on the meaning and context of 1798 as a result of his reliance on a straight reading of these deeply problematic texts. Following these unreliable narrators, he emphasises sectarianism and depoliticises the rebels: 'the disaffected had no serious political aims'; 1798 was 'the old agrarian war under a new name'; the rebels were 'a half disciplined mob with little idea beyond plunder' who represented 'the primitive force of the countryside'. The rebellion itself is portrayed as 'a noisy jacquerie of the local peasantry', carried out by 'aimless and leaderless' men, 'poor and politically unsophisticated'.[209]

The unsatisfactory end-product of this type of historical analysis of the 1790s can most obviously be seen in Roy Foster's synthesis, with its crudely reductionist dismissal of the origins of the 1798 rebellion as being due to 'an increase in taxes, land-hunger and sectarianism'.[210] This interpretation derives from a misreading of the post-'98 accounts, swallowing the depoliticised reading which was not aimed at understanding 1798 in its contemporary contexts, but was wielded as a weapon in post-rebellion politics. One can also see how attractive this early revisionism would be to a later revisionist project. Pakenham's book was written after the nationalist celebration of the fiftieth anniversary of the 1916 rising, with Northern Ireland on the brink of political dissolution. Foster's project aimed to explode the unitary narrative of Irish nationalism, in the service of an equally (but adversarial) politicised reading of Irish history.

In the 1990s a post-revisionist interpretation of the 1790s is gradually finding a voice.[211] The most striking feature of this new writing is its insistence on approaching the 1790s on its own terms, not from the viewpoint of carefully contrived post-rebellion polemics. A central thread has been the significance of politicisation as the principal theme of the decade. It has also discarded the 'spontaneous combustion' view of the rebellion itself, in favour of seeing it as a relatively sophisticated and co-ordinated endeavour, which failed because the linch-pin of the plan, Dublin, did not work, thereby giving a disjointed, spasmodic look to the wave of supporting mobilisations in a crescent around the capital.[212] The new writing has also discarded, perhaps with unseemly haste, the emphasis on economic and especially agrarian issues which has dominated and distorted, for example, the interpretation of the Defenders and the Orange Order. This has led to a far more sophisticated understanding of the nature of sectarianism in the 1790s, of the interplay of high and popular politics, and of counter-revolutionary as well as revolutionary mobilisation. In turn, the United Irishmen have been restored to their 1790s context and thereby rescued from the manipulative manoeuvres of their post-rebellion interpreters. As the bicentenary approaches and as the volume of work increases, the meaning of the rebellion is once more contested and once more reshaped. The very instability of the narrative of '98 since '98 is a salutary reminder that past and present are constantly imbricated and that the positivist reading of historical texts is no longer adequate to the enterprise of historical scholarship.

Sermon

Do not then approach the rotten tree of French liberty, if you desire to live. It bears forbidden fruit, fair to the eye but deadly to those who taste it. Rooted in corruption, it vegetates only to destory. Evils innumerable lie concealed under its branches and shining foliage, bending under an exuberant weight of crimes. Such is the boasted tree of liberty, and such its baleful fruit presented to us covered over with the fairest flowers of ill-applied oratory, and under the imposing names of Liberty, Equality, Amity, and Protection.

ARCHBISHOP JOHN THOMAS TROY (February 1797)

ABBREVIATIONS

B.L.	British Library
D.D.A.	Dublin Diocesan Archives
D.E.P.	*Dublin Evening Post*
F.D.J.	*Faulkner's Dublin Journal*
F.L.J.	*Finn's Leinster Journal*
G.O.	Genealogical Office, Dublin
H.M.C.	Historical Manuscripts Commission
I.H.S.	*Irish Historical Studies*
mic.	microfilm
N.A.	National Archives, Dublin
N.H.I.	*New History of Ireland*
N.L.I.	National Library of Ireland
N.M.I.	National Museum of Ireland
P.R.O., H.O.	Public Record Office, London: Home Office series
P.R.O.N.I.	Public Record Office of Northern Ireland
Parl. Reg.	*The Parliamentary Register*, or *History of the Proceedings and Debates of the House of Commons of Ireland* (17 vols, Dublin, 1782–1801)
R.I.A.	Royal Irish Academy
R.I.A. Proc./Trans.	*Proceedings/Transactions of the Royal Irish Academy*
R.P.	Rebellion Papers (N.A.)
R.S.A.I. Jn.	*Journal of the Royal Society of Antiquaries of Ireland*
Rep. Comm. Sec.	*Reports of the Committees of Secrecy of the House of Commons and the House of Lords of Ireland* (Dublin, 1798)
S.O.C.	State of the Country Papers (N.A.)
T.C.D.	Trinity College, Dublin

NOTES AND REFERENCES

An Underground Gentry

1. S. J. Connolly, *Religion, Law and Power: The Making of Protestant Ireland 1660–1760* (Oxford, 1992). For an alternative viewpoint, see Thomas Bartlett, "'A People made rather for Copies than Originals": The Anglo-Irish 1760–1800' in *Int. Hist. Rev.*, xii (1990), pp. 11–25; idem., 'The Rise and Fall of the Protestant Nation 1690–1800' in *Éire-Ireland*, xxvi (1991), pp. 7–18.

2. L. M. Cullen, *The Emergence of Modern Ireland 1600–1900* (London, 1981); Thomas Bartlett, 'An End to Moral Economy: The Irish Militia Disturbances of 1793' in *Past & Present*, xcix (1983), pp. 41–64; Connolly, *Religion, Law and Power*. For a general discussion of the literature on *mentalité* see Robert Darnton, *The Kiss of Lamourette: Reflections in Cultural History* (London, 1990); Peter Burke, *The French Historical Revolution: The* Annales' *School 1929–1989* (Cambridge, 1990).

3. David Dickson, 'Middlemen' in Thomas Bartlett and David Hayton (eds.), *Penal Era and Golden Age* (Belfast, 1979), pp. 162–85; L. M. Cullen, 'Catholic Social Classes under the Penal Laws' in T. P. Power and Kevin Whelan (eds.), *Endurance and Emergence: Catholics in Ireland in the Eighteenth Century* (Dublin, 1990), pp. 57–84.

4. 'A Letter to the Free Electors of the County of Londonderry', 9 Sept. 1775 (W.H. Crawford and Brian Trainor (eds.), *Aspects of Irish Social History 1750–1800* (Belfast, 1969), p. 163).

5. H. Moore (Dublin) to W. Ellis (Gowran, County Kilkenny), 16 Sept. 1746 (P.R.O.N.I., T3403/1/5).

6. For O'Mahony see references 65–6; for James O'Reilly see John Ainsworth, N.L.I. Reports on Collections in Private Keeping, no.6; for Whites see White Papers, T.C.D. MS.

7. Josiah Bateman, *A Just and True Relation of Josiah Bateman's Concerns under the Rt Hon. Richard, Earl of Burlington ever since the year 1713* (n.p., n.d., [c. 1734?]), p. 8.

8. Cited in J. H. Andrews, *Plantation Acres* (Belfast, 1985), p. 84. See also the land surveyor Thomas Moland's comments on the townland of Bealaghbehy on the Courtenay estate in 1709: 'The dwellers on the mountains are all Irish natives and live wretchedly. This farm has a multitude of these cottages and the inhabitants get good oats and potatoes out of their lands, without thought of any further improvement' (p. 270).

9. E. Cooke to W. Fownes, 17 Mar. 1737 (N.L.I., Cooke MS, mic. 1560).

10. L. M. Cullen, 'Catholics under the Penal Laws' in *Eighteenth-Century Ireland*, i (1986), pp. 23–36.

11. J. G. Simms, *The Williamite Confiscation in Ireland 1690–1703* (London, 1956), pp. 193–6.

12. *N.H.I.*, iv, p. 16.
13. Obituary in *Monthly Magazine*, July 1797, p. 70: Eileen O'Byrne (ed.), *The Convert Rolls* (Dublin, 1981), p. 115.
14. *Dialogue between a Protestant and a Papist* (Dublin, 1752), p. 10
15. T. P. Power, 'Converts' in Power and Whelan (eds.), *Endurance and Emergence*, pp. 101–28; W.N. Osborough, 'Catholics, Land and the Popery Acts of Anne', ibid., pp. 21–56.
16. Kavanagh estate papers (N.L.I., mic. 7155; G.O., MS 471; P.R.O.N.I., T3331).
17. *Census Ire.*, 1659, p. 358.
18. For the Butlers see Kevin Whelan, 'The Catholic Church in County Tipperary 1700–1900' in William Nolan (ed.), *Tipperary: History and Society* (Dublin, 1985), pp. 215–55. For the Clanricardes see P. Melvin, 'The composition of the Galway Gentry' in *Ir. Geneal.*, vii (1986), pp. 81–96. For Antrim see Jane Ohlmeyer, *Civil War and Restoration in the Three Stuart Kingdoms: The Career of Randal MacDonnell, Marquis of Antrim, 1609–83* (Cambridge, 1993), pp. 82–8, 240–57.
19. T. P. Power, *Land, Politics and Society in Eighteenth-Century Tipperary* (Oxford, 1993), p. 149.
20. W. J. Smyth, 'Exploring the Social and Cultural Topographies of Sixteenth- and Seventeenth-Century County Dublin' in F. H. A. Aalen and Kevin Whelan (eds.), *Dublin City and County: From Prehistory to Present* (Dublin, 1992), p. 173.
21. Kevin Whelan, 'The Catholic Community in Eighteenth-Century County Wexford' in Power and Whelan (eds.), *Endurance and Emergence*, pp. 137–44.
22. J. Percival (Cork) to ——, 16 Oct. 1658 (H.M.C., *Egmont*, i, pp. 599–600).
23. Cited in Dickson, 'Middlemen', p. 172.
24. William King, *The State of the Protestants of Ireland under the late King James's Government* (3rd ed., London, 1692), p. 36.
25. Samuel Madden, *Reflections and Resolutions proper to the Gentlemen of Ireland* (Dublin, 1738), p. 104.
26. R. Hedges (Ross Castle) to ——, 8 June 1714 (N.A., MS 757).
27. P. S. Dinneen and Tadhg O'Donoghue (eds.), *Dánta Aodhagáin Uí Rathaille: The Poems of Egan O'Rahilly* (London, 1911), p. 8.
28. N. J. A. Williams (ed.), *Pairlement Chloinne Tomáis* (Dublin, 1981), p. 55; see also the passage on pp 60–1.
29. Cited in P. H. Kelly (ed.), 'The Improvement of Ireland' in *Anal. Hib.*, xxxv (1992), pp. 83–4.
30. Tomás Ó Fiaich (ed.), *Art Mac Cumhaigh: Dánta* (Dublin, 1973), pp. 102–4, 105.
31. Breandán Ó Buachalla (ed.), *Peadar Ó Doirnín: Amhráin* (Dublin, 1969), p. 55.
32. Seán Ó Tuama (ed.), *Caoineadh Airt Uí Laoghaire* (Dublin, 1963), p. 62.
33. Cited in L. M. Cullen, *The Hidden Ireland: Reassessment of a Concept* (Gigginstown, 1988), pp. 20–1.
34. Miles Byrne, *Memoirs* (2 vols, Paris, 1863), i, p. 3.
35. John O'Keefe, *Recollections of the Life of John O'Keefe written by himself* (2 vols, London, 1826), i, pp. 8–9.
36. John Brady, *Catholics and Catholicism in the Eighteenth-Century Press* (Maynooth, 1965), p. 311.
37. Denis Taaffe, *Vindication of the Irish Nation* (Dublin, 1802), iii, p. 90.
38. G. O'Malley, 'The Present State of the Name and Fameyly of O'Malley in Ireland in yr of Our Lord 1776' in O. O'Malley, 'O'Malleys between 1651 and 1725' in *Galway Arch. Hist. Jn.*, xxv (1952), pp. 32–46.

39. R. O'Connell to M. Leyne, 20 Aug. 1779 (cited in M.J. O'Connell, *The Last Colonel of the Irish Brigade* (2 vols, London, 1892), i, pp. 223–4).

40. J. Taylor to Richard Wall, 21 Feb. 1775 (cited in Gerry Lyne, 'Landlord–Tenant Relations on the Shelburne Estate in Kenmare, Bonane and Tuosist 1770–1785' in *Kerry Arch. Hist. Soc. Jn.*, xii (1979), pp. 47–8).

41. Cited in J.H. Andrews, 'Charles Vallancey and the Map of Ireland' in *Geog. Jn.*, cxxxii (1966), p. 59.

42. Síle Ní Chinnéide (ed.), 'A New View of Eighteenth-Century Life in Kerry' in *Kerry Arch. Hist. Soc. Jn.*, vi (1973), p. 93.

43. 'The Ancient Inheritance of the Waddings of Ballycogley' (N.L.I., MS 5193, ff. 154–9).

44. Breandán Ó Buachalla, 'Irish Jacobite poetry' in *Ir. Review*, xii (1992), pp. 40–9; idem, 'Irish Jacobitism and Irish Nationalism: The Literary Evidence' in Michael O'Dea and Kevin Whelan (eds.), *Nations and Nationalisms: France, Britain, Ireland and the Eighteenth-Century Context* (Oxford, 1995), pp. 103–16; idem, *Aisling Ghéar: Na Stiobhartaigh agus an t-Aos Léinn 1603–1788* (Baile Átha Cliath, le teacht).

45. Risteárd Ó Foghludha (ed.), *Míl na hÉigse* (Dublin, 1945), p. 57.

46. *Dánta Aodhagáin Uí Rathaille*, p. 6.

47. *Míl na hÉigse*, p. 243.

48. Petition of fifteen gentlemen of County Cork, 3 June 1747 (cited in David Dickson, 'An Economic History of the Cork Region in the Eighteenth Century' (Ph.D. thesis, T.C.D., 1977, pp. 144–5). James Lyons, reporting to Rome on 18 August 1763 concerning a candidate for episcopal advancement in Dublin, observed: 'He is in the first place a man of low birth and that is something which does not pass unnoticed in this country' (*Collect. Hib.*, xi (1968), p. 104).

49. Kevin Whelan, 'The Regional Impact of Irish Catholicism 1700–1850' in W. J. Smyth and Kevin Whelan (eds.), *Common Ground: Essays on the Historical Geography of Ireland* (Cork, 1988), pp. 253–77.

50. Kieran O'Shea (ed.), 'Bishop Moylan's *relatio status*, 1785' in *Kerry Arch. Hist. Soc. Jn.*, vii (1974), pp. 24–5.

51. Thomas Molyneux, 'A Tour in Ireland, 1708' (T.C.D., MS 888, f. 19).

52. Edward MacLysaght (ed.), *The Kenmare Manuscripts* (Dublin, 1942), p. 230.

53. J. Taylor to Shelburne, 5 July 1773 (Marquis of Lansdowne, *Glanerought and the Petty-Fitzmaurices* (Oxford, 1937), p. 75).

54. Arthur Young, *A Tour in Ireland, with General Observations . . . 1776, 1777 and 1778* (2 vols, London, 1780), ii, app. p. 13; see also 'On the Tenantry of Ireland', ibid., pp. 17–25.

55. Ó Tuama (ed.), *Caoineadh*. Compare the description by Denis McCarthy, 'a reduced gentleman' of Nedeen (Kenmare), of his clothes when wealthy: he 'used to wear broad cloath and ruffles and a three legged wig with fringe of gold and Brussels lace and cravat and a fine beaver with gold lace and cockade' (Lansdowne, *Glanerought*, p. 90).

56. J. Taylor to Shelburne, 9 Nov. 1773 (cited in Lyne 'Kenmare, Bonane and Tuosist 1770–85', p. 50).

57. Seán Ó Tuama and Thomas Kinsella (eds.), *An Duanaire: Poems of the Dispossessed* (Dublin, 1990), p. 29.

58. Cited in R. Lightboum, 'Eighteenth- and Nineteenth-Century Visitors to Kilkenny' in *Old Kilk. Rev.*, iii, no. 1 (1983), pp. 6–7.

59. C. J. Woods (ed.), *Journals and Memoirs of Thomas Russell 1791–5* (Dublin, 1991).

60. Gabriel Stokes (ed.), *Pococke's Tour in Ireland in 1752* (Dublin, 1891), pp. 71–2. For examples in Carlow and Kilkenny cited by the Catholic Bishop of Ossory in the 1830s, see Emmet Larkin (ed.), *Alexis de Tocqueville's Journey in Ireland in 1835* (Dublin, 1990), p. 63.

61. Pilib Ó Mórdha, 'Colla Dubh MacMahon, his Ancestors and Descendants' in *Clogher Rec.*, viii (1974), pp. 194–206.

62. Pilib Ó Mórdha, *A History of Currin Parish* (Currin, 1986), p.134.

63. *F.L.J.*, 22–5 Aug. 1770, 30 Nov. – 2 Dec. 1774, 8–11 Dec. 1790, 26–30 Jan., 1793. Purcell's will added an unusual clause: 'My body shall be preceded to the grave by twelve of the best performers on the small pipes which can conveniently be had, to whom I will give one crown each for their trouble in playing my favourite tune of Granuail.'

64. *F.D.J.*, 29 Feb. 1752.

65. Lansdowne, *Glanerought*, p. 53.

66. M. Hickson, *Selections from Old Kerry Records* (London, 1874), p. 158.

67. Gerry Lyne, 'Dr Dermot Lyne: An Irish Catholic Landholder in Cork and Kerry under the Penal Laws' in *Kerry Arch. Hist. Soc. Jn.*, viii (1975), pp. 54–7; idem, 'The Mac Fínín Dubh O'Sullivans of Tuosist and Bearehaven', ibid., ix (1976), pp. 32–67; idem, 'Land Tenure in Kenmare and Tuosist 1696–1716', ibid., x (1977), pp. 19–54.

68. *Seasonable Advice to Protestants containing some Means of Reviving and Strengthening the Protestant Interest* (2nd ed., Cork, 1745), p. 23.

69. MacLysaght (ed.), *Kenmare Manuscripts*, pp. 183, 187, 190.

70. Lansdowne, *Glanerought*, p. 166. He similarly described John Lyne of Cashelkeelty as being 'so surrounded by a clan that he fears nothing'.

71. Ibid., p. 166.

72. [Henry Blake], *Letters from the Irish Highlands* (2nd ed., London, 1825), pp. 12–13. For a report of deliberate wrecking by this family at Inishboffin in 1741, see Brady, *Catholics*, p. 63.

73. R. St George Mansergh St George to Dublin Castle, 17 Mar. 1794 (N.A., R.P., 620/21/18); see also the smuggling song 'An Captín Máilleach' in Micheál Ó Tiománaidhe (ed.), *Amhrán Ghaeilge an Iarthair* (Indreabhán, 1992).

74. J. Burtchaell and D. Dowling, 'Social and Economic Conflict in County Kilkenny 1600–1800' in William Nolan and Kevin Whelan (eds.), *Kilkenny: History and Society* (Dublin, 1990), p. 257; William Healy, *History and Antiquities of Kilkenny* (Kilkenny, 1893), p. 283.

75. Caoimhín Ó Danachair 'An Rí, the King: An Example of Traditional Social Organisation' in *R.S.A.I. Jn.*, iii (1981), pp. 14–28. For an account of Ned Joyce and Edward O'Malley, see [Blake], *Letters*, pp. 41, 106. For Ó Flaitheartha see Tim Robinson, *Stones of Aran* (Dublin, 1986), p. 6.

76. J. Barry (ed.), 'The Groans of Ireland' in *Ir. Sword*, ii (1954–6), p. 134.

77. Edward Wakefield, *An Account of Ireland, Statistical and Political* (2 vols, London, 1812), ii, pp. 544–5. For confirmation, see Charles O Hara's comment in 1772 on the Sligo gentry as 'mostly the descendants of adventurers who have rather the spirit of domination handed down to them' (N.L.I., MS 20397).

78. E. Œ. Somerville and M. Ross, *Irish Memories* (London, 1917), p. 4. For similar comments see Robert Bell, *A Description of the Conditions and Manners as well as*

the Moral and Political Character, Education, etc. of the Peasantry of Ireland between the years 1780 and 1790 (London, 1804), p. 7.

79. J. Mannion, 'A Transatlantic Merchant Fishery: Richard Welsh of New Ross and the Sweetmans of Newbawn in Newfoundland 1734–1862' in Kevin Whelan (ed.), *Wexford: History and Society* (Dublin, 1987), pp. 373–421. For another example see Eoghan Ó Néill, *Gleann an Óir* (Dublin, 1988), a case study of the O'Neill family of south Tipperary and south Kilkenny; the thrust of this book is summarised in Kevin Whelan, 'Gaelic Survivals' in *Ir. Review*, vii (1989), pp. 139–43.

80. Kevin Whelan, 'The Catholic Parish, the Catholic Chapel and Village Development in Ireland' in *Ir. Geog.*, xvi (1983), pp. 1–15.

81. *Wexford People*, 21 Aug. 1909.

82. W. Grattan Flood (ed.), 'The Diocesan Manuscripts of Ferns during the Rule of Bishop Sweetman 1745–1786' in *Archiv. Hib.*, iii (1914), p. 117. For rows over precedence in Catholic chapels among these old families, see Lansdowne, *Glanerought*, p. 68; [Patrick Kennedy], *Evenings in the Duffry* (Dublin, 1869), pp. 299–312.

83. Whelan, 'Catholic Community', pp. 155–9.

84. Charles O'Conor, *Memoirs of the Life and Writings of the late Charles O'Conor of Belanagare* (Dublin, 1796), p. 162.

85. Young, *Tour*, i, p. 185.

86. *D.E.P.*, 4 Feb. 1786.

87. James Kelly (ed.), *The Letters of Lord Chief Baron Edward Willes 1757–1762* (Aberystwyth, 1990), pp. 90–1. One should, however, caution that this may be only another version of the description of Roderick O'Flaherty at Park near Galway, well known from earlier descriptions by John Dunton and Thomas Molyneux.

88. Angélique Day (ed.), *Letters from Georgian Ireland: The Correspondence of Mary Delany 1731–1768* (Belfast, 1991), p. 124.

89. [Blake], *Letters*, pp. 14–15.

90. Laurence Whyte, *Original Poems on Various Subjects* (Dublin, 1740), preface, p. vii.

91. *The Compleat Irish Traveller* (London, 1788), i, pp. 78–9.

92. C. Carroll to D. O'Carroll (London), 9 Sept. 1748 ('Charles Carroll's Correspondence' in *Maryland Hist. Mag.*, xxii (1927), p. 136).

93. Gerry Lyne, 'The O'Connell Family of Derrynane in the Eighteenth Century' (unpublished typescript).

94. Augustín Ravina, *Burguesía Extranjera y Comercio Atlántico: La Empresa Comercial Irlandesa en Canarias 1703–1771* (Tenerife, 1985): for an example see Edward M'Gauran, *The Memoirs of Major Edward M'Gauran (grandson of Colonel Bryan M'Gauran, Baron M'Gauran of Talaha in the county of Cavan)*, (2 vols, London, 1786), i, pp. 133–4.

95. Attestation of Noblesse, A. O'Callaghan to the daughters of Sir Peter Redmond, 15 Mar. 1732 (Windsor Palace, Stuart Papers, vol. clii, f. 126); see also A. Redmond to James III, 1 Jan. 1745 (ibid., cclxi, f. 96).

96. Síle Ní Chinnéide (ed.), 'A Journey from Mullingar to Loughrea in 1791' in *Old Athlone Soc. Jn.*, ii (1978), p. 18.

97. J. Condon, 'Don Jorge Rian of Inch, County Tipperary 1748–1805' in *Ir. Ancestor*, xvii, no. 1 (1986), pp. 5–10.

98. [James Little], 'A Diary of the French Landing in 1798' in *Anal. Hib.*, xi (1941), pp. 148–9.

99. J. O'Donovan, 5 July 1837, *O.S. Letters, Roscommon*, i, pp. 60–1.

100. T. O'Connor, 19 Dec. 1835, *O.S. Letters, Louth*, p. 10.

101. Charles Teeling, *Personal Narrative of the Irish Rebellion of 1798* (Glasgow, 1828), pp. 103–5.

102. Jonah Barrington, *Personal Sketches of His Own Times* (3 vols, Paris, 1827–32), i, p. 150.

103. Whyte, *Original Poems*, p. 72.

104. Lyne, 'O'Connell Family'.

105. [M. Whitty], article in Walsh scrapbook (N.L.I., MS 14040 (unpaginated)).

106. A. Griffith, 'An Account of the Barony of Forth', *Dublin Magazine*, 1765, p. 505. For a remarkably similar account *c.* 1780 see Bell, *Description*, pp. 18–19.

107. *D.E.P.*, 9 Feb. 1786.

108. W. H. Maxwell, *Wild Sports of the West* (London, 1832), pp. 375–6.

109. *F.L.J.*, 8–11 Aug. 1787.

110. Ibid., 26–9 Nov. 1788.

111. Ibid., 29 Nov. – 1 Dec. 1788.

112. Samuel Crumpe, *An Essay on the Best Means of providing Employment for the People* (Dublin, 1793), pp. 431–2.

113. Madden, *Reflections and Resolutions*, p. 103.

114. *A Letter from a Country Gentleman in the Province of Munster* (Dublin, 1741), p. 3.

115. Power, *Tipperary*, pp. 142–3.

116. Musgrave, *Memoirs of the Various Rebellions in Ireland* (Dublin, 1801), app., p. 151.

117. I am grateful to Caoimhín Ó Danachair for this elegant definition of a Limerick strong farmer.

118. Liam Ó Cathnia, *Scéal na hIomána* (Dublin, 1981); Kevin Whelan, 'The Geography of Hurling' in *History Ireland*, i, no. 1 (1993), pp. 25–8.

119. M. Weiner, *Matters of Felony* (London, 1967); see also *F.L.J.*, 21 Apr., 28 Aug. 1779, 2 Feb. 1780; L. M. Cullen, *The Emergence of Modern Ireland* (London, 1981), pp. 245–7; James Kelly, 'The Abduction of Women of Fortune in Eighteenth-Century Ireland' *Eighteenth-Century Ireland*, ix (1994), pp. 31–2.

120. S. J. Connolly, *Priests and People in Pre-Famine Ireland 1780–1845* (Dublin, 1982); Emmet Larkin, *The Historical Dimensions of Irish Catholicism* (Washington, 1984).

121. R.I.A., MS 12/M/11, p. 395.

122. Lansdowne, *Glanerought*, p. 171.

123. Cullen, 'Catholic Social Classes', pp. 57–84.

124. William Tighe, *Statistical Observations relative to the County of Kilkenny* (Dublin, 1802), pp. 384–6. For equivalent comments on the Walsh farm at Earlsrath see ibid., p. 387, and for the accuracy of Tighe's commentary, see *F.L.J.*, 11–13 Aug. 1794.

125. A. Atkinson, *The Irish Tourist* (Dublin, 1815), pp. 471–2.

126. J. H. Andrews, *A Paper Landscape: The Ordnance Survey in Nineteenth-Century Ireland* (Oxford, 1975), p. 223.

127. John Loveday, *Diary of a Tour in 1732 through parts of England, Wales, Ireland and Scotland made by John Loveday of Caversham* (Edinburgh, 1890), p. 58.

128. James Graves and James Prim, *The History, Architecture and Antiquities of the Cathedral Church of St Canice, Kilkenny* (Dublin, 1885), p. 137.

129. *Cinnlae Amhlaoibh Uí Shúilleabháin*, Michael McGrath (ed.) (4 vols, London, 1928–34), iii, p. 15 (my translation). Compare this with the description of the houses in Irishtown (Kilkenny) as 'swallows' nests' (*F.L.J.*, 31 Dec. 1791 – 4 Jan. 1792).

130. Wakefield, *Ire.*, ii, p. 628.
131. Will of Robert Keating, 1729, in *Ir. Geneal.*, iv (1938), p. 125. For the family see Kevin Whelan, 'Catholic Mobilisation 1750–1850' in L. Bergeron and L. M. Cullen (ed.), *Culture et pratiques politiques en France et en Irlande, xvie–xviiie siècle* (Paris, 1991), pp. 235–58.
132. Bernard Browne and Kevin Whelan, 'The Browne Families of County Wexford' in Whelan (ed.), *Wexford*, p. 478.
133. Cited in J. O'Donoghue, 'The Scullys of Kilfeakle: Catholic Middlemen of the 1770s' in *Tipp. Hist. Jn.*, ii (1989), pp. 38–51.
134. N.L.I., MS 27577.
135. J. Downes (Adamstown) to J. Colclough (Tintern Abbey), 2 Nov. 1801 (N.L.I., MS 29766 (25)).
136. M. Whitty to R. R. Madden, 14 May 1868 (cited in *The Past*, vii (1964), pp. 127–30).
137. Whelan, 'Catholic Community', pp. 159–64; James O'Shea, *Priests, Politics and Society in Post-Famine Ireland: A Study of County Tipperary 1850–1891* (Dublin, 1983), pp. 326–60.
138. Young, *Tour*, i, p. 126.
139. J. Burrows, 'A Tour in Ireland in 1773' (P.R.O.N.I., T 3551, p. 99); L. Ritchie, 'Ireland Picturesque and Romantic' in *Heath's Picturesque Annual* (London, 1837), p. 75.
140. Patrick Knight, *Erris in the Irish Highlands* (Dublin, 1836), p. 104.
141. Caesar Otway, *A Tour in Connacht* (Dublin, 1839), p. 252.
142. Cullen, *Hidden Ireland*; T. Jones Hughes, 'The Large Farm in Nineteenth-Century Ireland' in Alan Gailey and Dáithí Ó hÓgáin (ed.), *Gold under the Furze* (Dublin, 1982), pp. 92–100; Kevin Whelan, 'Society and Settlement in Eighteenth-Century Ireland' in G. Dawe and J. Foster (ed.), *The Poet's Place* (Belfast, 1991), pp. 45–62.
143. Young, *Tour*, ii, p. 54; see also Bell, *Description*, pp. 31–3.
144. David Thompson (ed.), *The Irish Journals of Elizabeth Smith 1840–1850* (Oxford, 1980), p. 6.
145. J. Walker, 'An Historical Essay on the Irish Stage' in *R.I.A. Trans.* (1785–9), pp. 75–6. See also H. Morris, 'Irish Wake Games', in *Béaloideas*, viii (1938), p. 123; *Anthologica Hibernica*, Dec. 1794; *Cinnlae Amhlaoibh Uí Shúilleabháin*, iii, p. 39.
146. Cited in Richard Bagwell, *Ireland under the Stuarts* (3 vols, London, 1909–16; repr. 1963), iii, pp. 32–5.
147. Longleat, Thynne MS, clxxix, ff. 125–6.
148. Arthur Dobbs, *An Essay on the Trade and Improvement of Ireland* (Dublin, 1731).
149. Richard Cox, *A Charge to the Grand Jury of County Cork* (Cork, 1740), p. 7.
150. Cited in E. M. Johnson, *Ireland in the Eighteenth Century* (Dublin, 1972), p. 230.
151. John Travers, *A Sermon preached at St Andrew's Church, Dublin* (Dublin, 1698), p. 15.
152. 'A Discourse concerning the Securing the Government of the Kingdom of Ireland to the Interest of England' [c. 1695] (B.L., Add. MS 28724, f. 4).
153. *The Axe Laid to the Root or Reasons humbly offered for Putting the Popish Clergy in Ireland under some Better Regulations* (Dublin, 1749), p. 5.
154. Kelly (ed.), *Willes*, p. 29.
155. Young, *Tour*, ii, p. 133.
156. Carrigan MS., St Kieran's College, Kilkenny.
157. Seamus Fenton, *It All Happened: Reminiscences* (Dublin, 1948), p. 171.
158. Kenneth Nicholls, 'Catholics and the Popery Laws' (unpublished paper), p. 2.
159. Hay MS, in possession of William Sweetman, Whitemills, Wexford.

160. Young, *Tour*, i, p. 249.

161. Chief Baron Willes referred to the 'red-hot' Protestants of Tipperary in the 1760s (Kelly (ed.), *Willes*, p. 46), while Forster Archer in 1801 commented: 'There is not in Ireland a county where the names of Englishman and Protestant are more hated than in the county of Cork. They are synonymous in their phrase and the object of their deep and bigotted hatred' (cited in P. Lysaght, 'Rev. Forster Archer's visit to Limerick and Clare, 1801' in *North Munster Antiq. Jn.*, xviii (1976), p. 53).

162. I am grateful to Máirín Ní Dhonnchadha for alerting me to these poems, which remain largely unedited.

163. Lyne, 'O'Connell Family'.

164. Power, *Tipperary*, p. 244.

165. See especially William Burke, *History of Clonmel* (Waterford, 1907), pp. 393, 404–5, for lists of those targeted. These incidents also left an indelible impression on Edmund Burke: see L. M. Cullen, 'Burke, Ireland and Revolution' in *Eighteenth-Century Life*, xvi (1992), pp. 21–42.

166. J. S. Donnelly, 'Irish Agrarian Rebellion: The Whiteboys of 1769–76' in *R.I.A. Proc.*, clxxxiii (1983), pp. 293–331.

167. Lansdowne, *Glanerought*, p. 62; see also J. A. Froude, *The English in Ireland in the Eighteenth Century* (3 vols, London, 1872–4), iii, p. 106, for similar comments by Townshend in 1770.

168. Lord Clonmell's diary in W. Fitzpatrick, *Curious Family History or Ireland before the Union*, 6th ed., Dublin, 1880, p. 33.

169. J. A. Froude, *The English in Ireland in the Eighteenth Century* (3 vols, London, 1872–4), ii, p. 553.

170. Ibid., iii, p. 386.

171. H.M.C., *Charlemont*, i, p. 48.

172. H.M.C., *Rutland*, iii, p. 281.

173. Ibid., p. 285.

174. Idem.

175. Thomas Bartlett, *The Fall and Rise of the Irish Nation: The Catholic Question 1690–1830* (Dublin, 1992), pp. 111–12: Power, *Tipperary*, p. 280.

176. *D.E.P.*, 24 Jan, 4 Feb., 9 Feb., 18 Feb., 25 Feb. 1786.

177. H.M.C., *Rutland*, iii, pp. 279–81. A. Zondari, Ab of Adana to Cardinal Buon-Compagni, 28 Jan., 7 Mar., 21 Mar. 1786 (cited in *Collect. Hib.*, xi (1968), pp. 73–4).

178. Address of the Roman Catholics of County Roscommon to the Lord Lieutenant, in *D.E.P.*, 28 Feb. 1786.

179. H.M.C., *Rutland*, iii, p. 284.

180. *F.L.J.*, 30 Sept. – 4 Oct. 1786. For another account of the O'Connor incident, see Bell, *Description*, pp. 27–8. For a truly extraordinary account of the O'Connor family, see Skeffington Gibbon, *The Recollections of Skeffington Gibbon from 1796 to the present year 1829, being an epitome of the lives and characters of the nobility and gentry of Roscommon, the genealogy of those who are descended from the kings of Connaught and a memoir of the late Madame O'Conor Dun* (Dublin, 1829).

181. Seamus Deane, 'Edmund Burke 1791–1797' in idem (ed.), *The Field Day Anthology of Irish Writing* (3 vols, Derry, 1991), ii, pp. 807–9; Conor Cruise O'Brien, *The Great Melody: A Thematic Biography of Edmund Burke* (London, 1992), esp. pp. 3–57; Cullen, 'Burke, Ireland and Revolution'; idem, 'Catholics of the Blackwater Valley 1730–1780' (lecture at T.C.D., 1991).

182. Compare Burke's view with Skeffington Gibbon's comments on those who celebrated the 1688 settlement in Ireland: 'I do not wonder at the progeny of those wolves and tigers idolizing those detestable and sanguinary times, as it rescued many of their ancestors from the worst and most abject stations in life and placed them and their posterity in the mansions and wide domains of the ancient nobles of the kingdom' (Gibbon, *Recollections*, pp. 153–4).

183. John O'Rourke, *The Case of Count O'Rourke presented to His Majesty in June 1784* (London, 1784) (copy in N.L.I., MS 52/K/4B).

184. Bartlett, *Fall and Rise*, p. 288. For two examples of this attitude in the 1790s, see James Coigley [Quigley], *The Life of the Rev. James Coigley* (London, 1798); Edward Sweetman, *Speech delivered to the Freeholders of County Wexford* (Dublin, 1792).

185. Byrne, *Memoirs*, i, p. 253.

186. Theobald Wolfe Tone, *Memoirs*, ed. W.T. Tone (2 vols, Washington), 1826, i, p. 245.

187. R.D. Edwards (ed.), 'The Minute Book of the Catholic Committee 1773–1792' in *Archiv. Hib.*, ix (1942), pp. 157–8. As late as 1826, the Catholic hierarchy still felt it necessary to declare: 'The Catholics of Ireland, far from claiming any right or title to forfeited lands, resulting from any right, title or interest which their ancestors may have had therein, declare upon oath that they will defend to the utmost of their power the settlement and arrangement of property in this country, as established by the laws now in being.' (J.W. Doyle, *An Essay on the Catholic Claims* (Dublin, 1826), p. 310.

188. Browne and Whelan, 'Browne Families', pp. 467–89.

189. J. Dougherty (Inishowen) to M. O'Connell (Derrynane), 22 Mar. 1765 (N.L.I. Reports on Private Collections, no. 361).

190. David Dickson, 'Derry's Backyard: The Barony of Inishowen 1660–1840' in M. Dunleavy (ed.), *Donegal. History and Society* (Dublin, 1995), pp. 405–46.

191. Wakefield, *Ire.*, ii, p. 745. See also his comment that Ulster Catholics 'are a miserable people, without an aristocracy to which they can fly, either for example or protection and who drag out a wretched existence in penury' (p. 649).

192. Thomas Bartlett, 'Defenders and Defenderism in 1795' in *I.H.S.*, xxiv (1984–5), pp. 376, 390.

193. Ibid., p. 385.

194. Jim Smyth, *The Men of No Property: Irish Radicals and Popular Politics in the Late Eighteenth Century* (Dublin, 1992), pp. 100–20: Marianne Elliott, 'The Defenders in Ulster' in David Dickson, Dáire Keogh and Kevin Whelan (ed.), *The United Irishmen: Republicanism, Radicalism and Rebellion* (Dublin, 1993), pp. 222–33.

195. Cited in Smyth, *Men of No Property*, p. 115.

196. T. Lane to Downshire, 12 Oct. 1799 (P.R.O.N.I., D607/6/200).

197. Teeling, *Personal Narrative*, p. 115.

198. Ibid., pp. 103–5.

199. L.M. Cullen, 'The Political Structures of the Defenders' in Hugh Gough and David Dickson (ed.), *Ireland and the French Revolution* (Dublin, 1990), pp. 117–38, idem, 'The Internal Politics of the United Irishmen' in Dickson, Keogh and Whelan (eds.), *United Irishmen*, pp. 176–96.

200. See my essay 'United and Disunited Irishmen' in this volume.

201. Bell, *Description*, p. 27.

202. [Little], 'Diary', p. 153.

203. Musgrave, *Rebellions*, app., p. 110.

204. Charles O'Conor, *Ortelius Improved* (Dublin, 1770). For its reissue in 1792 see *Hib. Jn.*, 15 Feb. 1792. For the context, see J. H. Andrews, 'The Cartographer as Antiquarian in Pre-Ordnance Survey Ireland' in C. Thomas (ed.), *Rural Landscape and Communities* (Dublin, 1986), pp. 31–63.

205. Westmorland to Pitt, 18 Feb. 1792 (P.R.O.N.I., T3319/12).

206. William Todd Jones, *A Letter to the Societies of United Irishmen of the Town of Belfast* (Dublin, 1792), pp. 21–2.

207. *The United Irishmen: A Tale Founded on Facts* (Dublin, 1798), pp. 5–6. For other references to the map see Wakefield, *Ire.*, ii, pp. 644–5; Horatio Townsend, *Statistical Survey of County Cork* (Dublin, 1810), p. 78.

208. *An Irishman's Letter to the People called Defenders* (Dublin, 1795), p. 4.

209. *Yelverton's Charge to the Antrim Grand Jury of Carrickfergus, 17 June 1797* (printed broadsheet in R.I.A., Day MS 12/10/13, p.75).

210. Westmorland to Dundas, 24 May 1793 (P.R.O., HO 100/43/319–20).

211. *Proceedings of the Irish Parliament in 1787* (Dublin, 1787), *sub* 19 Feb.

212. Froude, *Ire.*, iii, p. 116.

213. Rosse to Redesdale, 9 May 1822 (P.R.O.N.I., T3030/13/3).

214. Lansdowne, *Glanerought*, p. 165.

215. Wakefield, *Ire.*, i, p. 248.

216. A. Wolfe to E. Cooke, Dublin Castle, 27 Aug. 1795 (N.A., R.P., 620/22/136).

217. B. Chapman to Shelburne, 25 April 1797. (Ann Arbor, Shelburne MS). In a later letter, of 20 May 1797, Chapman made the remarkable comment: 'I should not omit to agree with all this kingdom in acknowledging the legitimate fairness of your lordship's great estates here. My family thought proper to get rid of that imputation in the County Kerry estate belonging to Lord Desmond; we sold to Lord Cork in the reign of James the 1st.'

218. Cited in T. Garvey, 'The Case of Edward Garvey of Rosmindle' in *Cathair na Mart*, vi (1986), p. 69.

219. *Report from the Committee of Secrecy . . . of the House of Commons of Ireland* (2nd ed., London, 1798) p. 28.

220. Byrne, *Memoirs*, i, p. 4.

221. Arthur O'Connor, *The State of Ireland* (London, 1798), p. 17.

222. Address by John Fottrell, provincial to the Dominican nuns of Dublin, 1738 (Hugh Fenning (ed.), *The Fottrell Papers 1721–39* (Belfast, 1980), p. 116).

223. *The Press*, no. 5, 1797, cited in Erhardt Rudebusche, *Irland im Zeitalter der Revolution* (Frankfurt, 1989), p. 185.

224. O'Connor, *State of Ireland*, p. 104.

225. *The Cry of the Poor for Bread* (Dublin, 1795) (broadsheet; copy in N.A., R.P., 620/18/14). For another printed Philanthropic handbill, see Bartlett, 'Defenders and Defenderism in 1795', p. 390.

226. *Christ in Triumph coming to Judgement* (Strabane, 1795), p. 31 (copy in N.A., R.P., 620/22/63).

227. *The Union Doctrine or Poor Man's Catechism* (Dublin, 1798), (copy in N.A., R.P., 620/43/1); reproduced in Musgrave, *Rebellions*, 2nd ed., pp. 166–70, where he notes that it was published and circulated since the rebellion was put down.

228. Tone, *Life*, i, p. 44.

229. *Union Doctrine or Poor Man's Catechism*, p. 6.

230. Judge Robert Day's charge to the Grand Jury of County Westmeath, 12 Apr. 1798 (R.I.A. MS 12/W/11, p. 39). Compare General Thomas Knox's comment to Pelham, 14 May 1797, that 'the present is a contest of the poor against the rich' (B.L., Add. MS 33104, f. 59).

231. F. Higgins to E. Cooke, [Jan.] 1797 (N.A., R.P., 620/18/14).

232. Musgrave, *Rebellions*, p. 224.

233. Ibid., pp 561–3

234. Ibid., app., p. 160.

235. *Old Ballymena: A History of Ballymena during the 1798 Rebellion* [Ballymena, 1857], p. 36.

236. Tom Dunne 'Edgeworthstown in Fact and Fiction 1760–1840' in Raymond Gillespie and Gerard Moran (ed.), *Longford: Essays in County History* (Dublin, 1991), pp. 95–122.

237. See the sequence of letters in Gerry Lyne, 'George Frederick Beltz, Lancaster Herald, and his Quest in Ireland in 1802 for the Ancestry of Sir Richard Joseph Sullivan', pt 2, in *Ir. Geneal.*, vi, no. 4 (1983), pp. 491–4; pt 3, ibid., vi, no. 5, (1985), p. 642.

238. Cited in R. B. McDowell, *The Irish Administration 1801–1914* (London, 1964), p. 272.

239. Cited in Andrews, *Paper Landscape*, p. 167.

240. P. MacWilliam and A. Day (ed.), *Ordnance Survey Memoir for County Fermanagh* (Belfast, 1991), p. 75.

241. Jane Barber, 'Memoir of my experiences in 1798', (typescript, N.L.I., p. 9).

242. A. Meadows (Wexford) to Dublin Castle, 8 May 1822, (N.A., S.O.C., 2509/11).

243. Edward Hay, *History of the Insurrection in the County of Wexford in the year of 1798* (Dublin, 1803), p. 204.

244. Larkin (ed.), *de Tocqueville*, p. 63.

245. Earl of Rosse to Lord Redesdale, 30 Mar. 1822 (P.R.O.N.I. T3030/13/1).

246. Rosse to Redesdale, 3 May 1822 (ibid., T3030/13/3).

247. J. Brownrigg to Lord Downshire, 31 Aug. 1815, (cited in W.A. Maguire, *The Downshire Estates in Ireland 1801–45* (Oxford, 1972), app. iv, pp. 262–4).

248. W. Armstrong (Armagh) to the Bursar, T.C.D., 10 May 1850 (cited in Robert MacCarthy, 'The Estates of Trinity College, Dublin, in the Nineteenth Century' (Ph.D. thesis, T.C.D., 1982, p. 196).

249. James Connery, *The Reformer or An Infallible Remedy to Prevent Pauperism and Periodical Return of Famine* (Cork, 1828), p. 60.

250. Kerby Miller, 'The Erosion of the Protestant Middle Class in Southern Ireland during the Pre-Famine Era' in *Huntington Lib. Quart.*, lix (1986), pp. 295–306.

251. H. Petty to F. Horner, 30 Sept. 1805 (cited in *Kerry Arch. & Hist. Soc. Jn.*, v (1972), p. 117).

252. Wakefield, *Ire.*, ii, p. 548.

253. T. J. Rawson, *Statistical Survey of the County of Kildare* (Dublin, 1807), p. 54; Whitley Stokes, *Observations on the Population and Resources of Ireland* (Dublin, 1821), p. 31.

254. *Census Ire., 1841*, County Cork.

255. Bell, *Description*, pp. 8–9. Compare this with Samuel Madden's account in 1738: 'rather huts than houses and those of our cottiers are built like birds' nests of dirt wrought together and a few sticks and some straw, and like those are generally removed once a year' (Madden, *Reflections and Resolutions*, p. 35).

256. *Seasonable advice to Protestants,* p. 32. Compare Edmund Burke's advice to his Catholic relatives in Cork to stick together (*Burke Corr.*, i, p. 289).

257. Wakefield, *Ire.*, ii, p. 645.

258. *F.L.J.*, 25–8 Feb. 1778.

259. Wakefield, *Ire.*, ii, p. 743; Tighe, *Statistical Observations relative to the County of Kilkenny*, p. 385.

260. W. Eastwood, 'An account of the parish of Tacumshane' in William Shaw Mason, *A Statistical Account or Parochial Survey of Ireland* (3 vols. Dublin, 1814–19), iii, p. 426; W. Parker, *Observations on the Intended Amendment of the Irish Grand Jury Laws* (Cork, 1816), p. 134.

261. Connery, *The Reformer*, p. 54.

262. *Devon Commission*, witness 431, question 55.

263. Memorandum of occurrences, 1831, (N.L.I. Drogheda, MS 9749).

264. Cited in Larkin (ed.), *de Tocqueville*, p. 41.

265. Wakefield, *Ire.*, ii, p. 545.

266. Cormac Ó Gráda, *A New Economic History of Ireland 1780–1939* (Oxford, 1995), p. 257.

267. Cited in Froude, *Ire.*, iii, p. 523.

The Republic in the Village

1. [T. W. Tone], *An Argument on behalf of the Catholics of Ireland* (Dublin, 1791).

2. Cited in W. Bailie, 'Rev. Samuel Barber 1738–1811, National Volunteer and United Irishman' in J. Haire (ed.), *Challenge and Conflict: Essays in Presbyterian History and Doctrine* (Antrim, 1981), p. 82.

3. *Rep. Comm. Sec.*, pp. 67, 71, 74.

4. *Northern Star*, 1 June 1795.

5. *Rep. Comm. Sec.*, p. 72.

6. I have used the 1777 Dublin edition of *The Complete Works of M. de Montesquieu translated from French* (4 vols). 'The Spirit of Laws' is in vol. i. My treatment is greatly influenced by Seamus Deane, 'The Irish Enlightenment' (lecture delivered to the Eighteenth-Century Ireland Society, Drumcondra, spring 1991).

7. Dying declaration of William Michael Byrne (N.A., R.P., 620/39/109).

8. Theobald Wolfe Tone, *Memoirs*, ed. W.T. Tone (2 vols, Washington, 1826), i, p. 51.

9. John Larkin (ed.), *The Trial of William Drennan* (Dublin, 1991), p. 40.

10. Arthur O' Connor, *The State of Ireland* (Dublin, 1798), p. 28.

11. *Rep. Comm. Sec.*, p. 27.

12. D. A. Chart (ed.), *The Drennan Letters 1776–1819* (Belfast, 1931), p. 228.

13. *Beauties of The Press* (London, 1800) p. 34.

14. *Northern Star*, 1 June 1795.

15. *Beauties of The Press*, p. 171.

16. L. McNally to E. Cooke, 12 Sept. 1795 (N.A., R.P., 620/10/121/27).

17. *A Letter on the State of the Parties and on the subject of Reform, addressed to the People* (Belfast, 1796), p. 13.

18. F. Archer to government, 6 Dec. 1797 (N.A., R.P., 620/33/123).

19. Information of John Smith, Dec. 1796 (ibid., 620/54/7).

20. This volume is in the Rare Books Library of Notre Dame University, South Bend, Indiana, to whom I am grateful for permission to consult it.

21. R. B. McDowell, 'The Personnel of the Dublin Society of the United Irishmen' in *I.H.S.*, ii, (1940–41), pp. 12–53.

22. 'An account of the numbers of persons surrendering themselves in the city of Dublin from 29 June to September 1798' in *Commons' Jn. Ire.*, app., pp. dccccxlvi–lix.

23. Larkin (ed.), *Trial of William Drennan*, p. 51.

24. Robert Burrowes, *Advice Religious and Political delivered in Four Sermons to a Congregation in the North of Ireland* [Cappagh, Co. Tyrone] (Dublin, 1801), p. 12.

25. D. Browne to government, 6 June 1793 (P.R.O., HO 100/44/115–8).

26. James Alexander, *Some Account of the First Apparent Symptoms of the Late Rebellion* (Dublin, 1800), p. 19.

27. L. McNally to E. Cooke, 12 Sept. 1795 (N.A., R.P., 620/10/121/27).

28. P. Dillon to E. Cooke, 14 Feb. 1795 (ibid., S.O.C., 30/159).

29. E. Newenham to T. Pelham, 31 May 1797 (ibid., R.P., 620/30/275).

30. Seamus Grimes (ed.), *Dublin in 1804* (Dublin, 1980), p. 18.

31. David Dickson, 'Centres of motion: Irish cities and the origins of popular politics' in Louis Bergeron and L. M. Cullen (eds.), *Culture et pratiques politiques en France et en Irlande, xvie–xviiie siècles* (Paris, 1991), pp. 101–22.

32. Lord Clonmell, 3 Mar. 1796, on the Defender trials in Thomas McNevin, *The Leading State Trials of Ireland* (Dublin, 1844), p. 478; Dean Dobbs, Carrickfergus, 'Digest of evidence on United Irishmen', 6 June 1795 (P.R.O., HO 100/58/190).

33. A. MacNevin to government, 9 July 1795 (P.R.O., HO 100/58/190).

34. Richard Musgrave, *Memoirs of the Various Rebellions in Ireland* (Dublin, 1801), p. 155.

35. *Northern Star*, 15 July 1796.

36. *The Union Doctrine or Poor Man's Catechism* (Dublin, 1798), p. 5 (copy in N.A., R.P., 620/43/1).

37. Musgrave, *Rebellions*, p. 155.

38. *A Letter on the State of the Parties*, p. 18.

39. A. O' Connor to C. Fox, n.d. (N.A., R.P., 620/15/3/8).

40. *Names of Persons who Took and Subscribed to the Oath of Allegiance to His Majesty before Baron Yelverton and Judge Chamberlain at an Adjourned Sessions held in Belfast in June 1797* (Belfast, 1797).

41. G. Knox to Abercorn, 16 Mar. 1793 (P.R.O.N.I., T2541/181/4/17).

42. Simon Davies, 'The *Northern Star* and the propogation of enlightened ideas' in *Eighteenth-Century Ireland*, vi (1990), pp. 43–52; R. C. Cole, *Irish Booksellers and English Writers 1740–1800* (London, 1986), p. 17.

43. C. J. Woods (ed.), *Journals and Memoirs of Thomas Russell 1791–5* (Dublin, 1991), p. 112.

44. Unattributed account of Ulster, 1796 (B.L., Add. MS 38759, p. 37).

45. Charles Moore, *Reflections on the Present State of our Country* (Dublin, 1798).

46. John Gray, 'A Tale of Two Newspapers: The Contest between the *Belfast News-letter* and the *Northern Star* in the 1790s' in idem (ed.), *An Uncommon Bookman: Essays in memory of J. R. R. Adams* (Belfast, forthcoming).

47. The following commentary is based on the *Northern Star* notebooks in N.A., R.P., 620/15/8–10.

48. The port hinterlands are given in R. Dickson, *Ulster Emigration to Colonial America 1718–1775* (London, 1966); the 1837 trade-flow map by W. D. Harkness is printed in the *Atlas to accompany the second part of the Report of the Commissioners appointed to Consider and Recommend a General System of Railways for Ireland* (H.C. 1838).

49. J. Schoales to Fitzwilliam, 7 May 1797 (N.L.I., Fitzwilliam MS, mic. 5641).

50. W. Richardson to Abercorn, 22 Feb. 1797 (P.R.O.N.I., Abercorn Papers, D623/A/156/5).

51. J. Richardson to government, 15 Oct. 1796 (N.A., R.P., 620/25/171).

52. *Rep. Comm. Sec.*, p. 12.

53. *F.D.J.*, 2 Jan. 1798.

54. Ibid., 9 Jan. 1798.

55. Transcript of the trial of Fr John Brookes (N.A., R.P., 620/41/66).

56. John Sweeney's papers (ibid., 620/48/47).

57. Mary Helen Thuente, *The Harp Restrung: The United Irishmen and the Rise of Irish Literary Nationalism* (Syracuse, 1994), p. 233.

58. Olive Smith, *The Politics of Language 1791–1819* (Oxford, 1984).

59. *Union Doctrine or Poor Man's Catechism*, p. 6.

60. R. Nevill to E. Cooke, 10 Dec. 1797 (N.A., R.P. 620/33/139).

61. M. Tracey to T. Pelham, 26 May 1797 (ibid., 620/30/198).

62. *Saunder's Newsletter*, 14 Dec. 1797.

63. J. Whyte to E. Cooke, 17 Mar. 1793 (P.R.O., HO 100/43/103).

64. Woods (ed.), *Russell*, pp. 66–7.

65. *Saunder's Newsletter*, 10 Dec. 1797; G. Holdcroft to J. Lees, 7 Apr. 1796 (N.A., R.P., 620/23/73); *The Press*, 5, 14 Dec. 1797.

66. Charles Jackson, *A Narrative of the Sufferings and Escape of Charles Jackson* (London, 1798), pp. 22–3.

67. Thuente, *The Harp Restrung, passim.*

68. *Northern Star*, 2 Sept. 1796.

69. T. Handcock, 'A Narrative of the Battle of Enniscorthy' (N.L.I., MS 16232, p. 116).

70. [Rev. C. Robinson] to E. Cooke, 29 May 1798 (N.A., R.P., 620/37/211a).

71. W. Birmingham to E. Cooke, 24 Dec. 1796 (ibid., 620/26/153).

72. *F.L.J.*, 2–6 Mar. 1793.

73. *D.E.P.*, 21 Mar. 1797.

74. Tom Paulin, *Minotaur: Poetry and the Nation State* (London, 1992), p. 167.

75. Ruth Bloch, *Visionary Republic: Millenial Themes in American Thought 1756–1801* (Cambridge, 1991).

76. A. Shackleton to J. Williams, 29 Nov. 1792 (N.L.I., Shackleton Papers, uncatalogued collection).

77. [James Little], 'A Diary of the French Landing in 1798' in *Anal. Hib.*, xi (1941), p. 122.

78. J. Beresford to Auckland, 4 Sept. 1796 (*Beresford Corr.*, ii, p. 128).

79. W. E. H. Lecky, *History of Ireland in the Eighteenth Century* (5 vols, London, 1892), iii, pp. 441–2.

80. *A Discourse on the Rise and Fall of Anti-Christ wherein the Revolution in France and the Downfall of Monarchy in this Kingdom are distinctly pointed out, delivered at London in the year 1701 by Robert Fleming* (Belfast, 1795), p. v. (copy in N.A., R.P., 620/22/63).

81. *Christ in Triumph coming to Judgement* (Strabane, 1795), p. 3 (copy in N.A., R.P., 620/22/63, with an accompanying letter).

82. T. A Emmet, 'Part of an Essay towards a History of Ireland' in W. J. MacNeven, *Pieces of Irish History* (New York, 1807), p. 77; see also J. S. Donnelly, 'Propagating the Cause of the United Irishmen' in *Studies*, lxix, (1980), pp. 5–23.

83. *The Press*, 20 Jan. 1798.

84. J. R. R. Adams, *The Printed Word and the Common Man: Popular Culture in Ulster, 1700–1900* (Belfast, 1987), p. 6.

85. L. M. Cullen, 'The Internal Politics of the United Irishmen' in David Dickson, Dáire Keogh and Kevin Whelan (eds.), *The United Irishmen: Radicalism, Republicanism and Rebellion* (Dublin, 1993), pp. 176–96.

86. Antonio Gramsci, *Selections from the Prison Notebooks* (London, 1973). I have benefited greatly from reading Terry Eagleton, 'Ascendancy and Hegemony' in *Heathcliff and the Great Hunger* (London, 1995), pp. 27–103.

87. H.M.C., *Charlemont*, ii, pp. 245–6.

88. Linen Hall Library, Henry Joy Papers, 8/15/3.

89. [James Porter], *Billy Bluff and Squire Firebrand* (Belfast, 1796), p. 21.

90. N.A., R.P., 620/41/112.

91. Clonmell, cited in *F.D.J.*, 5 Mar. 1796; Musgrave, *Rebellions*, p. 117; Dexter Club (N.A., R.P., 620/34/58); Shoe Club (ibid., 620/34/58); Strugglers (John Burk, *History of the Late War in Ireland, with an Account of the United Irish Association* (Philadelphia, 1799), p. 44); Cold Bone Club (N.L.I., MS 1429); Real United Traders (N.A., R.P., 620/24/171); Clady Club (ibid., 620/34/59); Shamrock Club (Musgrave, *Rebellions*, p. 113).

92. *F.D.J.*, 8 Mar. 1796.

93. Ibid., 26 Jan. 1796.

94. Ibid., 5 Jan. 1796.

95. Ian McCalman, *Radical Underworld: Prophets, Revolutionaries and Pornographers in London 1795–1840* (Oxford, 1993); Robert Darnton, *The Literary Underground of the Old Regime* (London, 1982); Marcus Wood, *Radical Satire and Print Culture, 1790–1822* (Oxford, 1994); R. Darnton and D. Roche (ed.), *Revolution in Print: The Press in France 1775–1800* (Berkeley, 1989); J. Landes, 'More than Words: The Printing Press and the French Revolution' in *Eighteenth-Century Studies*, xxv (1991), pp. 85–98; Robert Darnton, *Édition et sédition: L'univers de la littérature clandestine au xviie siècle* (Paris, 1991).

96. The information of Thomas Kennedy, 15 Mar. 1796 (N.A., R.P., 620/23/59). This is an account of the Huguenot Society by one of its members, including details of the production of *The Cry of the Poor for Bread*.

97. F. Higgins to E. Cooke, 15 Aug. 1796 (N.A., R.P., 620/18/14).

98. Thomas Bartlett, 'Defenders and Defenderism in 1795' in *I.H.S.*, xxiv (1984–5), p. 390.

99. E. P. Thompson, *The Making of the English Working Class* (London, 1963), pp. 107–8.

100. A copy of *The New Age* is in N.A., R.P., 620/18/14.

101. Denis Taaffe, *Ireland's Mirror, exhibiting a Picture of her Present State, with a Glimpse of her Future Prospects* (Dublin, 1796), p. 14.

102. *F.D.J.*, 5 Mar. 1796. This long report was probably written by Francis Higgins.

103. *Letter from a Gentleman in Ireland to his Friend at Bath* (Cork, 1798), p. 10.

104. *F.D.J.*, 8 Mar. 1796.

105. Burk, *History*, pp. 45–6.

106. F. Higgins to E. Cooke (various letters) (N.A., R.P. 620/18/14).

107. Bernard Mandeville, *The Fable of the Bees* (1714; repr. Harmondsworth, 1970), p. 191.

108. Musgrave, *Rebellions*, app., p. 826. Watty Cox claimed that in an English regiment of 700 men stationed in Dublin in 1798, only thirty could read (*Irish Magazine*, Nov. 1807, p. 12).

109. Address to the Grand Jury of County Kerry, 18 Mar. 1799 (R.I.A., MS 12/10/11).

110. *F.D.J.*, 3 Mar. 1796.

111. *Presbyterio-Catholicon* (Dublin, 1792), p. 19.

112. *F.D.J.*, 2 Jan. 1798.

113. James Caulfield, *The Reply of the Right Revd Dr Caulfield, Roman Catholic Bishop, and of the Roman Catholic Clergy of Wexford to the Misrepresentation of Sir Richard Musgrave* (Dublin, 1801), p. 84.

114. J. Arbuckle to Downshire, 18 Sept. 1796 (P.R.O.N.I., Downshire Papers, D607/D/180).

115. *The Speech of the Rt Hon. John, Earl of Clare, 17 February 1798* (Dublin, 1798), p. 33.

116. Brian Inglis, *The Freedom of the Press in Ireland 1784–1841* (London, 1954).

117. Castlereagh to Cornwallis, 8 Sept. 1798 (*Cornwallis Corr.*, ii, p. 448).

118. *Essay on the Present State of Manners and Education among the Lower Class of the People of Ireland and the Means of Improving Them* (Dublin, 1799), p. 7.

119. Whitley Stokes, *Projects for Re-establishing the Internal Peace and Tranquillity of Ireland* (Dublin, 1799), pp. 41–3.

120. *The Present State of Manners,* pp. 6–7.

121. Robert Day's report on the Cork disturbances, 1794 (R.I.A., MS 12/10/14).

122. Mary Pollard, *Dublin's Trade in Books 1550–1800* (Oxford, 1989); Hugh Fenning, 'The Catholic Press in Munster in the Eighteenth Century' and 'Dublin Imprints of Catholic Historical Interest 1700–1753' (unpublished papers).

123. *Address of the County Committee of Dublin City to their Constituents, 1 February 1798* (Dublin, 1798) (copy in N.A., R.P., 620/42/14).

124. Kevin Whelan, 'Politicisation in County Wexford and the Origins of the 1798 Rebellion' in Hugh Gough and David Dickson (eds.), *Ireland and the French Revolution* (Dublin, 1990), p. 174; Edward Hay, *History of the Insurrection in County Wexford* (Dublin, 1803), app., p. xxvi.

125. Kevin Whelan, 'The Catholic Community in Eighteenth-Century County Wexford' in Thomas Power and Kevin Whelan (eds.), *Endurance and Emergence: Catholics in Ireland in the Eighteenth Century* (Dublin, 1990), pp. 129–70.

126. Letter of R. Jephson, cited in Constantia Maxwell, *Dublin under the Georges 1714–1890* (London, 1938), p. 108.

127. Anne, Countess of Roden, to H. Skeffington, 21 Feb. 1793 (P.R.O.N.I., D562/2563).

128. Alexander, *Some Account of the First Apparent Symptoms*, p. 22.

129. *F.D.J.*, 3 May 1798.

130. *F.L.J.*, 5–8 Aug. 1795; Mona Ozouf, 'Du Mai de liberté à l'arbre de la liberté: symbolisme révolutionaire et tradition paysan', in *Ethnologie Française*, v (1975), pp. 9–34; Joel Barlow, Genealogy of the Tree of Liberty (Houghton Library, Harvard University, Barlow Papers).

131. Roger McHugh (ed.), *Carlow in '98: The Autobiography of William Farrell* (Dublin, 1949), p. 23.

132. *F.L.J.*, 20–23 July 1770, 13–16 Mar. 1776.

133. *Wexford People*, 3 July 1909; Miles Byrne, *Memoirs* (2 vols, Paris, 1863), i, p. 223; N.A., R.P. 620/11/138/43, 620/13/168/3; ibid., S.O.C., 1804, 1026/17, 1027/2.

134. Byrne, *Memoirs*, i, p. 94.
135. *The Tryal of William Byrne of Ballymanus* (Dublin, 1799), p. 19.
136. Members' registers, Grand Lodge of Free and Accepted Masons, Molesworth Street, Dublin; A. T. Q. Stewart, *A Deeper Silence: The Hidden Origins of the United Irishmen* (London, 1993); James Smyth, 'Freemasonry and the United Irishmen' in Dickson, Keogh and Whelan (eds.), *United Irishmen*, pp. 167–75; Philip Robinson, 'Hanging Ropes and Buried Secrets' in *Ulster Folklife*, xxxii (1986), pp. 3–15.
137. J. Knox to E. Cooke, 13 June 1798, (N.A., R.P., 620/38/141).
138. John Hewitt, *Rhyming Weavers and other Country Poets of Antrim and Down* (Belfast, 1974); John Gray, 'Folk Poetry and Working-Class Identity in Ulster: An Analysis of James Orr's *The Penitent*' in *Jn. Hist. Sociology*, vi (1993), pp. 249–75.
139. *Freeman's Journal*, 19 Mar. 1796.
140. T. Boyle to government, 13 Apr. 1797 (N.A., R.P., 620/18/3).
141. J. Smith to government, 16 June 1797 (ibid., S.O.C., 11/3086).
142. C. Colclough to government, 18 Jan. 1799 (ibid., R.P., 620/56/62).
143. [Little], 'Diary', pp 64–5, 67. For other references to confraternities see N.A., R.P., 620/26/64, 620/32/77, 620/31/180, 620/56/14.
144. L. Hyland to Glenworth, 8 Dec. 1796 (N.A., R.P., 620/26/105); *Northern Star*, 18 Jan. 1796; N.A., R.P., 620/23/53; Smyth, *Men of No Property* (London, 1992), *passim*.
145. *Saunder's Newsletter*, 2 June 1797; A. Cole-Hamilton to government, 24 Mar. 1796 (N.A., R.P., 620/25/53).
146. *F.L.J.*, 31 Aug. – 4 Sept. 1782. For similar examples see ibid., 21–25 Aug. 1773, 28–31 Aug. 1782, 20–27 Sept. 1783.
147. Ibid., 27–30 May 1795.
148. Information of James Sheridan, 21 Apr. 1795 (P.R.O., Digest on the United Irishmen, HO 100/58/189).
149. A. Newton to T. Pelham, 15 Aug. 1796 (N.A., R.P., 620/24/120).
150. B. Chapman to Shelburne, 25 Apr. 1797 (Michigan University Library, Ann Arbor, Shelburne Papers).
151. J. Walsh, *Sketches of Ireland Sixty Years Ago* (Dublin, 1849), p. 110.
152. H. Echlin to government, 17 May 1798 (N.A., R.P., 620/37/95).
153. George Moore, *Observations on the Union, Orange Associations and other subjects of Domestic Policy* (Dublin, 1799), pp. 11–12.
154. Hobart to Nepean, 17 June 1793 (P.R.O., HO 100/44/147–50).
155. *Rep. Comm. Sec.*, p. 6; see also Samuel McSkimin, *Annals of Ulster* (Belfast, 1849), pp. 37–9; *The Press*, 21 Dec. 1797; J. A. Froude, *The English in Ireland in the Eighteenth Century* (3 vols, London, 1872–4), iii, pp. 217–18.
156. 'The Exiled Irishman's Address to his Countrymen', (N.A., R.P. 620/42/14).
157. E. Cooke to T. Pelham, 6 Oct. 1795 (P.R.O.N.I., T755/2/225–7).
158. E. Hay to L. Teeling, 8 Sept. 1795, in N.L.I., Reports on Private Collections, no. 261.
159. E. Burke to T. Hussey, 9 June 1795 (cited in Hay, *History*, app., p. xxxviii).
160. *The Speech of Edward Sweetman at a Meeting of the Freeholders of the County of Wexford on 22 September 1792* (Dublin, 1792), p. 9.
161. Hay, *History*, p. 34.
162. J. Troy to E. Wakefield, 5 Apr. 1811 (cited in Edward Wakefield, *An Account of Ireland, Statistical and Political* (2 vols, London, 1812), ii, p. 592).
163. *D.E.P.*, 23 June 1791.

164. *F.L.J.*, 16–19 Feb. 1791; see also ibid., 2–6 May 1788, 23–6 Feb. 1791; *D.E.P.*, 23 June 1791.
165. *F.L.J.*, 3–7 Oct. 1789; Grimes (ed.), *Dublin in 1804*, p. 28.
166. Thomas Brennan, *Public Drinking and Popular Culture in Eighteenth-Century Paris* (Princeton, 1988).
167. *F.L.J.*, 13–16 Mar. 1793; Froude, *Ire.*, iii, p. 122.
168. Robert Day's charge to Kilmainham quarter-sessions, 12 Jan. 1796, in *F.D.J.*, 28 Jan. 1796.
169. *Address of the County Committee of Dublin City*, pp. 2–3.
170. *To the Friends of the Union of the County of Meath* (Trim, 1797) (copy in N.A., R.P., 620/54/37); *To the United Men of Ireland* (Dublin, 1797) (copy in ibid., 620/54/40).
171. Richard Musgrave, *Memoirs of the Various Rebellions in Ireland*, (Dublin, 1801), p. 232; Diary of Robert Day, 1829 (R.I.A., MS 12/W/16), p. 163.
172. *Grania's Lamentation* [ballad on Armagh expulsions] (copy in N.A., S.O.C., 1797, 30/46).
173. N.A., R.P., 620/39/10.
174. J. Laffan to government, 1 Oct. 1804 (P.R.O., HO 100/122/340–2).
175. Peter Burke, *Popular Culture in Early-Modern Europe* (London, 1978); see also my essay 'An Underground Gentry? Catholic Middlemen in Eighteenth-Century Ireland' in this volume.
176. Linda Colley, *Britons: Forging the Nation 1707–1837* (Yale, 1992).
177. Robert Bell, *A Description of the Conditions and Manners as well as the Moral and Political Character, Education, etc. of the Peasantry of Ireland between the years 1780 and 1790* (London, 1804), p. 1.
178. James Kelly (ed.), *The Letters of Lord Chief Baron Edward Willes 1757–1762* (Aberystwyth, 1990), p. 45.
179. *F.L.J.*, 12–15 July 1780; long account in collection of news cuttings (N.M.I., 6–1935, under 14 July 1780).
180. George O'Malley, Autobiography (N.L.I., mic. 208, p. 543).
181. Bell, *Description*, p. 1.
182. *Londonderry Jn.*, 25 Jan. 1831.
183. Peter Sahlins, *Forest Rites: The War of the Demoiselles in Nineteenth-Century France* (London, 1994).
184. Musgrave, *Rebellions*, app., p. 24.
185. Moore, *Observations on the Union*, p. 13.
186. S. Hoey to J. Forbes, 1 July 1788 (cited in M. Corcoran (ed.), 'Three Eighteenth-Century Drogheda Letters' in *Louth Arch. Soc. Jn. xxii* (1989), p. 31).
187. *F.L.J.*, 11–14 July 1792.
188. James Caulfield, *Advice to the Roman Catholic Clergy of the Diocese of Ferns, 12 April 1803* (Wexford, 1803), p. 3.
189. [Little], 'Diary', p. 70.

United and Disunited Irishmen

1. James Kelly, *Prelude to Union: Anglo-Irish Politics in the 1780s* (Cork, 1992), *passim*.
2. Thomas Bartlett, *The Fall and Rise of the Irish Nation: The Catholic Question 1690–1830* (Dublin, 1992), *passim*.
3. *Parl. Reg.*, vi (1786), p. 256.

4. Cited in J. A. Froude, *The English in Ireland in the Eighteenth Century* (3 vols, London, 1872–4), iii, p. 476.

5. Theobald Wolfe Tone, *Memoirs*, ed. W. T. Tone (2 vols, Washington, 1826), i, p. 356. For the general background, see Kevin Whelan, 'Catholics, Politicisation and the 1798 Rebellion', in R. Ó Muirí (ed.), *Irish Church History Today* (Armagh, 1991), pp. 63–83.

6. [T. W. Tone], *Argument on behalf of the Catholics of Ireland* (Dublin, 1791), p. 17.

7. See my essay 'The Republic in the Village' in this volume.

8. David Dickson, Dáire Keogh and Kevin Whelan (ed.), *The United Irishmen: Radicalism, Republicanism and Rebellion* (Dublin, 1993); Nancy Curtin, *The United Irishmen: Popular Politics in Ulster and Dublin 1791–1798* (Oxford, 1994).

9. E. P. Thompson, *Witness against the Beast: William Blake and the Moral Law* (Cambridge, 1993).

10. Colin Haydon, 'Anti-Catholicism in Eighteenth-Century England *c.* 1714–1780' (D.Phil. thesis, Oxford University, 1985).

11. Bartlett, *Fall and Rise, passim.*

12. *Mr Grattan's Letter to his Fellow Citizens of Dublin* (Edinburgh, 1797), p. 7.

13. These early addresses by the United Irishmen are conveniently collected in the *Reports of the Committees of Secrecy of the House of Commons and the House of Lords of Ireland, with appendices* (Dublin, 1798).

14. *Parl. Reg.*, xv (1795), p. 289.

15. *Polar Star and Boston Daily Advertiser*, 13 Oct. 1796.

16. *Political Register*, 13 Jan. 1821.

17. W. B. Kirwan, *A Discourse on Religious Innovations pronounced by the Rev. Walter Blake Kirwan at His Excellency the Neopolitan Ambassador's Chapel, 20 March 1786* (London, 1787), p. 3.

18. Longfield to Shannon, 16 July 1778 (P.R.O.N.I., Shannon, MS D2707/A2/2/40).

19. Diary of Henry Quin, 25 Dec. 1785 (T.C.D., MS 2261).

20. [W. J. MacNeven], *An Argument for Independence* (Dublin, 1799), p. 36.

21. Denis Taaffe, *An Impartial History of Ireland* (4 vols, Dublin, 1811), iv, p. 451.

22. W. Latimer, *A History of Irish Presbyterians* (Belfast, 1893), p. 359.

23. George Moore, *Observations on the Union* (Dublin, 1799), p. 74; see also J. Black, *British Foreign Policy in the Age of Revolution 1783–1793* (Cambridge, 1995).

24. *The Writings and Speeches of Edmund Burke*, vol. viii: *The French Revolution, 1790–1794*, ed. L. G. Mitchell (Oxford, 1989), p. 306; see also P. Schofield, 'British Politicians and French Arms: The Ideological War of 1793–1795' in *History* (June 1992), pp. 183–201.

25. Marc de Bombelles, *Journal de voyage en Grande Bretagne et en Irlande, 1784,* ed. Jacques Gury (Oxford, 1989), p. 239: 'It would be imprudent to admit to any kind of magistracy or public employment individuals other than those who profess the dominant religion of the country. Ireland is governed by the same laws that govern England and has adopted the same liturgy. She could not, without incurring the risk of new disorders, extend to Catholics, who are more numerous by two-thirds than the Protestants, prerogatives that only the latter must enjoy.'

26. Michel Fuchs, 'The French Face of Irish Nationalism in the Eighteenth Century' in Michael O'Dea and Kevin Whelan (eds.), *Nations and Nationalisms* (Oxford, 1995), pp. 119–28.

27. Seamus Deane, *The French Revolution and Enlightenment in England 1789–1832* (Harvard, 1988).

28. D. A. Chart, 'The Irish Levies during the Great French War' in *Eng. Hist. Rev.*, xxxii (1913), pp. 79–102.

29. Bartlett, *Fall and Rise*, passim.

30. Jacqueline Hill, 'National Festivals, the State and Protestant Ascendancy' in *I.H.S.*, xxiv (1984), pp. 30–51.

31. Thomas Russell, *A Letter to the People of Ireland* (Belfast, 1796), p. 4; see also *The Press*, 21 Oct. 1797.

32. P. Plunkett to J. Connolly, 12 Oct. 1796 (cited in Hugh Fenning, *The Irish Dominican Province 1698–1797* (Dublin, 1990), p. 576).

33. J. Connolly to P. Plunkett, 10 Nov. 1796 (cited in A. Cogan, *The Diocese of Meath, Ancient and Modern* (3 vols, Dublin, 1870), iii, p. 207).

34. Thomas Hussey, *A Sermon preached in the Spanish Chapel in London, 14 May 1798* (London, 1798), p. 6.

35. Cited in Froude, *Ire.*, ii, p. 553.

36. G. Knox to Abercorn, 16 Jan. 1793 (P.R.O.N.I., T2541/1B1/4/1).

37. Cited in Froude, *Ire.*, iii, pp. 60–1.

38. *F.L.J.*, 12–15 Sept. 1792.

39. James Kelly, 'Eighteenth-Century Ascendancy: A Commentary' in *Eighteenth-Century Ireland*, v (1990), pp 173–87. The most detailed treatment will be in Peter MacDonagh's forthcoming 'Church, State and Society in Ireland 1763–1800' (Ph.D. thesis, University of Cambridge).

40. Thomas Hussey, *A Pastoral Letter to the Catholics of the United Dioceses of Waterford and Lismore* (Waterford, 1797), p. 9.

41. United Irish declaration, 4 Sept. 1792 (cited in Richard Musgrave, *Memoirs of the Various Rebellions in Ireland* (Dublin, 1801), p. 86).

42. [T. A. Emmet, W. J. MacNeven and Arthur O'Connor], *Memoir or Detailed Statement of the Origin and Progress of the Irish Union* (London, 1802), pp 72, 80.

43. *Mr Grattan's Letter to his Fellow Citizens of Dublin*, pp. 5–6.

44. *The Works of the Rt Hon. Edmund Burke* (2 vols, London, 1834), ii, p. 454.

45. Patrick Duigenan, *The Speech of Dr Duigenan in the House of Commons, 4 February 1793* (Dublin, 1793), p. 46; see also Froude, *Ire.*, iii, p. 100.

46. Cited in Froude, *Ire.*, iii, p. 170.

47. Ibid., iii, p. 112.

48. Fitzgibbon to Townshend, 9 June 1795 (N.A., Townshend Papers, MS 725).

49. Cited in Froude, *Ire.*, iii, p. 114.

50. E. Cleaver to T. Grenville, 21 June 1797 (B.L., Grenville Papers, Add. MS 41855, f. 130).

51. Burke, *Works*, ii, p. 558.

52. Ibid., i, p. 560.

53. Ibid., ii, p. 542.

54. Ibid., p. 553.

55. Ibid., p. 456.

56. Ibid., p. 478.

57. Portland to Camden, 26 Mar. 1795 (P.R.O., HO 100/56/455–6).

58. Camden to Portland, 30 Apr. 1795 (ibid., HO 100/57/227–8).

59. L. M. Cullen, 'The United Irishmen: Heirs to the French Revolution' (paper delivered to the conference 'The Causes and Consequences of 1798', Ferrycarrig Hotel, Wexford, 4 Feb. 1995).

60. Camden to Portland, 17 June 1796 (P.R.O., HO 100/69/398).

61. J. Beresford to Auckland, 20 Aug. 1796 (*Beresford Corr.*, iii, p. 355).

62. M. Edgeworth to M. Ruxton, 20 Apr. 1795 (N.L.I., Edgeworth Papers); *Memoirs of Richard Lovell Edgeworth begun by himself and concluded by his daughter Maria Edgeworth* (2 vols, London, 1820), i, pp. 205–6. I am grateful to Tom Dunne for this reference.

63. James [Quigley], *The Life of the Rev. James Coigley* (London, 1798), p. 23.

64. Diary of Robert Day, 1 Aug. 1801 (R.I.A., MS W/12/15).

65. Bartlett, *Fall and Rise*, p. 60.

66. W. Richardson, *History of the Origin of the Irish Yeomanry* (Dublin, 1801), pp. 13–14.

67. J. Beresford to Auckland, 4 Sept. 1796 (*Beresford Corr.*, ii, p. 129).

68. Alan Blackstock, 'The Origins and Development of the Irish Yeomanry 1796–c. 1807' (Ph.D. thesis, Queen's University, Belfast, 1993).

69. J. Beresford to Auckland, 4 Sept. 1796 (*Beresford Corr.*, ii, pp. 127–8).

70. 'The number of yeomanry in Ireland, 1797–1799' (N.A., R.P., 620/48/56).

71. E. Newenham to T. Pelham, 15 July 1795 (ibid., 620/22/16).

72. Gosford to E. Cooke, 13 July 1796 (P.R.O.N.I., D1606/1/1/188).

73. The old orthodoxy is most evident in Peter Gibbon, *The Origins of Ulster Unionism: The Formation of Popular Protestant Politics and Ideology in Nineteenth-Century Ireland* (Manchester, 1975).

74. J. Ogle to E. Cooke, 15 July 1796 (N.A., R.P., 620/24/37).

75. *The Formation of the Orange Order 1795–1798: The Edited Papers of Colonel William Blacker and Colonel Robert H. Wallace* (Belfast, 1994), pp. 18–19.

76. Cited in M. MacDonagh, *The Viceroy's Postbag: Correspondence hitherto unpublished of the Earl of Hardwicke, first Lord Lieutenant after the Union* (London, 1904), p. 24.

77. Ibid., pp 24–5.

78. *The Formation of the Orange Order*, p. 65.

79. MacDonagh, *Viceroy's Postbag*, p. 27.

80. *Resolutions of the Masters of the different Orange Lodges in the Province of Ulster, held in the town of Armagh*, 21 May 1797 (copy in R.I.A., Halliday pamphlets, vol. 730).

81. J. Beresford to Auckland, 27 Sept. 1796 (*Beresford Corr.*, ii, p. 136).

82. W. Richardson to Abercorn, 14 Feb. 1797 (P.R.O.N.I., Abercorn MS D623/A /156/4).

83. Hill, 'National Festivals'.

84. [N. Alexander], Report on Defenderism, [Nov.] 1796 (N.A., R.P., 620/26/51).

85. T. Knox to E. Cooke, 13 Aug. 1796 (ibid., 620/24/106).

86. J. Knox to T. Pelham, 23 May 1797 (P.R.O.N.I., T755/5/101).

87. T. Pelham to J. Knox, 28 May 1797 (N.L.I., Knox MS 56).

88. J. Knox to T. Pelham, 1 June 1797 (N.A., R.P., 620/30/92).

89. J. Knox to G. Lake, 11 Mar. 1797 (B.L., Add MS 33101).

90. J. Knox to Abercorn, 11 May 1797 (P.R.O.N.I., T2541/1B3/6/12).

91. Cited in Musgrave, *Rebellions* p. 73.

92. J. Knox to G. Lake, 18 Mar. 1797 (cited in W. E. H. Lecky, *History of Ireland in the Eighteenth Century* (5 vols, London, 1892), iv, p. 52).

93. Camden to Portland, 25 Sept. 1795 (P.R.O., HO 100/58/334–43).

94. T. Pelham to Duke of York, 4 Jan. 1797 (J. T. Gilbert (ed.), *Documents relating to Ireland 1795–1804* (Dublin, 1893), pp. 102–3).

95. Musgrave, *Rebellions*, p. 73.

96. J. Knox to E. Cooke, 6 June 1798 (N.A., R.P., 620/38/61); see also my essay 'The Republic in the Village' in this volume.

97. C. Warburton to Fitzwilliam, 2 Jan. 1799 (Sheffield City Library, Fitzwilliam MS, f. 30).

98. W. Richardson to Abercorn, 22 Feb. 1797 (P.R.O.N.I., Abercorn MS D623/A/156/5).

99. W. Richardson to Abercorn, 28 Mar. 1797 (ibid., D623/A/156/11).

100. T. Higginson to J. Foster, 22 Aug. 1796 (N.A., R.P., 620/24/156).

101. Abercorn to W. Richardson, 17 Mar. 1797 (P.R.O.N.I., Abercorn MS D623/A/80/41).

102. W. Richardson to Viscount Kilwarden, 2 May 1803 (B.L., Add. MS 35739).

103. R. Jephson to Charlemont, 9 Oct. 1795 (H.M.C., *Charlemont*, app., pp. 7–8).

104. J. Short to G. Geraghty, 6 Jan. 1796 (N.L.I., Fitzwilliam MS, mic. 5641).

105. B. Brannon to P. Kerr, 14 Aug. 1796 (N.A., R.P., 620/24/131).

106. John Lennon, *The Irish Repealer's Mountain Harp of the Triumphant Year of 1843* (Dublin, 1843), p. v.

107. L. Cullen, 'Politics and Rebellion in Wicklow in the 1790s' in Ken Hannigan and William Nolan (eds.), *Wicklow: History and Society* (Dublin, 1994), pp. 411–501.

108. *The Press*, 7 Oct. 1797.

109. Aiken McClelland, *The Formation of the Orange Order* (n.p., n.d).

110. Musgrave, *Rebellions*, p. 72.

111. *Orange Vindicated in a Reply to Theobald McKenna* (Dublin, 1799), pp. 7–9.

112. J. Knox to T. Pelham, 22 May 1797 (P.R.O.N.I., T755/5/729).

113. [N. Alexander], Report on Defenderism [Nov. 1796] (N.A., R.P., 620/26/51).

114. P. Burrowes to A. Hamilton, 2 Oct. 1796 (P.R.O.N.I., T3489/D/2/2); P. Burrowes to L. Parsons, 23 Oct. 1800 (ibid., T3489/D/2/11|).

115. Clare to Camden, 7 Sept. 1796 (ibid., T2627/4/201).

116. *F.L.J.*, 3–6 Feb. 1796.

117. T. Pelham to G. Lake, 3 Mar. 1797 (N.L.I., Knox MS 56).

118. Camden to Portland, 9 Mar. 1797 (P.R.O., HO 100/69/132–3).

119. J. Knox to T. Pelham, 16 June 1797 (P.R.O.N.I., T755/5/165).

120. T. Pelham to Portland, 24 Mar. 1796 (B.L., Add. MS 33113, p. 43).

121. *The speech of the Rt Hon. John, Earl of Clare, 19 February 1798* (Dublin, 1798), p. 34.

122. *The Press*, 20 Jan. 1798.

123. H. Grattan to Fitzwilliam, [Apr.] 1796 (N.L.I., Fitzwilliam MS, mic. 5641).

124. *Parl. Reg.*, xvii (1796), p. 13.

125. Grattan to Fitzwilliam, 15 Nov. 1796 (N.L.I., Fitzwilliam MS, mic. 5641).

126. *Mr Grattan's Letter to his Fellow Citizens of Dublin*, p. 11.

127. L. McNally to E. Cooke, [Apr.] 1798 (N.A., R.P., 620/10/121).

128. Clare to Shannon, 13 Feb. 1801 (P.R.O.N.I., D2707/A/2/2/156).

129. Coigley [Quigley], *Life*, p. 14.

130. Russell, *Letter to the People of Ireland*, pp. 14–15.

131. *Beauties of The Press*, p. 362.

132. *The Press*, 23 Jan. 1798.

133. Tone, *Memoirs*, i, p. 290: Charles H. Teeling, *Observations on the History and Consequences of the Battle of the Diamond* (Belfast, 1838), pp. 7, 15, 48.

134. Day, Diary, 1 Aug. 1801.

135. C. Warburton to Fitzwilliam, 12 Jan. 1799 (N.L.I., Fitzwilliam MS, mic. 5641).

136. G. Knox to P. Burrowes, 6 Aug. 1803 (R.I.A., Burrowes Papers, MS 23/K/53).

137. Marianne Elliott, 'The Origins and Transformation of Irish Republicanism' in *International Rev. of Soc. Hist.*, xxiii (1978), pp. 405–28; Curtin, *United Irishmen*.

138. Kevin Whelan, 'Catholic Mobilisation 1750–1850' in Louis Bergeron and L. M. Cullen (eds.), *Culture et practiques politiques en France et en Irelande xvie–xviiie siècles* (Dublin, 1990), pp. 235–58.

'98 After '98

1. Robert Gildea, *The Past in French History* (New Haven, 1994), p. 12; Pierre Nora, *Les lieux de mémoire* (3 vols, Paris, 1984–92)

2. J. Beresford to Auckland, 15 Mar. 1798 (P.R.O.N.I., T3229/2/30).

3. E. Cooke to Auckland, 19 Mar. 1798 (*Auckland Corr.*, iii, pp. 392–3).

4. [Rev. C. Robinson] to E. Cooke, 29 May 1798 (N.A., R.P., 620/37/211A).

5. Clare to Auckland, 31 May 1798 (*Auckland Corr.*, iii, p. 438).

6. J. Beresford to Auckland, 31 May 1798 (ibid., pp. 439–40).

7. *F.D.J.*, 5 June 1798.

8. *Freeman's Journal*, 7 June 1798.

9. A. Averell to J. Benson, 7 June 1798 (Irish Wesleyan Historical Society Archive, Belfast).

10. Clare to Auckland, 5 June 1798 (*Auckland Corr.*, iv, p. 4).

11. E. Cleaver to T. Grenville, 8 June 1798 (B.L., Grenville Papers, Add. MS 41855, ff. 156–60).

12. J. Beresford to Auckland, 8 June 1798 (*Auckland Corr.*, iv, pp. 9–10).

13. J. Beresford to Auckland, 9 June 1798 (ibid., pp. 12–14).

14. E. Hudson to Charlemont, 18 July 1798 (H.M.C., *Charlemont*, ii, p. 327).

15. E. Hudson to Charlemont, 5 July 1799 (ibid., p. 350).

16. David Dickson, Introduction to Richard Musgrave, *Memoirs of the Various Rebellions in Ireland* (repr., Fort Wayne, 1995).

17. L. M. Cullen, *The Emergence of Modern Ireland 1600–1900* (London, 1981); idem, 'Burke, Ireland and Revolution' in *Eighteenth–Century Life,* vii (1992), pp. 21–42.

18. W. J. McCormack, *The Dublin Paper War of 1786–1788* (Dublin, 1993).

19. Thomas Bartlett, *The Fall and Rise of the Irish Nation: The Catholic Question 1690–1830* (Dublin, 1992), p. 7; T. C. Barnard, '1641: A Bibliographical Essay' in Brian Mac Cuarta (ed.), *Ulster, 1641: Aspects of the Rising* (Belfast, 1994); idem, 'The Uses of 23 October 1641 and Irish Protestant Celebrations' in *Eng. Hist. Rev.*, cvi (1991), pp. 889–920; James Kelly, '"The Glorious and Immortal Memory": Commemoration and Protestant Identity in Ireland 1660–1800' in *R.I.A. Proc.*, clxliv (1994), pp. 25–52.

20. Musgrave, *Rebellions*, 3rd ed. (Dublin, 1802), preface.

21. Depositions sent to Richard Musgrave (T.C.D., MSS 871–2).

22. William Bingley, *An Examination into the Origins and Continuance of the Discontents in Ireland and the True Cause of Rebellion, being a faithful narrative of the particular suffering of the Irish peasantry* (London, 1799), p. 20.

23. R. Musgrave to G. Lenox–Conyngham, 27 Apr. 1799 (P.R.O.N.I., D1449/12/292).

24. Musgrave, *Rebellions*, p. 503; T. Percy to R. Musgrave, 6 June 1799 (N.L.I., MS 4156).

25. Hope's memoir, written in 1843, is printed in R. R. Madden, *The United Irishmen, their Lives and Times* (7 vols, London, 1842–6), 3rd series, i, pp. 218–313; Charles Teeling, *Personal Narrative of the Irish Rebellion of 1798* (London, 1828).

26. Musgrave, *Rebellions*, pp. 184, 224, 258, 287.

27. R. Musgrave to T. Percy, [June] 1799 (N.L.I., MS 4157).

28. Musgrave, *Rebellions*, p. 568.

29. Ibid., p. 858.

30. Idem.

31. J. W. Croker, *A Sketch of the State of Ireland Past and Present* (Dublin, 1803), p. 13.

32. R. Musgrave to T. Percy, 15 Jan. 1799 (N.L.I., MS 4157).

33. Idem.

34. R. Musgrave to T. Percy, 15 Jan., 15 Feb. 1799 (ibid.).

35. Musgrave, *Rebellions, passim.*

36. *Considerations upon the State of Public Affairs in Ireland in the year 1799* (Dublin, 1799) p. 41.

37. Linda Colley, *Britons: Forging the Nation 1707–1837* (New Haven, 1992).

38. David Hempton and Myrtle Hill, *Evangelical Protestantism in Ulster Society 1740–1890* (London, 1992).

39. Minutes of the Burgher Presbytery of Down, 3 July 1798 (P.R.O.N.I., Stewart MSS, D1759/1D/17).

40. *First Report of the Commissioners of Irish Education Inquiry*, H.C. 1825 (400) xii, p. 66; *Report of the Committee of the London Hibernian Society* (Dublin, 1810), p. 24.

41. Musgrave, *Rebellions*, p. vii.

42. *Orange Vindicated in a Reply to Theobald McKenna* (Dublin, 1799), p. 33.

43. *Union or not? By an Orangeman* (Dublin, 1799), p. 22.

44. *Orange Vindicated*, pp. 10–11.

45. *Public Spirit — a poem* (Dublin, 1798), p. 12; *A Sermon preached at Mullingar on 1 July 1798* (Dublin, 1798), p. 6; Robert Day, charge to the Grand Jury of County Cork, Sept. 1798 (R.I.A., MS 12/10/11).

46. *Orange Vindicated*, p. 11.

47. *Union or Not?*, p. 23.

48. Musgrave, *Rebellions*, p. vi.

49. *The Sun*, 3 Nov. 1802.

50. William Bennet, Notes on Musgrave's *Rebellions* (N.L.I., MS 637).

51. E. Gibbon to Lord Sheffield, cited in R. L. Edgeworth, *A Letter to the Earl of Charlemont on the Tellograph and on the Defence of Ireland* (Dublin, 1797), p. 39.

52. C. Warburton to Fitzwilliam, 31 July 1798 (N.L.I., mic. 5641).

53. C. Mordaunt to ———, 2 July 1798 (E. Hamilton, *The Mordaunts: An Eighteenth-Century Family* (London, 1965), p. 242).

54. Idem.

55. George Moore, *Observations on the Union, Orange Associations and other Subjects of Domestic Policy* (Dublin, 1799), p. 34.

56. Buckingham to Grenville, 6 July 1798 (H.M.C., *Fortescue*, v, p. 245).

57. C. Warburton to Fitzwilliam, 31 July 1798 (N.L.I., mic. 5641).

58. B. Chapman to Shelburne, 13 Oct. 1798 (Ann Arbor Library, Michigan, Shelburne MS).

59. R. Musgrave to T. Percy, 22 July 1799 (N.L.I., MS 4157).

60. Cited in F. S. B[ourke], 'Musgrave's History' in *Ir. Sword*, ii (1954–6), p. 298.

61. Idem.

62. Patrick Duigenan, *A Fair Representation of the Present Political State of Ireland* (Dublin, 1799).

63. James Gordon, *History of the Rebellion in Ireland in the year 1798* (Dublin, 1801); Joseph Stock, *A Narrative of what passed at Killala in the County of Mayo* (Dublin, 1800); Francis Plowden, *An Historical Review of the State of Ireland, from the invasion of that country under Henry II, to its Union with Great Britain* (2 vols, London, 1803).

64. Altamont to Dublin Castle, 18 May 1800 (cited in *Cathair na Mart*, iv (1992), p. 25).

65. Jonah Barrington, *Personal Sketches of His Own Times* (3 vols, Paris, 1827–32), ii, p. 202.

66. L. M. Cullen, 'The 1798 Rebellion in its Eighteenth-Century Context' in P. J. Corish (ed.), *Radicals, Rebels and Establishments* (Belfast, 1985), pp. 91–113.

67. Bartlett, *Fall and Rise*, *passim*.

68. Fitzwilliam to T. L. O'Beirne, 2 Sept. 1798 (N.L.I., mic. 5641).

69. Moore, *Observations*, p. 32.

70. Ibid., p. 35.

71. *A Refutation of Dr Duigenan's appendix* (London, 1800), p. 76.

72. Ibid., p. 77.

73. Idem.

74. George Cooper, *Letters on the Irish Nation written during a visit to that kingdom in the autumn of the year 1799* (London, 1800), p. xxii.

75. H. Grattan to F. Plowden, 23 Dec. 1803 (N.A., Frazer MS).

76. Fitzwilliam to F. Plowden, 25 Sept. 1803 (ibid.).

77. Cornwallis to Portland, 28 June 1798 (P.R.O., HO 100/77/200–1).

78. C. Erskine to J. Troy, 23 June 1798 (D.D.A., Troy MS).

79. Thomas Bartlett, '"A People made rather for Copies than Originals": The Anglo-Irish 1760–1800' in *International Hist. Rev.*, xii (1990), pp. 11–25.

80. *The Works of the Rt Hon. Edmund Burke* (2 vols, London, 1834), i, p. 557.

81. T. Hussey to J. Clinch, 10 June 1800 (D.D.A., Troy MS).

82. Memorandum of J. Foster, [*c.* 1799] (P.R.O.N.I., T2965/178).

83. Cooper, *Letters*, p. 129; postulation of forty Connacht priests in favour of the Bishop of Achonry, 26 July 1798 (Vatican Archives, Congressi Irlanda, xvii, ff. 515–20); *Declaration of the Parochial Roman Catholic Clergy of the Diocese of Kilmacduagh and Kilfenora* (London, 1798).

84. *Protestant Ascendancy and Catholic Emancipation reconciled in a Legislative Union* (Dublin, 1800), p. 57.

85. Kevin Whelan, 'The Role of the Catholic Priest in the 1798 Rebellion in County Wexford' in idem (ed.), *Wexford: History and Society* (Dublin, 1987), pp. 296–315.

86. Dáire Keogh, *The French Disease: The Catholic Church and Radicalism in Ireland 1790–1800* (Dublin, 1993), pp. 200–13.

87. Ibid., pp. 83–97.

88. [James Caulfield], *A Vindication of the Roman Catholic Clergy of the Town of Wexford during the late Unhappy Rebellion* (Dublin, 1799), p. 18.

89. Veritas, *The State of His Majesty's Subjects in Ireland professing the Roman Catholic Religion*, pt 1 (2nd ed., Dublin, 1799), p. iii.

90. J. Caulfield to J. Troy, 15 July 1799 (D.D.A., Troy MS).

91. E. Sproule to E. Cooke, 21 July 1798 (N.A., R.P., 620/39/2).

92. J. Troy to L. Concanen [Apr.], 1800 (D.D.A., Troy MS).

93. J. Caulfield to J. Troy, 25 June 1799 (ibid.).

94. F. Higgins to E. Cooke, 7 Mar. 1798 (N.A., R.P., 620/18/14).

95. *Evidence taken before the Select Committee of Lords and Commons appointed in the Sessions of 1824 and 1825 to Inquire into the State of Ireland* (London, 1825), p. 186.

96. *Freeman's Journal*, 22 May 1841.

97. W. O'Neill Daunt, *Personal Recollections of the late Daniel O'Connell* (2 vols, London, 1848), ii, p. 7.

98. Redesdale to Percival, 23 Oct. 1803 (P.R.O.N.I., T3030/7/10).

99. Kevin Whelan, 'Catholic Mobilisation 1750–1850' in Louis Bergeron and L. M. Cullen (eds.), *Culture et pratiques politiques en France et en Irlande xvie–xviie siècles* (Paris, 1991), pp. 235–58.

100. Gary Owens, 'Hedge School of Politics: O'Connell's Monster Meetings' in *History Ireland*, ii, no. 1 (1994), pp. 35–40.

101. Ian McBride, 'William Drennan and the Dissenting Tradition' in David Dickson, Dáire Keogh and Kevin Whelan (eds.), *The United Irishmen: Radicalism, Republicanism and Rebellion* (Dublin, 1993), pp. 49–61; idem., 'Presbyterians in the Penal Era' in *Bullán*, i, no. 2 (1995), pp. 73–86; G. Chambers, 'Divided Loyalties in the Business Community of Belfast in 1798' in *Familia*, ii (1994), pp. 13–38.

102. H. J. McCracken to M. McCracken, 18 June 1798 (cited in Mary McNeill, *The Life and Times of Mary Ann McCracken 1770–1856* (Belfast, 1988), p. 177).

103. Minutes of the Burgher Presbytery of County Down, 3 July 1798 (P.R.O.N.I., Stewart MSS, D1759/1D/17).

104. Robert Day, Charge to the Grand Jury of County Antrim, 9 Aug. 1799 (R.I.A., MS 12/W/13, p. 84).

105. Hempton and Hill, *Evangelical Protestantism, passim.*

106. Peter Brooke, *Ulster Presbyterianism: The Historical Perspective 1610–1970* (Dublin, 1987).

107. L. M. Cullen, 'The Internal Politics of the United Irishmen' in Dickson, Keogh and Whelan (eds.), *United Irishmen*, pp. 176–96.

108. L. M. Cullen, 'The Political Structure of the Defenders' in Hugh Gough and David Dickson (eds.), *Ireland and the French Revolution* (Dublin, 1990), pp. 117–38.

109. Nancy Curtin, 'The Transformation of the Society of United Irishmen into a Mass-Based Revolutionary Organisation 1794–6' in *I.H.S.*, xxiv (1985), pp. 463–92.

110. Tommy Graham, '"An Union of Power": The United Irish Organisation' in Dickson, Keogh and Whelan (eds.), *United Irishmen*, pp. 244–55.

111. W. J. MacNeven, 'An Account of the Treaty between the United Irishmen and the Anglo-Irish Government in 1798' in idem, *Pieces of Irish History* (New York, 1807), p. 155.

112. *Memoir or Detailed Statement of the Origin and Progress of the Irish Union delivered to the Irish Government by Messrs Emmet, O'Connor and McNevin* (London, 1802).

113. Ibid., p. 144.

114. T. A. Emmet, 'Part of an Essay towards the History of Ireland' in MacNeven, *Pieces of Irish History*, pp. 1–121; William Sampson, *Memoirs* (New York, 1807); D. A. Chart (ed.), *The Drennan Letters 1776–1819* (Belfast, 1931).

115. Cullen, 'The Internal Politics of the United Irishmen'.

116. Edward Hay, *History of the Insurrection in the County of Wexford, A.D. 1798* (Dublin, 1803); Thomas Cloney, *A Personal Narrative of those Transactions in the County of Wexford in which the author was engaged during the awful period of 1798* (Dublin, 1832).

117. Hay, *History*, pp. xii–xliv; Cloney, *Personal Narrative*, pp. 237–76.

118. Hay, *History*, *passim*.

119. L. M. Cullen, 'The 1798 Rebellion in Wexford: United Irishman Organisation, Membership, Leadership' in Whelan (ed.), *Wexford*, pp. 248–95. For good examples, see statement of Edward Roche, 25 Aug. 1798 (N.A., R.P., 620/39/206); R. J. Carthy, 'A Detail of Facts relating to the Arrest and Subsequent Imprisonment of Robert Joseph Carthy, both in England and Ireland [20 Dec. 1808]' in *Report from the Commissioners of the Prisons in Ireland* (Dublin, 1809), app., pp. 120–24.

120. Robert Day, Charge to the Grand Jury of County Waterford (R.I.A., MS 12/10/11, pp. 105–9).

121. I am grateful to Fiachra Ó Lionnáin (Coolgreany) for this piece of oral history.

122. *Rep. Comm. Sec.*; Hay, *History*, p. 55.

123. Hay, *History*, p. 122.

124. Ibid., p. 123.

125. Ibid., p. 56.

126. Ibid., p. 123.

127. Whelan, 'Role of the Catholic Priest'.

128. Hay, *History*, p. 169.

129. Edward Hay, *Authentic Detail of the Extravagant and Inconsistent Conduct of Sir Richard Musgrave* (Dublin, 1803), p. 18.

130. E. Hay to Fitzwilliam, 19 Feb. 1803 (N.A., Frazer MS).

131. Hay, *History*, p. 11.

132. William Bennet, Notes on Musgrave's *Rebellions* (N.L.I., MS 637).

133. A. Marsden to W. Wickham, 9 Mar. 1803 (P.R.O.N.I., Wickham MS, T2627/5/k/166).

134. [Richard Musgrave], *Observations on the Remonstrance of the Rev. Peter O'Neill, Parish Priest of Ballymacoda in the County of Cork* (Dublin, 1804), p. iv.

135. T. C. Croker (ed.), *Memoirs of Joseph Holt* (2 vols, London, 1838).

136. Ruan O'Donnell and Bob Reece, ' "A Clean Beast": Crofton-Croker's Fairy-Tale of General Holt' in *Eighteenth-Century Ireland*, vii (1992), pp. 7–42.

137. Cited in ibid., p. 15.

138. Croker (ed.), *Memoirs of Holt*, i, p. 17.

139. Ibid., p. 123.

140. Ibid., p. 16.

141. Ibid., p. 18.

142. 'The Live [sic] and Adventures of Joseph Holt' (Mitchell Library, Sydney, MS A2024). I am grateful to Perry McIntyre for facilitating my inspection of the manuscript and to Peter Shaughnessy for drawing my attention to it.

143. Roger McHugh (ed.) *Carlow in '98: The Autobiography of William Farrell of Carlow*, (Dublin, 1949).

144. Pádraig Ó Snodaigh, *'98 and Carlow: A Look at the Historians* (Carlow, 1979).

145. H. Alexander to T. Pelham, 4 Aug. 1798 (J. T. Gilbert (ed.), *Documents relating to Ireland 1795–1804* (Dublin, 1893), p. 202.

146. Statement of S. Neilson (N.A., R.P., 620/52/112).

147. S. Neilson to A. H. Rowan, 12 July 1802 (W. Drummond (ed.), *The Autobiography of Archibald Hamilton Rowan* (Dublin, 1840), pp. 435–6).

148. Memoir of James Hope, (Madden, *United Irishmen*, 3rd series, i), p. 222.

149. Dorothy Thompson, 'Seceding from the Seceders: The Decline of the Jacobin Tradition in Ireland 1790–1850' in idem, *Outsiders* (London, 1994), pp. 134–63.

150. Cited in E. P. Thompson, *The Making of the English Working Class,* 2nd ed. (London, 1968), p. 193.

151. K. Coburn (ed.), *The Notebooks of Samuel Taylor Coleridge* (Princeton, 1957), entry no. 1522.

152. *The Union Doctrine or Poor Man's Catechism* (Dublin, 1798) (copy in N.A., R.P., 620/43/1).

153. Beresford to Auckland, 6 Feb. 1799 (*Auckland Corr.*, iv, p. 211).

154. Marianne Elliott, *Partners in Revolution: The United Irishmen and France* (New Haven, 1982), p. 343.

155. See my essay 'The Republic in the Village' in this volume.

156. Denis Taaffe, *A Succinct View of Catholic Affairs* (Dublin, 1805), p. 15.

157. *Irish Magazine*, Oct. 1810, p. 482.

158. Ibid., Aug. 1800, frontispiece.

159. R. R. Madden, *Literary Remains of the United Irishmen* (London, 1887); G. D. Zimmerman, *Songs of Irish Rebellion: Political Street Ballads and Rebel Songs 1780–1900* (Dublin, 1967), pp. 35–58.

160. Tom Dunne, 'Revolution or Restoration? The French as Saviours in Gaelic Poetry' (paper delivered at the symposium, 'L'Irlande et la Révolution Française', Paris, May 1989).

161. [Denis Taaffe], *Antidote to Cure the Catholicophobia and Ierneophobia, efficacious to eradicate the horrors against Catholics and Irishmen by early instilled prejudices* (Dublin, 1804), p. ix.

162. D[enis] T[aaffe], *Ireland's Mirror, exhibiting a Picture of her Present State with a Glimpse of her Future Prospects* (Dublin, 1796), pp. 14–15.

163. Taaffe, *Antidote*, p. 4.

164. John Burk, *History of the Late War in Ireland, with an Account of the United Irish Association* (Philadelphia, 1799); Thomas Ledlie Birch, *A Letter from an Irish Emigrant to his Friend in the United States, giving an Account of the Commotions in Ireland, of the United Irishmen and Orange Society and of the Several Battles and Military Executions* (Philadelphia, 1799); [E. Byrne], *Hibernicus, or Memoirs of an Irishman now in America, containing an Account of the Principal Events of his Life both before and since his Emigration* (Pittsburgh, 1828).

165. Birch, *Letter*, p. 62. For Birch see Aiken McClelland, 'Thomas Ledlie Birch, United Irishman' in the *Belfast Natural Hist. & Phil. Soc. Jn.*, vii (1965), pp. 24–42.

166. Sampson, *Memoir*, p. v.

167. MacNeven, *Pieces of Irish History*, p. 156.

168. [Byrne], *Hibernicus*, p. 59.

169. Ibid., p. 57.

170. Martin Burke, 'Piecing Together a Shattered Past: The Historical Writings of the United Irish Exiles in America' in Dickson, Keogh and Whelan (eds.), *United Irishmen*, pp. 297–306.

171. *The Shamrock or Hibernian Chronicle*, 1810–1817. A file of this paper is housed in the library of the American–Irish Historical Society in New York, to whom I am grateful for permission to consult it. See also Kieran McShane, 'A Study of Two New York Irish-American Newspapers in the Early Nineteenth Century' in *New York Irish History*, viii (1994), pp. 13–21.

172. T. A. Emmet to P. Burrowes, 19 Nov. 1806 (R.I.A., MS 23/K/53).

173. Legal papers of Thomas Cloney (Burrowes MS, ibid.).

174. Madden, *United Irishmen*; see also R. R. Madden, *Memoirs (chiefly autobiographical) 1798–1886*, ed. T. M. Madden (New York, 1892).

175. Anna Kinsella, 'Who Fears to Speak of '98? The Nineteenth-Century Interpretation of 1798 (M.Litt. thesis, T.C.D., 1992), p. 42.

176. Madden, *United Irishmen*, first series, ii, pp. 342–3: 'There was never a greater mistake than to call their struggle a popish rebellion.'

177. *The Nation*, 3 Dec. 1842.

178. C. J. Woods, 'Tone's Grave at Bodenstown: Memorials and Commemorations 1798–1913' in D. Siegmund-Schultze (ed.), *Irland Gesellschaft und Kultur*, vi (Halle, 1989), pp. 138–48.

179. Miles Byrne, *Memoirs* (repr., Dublin, 1972); see also Thomas Bartlett, Introduction to Miles Byrne, *Memoirs* (Enniscorthy, forthcoming).

180. Byrne, *Memoirs* (1863 ed.), i, pp. 348–58.

181. Ibid., p. 40.

182. Ibid., p. 38.

183. Ibid., p. 39.

184. Ibid., iii, p. 244.

185. Emmet Larkin, *The Historical Dimensions of Irish Catholicism* (Washington, 1984), pp. 107–8.

186. P. Cullen to T. Kirby, 30 Sept. 1856 (cited in *Archiv. Hib.*, xxxi (1973), p. 62).

187. Kinsella, 'Who Fears to Speak of '98?'

188. W. J. Fitzpatrick, *Curious Family History, or Ireland before the Union* (6th ed., Dublin, 1880), p. 263.

189. M. V. Ronan (ed.), *Personal Recollections of Wexford and Wicklow Insurgents of 1798 as collected by the Rev. Br. Luke Cullen 1798–1859* (Enniscorthy, 1958).

190. Luke Cullen Papers (T.C.D., Madden MS 1472; N.L.I., MSS 9760–62).

191. Patrick Kavanagh, *A Popular History of the Insurrection of 1798* (Dublin, 1870). A copy of this rare first edition is in the Franciscan Library, Killiney.

192. Nuala Johnson, 'Sculpting Heroic Pictures: Celebrating the Centenary of the 1798 Rebellion in Ireland' in *Trans. Inst. Brit. Geog.*, xix (1994), pp. 78–93.

193. 'The Principal Persons concerned in Treasonable Practices about London [winter 1798] (N.L.I., MS 33043).

194. *Wexford People*, 15 June 1898.

195. John Turpin, 'Oliver Sheppard's 1798 Memorials' in *Irish Arts Review* (1991), pp 71–80; Chief Secretary's Office, volumes of Irish newspaper cuttings re 1798 centenary (N.L.I., vols 56–7).

196. P. Kavanagh to T. Byrne, 18 Dec. 1897 (in possession of Father Lory Kehoe, P.P., Craanford, to whom I am grateful for permission to consult it).

197. I am grateful to Kathleen Kane, Courthoyle, Newbawn, County Wexford, for making available a set of the mummer's rhymes printed by Evoy which identifies Sinnott as their author.

198. Cheryl Herr, *For the Land They Loved: Irish Political Melodramas 1890–1925* (Syracuse, 1991); Thomas Flanagan, *The Year of the French* (London, 1979); Brian Friel, *Translations* (London, 1981); Seamus Heaney, 'Requiem for the Croppies' in *Door into the Dark* (London, 1969).

199. Pers. comm., Roisín McCauley, B.B.C. Radio 3 producer, Ballyvaughan, County Clare, Aug. 1994.

200. Murphy Papers, Mission House, Enniscorthy, County Wexford.

201. Timothy O'Keeffe, 'The 1898 Efforts to Celebrate the United Irishmen: The '98 Centennial' in *Éire–Ireland*, xxiii (1988), pp. 51–73; idem, 'Who Fears to Speak of '98? The Rhetoric and Rituals of the United Irishmen Centennial 1898' in *Éire–Ireland*, xxvii (1992), pp. 67–91.

202. Kinsella, 'Who Fears to Speak of '98?', pp. 62–91; Gary Owens, 'Nationalist Monuments in Ireland *c.* 1870–1914: Symbolism and Ritual' in Brian Kennedy and Raymond Gillespie (eds.), *Ireland: Art into History* (Dublin, 1994), pp 103–17; idem, 'The Symbolism and Ritual of Nationalist Monuments in Post-Famine Ireland' (paper delivered to Parnell Summer School, August 1995).

203. Woods, 'Tone's Grave at Bodenstown'.

204. Kinsella, 'Who Fears to Speak of '98?', pp. 43–61.

205. Woods, 'Tone's Grave at Bodenstown'.

206. *Diary and Correspondence of Charles Abbot, Lord Colchester*, ed. Lord Colchester (3 vols, London, 1861); *The Journal and Correspondence of William, Lord Auckland*, ed. Bishop of Bath (4 vols, London, 1861–2); *The Correspondence of the Rt Hon. John Beresford*, ed. W. Beresford, (2 vols, London, 1854); *Memoirs and Correspondence of Viscount Castlereagh*, ed. Marquis of Londonderry (12 vols, London, 1848–53); *The Manuscripts and Correspondence of James, first Earl of Charlemont* (2 vols, H.M.C., London, 1891–4); *The Correspondence of Charles, 1st Marquis of Cornwallis*, ed. C. Ross (3 vols, London, 1859); *The Manuscripts of J. B. Fortescue, Esq., preserved at Dropmore* (10 vols, H.M.C., London, 1892–1927); *Correspondence between the Rt Hon. William Pitt and Charles, Duke of Rutland*, ed. John, Duke of Rutland (London, 1890); *The Diary of Sir John Moore*, ed. J. F. Maurice (London, 1904).

207. W. E. H. Lecky, *History of Ireland in the Eighteenth Century* (5 vols, London, 1892); J. A. Froude,*The English in Ireland in the Eighteenth Century* (3 vols, London, 1872–4); Donal McCartney, *W. E. H. Lecky: Historian and Politician 1838–1903* (Dublin, 1994).

208. Thomas Pakenham, *The Year of Liberty: The Great Irish Rebellion of 1798* (London, 1969); R. B. McDowell, 'The Age of the United Irishmen' in *N.H.I.*, iv, pp. 339–73.

209. Pakenham, *Year of Liberty*, pp. 66, 87, 101, 130, 150.

210. R. F. Foster, 'Ascendancy and Union' in idem, (ed.), *The Oxford Illustrated History of Ireland* (Oxford, 1989), p. 183.

211. S. J. Connolly, 'The United Irishmen at Trinity' in *Bullán*, i (1994), pp. 148–50.

212. Daniel Gahan, 'The Military Strategy of the Wexford United Irishmen in 1798' in *History Ireland*, i, no. 4 (1993), pp. 28–32.

BIBLIOGRAPHY

Manuscripts

Ann Arbor, Michigan
  W. L. Clements Library
    Shelburne Papers

Belfast
  Irish Wesleyan Historical Society Archive
    Averell Papers

  Linen Hall Library
    Joy Papers, MS 8/15/3

  Public Record Office of Northern Ireland

Abercorn,	D623/T2541
Auckland,	T3229
Camden,	T2627
Downshire,	D607
Ellis,	T3403
Foster,	T2965
Gosford,	D1606
Lenox-Conyngham,	D1449
Pelham,	T755
Redesdale,	T3030
Rosse,	T3489
Shannon,	D2707
Stewart,	S1759
Westmorland,	T3319

Birr
  Birr Castle
    Rosse Papers

Boston
  Houghton Library
    Barlow Papers

Dublin
  Dublin Diocesan Archives
    Troy Papers
    Hay Papers

Grand Lodge of Free and Accepted Masons
  Members' Registers

National Archives of Ireland
  Frazer MS
  Hedges MS 757
  Rebellion Papers
  State of the Country Papers
  Townshend MS 725

National Library of Ireland
  William Bennet MS 637
  Colclough MS 29766
  Cooke MS, mic. 1560
  Luke Cullen Papers, 9760–2
  Drogheda MS, 9749
  Edgeworth MSS 7362–4
  Fitzwilliam MSS, mic. 5640–1
  Thomas Handcock MS 16232
  Informers report on United Irishmen in London, MS 33043
  Kavanagh Papers, mic. 7155
  John Knox MS 56
  Richard Musgrave MSS 4155–6
  O'Hara Papers, 20397
  George O'Malley autobiography, mic. 208
  Scully Papers, 27, 777
  Shackleton Papers (uncatalogued)
  Wadding MS 5193
  Walsh scrapbook, MS 14040

National Museum of Ireland
  Eighteenth-century newspaper cuttings, N.M.I. 6–1935

Royal Irish Academy
  Burrowes MS
  Cloney MS
  Day MS

Trinity College Dublin
  Luke Cullen Papers, 1472
  Henry Quin Diary, 2261
  R. R. Madden MS 873
  Molyneux MS 888
  Richard Musgrave MSS 871–2
  Sirr Papers, MS 869
  White MS

Enniscorthy
  Mission House
    Patrick Murphy Papers

Kilkenny
  St Kieran's College
    Carrigan MS

London
  British Library
    Grenville, Add., MS 41855
    Lake, Add. MS 33101
    Pelham, Add. MS 33104
    Tour in Ulster, 1796, Add. MS 28724

  Public Record Office
    Home Office Papers (HO 100/1–22)

  Windsor Palace
    Stuart Papers

Longleat
    Thynne MS

Paris
  Collège Irlandaise
    Miles Byrne Papers

Rome
  Anchivio Segreto Vaticano
    Congressi Irlanda

Sydney
  Mitchell Library
    Holt MS A2024

  Manuscripts in private possession
    Patrick Kavanagh letters, in possession of Lory Kehoe, P.P., Craanford,
      Country Wexford
    Hay Papers, in possession of William Sweetman, Whitemills, County
      Wexford

Published Sources: Contemporary Material

Abbot, Charles, *Diary and Correspondence of Charles Abbot, Lord Colchester*, ed. Lord Colchester (3 vols, London, 1861)

Atkinson, A. *The Irish Tourist* (Dublin, 1815)

Auckland, WIlliam, Lord, *The Journal and Correspondence of William, Lord Auckland*, ed. Bishop of Bath (4 vols, London 1861–2)

Barrington, Jonah, *Personal Sketches of His Own Times* (3 vols, Paris 1827–32)

Beresford, John, *The Correspondence of Rt Hon. John Beresford*, ed. W. Beresford (2 vols, London, 1854)

Birch, Thomas Ledlie, *A Letter from an Irish Emigrant to his Friend in the United States, giving an account of the commotions in Ireland, of the United Irishmen and Orange Society and of the several battles and military executions* (Philadelphia, 1799)

Blacker, William, and Wallace, Robert H., *The Formation of the Orange Order 1795–98: The Edited Papers of Colonel William Blacker and Colonel Robert H. Wallace* (Belfast, 1994)

[Blake, Henry], *Letters from the Irish Highlands* (2nd ed., London 1825)

Bombelles, Marc de, *Journal des voyages en Grand Bretagne et en Irlande, 1784*, ed. Jacques Gury (Oxford, 1989)

Burk, John, *History of the late War in Ireland, with an Account of the United Irish Association* (Philadelphia, 1799)

Burke, Edmund, *The Works of the Rt Hon. Edmund Burke* (2 vols, London, 1834)

—— *The Writings and Speeches of Edmund Burke*, vol. iii: *The French Revolution*, ed. L. G. Mitchell (Oxford, 1989)

—— *The Correspondence of Edmund Burke*, ed. T. W. Copeland et al. (10 vols, Cambridge, 1958–78)

[Byrne, Edward], *Hibernicus, or Memoirs of an Irishman now in America, containing an Account of the Principal Events of his Life both before and since his Emigration* (Pittsburgh, 1828)

Byrne, Miles, *Memoirs of Miles Byrne, Chef de Bataillon in the Service of France*, edited by his widow (2 vols, Paris, 1863)

Carroll, Charles, 'Charles Carroll's correspondence' in *Maryland Hist. Mag*, xxii (1927)

Castlereagh, Viscount, *Memoirs and Correspondence of Viscount Castlereagh*, ed. Marquis of Londonderry (12 vols, London, 1848–53)

Charlemont, Earl of, *The Manuscripts and Correspondence of James, First Earl of Charlemont* (2 vols, London, 1891–4)

Cloney, Thomas, *A Personal Narrative of those Transactions in the County of Wexford in which the author was engaged at the awful period of 1798* (Dublin, 1832)

The Compleat Irish Traveller (London, 1788)

Cornwallis, Marquis of, *The Correspondence of Charles, 1st Marquis of Cornwallis*, ed. C. Ross (3 vols, London, 1859)

Delany, Mary, *Letters from Georgian Ireland: The Correspondence of Mary Delany 1731–1768*, ed. Angélique Day (Belfast, 1991)

Drennan, William, *The Drennan Letters 1776–1814*, ed. D. A. Chart (Belfast, 1931)

—— *The Trial of William Drennan*, ed. John Larkin (Dublin, 1991)

Edwards, R. D., (ed.), 'The Minute Books of the Catholic Committee 1773–1792', in *Anal. Hib.*, ix (1942), pp. 1–172

Edgeworth, R. L., *Memoirs of Richard Lovell Edgeworth, begun by himself and concluded by his daughter Maria Edgeworth* (2 vols, London, 1820)

Farrell, William, *Carlow in '98: The Autobiography of William Farrell*, ed. Roger McHugh (Dublin, 1949)

The Fottrell Papers, 1721–39, ed. Hugh Fenning (Belfast, 1980)

The Manuscripts of J. B. Fortescue, Esq., preserved at Dropmore (10 vols, London, 1892–1927)

Gibbon, Skeffington, *The Recollections of Skeffington Gibbon from 1796 to the present year 1829, being an epitome of the lives and characters of the nobility and gentry of Roscommon, the genealogy of those who are descended from the Kings of Connaught, and a memoir of the late Madam O'Conor Dun* (Dublin, 1829)

Gilbert, J. T., (ed.), *Documents relating to Ireland 1795–1804* (Dublin, 1893)

Gordon, James, *History of the Rebellion in Ireland in the year 1798* (Dublin, 1801)

Hardwicke, Earl of, *The Viceroy's Postbag: Correspondence hitherto unpublished of the Earl of Hardwicke, first Lord Lieutenant after the Union*, ed. Michael MacDonagh (London, 1904)

Hay, Edward, *History of the Insurrection in the County of Wexford*, A.D. *1798* (Dublin, 1803)

Holt, Joseph, *Memoirs*, ed. T. C. Croker (2 vols, London, 1838)

Journals of the House of Commons of the Kingdom of Ireland (4th ed., 20 vols, Dublin, 1796–1800)

Kelly, Patrick, (ed.), 'The Improvement of Ireland', in *Anal. Hib.*, xxv (1992), pp. 45–86

Knight, Patrick, *Erris in the Irish Highlands* (Dublin, 1836)

[Little, James], 'A Diary of the French Landing in 1798' in *Anal. Hib.*, xi (1941), pp. 58–168

Loveday, John, *Diary of a Tour in 1732 through Parts of England, Wales, Ireland and Scotland* (Edinburgh, 1890)

Mac Cumhaigh, Art, *Dánta*, ed. Tomás Ó Fiaich (Dublin, 1973)

McGauran, Edward, *The Memoirs of Major Edward McGauran, grandson of Colonel Bryan McGauran, Baron McGauran of Talaha in the County of Cavan* (2 vols, London, 1786)

MacLysaght, Edward, (ed.), *The Kenmare Manuscripts* (Dublin, 1942)

MacNeven, William J., *Pieces of Irish History* (New York, 1807)

MacNevin, Thomas, *The Leading State Trials of Ireland* (Dublin, 1844)

McSkimin, Samuel, *Annals of Ulster* (Belfast, 1949)

Madden, R. R., *The United Irishmen, their Lives and Times* (7 vols, London, 1842–6)

—— *Literary remains of the United Irishmen* (London, 1887)

Mason, William Shaw, *A Statistical Account or Parochial Survey of Ireland* (3 vols, Dublin, 1814–19)

Maxwell, W. H., *Wild Sports of the West* (London, 1832)

Montesquieu, Charles de Secondat, Baron de, *Complete Works, translated from the French* (4 vols, Dublin, 1787)

Moore, John, *The Diary of Sir John Moore*, ed. J. F. Maurice (London, 1904)

'Bishop Moylan's *Relatio Status* 1785', ed. Kieran O'Shea, *in Kerry Arch. Hist. Soc. Jn.*, vii (1974), pp. 21–36

Musgrave, Richard, *Memoirs of the Various Rebellions in Ireland* (Dublin, 1801)

O'Byrne, Eileen, (ed.), *The Convert Rolls* (Dublin, 1981)

O'Conor, Charles, *Memoirs of the Life and Writings of the late Charles O'Conor of Belanagare* (Dublin, 1796)

Ó Doirnín, Peadar, *Amhráin*, ed. Breandán Ó Buachalla (Dublin, 1969)

O'Keefe, John, *Recollections of the Life of John O'Keefe, written by himself* (2 vols, London, 1826)

Ó Rathaille, Aodhagán, *Dánta Aodhagán Uí Rathaille: The Poems of Egan O'Rahilly*, ed. P. S. Dinneen and Tadhg O'Donoghue (London, 1911)

Ordnance Survey Memoir for County Fermanagh, ed. P. MacWilliams and A. Day (Belfast, 1991)

Ordnance Survey Letters for County Louth, ed. Michael O'Flanagan (Dublin, 1931)

Ordnance Survey Letters for County Roscommon, ed. Michael O'Flanagan (Dublin, 1931)

Ó Súilleabháin, Amhlaoibh, *Cinnlae Amhlaoibh Uí Shúilleabháin: The Diary of Humphrey O'Sullivan,* ed. Michael McGrath (4 vols, London, 1928–34)

Otway, Caesar, *A Tour in Connacht* (Dublin, 1839)

The Parliamentary Register, or History of the Proceedings and Debates of the House of Commons of Ireland 1781–1797 (17 vols, Dublin, 1782–1801)

Pender, Seamus, (ed.), *A Census of Ireland in 1659* (Dublin, 1949)

Plowden, Francis, *An Historical Review of the State of Ireland from the Invasion of that Country under Henry II to its Union with Great Britain* (2 vols, London, 1803)

Pococke, Richard, *Pococke's Tour in Ireland in 1752*, ed. G. T. Stokes (Dublin, 1891)

Rawson, Thomas, *Statistical Survey of the County of Kildare* (Dublin, 1807)

Reports of the Committee of Secrecy of the House of Commons and the House of Lords of Ireland (Dublin, 1798)

Rowan, Archibald Hamilton, *Autobiography*, ed. W. Drummond (Dublin, 1840)

Russell, Thomas, *Journals and Memoirs* ed. C. J. Woods (Dublin, 1991)

Rutland, Charles, Duke of, *The Correspondence between the Rt Hon, William Pitt and Charles, Duke of Rutland*, ed. Lord Mahon (London, 1890)

Sampson, William, *Memoirs* (New York, 1807)

Smith, Elizabeth, *The Irish journals of Elizabeth Smith 1840–1850*, ed. David Thompson (Oxford, 1980)

Stock, Joseph, *A Narrative of what passed at Killala in the County of Mayo* (Dublin, 1800)

Teeling, Charles, *Personal Narrative of the Irish Rebellion of 1798* (London, 1828)

Tighe, William, *Statistical Observations relative to the County of Kilkenny* (Dublin, 1802)

Tocqueville, Alexis de, *Journey in Ireland in 1835*, ed. Emmet Larkin (Dublin, 1990)

Tone, Theobald Wolfe, *Memoirs,* ed. W. T. Tone (2 vols, Washington, 1826)

Townshend, Horatio, *Statistical Survey of the County of Cork* (Dublin, 1810)

Wakefield, Edward, *An Account of Ireland, Statistical and Political* (2 vols, London, 1812)

[Walsh, J. E.], *Sketches of Ireland Sixty Years Ago* (Dublin, 1849)

Whyte, Laurence, *Original Poems on Various Subjects* (Dublin, 1740)

Willes, Edward, *The Letters of Lord Chief Baron Edward Willes, 1757–1762,* ed. James Kelly (Aberystwyth, 1990)

Young, Arthur, *A Tour in Ireland, with General Observations on the Present State of the Kingdom, made in the year 1776, 1777 and 1778 and brought down to the end of 1779* (2 vols, London, 1780)

Contemporary Pamphlets

Address of the County Committee of Dublin City to their Constituents, 1 February 1798 (Dublin, 1798)

Alexander, James, *Some Account of the First Apparent Symptoms of the Late Rebellion* (Dublin, 1800)

The Axe Laid to the Root, or Reasons humbly offered for putting the Popish Clergy in Ireland under some Better Regulation (Dublin, 1749)

Bateman, Josiah, *A Just and True Relation of Josiah Bateman's Concerns under the Rt Hon. Richard, Earl of Burlington, ever since the year 1713* (n.p., [1734?])

Beauties of The Press (London, 1800)

Bell, Robert, *A Description of the Conditions and Manners as well as the Moral and Political Character, Education, etc., of the Peasantry of Ireland between the years 1780 and 1790* (London, 1804)

Bingley, William, *An Examination into the Origins and Continuance of the Discontents of Ireland and the True Cause of Rebellion, being a Faithful Narrative of the Particular Sufferings of the Irish Peasantry* (London, 1799)

Burrowes, Robert, *Advice Religious and Political delivered in Four Sermons to a Congregation in the North of Ireland* (Dublin, 1801)

Caulfield, James, *The Reply of the Rt Revd Dr Caulfield, Roman Catholic Bishop, and the R. C. Clergy of Wexford to the Misrepresentations of Sir Richard Musgrave, Bart* (Dublin, 1801)

—— *Advice to the R. C. Clergy of the Diocese of Ferns, 12 April 1803* (Wexford, 1803)

Christ in Triumph Coming in Judgement (Strabane, 1795)

Connery, James, *The Reformer, or An Infallible Remedy to Prevent Pauperism and periodical Return of the Famine* (Cork, 1828)

Considerations upon the State of Public Affairs in Ireland in the year 1799 (Dublin, 1799)

Cooper, George, *Letters on the Irish Nation written during a Visit to that Kingdom in the autumn of the year 1799* (London, 1800)

Cox, Richard, *A Charge to the Grand Jury of County Cork* (Cork, 1740)

Croker, John Wilson, *A Sketch of the State of Ireland Past and Present* (Dublin, 1803)

Crumpe, Samuel, *An Essay on the Best Means of Providing Employment for the People* (Dublin, 1793)

The Cry of the Poor for Bread (Dublin, 1795)

Declaration of the Parochial Roman Catholic Clergy of the Diocese of Kilmacduagh and Kilfenora (London, 1798)

Dialogue between a Protestant and a Papist (Dublin, 1752)

Dobbs, Arthur, *An Essay on the Trade and Improvement of Ireland* (Dublin, 1731)

[Doyle, James Warren], *An Essay on the Catholic Claims* (Dublin, 1826)

Duigenan, Patrick, *The Speech of Dr Duigenan in the House of Commons, 4 February 1793* (Dublin, 1793)

—— *A Fair Representation of the Present Political State of Ireland* (Dublin, 1799)

Edgeworth, R. L., *A Letter to the Earl of Charlemont on the Tellograph and on the Defence of Ireland* (Dublin, 1797)

Essay on the Present State of Manners and Education among the Lower Class of the People of Ireland and the Means of Improving Them (Dublin, 1799)

Fitzgibbon, John, *The Speech of the Rt Hon. John, Earl of Clare, 17 February 1798* (Dublin, 1798)

[Fleming, Robert], *A Discourse on the Rise and Fall of Anti-Christ, wherein the Revolution in France and the Downfall of Monarchy in this Kingdom are distinctly pointed out, delivered at London in the year 1701* (Belfast, 1795)

Grattan, Henry, *Mr Grattan's Letter to his Fellow Citizens of Dublin* (Edinburgh, 1797)

Hay, Edward, *Authentic Detail of the Extravagant and Inconsistent Conduct of Sir Richard Musgrave* (Dublin, 1803)

Hussey, Thomas, *A Pastoral Letter to the Catholics of the United Dioceses of Waterford and Lismore* (Waterford, 1797)

—— *A Sermon preached at the Spanish Chapel in London, 14 May 1798* (London, 1798)

An Irishman's letter to the People called Defenders (Dublin, 1795)

Jackson, Charles, *A Narrative of the Sufferings and Escape of Charles Jackson* (London, 1798)

Jones, William Todd, *A Letter to the Societies of United Irishmen of the Town of Belfast* (Dublin, 1792)

Kirwan, Walter Blake, *A Discourse on Religious Innovation pronounced . . . at His Excellency's the Neapolitan Ambassador's Chapel, 20 March 1786* (London, 1787)

Lennon, John, *The Irish Repealer's Mountain Harp of the Triumphant Year of 1843* (Dublin, 1843)

A Letter from a Gentleman in Ireland to his Friend at Bath (Cork, 1798)

A Letter from a Country Gentleman in the Province of Munster (Dublin, 1741)

A Letter on the State of the Parties and on the Subject of Reform, addressed to the People (Belfast, 1796)

[MacNeven, W. J.], *An Argument for Independence* (Dublin, 1799)

Madden, Samuel, *Reflections and Resolutions proper to the Gentlemen of Ireland* (Dublin, 1738)

Moore, Charles, *Reflections on the Present State of our Country* (Dublin, 1798)

Moore, George, *Observations on the Union, Orange Associations and other Subjects of Domestic Policy* (Dublin, 1799)

Musgrave, Richard, *Observations on the Remonstrance of the Rev. Peter O'Neill, P.P. of Ballymacoda in the County of Cork* (Dublin, 1804)

Names of Persons who Took and Subscribed to the Oath of Allegiance to His Majesty before Baron Yelverton and Judge Chamberlain at an Adjourned Sessions held in Belfast in June 1797 (Belfast, 1797)

The New Age, addressed to the People of Great Britain and Ireland (Dublin, 1796)

O'Connor, Arthur, *The State of Ireland* (London, 1798)

——, Emmet, Thomas Addis, and MacNeven, W. J., *Memoir or Detailed Statement of the Origin and Progress of the Irish Union* (London, 1802)

O'Conor, Charles, *Ortelius Improved* (Dublin, 1770)

Orange Vindicated in a Reply to Theobald McKenna (Dublin, 1799)

O'Rourke, John, *The Case of Count O'Rourke presented to His Majesty in June 1784* (London, 1784)

Parker, William, *Observations on the Intended Amendment to the Irish Grand Jury Laws* (Cork, 1816)

[Porter, James], *Billy Bluff and Squire Firebrand* (Belfast, 1796)

[Quigley, James], *The Life of the Rev. James Coigley* (London, 1798)

Presbyterio-Catholicon; or A Refutation of the Modern Catholic Doctrines (Dublin, 1792)

Protestant Ascendancy and Catholic Emancipation reconciled in a Legislative Union (Dublin, 1800)

Public Spirit – a Poem (Dublin, 1798)

A Refutation of Dr Duigenan's Appendix (London, 1800)

Richardson, William, *History of the Origin of the Irish Yeomanry* (Dublin, 1801)

Russell, Thomas, *A Letter to the People of Ireland* (Belfast, 1796)

Seasonable Advice to Protestants containing some means of Reviving and Strengthening the Protestant Interest (2nd ed., Cork, 1745)

A Sermon preached at Mullingar on 1 July 1798 (Dublin, 1798)

Stokes, Whitley, *Projects for Re-establishing the Internal Peace and Tranquillity of Ireland* (Dublin, 1799)

—— *Observations on the Population and Resources of Ireland* (Dublin, 1792)

[Sweetman, Edward], *The Speech of Edward Sweetman delivered at a Meeting of the Freeholders of the County of Wexford on 22 September 1792* (Dublin, 1792)

Taaffe, Denis, *Ireland's Mirror, exhibiting a Picture of her Present State with a Glimpse of her Future Prospects* (Dublin, 1796)

—— *Vindication of the Irish Nation* (Dublin, 1802)

—— *Antidote to Cure the Catholicophobia and Ierneophobia efficacious to eradicate the Horrors against Catholics and Irishmen by early instilled Prejudices* (Dublin, 1804)

—— *A Succinct View of Catholic Affairs* (Dublin, 1805)

Teeling, Charles H., *Observations on the History and Consequences of the Battle of the Diamond* (Belfast, 1838)

[Tone, Theobald Wolfe], *An Argument on behalf of the Catholics of Ireland* (Dublin, 1791)

Travers, John, *A Sermon preached at St Andrew's Church, Dublin* (Dublin, 1698)

The Tryal of William Byrne of Ballymanus (Dublin, 1799)

The Union Doctrine or Poor Man's Catechism (Dublin, 1798)

Union or not? By an Orangeman (Dublin, 1799)

The United Irishmen: A Tale founded on Facts (Dublin, 1798)

Veritas, *The State of His Majesty's Subjects in Ireland professing the Roman Catholic Religion* (2nd ed., Dublin, 1799)

A Vindication of the Roman Catholic Clergy of the Town of Wexford during the Unhappy Rebellion (Dublin, 1799)

Yelverton's Charge to the Grand Jury of Carrickfergus, 17 June 1797 (Belfast, 1791)

Newspapers and contemporary periodical publications

Anthologica Hibernia (Dublin)
Dublin Evening Post
Dublin Magazine
Faulkner's Dublin Journal (Dublin)
Finn's Leinster Journal (Kilkenny)
Freeman's Journal (Dublin)
Hibernian Journal (Dublin)
Irish Magazine (Dublin)
Londonderry Journal
The Nation (Dublin)
Northern Star (Belfast)
Polar Star and Boston Daily Advertiser
Political Register (London)
The Press (Dublin)
Saunder's Newsletter (Dublin)
The Shamrock or Hibernian Chronicle (New York)
The Sun (London)
Wexford People

Secondary published works

Adams, J. R. R., *The Printed Word and the Common Man: Popular Culture in Ulster 1700–1900* (Belfast, 1987)

Andrews, J. H., *Plantation Acres* (Belfast, 1985)

Barnard, T. C., 'The Uses of 23 October 1641 and Irish Protestant Celebrations' in *Eng. Hist. Rev*, cvi (1991), pp. 889–920

—— 'The End of Old Ireland' in *Hist. Jn.*, xxxvi (1993), pp. 909–28

Bartlett, Thomas, 'An End to Moral Economy: The Irish Militia Disturbances of 1793' in *Past & Present*, lxc (1983), pp. 41–64

—— 'Defenders and Defenderism in 1795' in *I.H.S.*, xxiv (1984–5), pp. 373–94

—— '"A People Made Rather for Copies than Originals": The Anglo-Irish 1760–1800' in *Int. Hist. Rev.*, xii (1990), pp. 11–25

—— 'The Rise and Fall of the Protestant Nation 1690–1800' in *Éire–Ireland*, xxvi (1991), pp. 7–18

—— *The Fall and Rise of the Irish Nation: The Catholic Question 1690– 1830)* (Dublin, 1992)

—— 'Nationalism in Eighteenth-Century Ireland' in O'Dea and Whelan (eds.), *Nations and Nationalisms*, pp. 79–88

—— and Hayton, David, (ed.), *Penal Era and Golden Age* (Belfast, 1979)

Bergeron, Louis, and Cullen, L. M., (ed.), *Culture et pratiques politiques en France et en Irlande, xvie-xviiie siècles* (Paris, 1991)

Black, Jeremy, *British Foreign Policy in the Age of Revolution 1783–1793* (Cambridge, 1995)

Bloch, Ruth, *Visionary Republic: Millenial Themes in American Thought 1756–1801* (Cambridge, 1991)

Brady, John, *Catholics and Catholicism in the Eighteenth-Century Press* (Maynooth, 1965)

Brennan, Thomas, *Public Drinking and Popular Culture in Eighteenth-Century Paris* (Princeton, 1988)

Brooke, Peter, *Ulster Presbyterianism: The Historical Perspective 1610–1975* (Dublin, 1987)

Browne, Bernard, and Whelan, Kevin, 'The Browne Families of County Wexford' in Whelan (ed.), *Wexford*, pp. 467–89

Burke, Martin, 'Piecing Together a Shattered past: The Historical Writings of the United Irish Exiles in America' in Dickson, Keogh and Whelan (eds.), *United Irishmen*, pp. 297–306

Burke, Peter, *Popular Culture in Early Modern Europe* (London, 1978)

—— *The French Historical Revolution: The Annales School 1929–1989* (Cambridge, 1990)

Burke, William, *History of Clonmel* (Waterford, 1907)

Chart, D. A., 'The Irish Levies during the Great French War' in *Eng. Hist. Rev.*, xxxii (1913), pp. 79–102

Coburn, Kathleen, (ed.), *The Notebooks of Samuel Taylor Coleridge* (Princeton, 1957)

Cole, R. C., *Irish Booksellers and English Writers 1740–1800* (London, 1986)

Colley, Linda, *Britons: Forging the Nation 1707–1837* (New Haven, 1992)

—— 'Britishness and Otherness: An Argument' in O'Dea and Whelan (eds.), *Nations and Nationalisms*, pp. 61–77

Connolly, Sean, *Religion, Law and Power: The Making of Protestant Ireland 1660–1800* (Oxford, 1992)

Cullen, L. M., *The Emergence of Modern Ireland 1600–1900* (London, 1981)

—— 'The 1798 Rebellion in its Eighteenth-Century Context' in P. J. Corish (eds.), *Radicals, Rebels and Establishments* (Belfast, 1985), pp. 91–113

—— 'Catholics under the Penal Laws' in *Eighteenth-Century Ireland*, i (1986), pp. 23–36

—— 'The 1798 Rebellion in Wexford: United Irish Organisation, Membership, Leadership' in Whelan (ed.), *Wexford*, pp. 248–95

—— 'The Political Structures of the Defenders' in Gough and Dickson (eds.), *Ireland and the French Revolution*, pp. 117–38

—— 'Catholic Social classes under the Penal Laws' in Power and Whelan (eds.), *Endurance and Emergence*, pp. 57–84

—— 'Burke, Ireland and Revolution' in *Eighteenth-Century Life*, xvi (1992), pp. 21–42

—— 'The Internal Politics of the United Irishmen' in Dickson, Keogh and Whelan (eds.), *United Irishmen*, pp. 176–96

—— 'Politics and Rebellion in Wicklow in the 1790s' in Ken Hannigan and William Nolan (eds.), *Wicklow: History and Society* (Dublin, 1994), pp. 411–501

Curtin, Nancy, 'The Transformation of the Society of United Irishmen into a Mass-Based Revolutionary Organisation 1794–6' in *I.H.S.*, xxiv (1985), pp. 463–72

—— *The United Irishmen: Popular Politics in Ulster and Dublin 1791–1798* (Oxford, 1994)

Davies, Simon, 'The *Northern Star* and the Propagation of Enlightened Ideas' in *Eighteenth-Century Ireland*, vi (1990), pp. 43–52

Darnton, Robert, *The Literary Underground of the Old Regime* (London, 1982)

—— *The Kiss of Lamourette: Reflections in Cultural History* (London, 1990)

Deane, Seamus, *The French Revolution and Enlightenment in England 1789–1832* (Harvard, 1988)

—— 'Edmund Burke 1791–1797' in Seamus Deane (ed.), *The Field Day Anthology of Irish Writing* (3 vols, Derry, 1991), ii, pp. 807–09

Dickson, David, 'Middlemen' in Bartlett and Hayton (eds.), *Penal Era and Golden Age*, pp. 162–85

—— 'Centres of Motion: Irish Cities and the Origins of Popular Politics' in Bergeron and Cullen (ed.), *Culture et pratiques*, pp. 101–22

—— Introduction to Richard Musgrave, *Memoirs of Various Rebellions in Ireland* (repr., Fort Wayne, 1995)

—— 'Derry's Backyard: The Barony of Inishowen, 1660–1840' in M. Dunleavy (ed.), *Donegal: History and Society* (Dublin, 1995), pp. 405–46

——, Keogh, Dáire, and Whelan, Kevin (eds.), *The United Irishmen: Radicalism, Republicanism and Rebellion* (Dublin, 1993)

Donnelly, James, 'Irish Agrarian Rebellion: The Whiteboys of 1769–1776' in *R.I.A Proc.*, clxxxiii (1983), pp. 293–331

—— 'Propagating the Cause of the United Irishmen' in *Studies*, lxix (1980), pp. 5–23

Dunne, Tom, 'Edgeworthstown in Fact and Fiction 1760–1840' in Raymond Gillespie and Gerald Moran (eds.), *Longford: Studies in County History* (Dublin, 1991), pp. 95–122

Eagleton, Terry, *Heathcliff and the Great Hunger: Studies in Irish Culture* (London, 1995)

Elliott, Marianne, 'The Origins and Transformation of Irish Republicanism' in *Int. Rev. of Social Hist.*, xxiii (1978), pp. 405–28

—— *Partners in Revolution: The United Irishmen and France* (New Haven, 1982)

—— 'The Defenders in Ulster', in Dickson, Keogh and Whelan (eds.), *United Irishmen*, pp. 222–33

Fenning, Hugh, *The Irish Dominican Province 1698–1797* (Dublin, 1990)

Fitzpatrick, William J., *Curious Family History, or Ireland before the Union* (6th ed., Dublin, 1880)

Foster, R. F., 'Ascendancy and Union' in R. F. Foster (ed.), *The Oxford Illustrated History of Ireland* (Oxford, 1989), pp. 161–212

Froude, James Anthony, *The English in Ireland in the Eighteenth Century* (3 vols, London 1872–74)

Fuchs, Michel, 'The French Face of Irish Nationalism in the Eighteenth Century' in O'Dea and Whelan (eds.), *Nations and Nationalisms*, pp. 119–28

Furlong, Nicholas, *Father John Murphy of Boolavogue 1753–1798* (Dublin, 1992)

Gahan, Daniel, 'The Military Strategy of the Wexford United Irishmen in 1798' in *History Ireland*, i, no. 4 (1993), pp. 28–32

Gibbon, Peter, *The Origins of Ulster Unionism: The Formation of Popular Protestant Politics and Ideology in Nineteenth-Century Ireland* (Manchester, 1975)

Gildea, Robert, *The Past in French History* (New Haven, 1994)

Gilroy, Paul, *The Black Atlantic: Modernity and Double Consciousness* (Harvard, 1993)

Gough, Hugh and Dickson, David, (eds.), *Ireland and the French Revolution* (Dublin, 1990)

Graham, Tommy, 'An Union of Power: The United Irish Organisation' in Dickson, Keogh and Whelan (ed.), *United Irishmen*, pp. 244–55

Gramsci, Antonio, *Selections from the Prison Notebooks* (London, 1973)

Gray, Jane, 'Folk Poetry and Working-Class Identity in Ulster: An Analysis of James Orr's "The Penitent"', in *Jn. Hist. Sociology*, vi (1993), pp. 249–75

Gray, John, 'A Tale of Two Newspapers: The Contest between the *Belfast News-letter* and the *Northern Star* in the 1790s' in John Gray (ed.), *An Uncommon Bookman: Essays in memory of J. R. R. Adams* (Belfast, forthcoming)

Grimes, Seamus, (ed.), *Dublin in 1804* (Dublin, 1980)

Hempton, David, and Hill, Myrtle, *Evangelical Protestantism in Ulster Society 1740 –1890* (London, 1992)

Herr, Cheryl, *For the Land They Loved: Irish Political Melodrama 1890–1925* (Syracuse, 1991)

Hewitt, John, *Rhyming Weavers and other Country Poets of Antrim and Down* (Belfast, 1974)

Hill, Jacqueline, 'National Festivities, the State and Protestant Ascendancy' in *I.H.S.*, xxiv (1984), pp. 30–51

Johnson, Nuala, 'Sculpting Heroic Pictures: Celebrating the Centenary of the 1798 Rebellion in Ireland' in *Trans. Inst. Brit. Geog.*, xix (1994), pp. 117–93

Jones Hughes, Thomas, 'The Large Farm in Nineteenth-Century Ireland' in Alan Gailey and Dáithí Ó hÓgáin (eds.), *Gold under the Furze* (Dublin, 1982), pp. 92–100

Kavanagh, Patrick, *A Popular History of the Insurrection of 1798* (Dublin, 1870)

Kelly, James, 'Eighteenth-Century Ascendancy: A Commentary' in *Eighteenth-Century Ireland*, v (1990), pp. 173–87

—— *Prelude to Union: Anglo-Irish Politics in the 1780s* (Cork, 1992)

—— 'The Abduction of Women of Fortune in Eighteenth-Century Ireland' in *Eighteenth-Century Ireland*, ix (1994), pp. 7–43

—— '"The Glorious and Immortal Memory": Commemoration and Protestant Identity in Ireland 1660–1800' in *R.I.A. Proc.*, clxliv (1994), pp. 25–52

Keogh, Dáire, *The French Disease: The Catholic Church and Radicalism in Ireland 1790–1800* (Dublin, 1993)

Lansdowne, Marquis of, *Glanerought and the Petty-Fitzmaurices* (Oxford, 1937)

Larkin, Emmet, *The Historical Dimensions of Irish Catholicism* (Washington, 1984)

Lecky, W. E. H., *History of Ireland in the Eighteenth Century* (5 vols, London, 1892)

Linebaugh, Peter, 'All the Atlantic Mountains Shook' in *Labour/Le Travail: Journal of Canadian Labour Studies*, x (1982)

—— 'Jubilating, or How the Atlantic Working Class used the Biblical Jubilee against Capitalism with Some Success' in *Radical History Review*, l (1991), pp. 142–80

—— and Rediker, Marcus, 'The Many-Headed Hydra: Sailors, Slaves and the Atlantic Working Class in the Eighteenth Century' in *Jn. Hist. Sociology*, iii, no. 3 (1990), pp. 205–52

Lyne, Gerry, 'Dr Dermot Lyne: an Irish Catholic landholder in Cork and Kerry under the Penal Laws' in *Kerry Arch. Hist. Soc. Jn.*, vii (1975), pp. 45–72

—— 'The Mac Fínín Dubh O Sullivan of Tuosist and Bearehaven, ibid., ix (1976), pp. 32–67

—— 'Land Tenure in Kenmare and Tuosist 1696–1716', ibid., x (1977), pp. 19–54

—— 'Landlord–Tenant Relations on the Shelburne Estate in Kenmare, Bonane and Tuosist 1770–1785', ibid., xii (1979), pp. 19–62

McBride, Ian, 'William Drennan and the Dissenting Tradition' in Dickson, Keogh and Whelan (eds.), *United Irishmen*, pp. 49–61

—— 'Presbyterianism in the Penal Era' in *Bullán*, i, no. 2 (1995), pp. 73–86

McCalman, Ian, *Radical Underworld: Prophets, Revolutionaries and Pornographers in London 1795–1840* (Oxford, 1993)

McClelland, Aiken, *The Formation of the Orange Order* ([Belfast], [1971])

—— 'Thomas Ledlie Birch, United Irishman' in *Belfast Natural Hist. & Phil. Soc. Jn.*, vii (1965), pp. 24–42

McDowell, R. B., 'The Personnel of the Dublin Society of the United Irishmen' in *I.H.S.*, ii (1940–41), pp. 12–53

MacNeill, Mary, *The Life and Times of Mary Anne McCracken 1770–1856* (Dublin, 1960)

McShane, Kieran, 'A Study of Two New York Irish-American Newspapers in the Early Nineteenth Century' in *New York Irish History*, viii (1994), pp. 13–21

Miller, Kerby, 'The Erosion of the Protestant Middle Class in Southern Ireland during the Pre-Famine era' in *Huntington Lib. Quart.*, lix (1986), pp. 295–306

Nora, Pierre, *Les lieux de mémoire*, (3 vols, Paris, 1984–92)

O'Brien, Conor Cruise, *The Great Melody: A Thematic Biography of Edmund Burke* (London, 1992)

Ó Buachalla, Breandán, 'Irish Jacobite Poetry' in *Irish Review*, xii (1992), pp. 40–49

—— 'Irish Jacobitism and Irish Nationalism: The Literary Evidence' in O'Dea and Whelan (eds.), *Nations and Nationalisms*, pp. 103–16

Ó Caithnia, Liam, *Scéal na hIomána* (Dublin, 1981)

O'Connell, Mrs Morgan John, *The Last Colonel of the Irish Brigade* (2 vols, London, 1892)

Ó Danachair, Caoimhín, 'An Rí, the King: An Example of Traditional Social Organisation' in *R.S.A.I. Jn.*, iii (1981), pp. 14–28

O'Dea, Michael, and Whelan, Kevin (eds.), *Nations and Nationalisms: France, Britain, Ireland and the Eighteenth-Century Context* (Oxford, 1995)

O'Donnell, Ruan, and Reece, Bob, ' "A Clean Beast": Crofton Croker's Fairy Tale of General Holt' in *Eighteenth-Century Ireland*, vii (1992), pp. 7–42

Ó Gráda, Cormac, *A New Economic History of Ireland 1780–1939* (Oxford, 1995)

O'Keeffe, Timothy, 'The 1898 Efforts to Celebrate the United Irishmen: The '98 centennial' in *Éire–Ireland*, xxiii (1988), pp. 51–73

—— 'Who Fears to Speak of '98? The Rhetoric and Rituals of the United Irishmen Centennial, 1898' in *Éire–Ireland*, xxvii (1992), pp. 67–91

Ó Mórdha, Pilíb, 'Colla Dubh MacMahon, his Ancestors and Descendants' in *Clogher Rec.*, viii (1974), pp. 194–206

Ó Néill, Eoghan, *Gleann an Óir* (Dublin, 1988)

Ó Foghludha, Risteárd (ed.), *Míl na hÉigse* (Dublin, 1945)

Ó Snodaigh, Pádraig, *'98 and Carlow: A Look at the Historians* (Carlow, 1979)

Ó Tuama, Seán, and Kinsella, Thomas (eds.), *An Duanaire: Poems of the Dispossessed* (Dublin, 1990)

Owens, Gary, 'Hedge School of Politics: O'Connell's Monster Meetings' in *History Ireland*, ii, no. 1 (1994), pp. 35–40

—— 'Nationalist monuments in Ireland *c.* 1870–1914: Symbolism and Ritual' in Brian Kennedy and Raymond Gillespie (eds.), *Ireland: Art into History* (Dublin, 1994), pp. 103–17

Ozouf, Mona, 'Du mai de liberté à l'arbre de la liberté: symbolisme révolutionnaire et tradition paysan' in *Ethnologie Française*, v (1975), pp. 9–34

Paulin, Tom, *Minotaur: Poetry and the Nation State* (London, 1992)

Pollard, Mary, *Dublin's Trade in Books 1550–1800* (Oxford, 1989)

Power, T. P., *Land, Politics and Society in Eighteenth-Century Tipperary* (Oxford, 1993)

—— and Whelan, Kevin (ed.), *Endurance and Emergence: Catholics in Ireland in the Eighteenth Century* (Dublin, 1990)

Ravina, Agustín, *Burguesia Extranjera y Comercio Atlántico: La Empresa Comercial Irlandesa en Canarias 1703–1771* (Tenerife, 1985)

Robinson, Philip, 'Hanging Ropes and Buried Secrets' in *Ulster Folklife*, xxxii (1986), pp. 3–15

Ronan, M. V. (ed.), *Personal Recollections of Wexford and Wicklow Insurgents of 1798 as collected by the Rev. Br. Luke Cullen 1798–1859* (Enniscorthy, 1958)

Rudebusche, Erhardt, *Irland im Zeitalter der Revolution* (Frankfurt, 1989)

Sahlins, Peter, *Forest Rites: The War of the Demoiselles in Nineteenth-Century France* (London, 1994)

Smith, Olive, *The Politics of Language 1791–1819* (Oxford, 1984)

Smyth, Jim, *The Men of No Property: Irish Radicals and Popular Politics in the late Eighteenth Century* (Dublin, 1992)

—— 'Freemasonry and the United Irishmen' in Dickson, Keogh and Whelan (eds.), *United Irishmen*, pp. 167–75

Somerville, E. Œ., and Ross, Martin, *Irish Memories* (London, 1917)

Stewart, A. T. Q., *A Deeper Silence: The Hidden Origins of the United Irishmen* (London, 1993)

Thuente, Mary Helen, *The Harp Restrung: The United Irishmen and the Rise of Irish Literary Nationalism* (Syracuse, 1994)

Thompson, Dorothy, *Outsiders: Class, Gender and Nation* (London, 1993)

Thompson, E. P., *The Making of the English Working Class* (2nd. ed., London, 1968)

—— *Witness against the Beast: William Blake and the Moral Law* (Cambridge, 1993)

—— *Making History: Writings on History and Culture* (New York, 1994)

Turpin, John, 'Oliver Sheppard's 1798 Memorials' in *Irish Arts Review* (1991), pp. 71–80

Walsh, Walter, 'Religion, Ethnicity and History: Clues to the Cultural Construction of Law' in Ronald Bayor and T. J. Meagher (eds.), *The New York Irish* (Baltimore, 1995), pp. 48–69

Whelan, Kevin, 'The Catholic Parish, the Catholic Chapel and Village Development in Ireland' in *Ir. Geog.*, xvi (1983), pp. 1–15

—— 'The Catholic Church in County Tipperary 1700–1900' in William Nolan (ed.), *Tipperary: History and Society* (Dublin, 1985), pp. 215–55

—— (ed.), *Wexford: History and Society* (Dublin, 1987)

—— 'The Role of the Catholic Priest in the 1798 Rebellion in County Wexford' in Whelan (ed.), *Wexford*, pp. 296–315

—— 'The Regional Impact of Irish Catholicism 1700–1850' in W. J. Smyth and Kevin Whelan (eds.), *Common Ground: Essays on the Historical Geography of Ireland* (Cork, 1988), pp. 253–77

—— 'Gaelic Survivals' in *Ir. Review*, vii (1989), pp. 139–43

—— 'Politicisation in County Wexford and the origins of the 1798 Rebellion' in Gough and Dickson (ed.), *Ireland and the French Revolution*, pp. 156–78

—— 'The Catholic Community in Eighteenth-Century County Wexford' in Power and Whelan (ed.), *Endurance and Emergence*, pp. 156–78

—— 'Catholic Mobilisation 1750–1850' in Bergeron and Cullen (ed.), *Culture et pratiques*, pp. 235–58

—— 'Catholics, Politicisation and the 1798 Rebellion' in Réamóinn Ó Muirí (ed.), *Irish Church History Today* (Armagh, 1991), pp. 63–83

—— 'Settlement and Society in Eighteenth-Century Ireland' in Gerald Dawe and J. W. Foster (eds.), *The Poet's Place* (Belfast, 1991), pp. 45–62

—— 'The Geography of Hurling' in *History Ireland*, i., no. 1 (1993), pp. 25–28

Williams, N. J. A. (ed.), *Pairlement Chloinne Tomáis* (Dublin, 1981)

Wood, Marcus, *Radical Satire and Print Culture 1790–1822* (Oxford, 1994)

Woods, C. J., 'Tone's Grave at Bodenstown: Memorials and Commemorations 1798–1913' in D. Siegmund-Schultze (ed.), *Irland Gesellschaft und Kultur*, vi (Halle, 1989), pp. 138–48

Zimmerman, G. D., *Songs of Irish Rebellion: Political Street Ballads and Rebel Songs 1780–1900* (Dublin, 1967)

Unpublished theses

Blackstock, Alan, 'The Origins and Development of the Irish Yeomanry 1796–1807' (Ph.D. thesis, Queen's University, Belfast, 1993)

Dickson, David, 'An Economic History of the Cork Region in the Eighteenth Century' (Ph.D. thesis, Trinity College, Dublin, 1977)

Haydon, Colin, 'Anti-Catholicism in Eighteenth-Century England *c.* 1714–1780' (D.Phil. thesis, Oxford University, 1985)

Kinsella, Anna, '"Who Fears to Speak of '98?" The Nineteenth-Century Interpretation of 1798' (M.Litt. thesis, University College, Dublin, 1991)

O'Donnell, Ruan, 'General Joseph Holt and the Rebellion of 1798 in County Wicklow' (M.A. thesis, University College, Dublin, 1991)

Whelan, Margaret, 'Edward Hay, styled Mr Secretary Hay: Catholic Politics, 1792–1822' (M.A. thesis, University College, Galway, 1991)

INDEX

Abbot, Charles, Chief Secretary, 173
abductions, 27
Abercorn, Lord, 120, 121
Adair, Sir Robert, 48
Adams, J. R. R., librarian, 74
Addington, Henry, Prime Minister, 147
Ahoghill, county Antrim, 67
aisling, 11, 35
Alexander, James, 64
Allan, Frederick, Fenian, 172
Altamont, Lord, 145
America, 165–7
American Revolution, 73, 101
Amnesty Act, 158
Andrews, J.H., geographer, 186n
Anglicans, 103–4, 117, 142, 154, 155
Annales school, 3
Antrim, county, 39, 44, 65, 70, 86, 95, 113,
    118, 138, 154
Arbuckle, James, 81
Archer, Rev Forster, 184n
Ardboe, county Derry, 88
Armagh city, 67, 68, 118
Armagh, county, 41, 104, 113, 116, 117, 118,
    119, 120, 121, 122–5, 127, 128
Armstrong, William, 51
artisan combinations, 75
Athenian club, 77, 79
Athlone, county Westmeath, 64
Athy, county Kildare, 14
Atkinson, A.L., 28
Atkinson, A.W., 124
Atkinson family of Crowhill, Armagh, 118
Auckland, Lord, 134, 173
Aughnacloy, county Tyrone, 121
Averell, Adam, 134
Aylward family, county Kilkenny, 28

Back Lane Parliament, *see* Catholic
    Convention
Bacon, Thomas, 138
Bagwell family, of county Tipperary, 37
Balbriggan, county Dublin, 88
Ballibritt, county Offaly, 20
Ballina, county Mayo, 34
Ballinacoola, county Carlow, 7
Ballinderry, county Antrim 118
Ballybeg, county Carlow, 6

Ballybrishan, county Kilkenny, 28
Ballybur, county Carlow, 7
Ballycroy, county Mayo, 31
Ballygurteen, county Cork, 83
Ballymanus corps, county Wicklow, 85
Ballymena, county Antrim, 48
Ballymore Eustace, county Kildare, 87
Ballynahinch, county Down, 66, 137, 151
Ballynattin, county Carlow, 7
Ballyraggett, county Kilkenny, 14
Ballyshannon, county Donegal, 14, 67
Ballyvaghan, county Tipperary, 14
Baltinglass, county Wicklow, 72
Bandon, county Cork, 141
Bantry Bay, county Cork, 48, 115, 123, 124
Baptists, 165
Barber, Jane, 49
Barber, Rev Samuel, 59
Barrington, Jonah, 22, 146
Bartlett, Thomas, historian, x, 3, 114
Bastille Day celebrations, 80, 100, 106
Bateman, Josiah, 5,
Bayley, Rev Edward, 136
Belfast, 62, 63, 64, 65, 66, 67, 68, 69, 72, 73,
    75, 81, 86, 90, 95, 101, 113, 121, 154, 155
Belfast Harp Festival, 61
Bell, Robert, 42, 53, 92
Beltz, George, 48
Bennet, William, Bp of Cloyne, 136, 143, 160
Beresford family, 37, 123
Beresford, John, 76–7, 112, 113, 114, 118,
    123, 126, 127, 133, 134, 136, 143, 163,
    164, 173
Bermingham, Walter, 73
Bessborough, county Kilkenny, 16
Betham, Sir William, 48
Big Barn, county Wexford, 30
Binns, John, 167
Birch, Rev Thomas Ledlie, 67, 165
Birr Castle, 50
Blacker family of county Armagh, 118
Blackwater, county Wexford, 50
Blake estate, county Galway, 16
Blake, Henry, 180n
Blackney family of county Carlow, 7
Blarney, county Cork, 8, 14, 27, 85
Blyth, John, printer, 63
Bodenstown, county Kildare, 168, 172

227